COMMANDERS IN CRISIS

STEVE ORLANDO · DAVIDE TINTO

BOOK 1

THE ACTION

STEVE ORLANDO
CREATOR, WRITER

DAVIDE TINTO
CREATOR, ARTIST

FRANCESCA CAROTENUTO
COLORIST

FABIO AMELIA
LETTERER

DAVIDE G.G. CACI
EDITOR

ANTONIO SOLINAS
ASSOCIATE EDITOR

FABRIZIO VERROCCHI
DESIGN

COMMANDERS IN CRISIS: THE ACTION, VOL. 1. First printing. April 2021. Published by Image Comics, Inc. Office of publication: PO BOX 14457, Portland, OR 97293. "Commanders in Crisis," created by Steve Orlando and Davide Tinto. Copyright © 2021 Orlando, Arancia Studio s.n.c. All rights reserved. Contains material originally published in single magazine form as COMMANDERS IN CRISIS #1-6. "Commanders in Crisis", its logos, and the likenesses of all characters herein are trademarks of Steve Orlando, Arancia Studio s.n.c., unless otherwise noted. "Image" and the Image Comics logos are registered trademarks of Image Comics, Inc. No part of this publication may be reproduced or transmitted, in any form or by any means (except for short excerpts for journalistic or review purposes), without the express written permission of Steve Orlando, Arancia Studio s.n.c. or Image Comics, Inc. All names, characters, events, and locales in this publication are entirely fictional. Any resemblance to actual persons (living or dead), events, or places, without satirical intent, is coincidental. Printed in the USA. For international rights, contact: licensing@aranciastudio.com. ISBN: 978-1-5343-1866-3.

IMAGE COMICS, INC. • **Todd McFarlane:** President • **Jim Valentino:** Vice President • **Marc Silvestri:** Chief Executive Officer • **Erik Larsen:** Chief Financial Officer • **Robert Kirkman:** Chief Operating Officer • **Eric Stephenson:** Publisher / Chief Creative Officer • **Nicole Lapalme:** Controller • **Leanna Caunter:** Accounting Analyst • **Sue Korpela:** Accounting & HR Manager • **Marla Eizik:** Talent Liaison • **Jeff Boison:** Director of Sales & Publishing Planning • **Dirk Wood:** Director of International Sales & Licensing • **Alex Cox:** Director of Direct Market Sales • **Chloe Ramos:** Book Market & Library Sales Manager • **Emilio Bautista:** Digital Sales Coordinator • **Jon Schlaffman:** Specialty Sales Coordinator • **Kat Salazar:** Director of PR & Marketing • **Drew Fitzgerald:** Marketing Content Associate • **Heather Doornink:** Production Director • **Drew Gill:** Art Director • **Hilary DiLoreto:** Print Manager • **Tricia Ramos:** Traffic Manager • **Melissa Gifford:** Content Manager • **Erika Schnatz:** Senior Production Artist • **Ryan Brewer:** Production Artist • **Deanna Phelps:** Production Artist

imagecomics.com

COMMANDERS IN CRISIS is proudly produced at Arancia Studio, Torino, Italy • #weArancia

ARANCIA STUDIO S.N.C.: • **Davide G.G. Caci:** Chief Executive Officer • **Andrea Meloni:** Chief Creative Officer • **Mirka Andolfo:** Art Director • **Fabrizio Verrocchi:** Marketing, Design, and Communication Guru • **Fabio Amelia:** Editorial Production Manager • **Antonio Solinas:** Talent Relations Manager • **Luca Blengino:** Senior Editor • **Elena Fontana:** Talent Relations, Editorial Assistant • **Giulia Dell'Accio:** Executive Assistant, Administrative Assistant • **Silvia Bellucci:** PR • **Cecilia Raneri:** Junior Associate Agent • **Fulvio Gambotto:** Special Projects

aranciastudio.com

★ INTRODUCTION ★

With a pen in his hand, a fire in his heart, and an extremely cool name that is very catchy, Steve Orlando has done it again. At just the right moment, too. When I first read COMMANDERS IN CRISIS #1, my initial thought was "This couldn't have come at a better time." It's rare enough that we get a positive and uplifting superhero adventure, but there truly was no year that needed this story more than the cursed 2020—a time so soul-crushingly terrible that even referencing it is quickly getting cliche.

I first met Steve when we were connected by a mutual friend of ours, a feisty young man named Anthony Smith. I was lamenting to Anthony, who is a writer/journalist, about trying and failing to find a job at a comic book store near me. Anthony suggested I reach out to Steve, who he quickly learned to love after hearing Steve talk about comics, "unprompted and unsolicited," for hours the first time they met. Instantly, I could relate. Shutting me up about comic books is a gargantuan task.

Since then, Steve has had my back as I have tried my own hand at writing. If I have an idea and it involves people wearing capes and beating each other senseless, he is there to point out all of the inevitable glaring plot holes. But he's tough on me for a reason—he had a writing mentor of his own growing up, a guy named Steven T. Seagle (a great man, cursed to be confused with the reprehensible Steven Seagal), and Seagle did not let Orlando get away with any bad writing. A young Steve Orlando would come to comic cons year after year, pitching idea after idea to Seagle. For many years, Seagle told him the same thing: "Come back next year, this isn't good enough yet." As you could imagine, one day it was in fact 'good enough,' and Seagle sent him off to Image Comics where he would go on to write some iconic runs and change the way we see certain characters forever. The apprentice has become the master, and only a master could create something like COMMANDERS IN CRISIS.

In other words, folks, get pumped. You're entering a whole new universe. COMMANDERS IN CRISIS, at least in the cover art, looks like an action-packed story about a handful of superheroes coming together to save the world. And sure, I guess, it is definitely that. In a sense. But that framework is familiar, and this book is anything but. COMMANDERS IN CRISIS gives us superheroes whose identities are more heroic than their power sets. It introduces us to presidents who (at least) try to be good people, a concept that most Americans will find even more fantastical than a man who derives his super strength from the power of adoring fans and cheering crowds (you'll see what I mean on page four).

At long last, 2021 has arrived—and the heroes of the Crisis Command are here to usher us in. Commanders in Crisis is a big, superheroic punch in the face to the grim reality of a country ravaged by hate and apathy. It finds light in the darkness of the world, and does so in a colorful, energetic, and unapologetically Steve Orlando manner. This book is everything a massive superhero comic should be and does so much that superhero comics have needed to do. I'm so excited for you to dive right in.

CAMERON KASKY

Cameron Kasky is an American activist, writer, and advocate against gun violence who co-founded the student-led gun violence prevention group Never Again MSD. He is a survivor of the February 2018 mass shooting at Marjory Stoneman Douglas High School. Kasky is notable for helping to organize the March for Our Lives, a nationwide student protest in March 2018. In 2018, Kasky was included in TIME magazine's 100 Most Influential People. In addition, he is working for Andrew Yang's 2021 mayoral campaign in New York City.

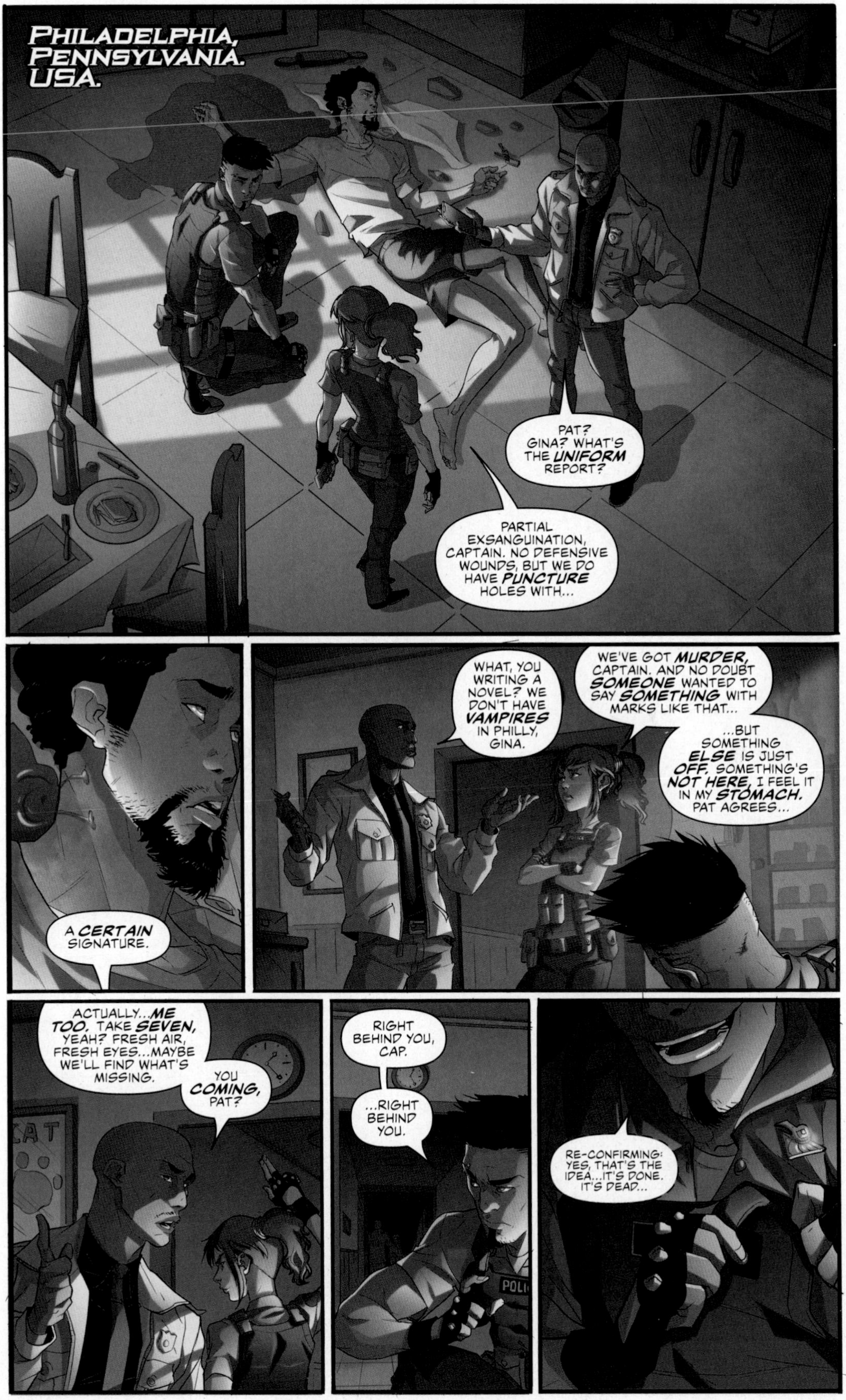
PHILADELPHIA, PENNSYLVANIA. USA.
PAT? GINA? WHAT'S THE UNIFORM REPORT?
PARTIAL EXSANGUINATION, CAPTAIN. NO DEFENSIVE WOUNDS, BUT WE DO HAVE PUNCTURE HOLES WITH...
A CERTAIN SIGNATURE.
WHAT, YOU WRITING A NOVEL? WE DON'T HAVE VAMPIRES IN PHILLY, GINA.
WE'VE GOT MURDER, CAPTAIN. AND NO DOUBT SOMEONE WANTED TO SAY SOMETHING WITH MARKS LIKE THAT...
...BUT SOMETHING ELSE IS JUST OFF. SOMETHING'S NOT HERE. I FEEL IT IN MY STOMACH. PAT AGREES...
ACTUALLY...ME TOO. TAKE SEVEN, YEAH? FRESH AIR, FRESH EYES...MAYBE WE'LL FIND WHAT'S MISSING.
YOU COMING, PAT?
RIGHT BEHIND YOU, CAP.
...RIGHT BEHIND YOU.
RE-CONFIRMING: YES, THAT'S THE IDEA...IT'S DONE. IT'S DEAD...

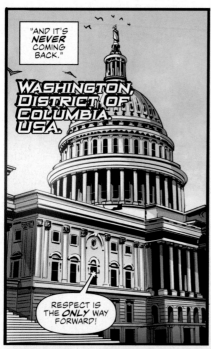

"AND IT'S *NEVER* COMING BACK."

WASHINGTON, DISTRICT OF COLUMBIA, USA.

RESPECT IS THE *ONLY* WAY FORWARD!

THE CONSTITUTION OF THE UNITED STATES IS THE GREATEST DOCUMENT IN THE *HISTORY* OF THE WORLD.

AND *CHIEF* AMONG ITS VIRTUES IS ITS ABILITY TO *CHANGE*. THIS COUNTRY WAS *FOUNDED* ON THE CONCEPT OF *UNITY*, BUT IN THE *CENTURIES* SINCE...

AMERICA HAS CHANGED! IRREVOCABLY!

WE *MUST* RESPECT THAT! WE *MUST* RESPECT OUR DIFFERENCES! WE *CAN* AGREE TO DISAGREE...

THE *AMERICAN INDIVIDUALITY ACT* IS HOW! SIMULTANEOUS, CONSENSUAL SECESSION FROM THE *UNITED* STATES...

...AND THE *INSTANT FORMATION* OF A *COMMUNITY* OF *52 NATION STATES*...

...EACH AGREEING TO SUPPORT THE OTHER FROM *OUTSIDE THREATS!*

THIS IS HOW *WE*, AS AMERICANS, PROTECT OUR FUTURE...

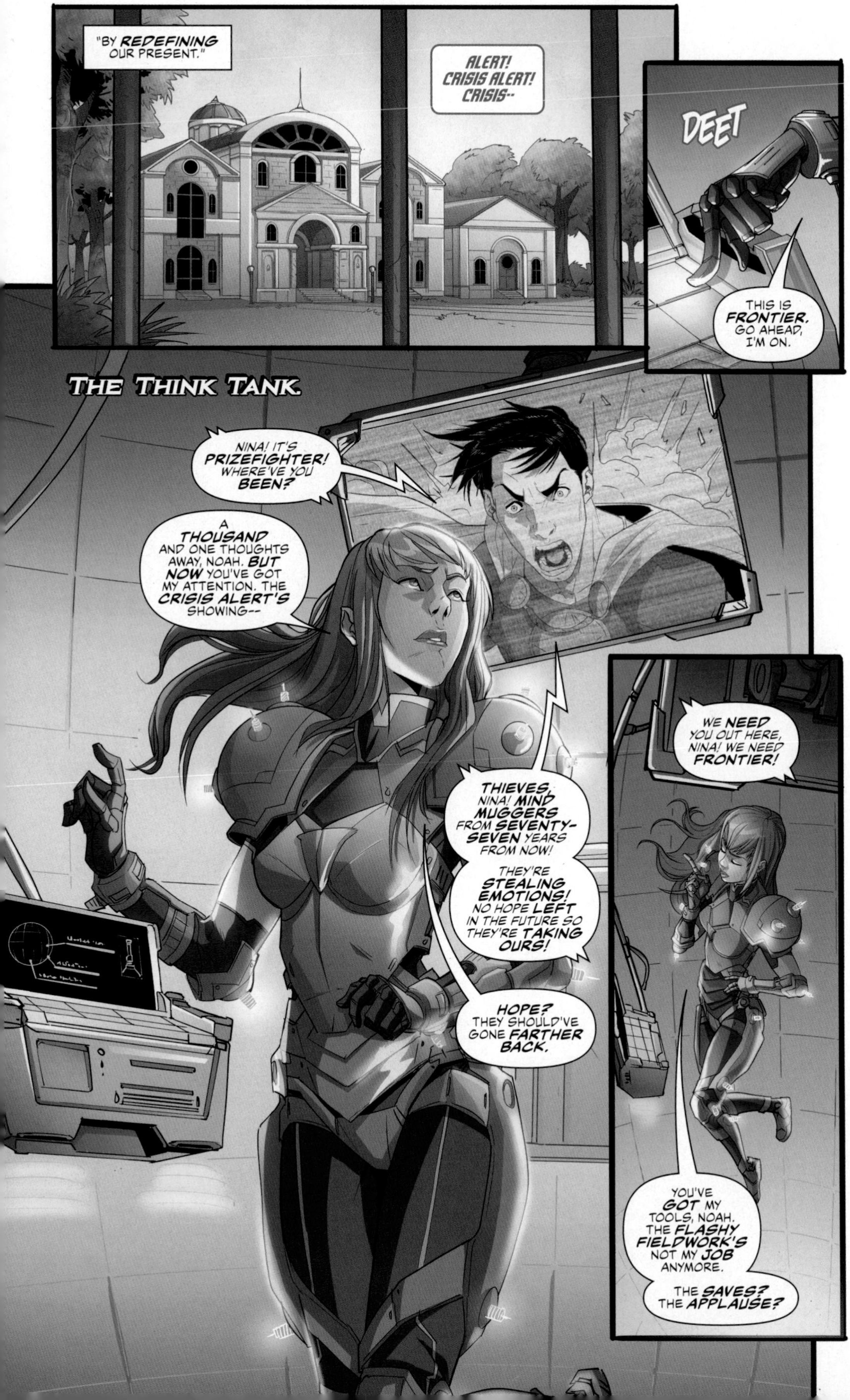
"BY REDEFINING OUR PRESENT."
ALERT! CRISIS ALERT! CRISIS--
DEET
THIS IS FRONTIER. GO AHEAD, I'M ON.
THE THINK TANK.
NINA! IT'S PRIZEFIGHTER! WHERE'VE YOU BEEN?
A THOUSAND AND ONE THOUGHTS AWAY, NOAH. BUT NOW YOU'VE GOT MY ATTENTION. THE CRISIS ALERT'S SHOWING--
THIEVES, NINA! MIND MUGGERS FROM SEVENTY-SEVEN YEARS FROM NOW!
THEY'RE STEALING EMOTIONS! NO HOPE LEFT IN THE FUTURE SO THEY'RE TAKING OURS!
HOPE? THEY SHOULD'VE GONE FARTHER BACK.
WE NEED YOU OUT HERE, NINA! WE NEED FRONTIER!
YOU'VE GOT MY TOOLS, NOAH. THE FLASHY FIELDWORK'S NOT MY JOB ANYMORE.
THE SAVES? THE APPLAUSE?

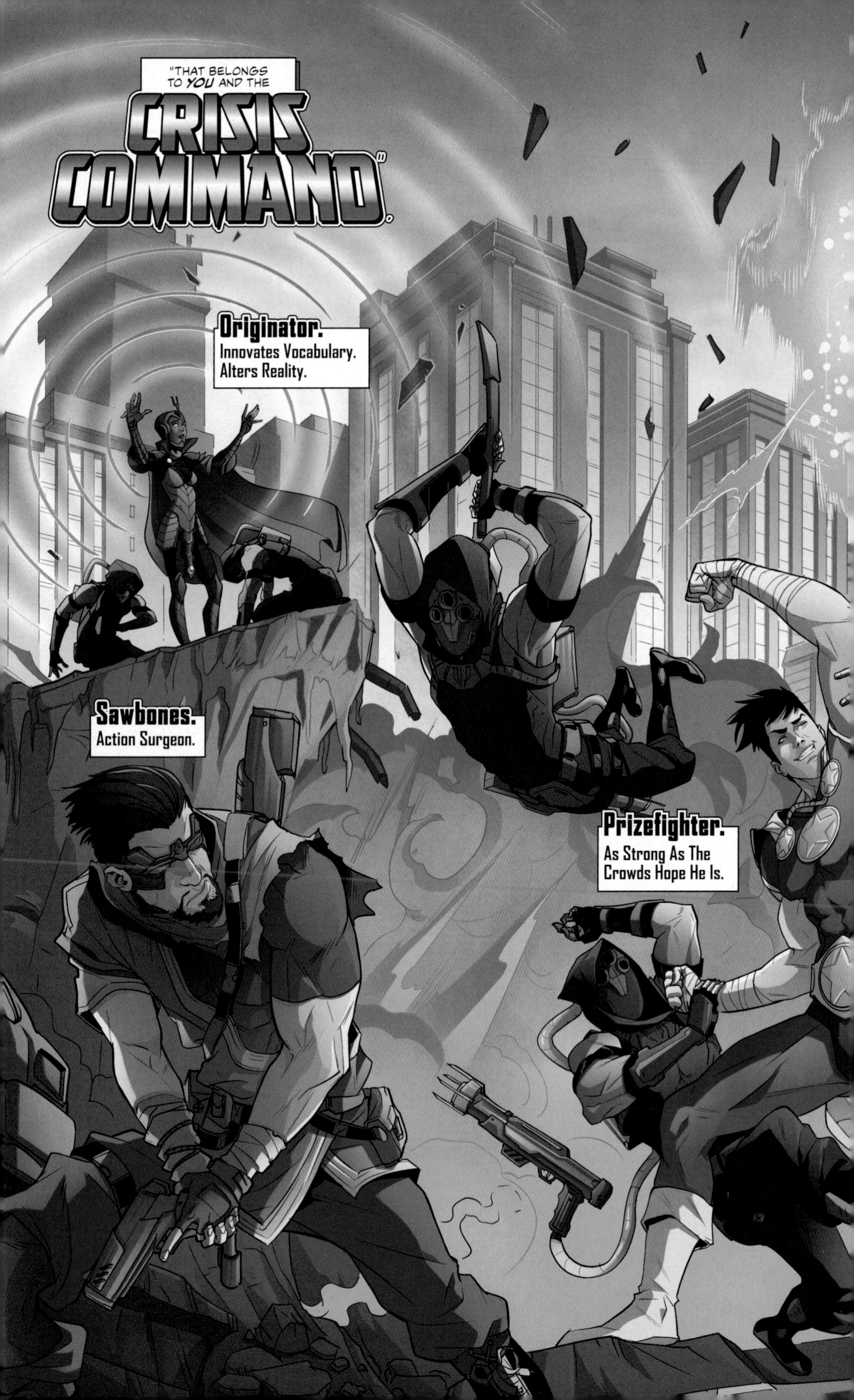
"THAT BELONGS TO YOU AND THE
CRISIS COMMAND"
Originator.
Innovates Vocabulary. Alters Reality.
Sawbones.
Action Surgeon.
Prizefighter.
As Strong As The Crowds Hope He Is.

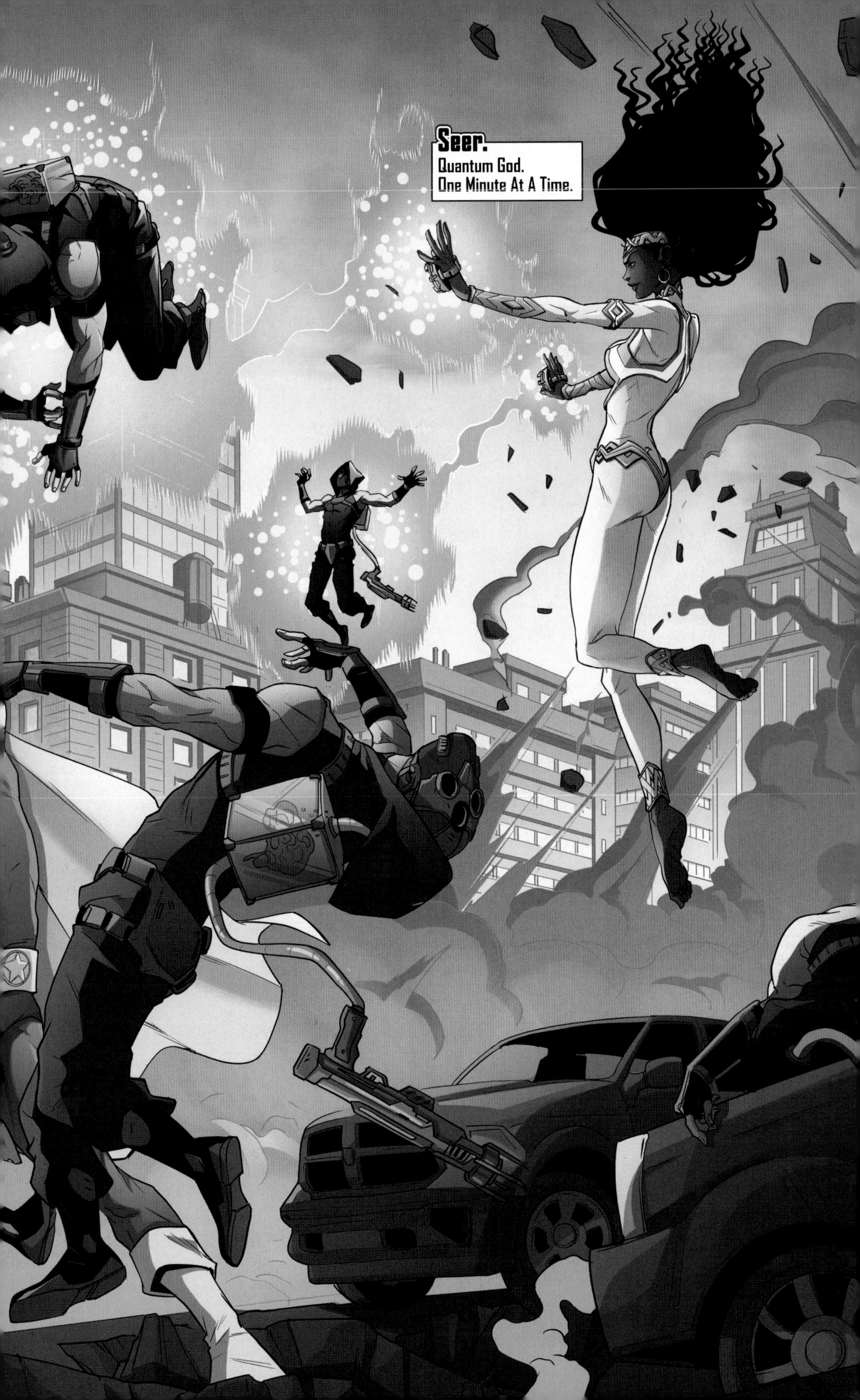
Seer.
Quantum God.
One Minute At A Time.

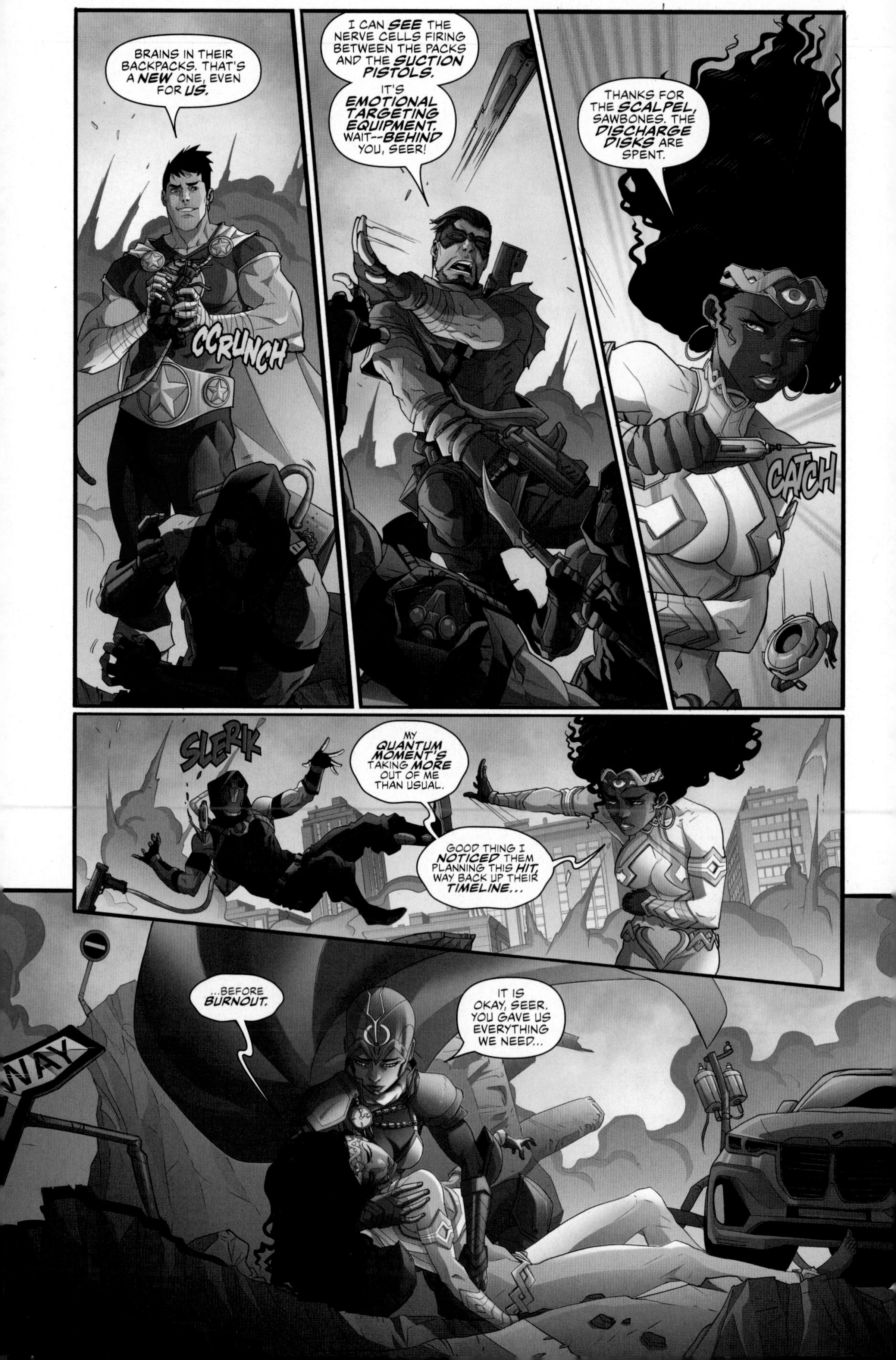
BRAINS IN THEIR BACKPACKS. THAT'S A NEW ONE, EVEN FOR US.
CCRUNCH
I CAN SEE THE NERVE CELLS FIRING BETWEEN THE PACKS AND THE SUCTION PISTOLS.
IT'S EMOTIONAL TARGETING EQUIPMENT. WAIT--BEHIND YOU, SEER!
THANKS FOR THE SCALPEL, SAWBONES. THE DISCHARGE DISKS ARE SPENT.
CATCH
SLERIK
MY QUANTUM MOMENT'S TAKING MORE OUT OF ME THAN USUAL.
GOOD THING I NOTICED THEM PLANNING THIS HIT, WAY BACK UP THEIR TIMELINE...
...BEFORE BURNOUT.
IT IS OKAY, SEER. YOU GAVE US EVERYTHING WE NEED...
WAY

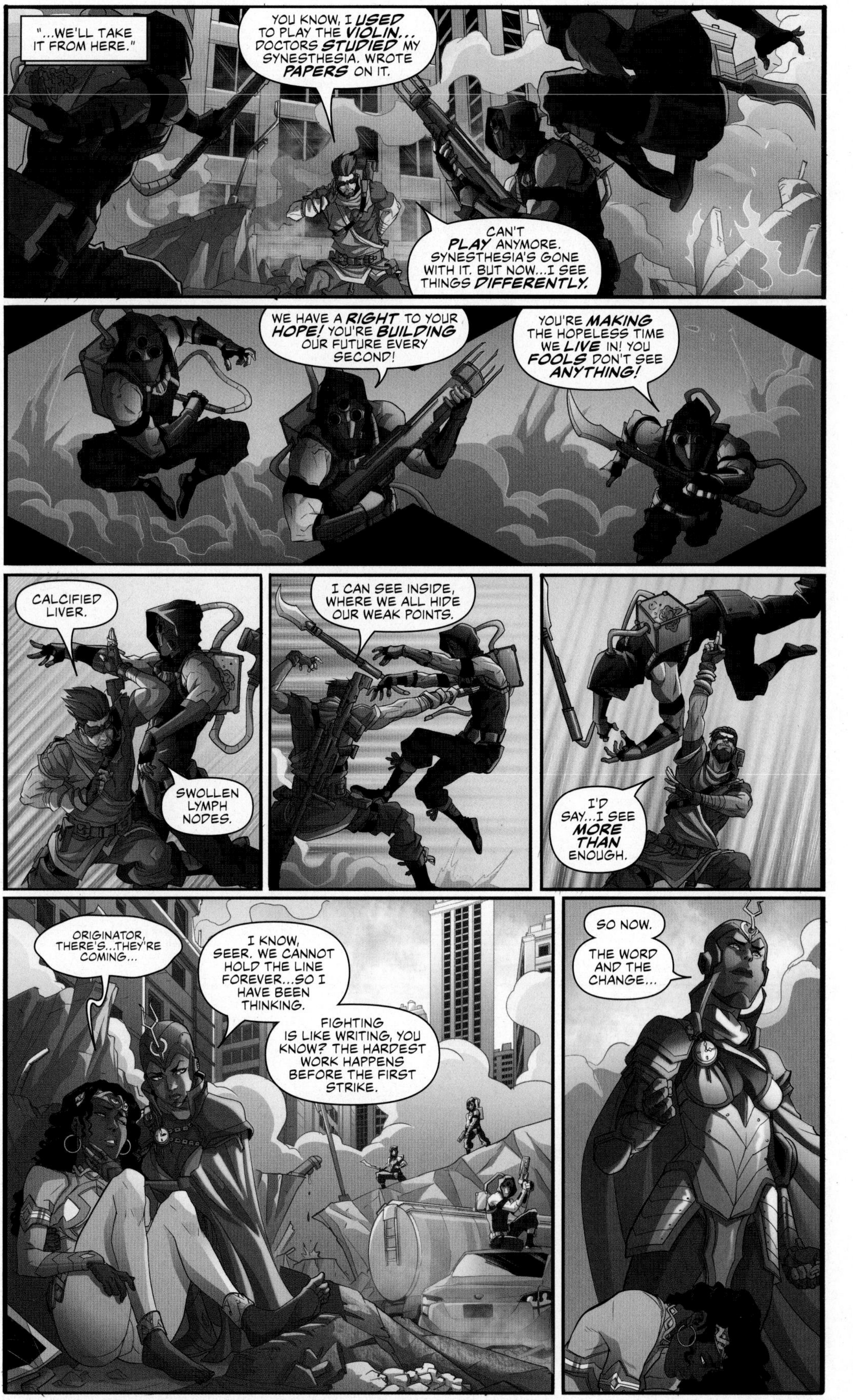
"...WE'LL TAKE IT FROM HERE."
YOU KNOW, I USED TO PLAY THE VIOLIN... DOCTORS STUDIED MY SYNESTHESIA. WROTE PAPERS ON IT.
CAN'T PLAY ANYMORE. SYNESTHESIA'S GONE WITH IT. BUT NOW...I SEE THINGS DIFFERENTLY.
WE HAVE A RIGHT TO YOUR HOPE! YOU'RE BUILDING OUR FUTURE EVERY SECOND!
YOU'RE MAKING THE HOPELESS TIME WE LIVE IN! YOU FOOLS DON'T SEE ANYTHING!
CALCIFIED LIVER.
SWOLLEN LYMPH NODES.
I CAN SEE INSIDE, WHERE WE ALL HIDE OUR WEAK POINTS.
I'D SAY...I SEE MORE THAN ENOUGH.
ORIGINATOR, THERE'S...THEY'RE COMING...
I KNOW, SEER. WE CANNOT HOLD THE LINE FOREVER...SO I HAVE BEEN THINKING.
FIGHTING IS LIKE WRITING, YOU KNOW? THE HARDEST WORK HAPPENS BEFORE THE FIRST STRIKE.
SO NOW.
THE WORD AND THE CHANGE...

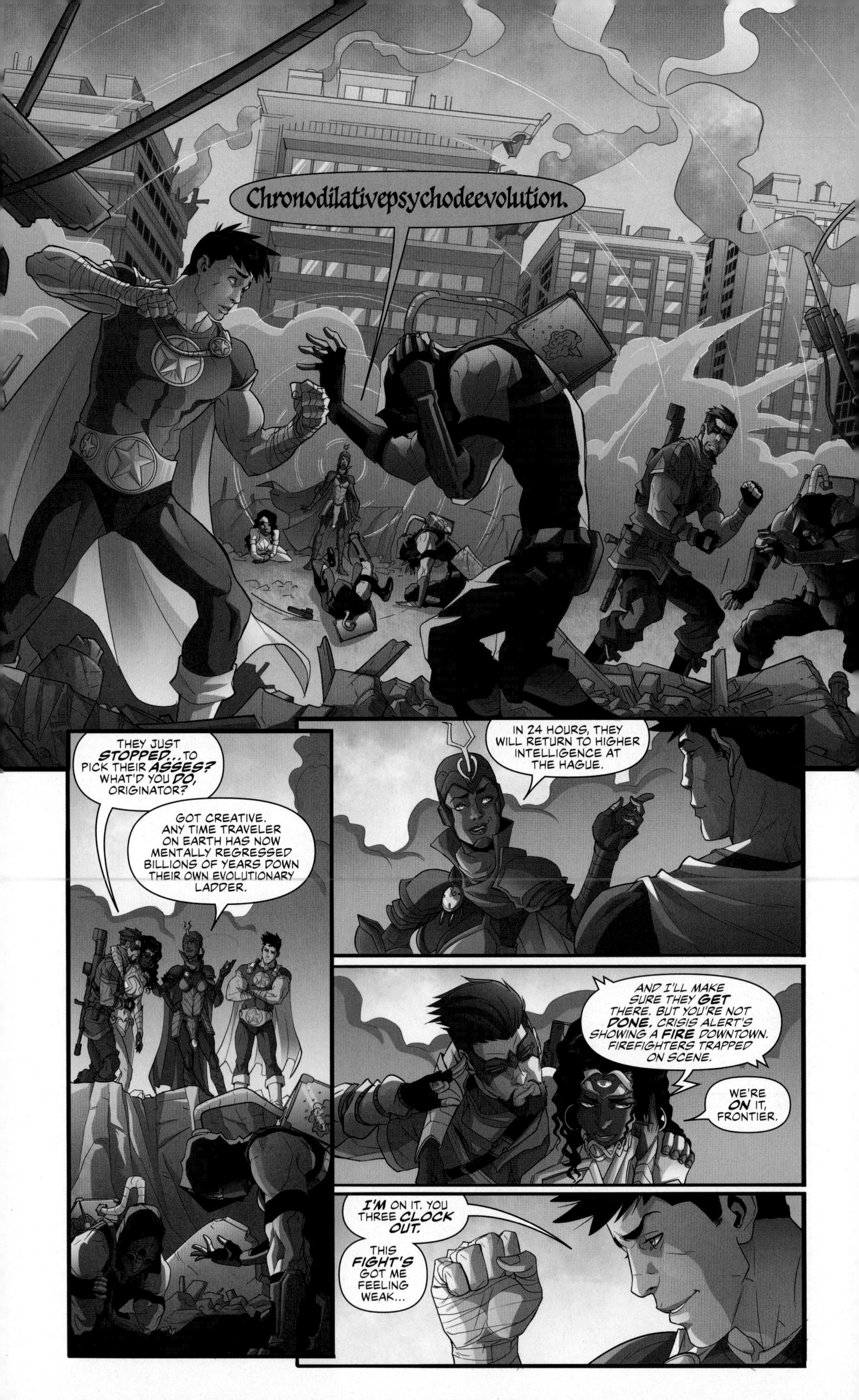
Chronodilativepsychodeevolution.
THEY JUST STOPPED... TO PICK THEIR ASSES? WHAT'D YOU DO, ORIGINATOR?
GOT CREATIVE. ANY TIME TRAVELER ON EARTH HAS NOW MENTALLY REGRESSED BILLIONS OF YEARS DOWN THEIR OWN EVOLUTIONARY LADDER.
IN 24 HOURS, THEY WILL RETURN TO HIGHER INTELLIGENCE AT THE HAGUE.
AND I'LL MAKE SURE THEY GET THERE. BUT YOU'RE NOT DONE. CRISIS ALERT'S SHOWING A FIRE DOWNTOWN. FIREFIGHTERS TRAPPED ON SCENE.
WE'RE ON IT, FRONTIER.
I'M ON IT. YOU THREE CLOCK OUT.
THIS FIGHT'S GOT ME FEELING WEAK...

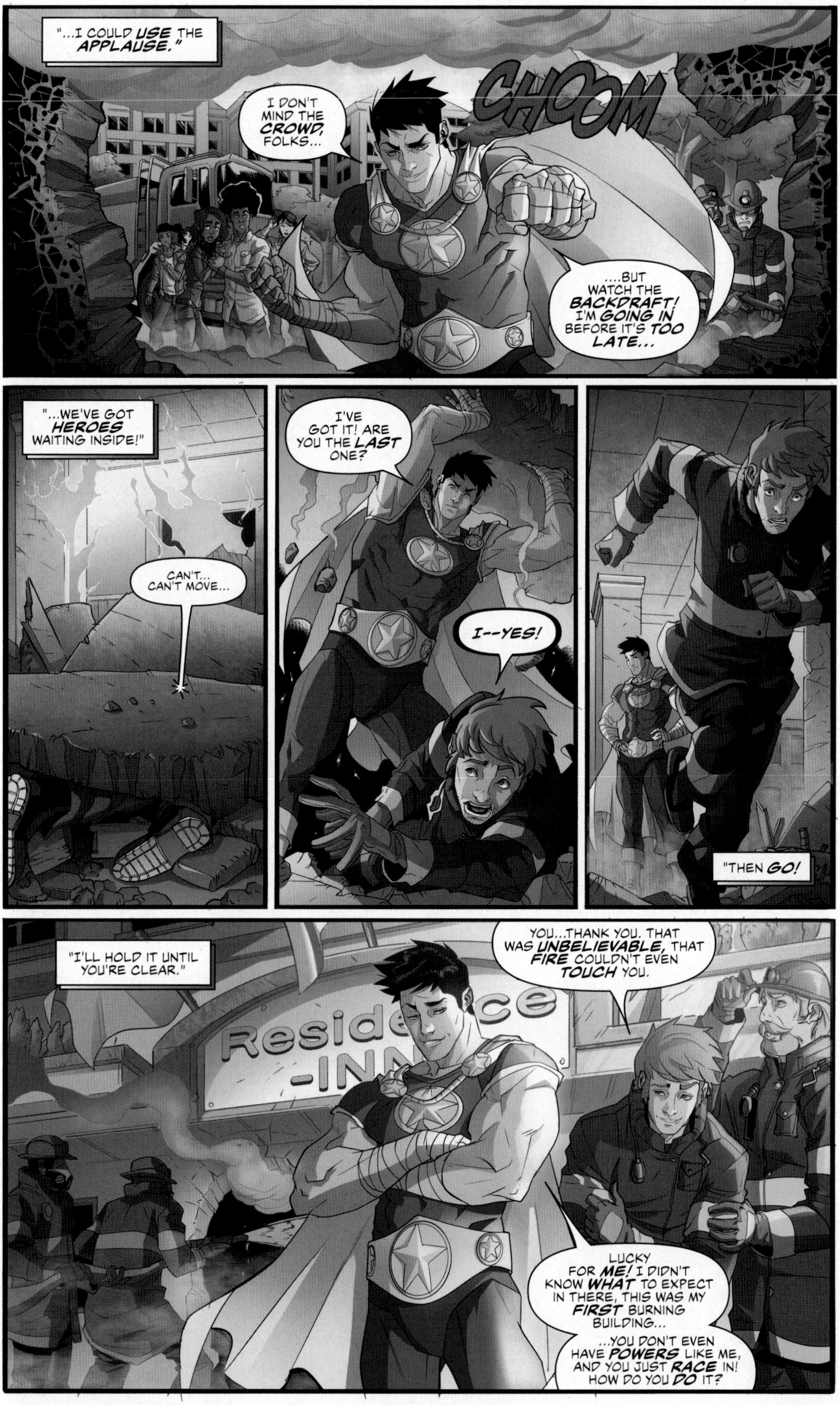
"...I COULD USE THE APPLAUSE."
I DON'T MIND THE CROWD, FOLKS...
CHOOM
....BUT WATCH THE BACKDRAFT! I'M GOING IN BEFORE IT'S TOO LATE...
"...WE'VE GOT HEROES WAITING INSIDE!"
CAN'T... CAN'T MOVE...
I'VE GOT IT! ARE YOU THE LAST ONE?
I--YES!
"THEN GO!
"I'LL HOLD IT UNTIL YOU'RE CLEAR."
YOU...THANK YOU. THAT WAS UNBELIEVABLE, THAT FIRE COULDN'T EVEN TOUCH YOU.
Residence -INN
LUCKY FOR ME! I DIDN'T KNOW WHAT TO EXPECT IN THERE, THIS WAS MY FIRST BURNING BUILDING...
...YOU DON'T EVEN HAVE POWERS LIKE ME, AND YOU JUST RACE IN! HOW DO YOU DO IT?

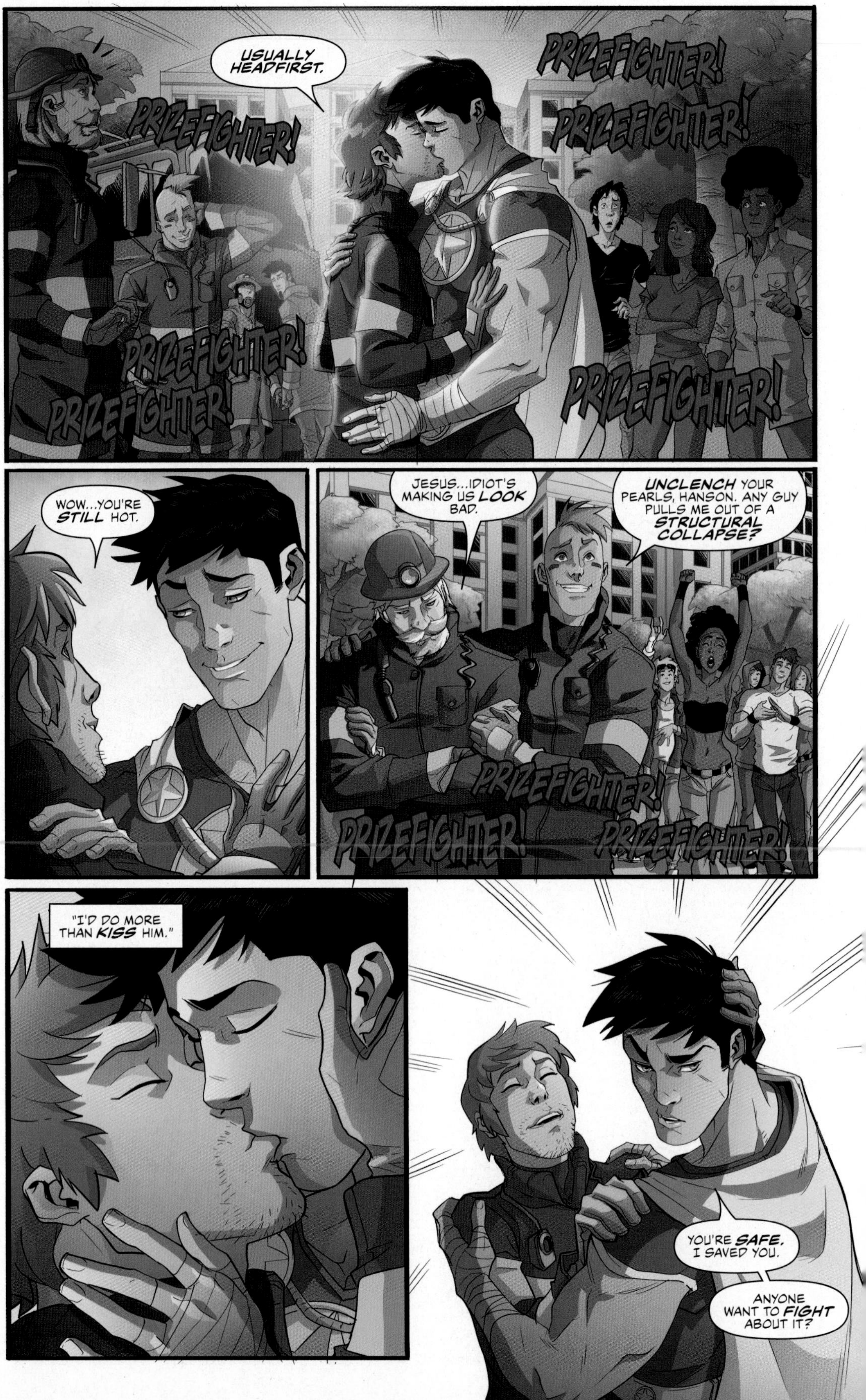
USUALLY HEADFIRST.
PRIZEFIGHTER!
PRIZEFIGHTER!
PRIZEFIGHTER!
PRIZEFIGHTER!
PRIZEFIGHTER!
PRIZEFIGHTER!
WOW...YOU'RE STILL HOT.
JESUS...IDIOT'S MAKING US LOOK BAD.
UNCLENCH YOUR PEARLS, HANSON. ANY GUY PULLS ME OUT OF A STRUCTURAL COLLAPSE?
PRIZEFIGHTER!
PRIZEFIGHTER!
PRIZEFIGHTER!
"I'D DO MORE THAN KISS HIM."
YOU'RE SAFE. I SAVED YOU.
ANYONE WANT TO FIGHT ABOUT IT?

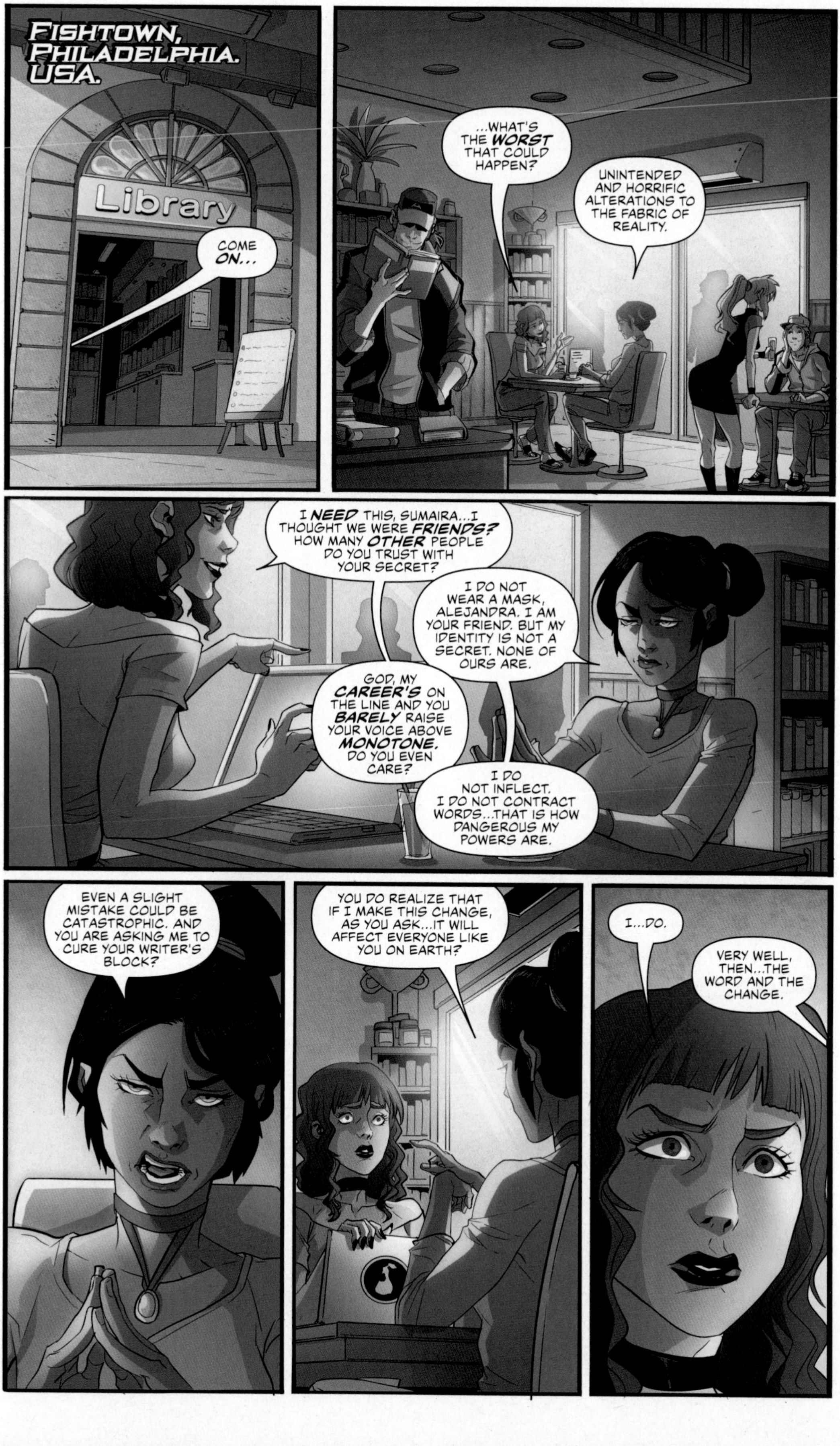
FISHTOWN, PHILADELPHIA. USA.
Library
COME ON...
...WHAT'S THE WORST THAT COULD HAPPEN?
UNINTENDED AND HORRIFIC ALTERATIONS TO THE FABRIC OF REALITY.
I NEED THIS, SUMAIRA...I THOUGHT WE WERE FRIENDS? HOW MANY OTHER PEOPLE DO YOU TRUST WITH YOUR SECRET?
I DO NOT WEAR A MASK, ALEJANDRA. I AM YOUR FRIEND. BUT MY IDENTITY IS NOT A SECRET. NONE OF OURS ARE.
GOD, MY CAREER'S ON THE LINE AND YOU BARELY RAISE YOUR VOICE ABOVE MONOTONE. DO YOU EVEN CARE?
I DO NOT INFLECT. I DO NOT CONTRACT WORDS...THAT IS HOW DANGEROUS MY POWERS ARE.
EVEN A SLIGHT MISTAKE COULD BE CATASTROPHIC. AND YOU ARE ASKING ME TO CURE YOUR WRITER'S BLOCK?
YOU DO REALIZE THAT IF I MAKE THIS CHANGE, AS YOU ASK...IT WILL AFFECT EVERYONE LIKE YOU ON EARTH?
I...DO.
VERY WELL, THEN...THE WORD AND THE CHANGE.

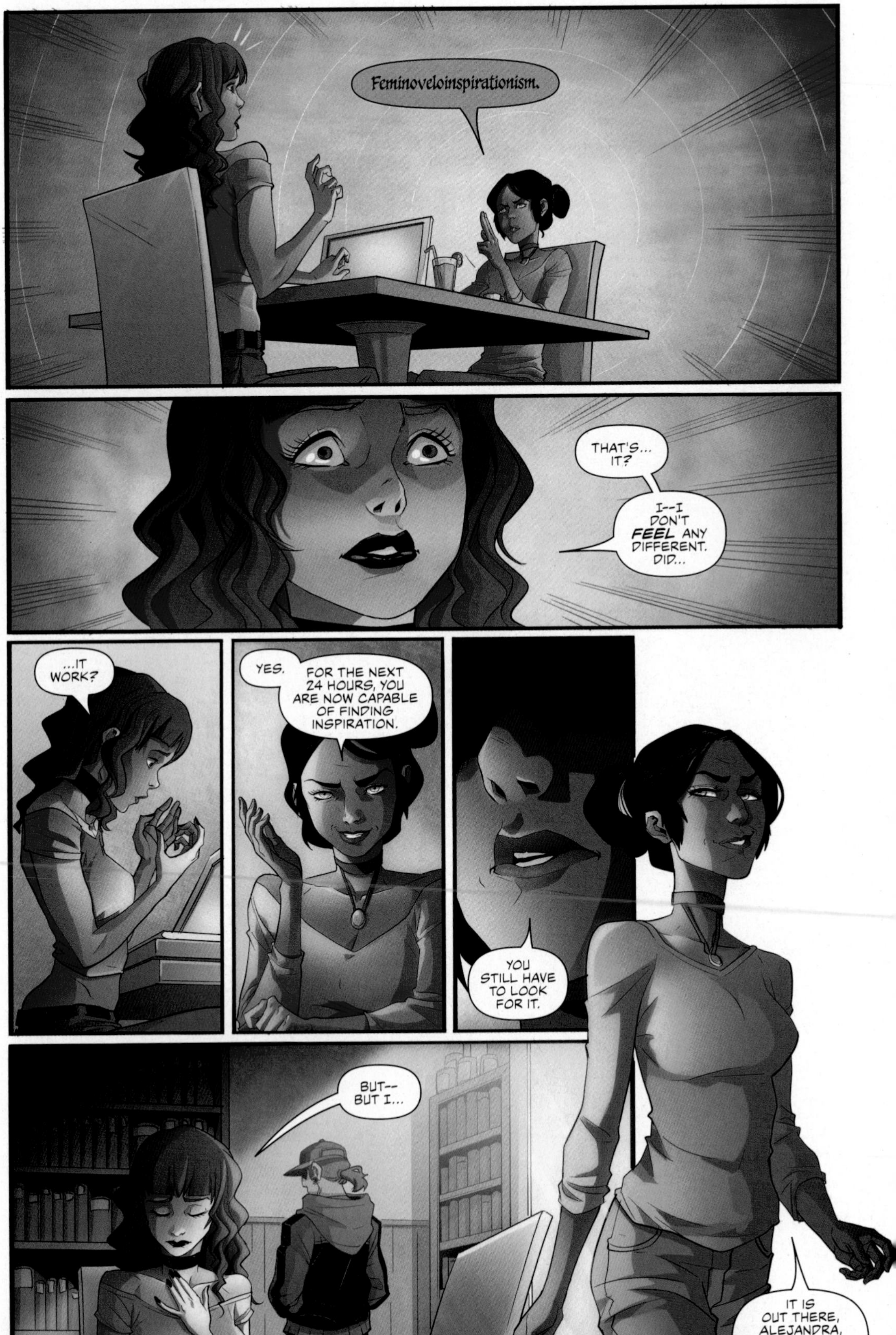
Feminoveloinspirationism.
THAT'S... IT?
I--I DON'T FEEL ANY DIFFERENT. DID...
...IT WORK?
YES.
FOR THE NEXT 24 HOURS, YOU ARE NOW CAPABLE OF FINDING INSPIRATION.
YOU STILL HAVE TO LOOK FOR IT.
BUT-- BUT I...
IT IS OUT THERE, ALEJANDRA, WHEN BEFORE IT WAS NOT. BUT EVEN SO...

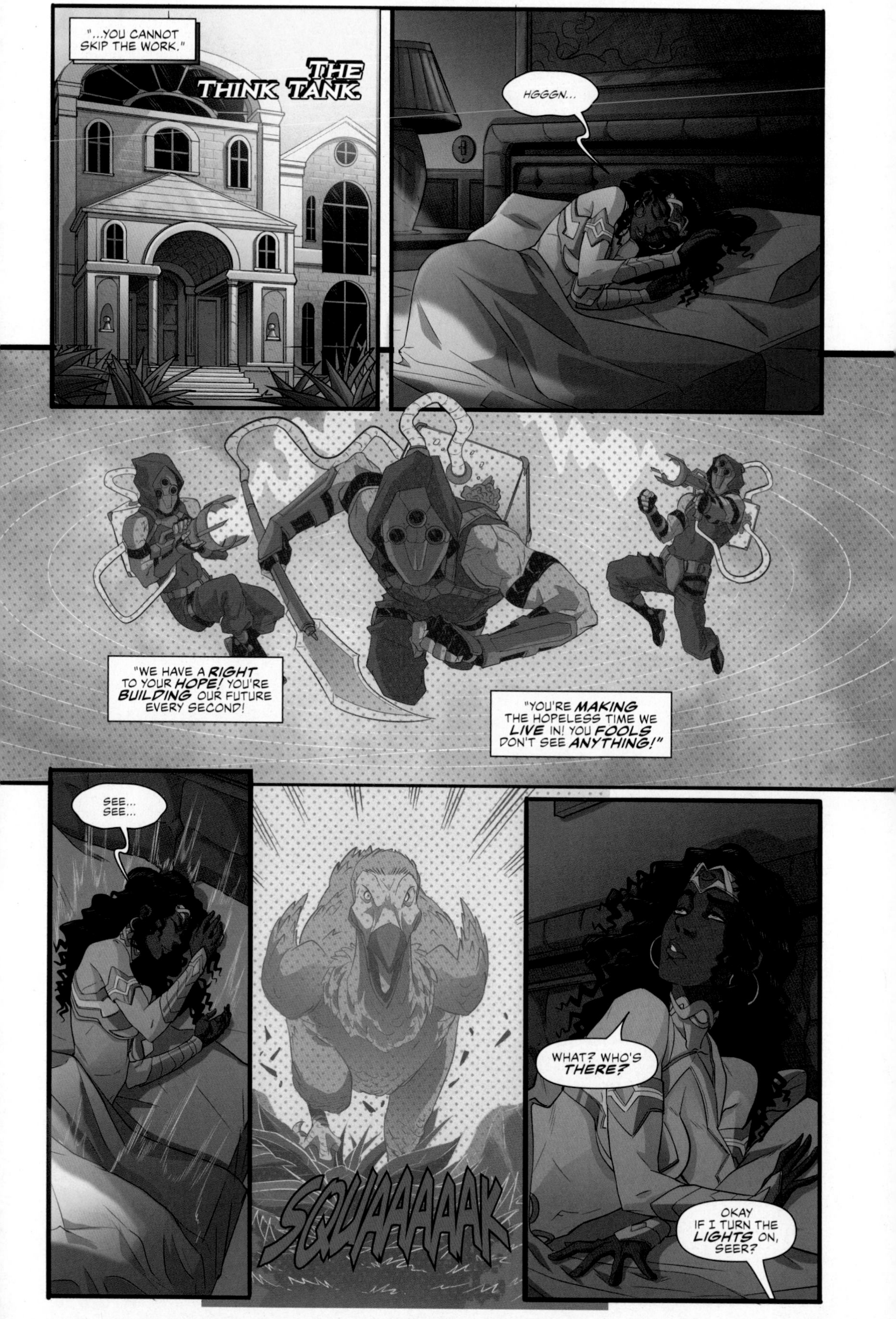
"...YOU CANNOT SKIP THE WORK."
THE THINK TANK
HGGGN...
"WE HAVE A RIGHT TO YOUR HOPE! YOU'RE BUILDING OUR FUTURE EVERY SECOND!
"YOU'RE MAKING THE HOPELESS TIME WE LIVE IN! YOU FOOLS DON'T SEE ANYTHING!"
SEE... SEE...
SQUAAAAAK
WHAT? WHO'S THERE?
OKAY IF I TURN THE LIGHTS ON, SEER?

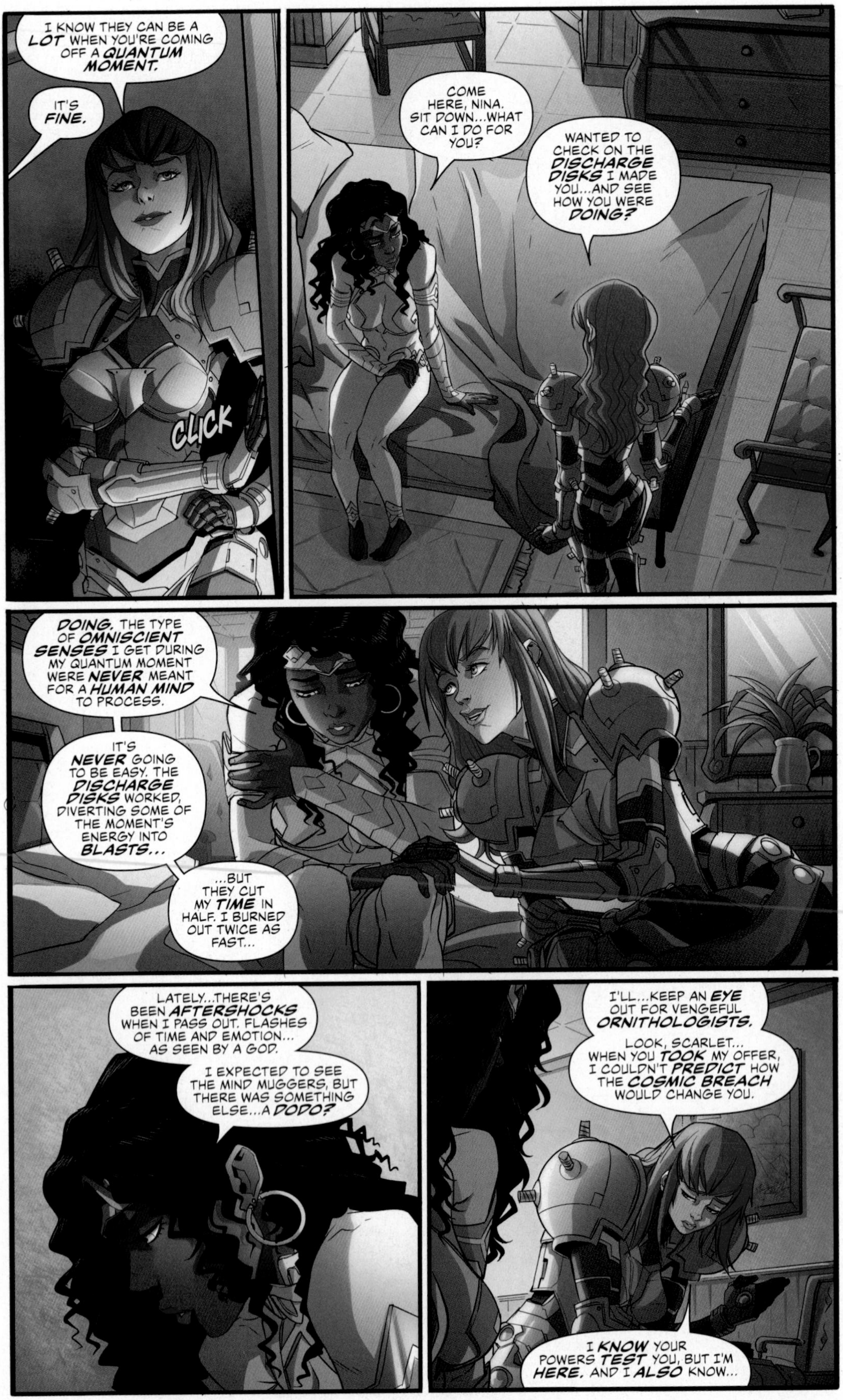
I KNOW THEY CAN BE A LOT WHEN YOU'RE COMING OFF A QUANTUM MOMENT.
IT'S FINE.
CLICK
COME HERE, NINA. SIT DOWN...WHAT CAN I DO FOR YOU?
WANTED TO CHECK ON THE DISCHARGE DISKS I MADE YOU...AND SEE HOW YOU WERE DOING?
DOING. THE TYPE OF OMNISCIENT SENSES I GET DURING MY QUANTUM MOMENT WERE NEVER MEANT FOR A HUMAN MIND TO PROCESS.
IT'S NEVER GOING TO BE EASY. THE DISCHARGE DISKS WORKED, DIVERTING SOME OF THE MOMENT'S ENERGY INTO BLASTS...
...BUT THEY CUT MY TIME IN HALF. I BURNED OUT TWICE AS FAST...
LATELY...THERE'S BEEN AFTERSHOCKS WHEN I PASS OUT. FLASHES OF TIME AND EMOTION... AS SEEN BY A GOD.
I EXPECTED TO SEE THE MIND MUGGERS, BUT THERE WAS SOMETHING ELSE...A DODO?
I'LL...KEEP AN EYE OUT FOR VENGEFUL ORNITHOLOGISTS.
LOOK, SCARLET... WHEN YOU TOOK MY OFFER, I COULDN'T PREDICT HOW THE COSMIC BREACH WOULD CHANGE YOU.
I KNOW YOUR POWERS TEST YOU, BUT I'M HERE. AND I ALSO KNOW...

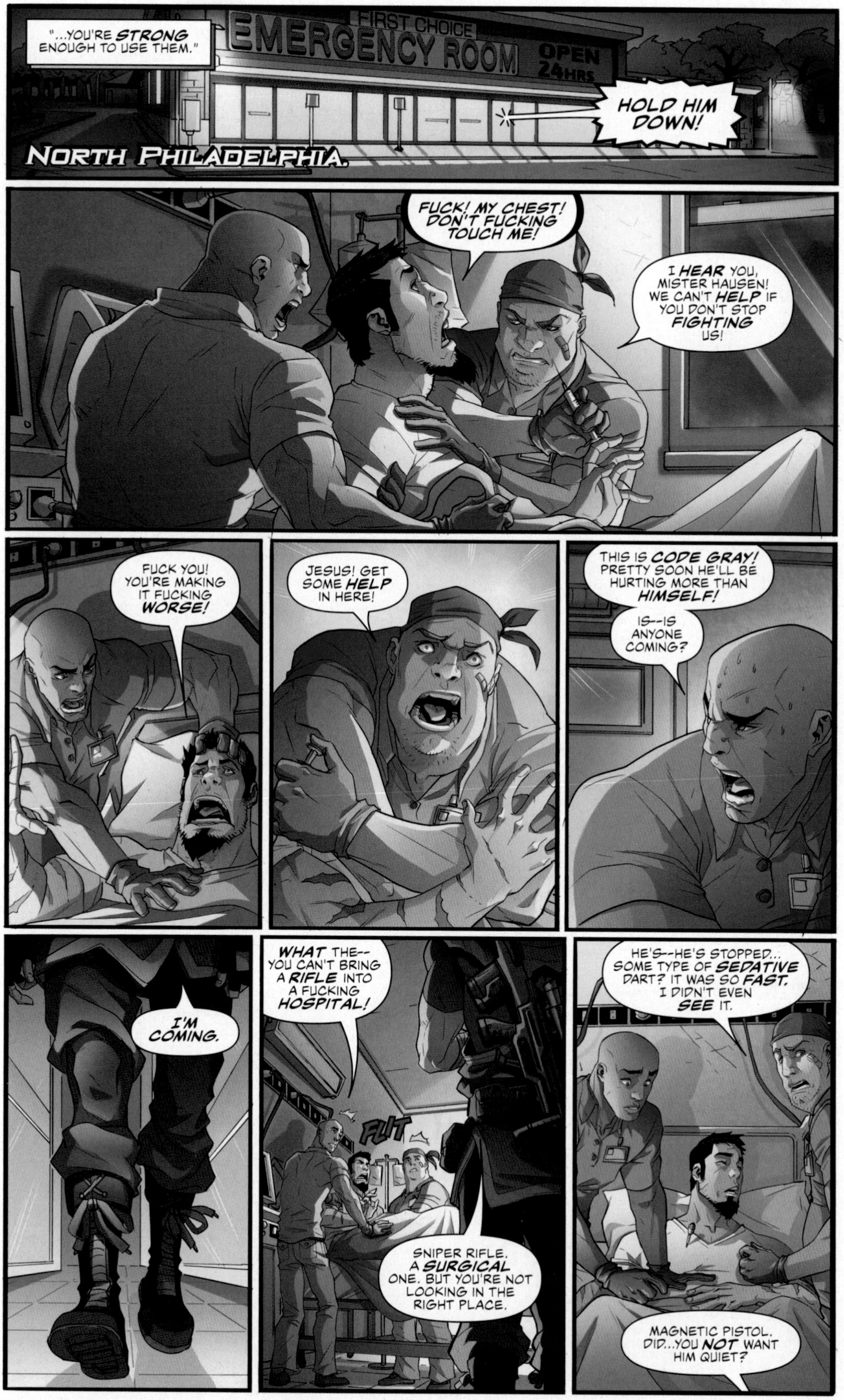
"...YOU'RE STRONG ENOUGH TO USE THEM."
FIRST CHOICE
EMERGENCY ROOM
OPEN 24HRS
HOLD HIM DOWN!
NORTH PHILADELPHIA.
FUCK! MY CHEST! DON'T FUCKING TOUCH ME!
I HEAR YOU, MISTER HAUSEN! WE CAN'T HELP IF YOU DON'T STOP FIGHTING US!
FUCK YOU! YOU'RE MAKING IT FUCKING WORSE!
JESUS! GET SOME HELP IN HERE!
THIS IS CODE GRAY! PRETTY SOON HE'LL BE HURTING MORE THAN HIMSELF!
IS--IS ANYONE COMING?
I'M COMING.
WHAT THE-- YOU CAN'T BRING A RIFLE INTO A FUCKING HOSPITAL!
FLIT
SNIPER RIFLE. A SURGICAL ONE. BUT YOU'RE NOT LOOKING IN THE RIGHT PLACE.
HE'S--HE'S STOPPED... SOME TYPE OF SEDATIVE DART? IT WAS SO FAST. I DIDN'T EVEN SEE IT.
MAGNETIC PISTOL. DID...YOU NOT WANT HIM QUIET?

I'M NOT A *DOCTOR*, BUT I CAN *HELP*. WHAT DO WE *KNOW?*

DANIEL HAUSEN. TWENTY-NINE. IF YOU COULDN'T TELL FROM THE SCARS...BACKYARD WRESTLER.

HIS COWORKERS OR...WHATEVER, DROPPED HIM IN THE E.D. AND LEFT.

NOW THAT HE'S *CALM*, LET'S SEE WHAT'S ACTUALLY GOING ON WITH HIM.

WHATEVER IT IS, IT'S *INTERNAL*. WE *CALLED* FOR AN X-RAY.

DON'T *NEED* ONE...

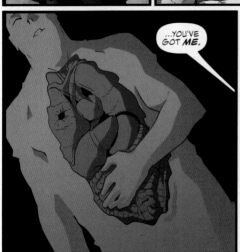

...YOU'VE GOT *ME*.

HOLE IN HIS LUNG, BRUISING *ALL OVER* HIS ORGANS.

A PNEUMOTHORAX? YOU KNOW WHAT'S *WRONG* WITH HIM BUT YOU'RE TALKING ABOUT IT LIKE A *MECHANIC*.

I *SAID* I WASN'T A *DOCTOR*...JUST GOT *GOOD* EYES.

BUT I'M *LEARNING*. THE NAME'S *SAWBONES*...

...MERCENARY MEDIC IN A *WORLD* THAT'S *FIGHTING ITSELF*.

JUST *HERE* TO MAKE SURE, NO MATTER THE *BATTLE*...

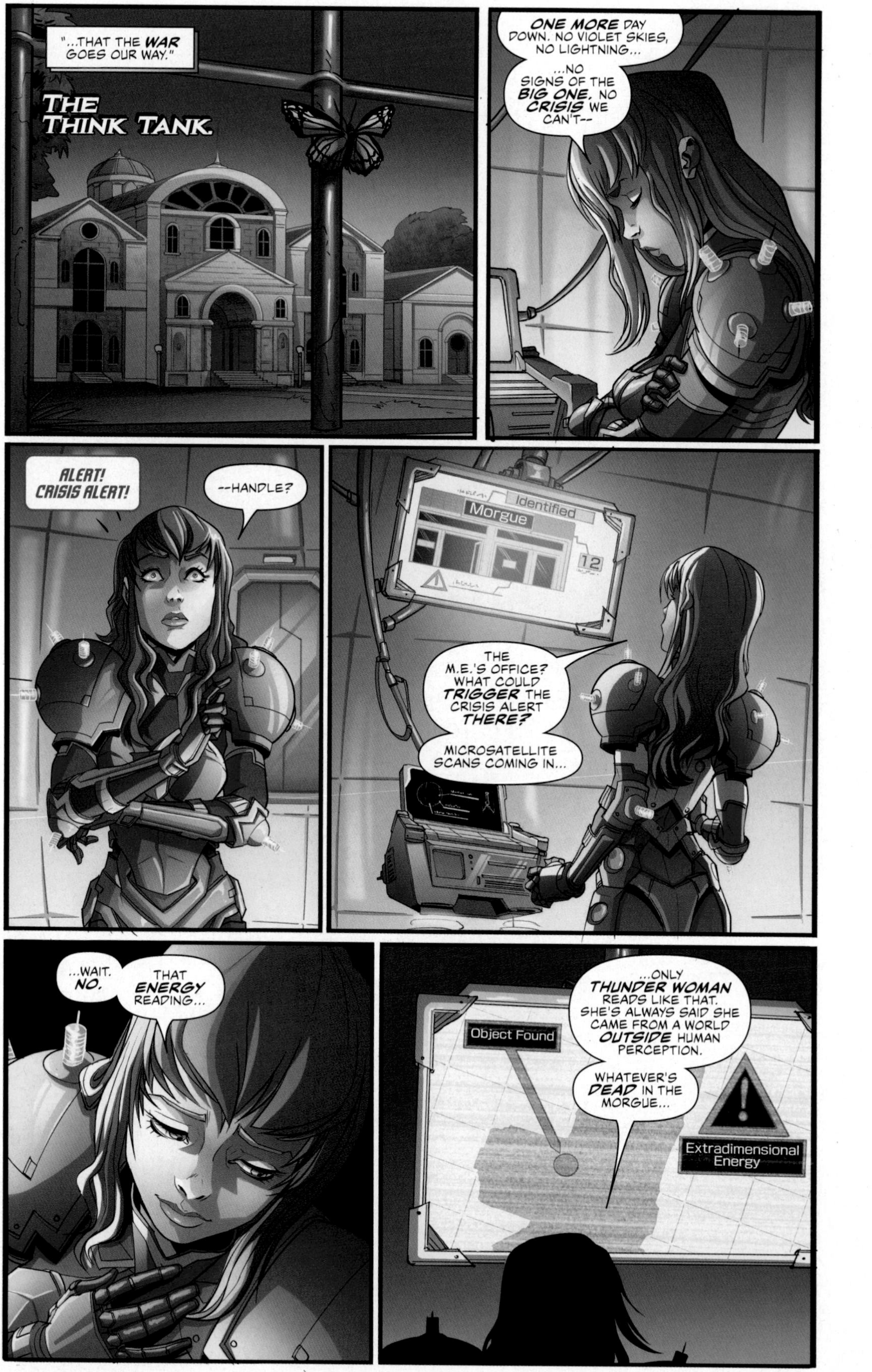
"...THAT THE WAR GOES OUR WAY."
THE THINK TANK.
ONE MORE DAY DOWN. NO VIOLET SKIES, NO LIGHTNING...
...NO SIGNS OF THE BIG ONE. NO CRISIS WE CAN'T--
ALERT! CRISIS ALERT!
--HANDLE?
Identified
Morgue
12
THE M.E.'S OFFICE? WHAT COULD TRIGGER THE CRISIS ALERT THERE?
MICROSATELLITE SCANS COMING IN...
...WAIT. NO.
THAT ENERGY READING...
Object Found
...ONLY THUNDER WOMAN READS LIKE THAT. SHE'S ALWAYS SAID SHE CAME FROM A WORLD OUTSIDE HUMAN PERCEPTION.
WHATEVER'S DEAD IN THE MORGUE...
Extradimensional Energy

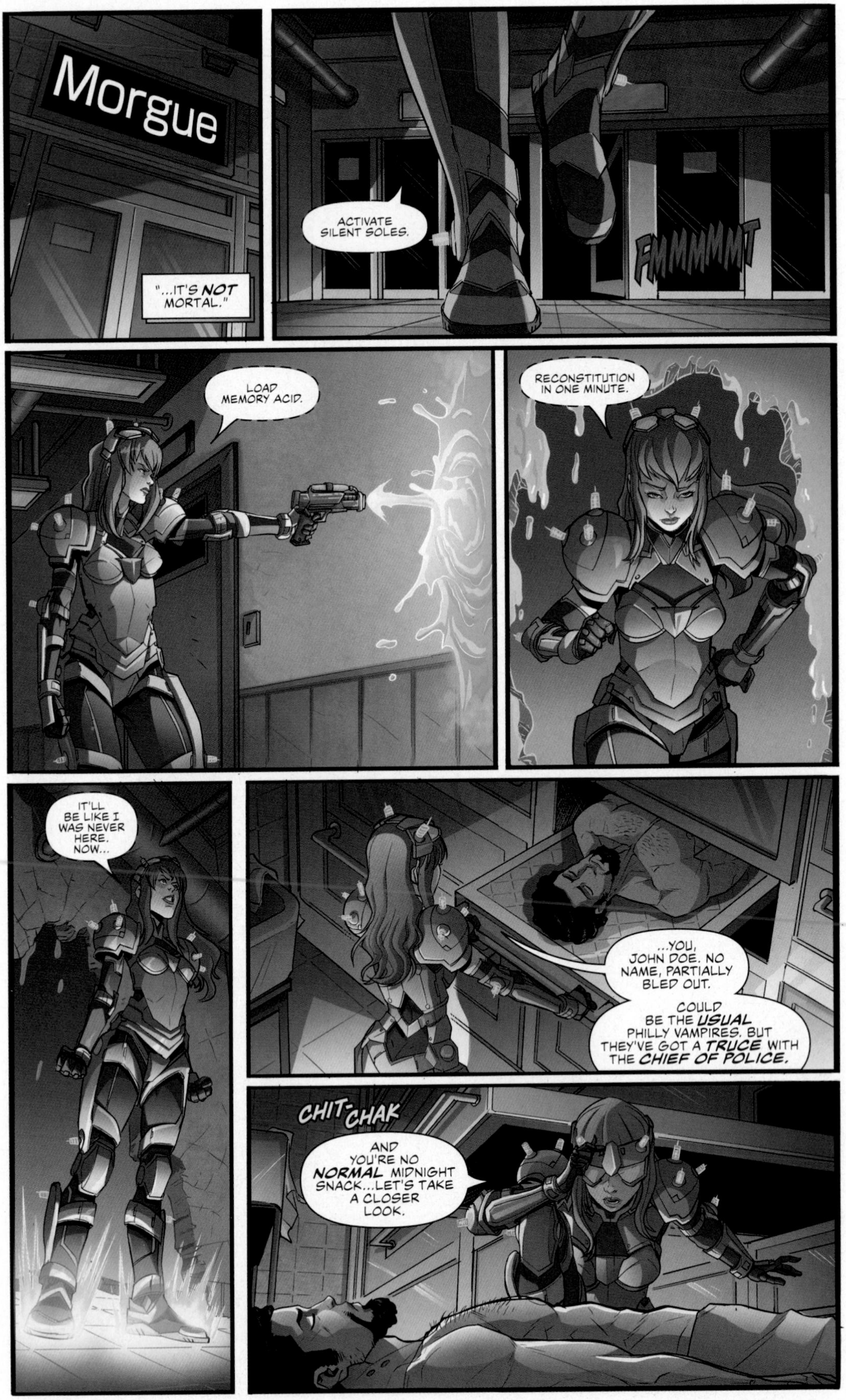
Morgue
"...IT'S NOT MORTAL."
ACTIVATE SILENT SOLES.
FMMMMMT
LOAD MEMORY ACID.
RECONSTITUTION IN ONE MINUTE.
IT'LL BE LIKE I WAS NEVER HERE. NOW...
...YOU, JOHN DOE. NO NAME, PARTIALLY BLED OUT.
COULD BE THE USUAL PHILLY VAMPIRES. BUT THEY'VE GOT A TRUCE WITH THE CHIEF OF POLICE.
CHIT-CHAK
AND YOU'RE NO NORMAL MIDNIGHT SNACK...LET'S TAKE A CLOSER LOOK.

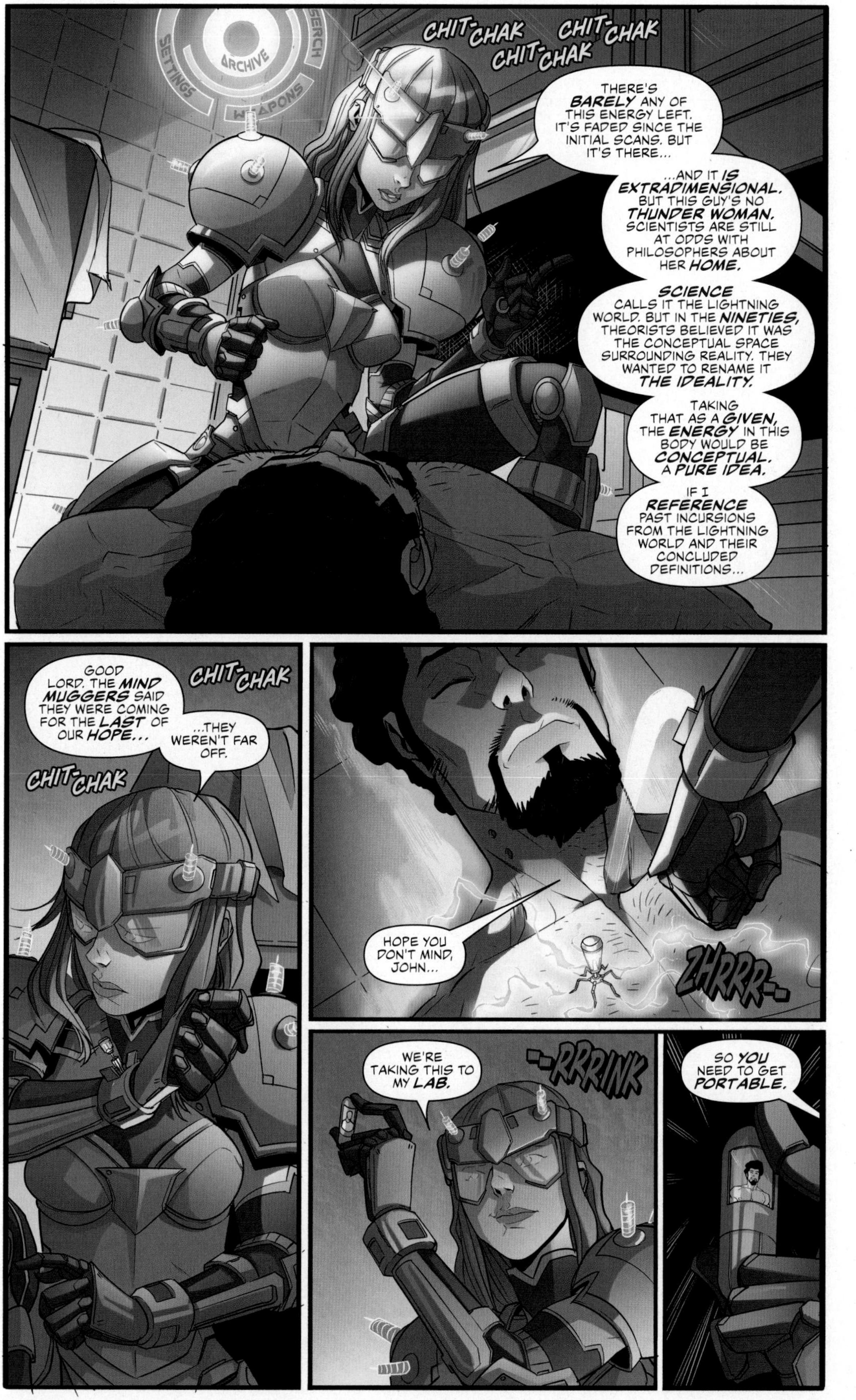
SETTINGS
ARCHIVE
SERCH
WEAPONS
CHIT-CHAK CHIT-CHAK
CHIT-CHAK
THERE'S BARELY ANY OF THIS ENERGY LEFT. IT'S FADED SINCE THE INITIAL SCANS. BUT IT'S THERE...
...AND IT IS EXTRADIMENSIONAL. BUT THIS GUY'S NO THUNDER WOMAN. SCIENTISTS ARE STILL AT ODDS WITH PHILOSOPHERS ABOUT HER HOME.
SCIENCE CALLS IT THE LIGHTNING WORLD. BUT IN THE NINETIES, THEORISTS BELIEVED IT WAS THE CONCEPTUAL SPACE SURROUNDING REALITY. THEY WANTED TO RENAME IT THE IDEALITY.
TAKING THAT AS A GIVEN, THE ENERGY IN THIS BODY WOULD BE CONCEPTUAL. A PURE IDEA.
IF I REFERENCE PAST INCURSIONS FROM THE LIGHTNING WORLD AND THEIR CONCLUDED DEFINITIONS...
GOOD LORD. THE MIND MUGGERS SAID THEY WERE COMING FOR THE LAST OF OUR HOPE...
CHIT-CHAK
...THEY WEREN'T FAR OFF.
CHIT-CHAK
HOPE YOU DON'T MIND, JOHN...
ZHRRR--
WE'RE TAKING THIS TO MY LAB.
--RRRINK
SO YOU NEED TO GET PORTABLE.

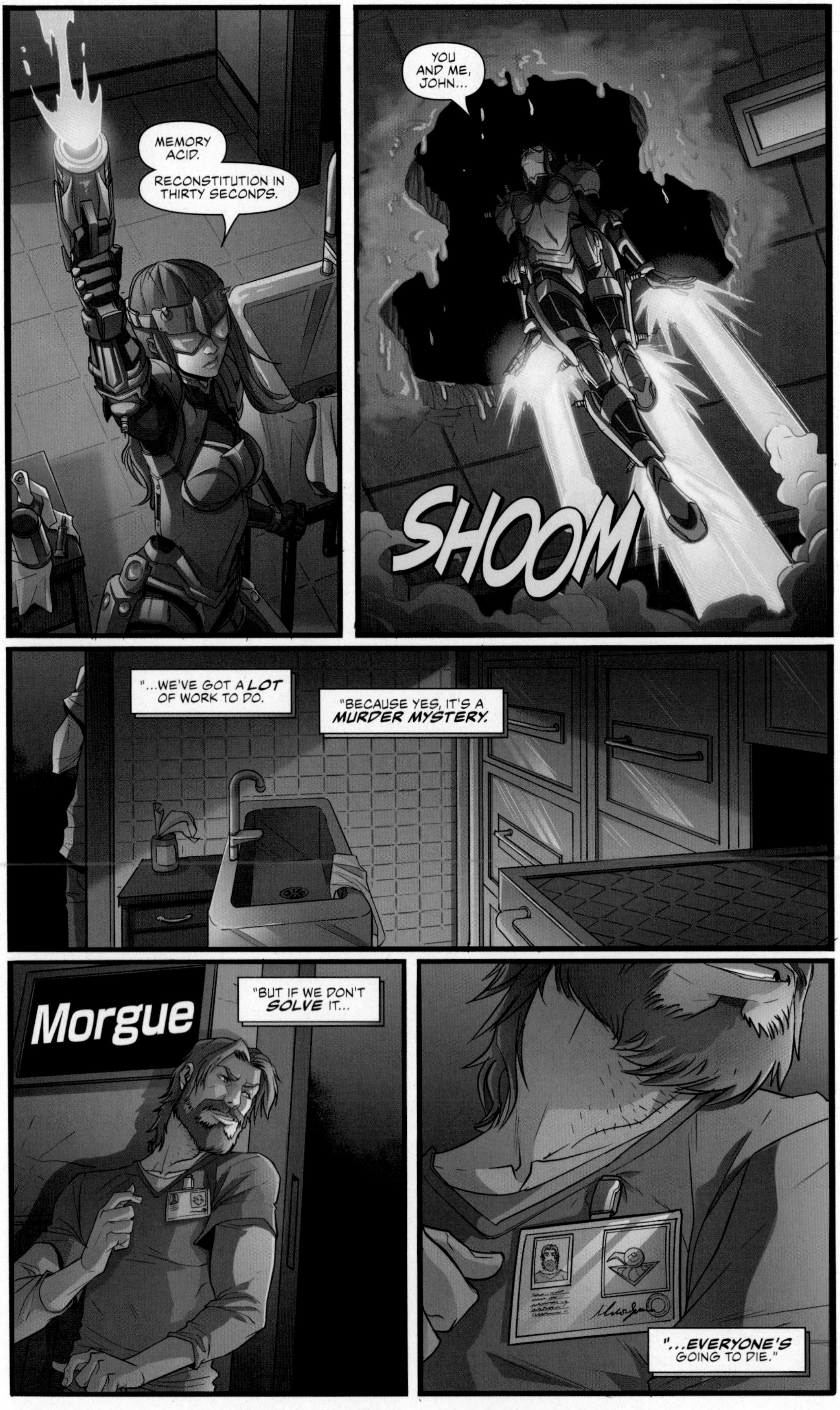
MEMORY ACID.
RECONSTITUTION IN THIRTY SECONDS.
YOU AND ME, JOHN...
SHOOM
"...WE'VE GOT A *LOT* OF WORK TO DO.
"BECAUSE YES, IT'S A *MURDER MYSTERY.*
Morgue
"BUT IF WE DON'T *SOLVE* IT...
"...*EVERYONE'S* GOING TO DIE."

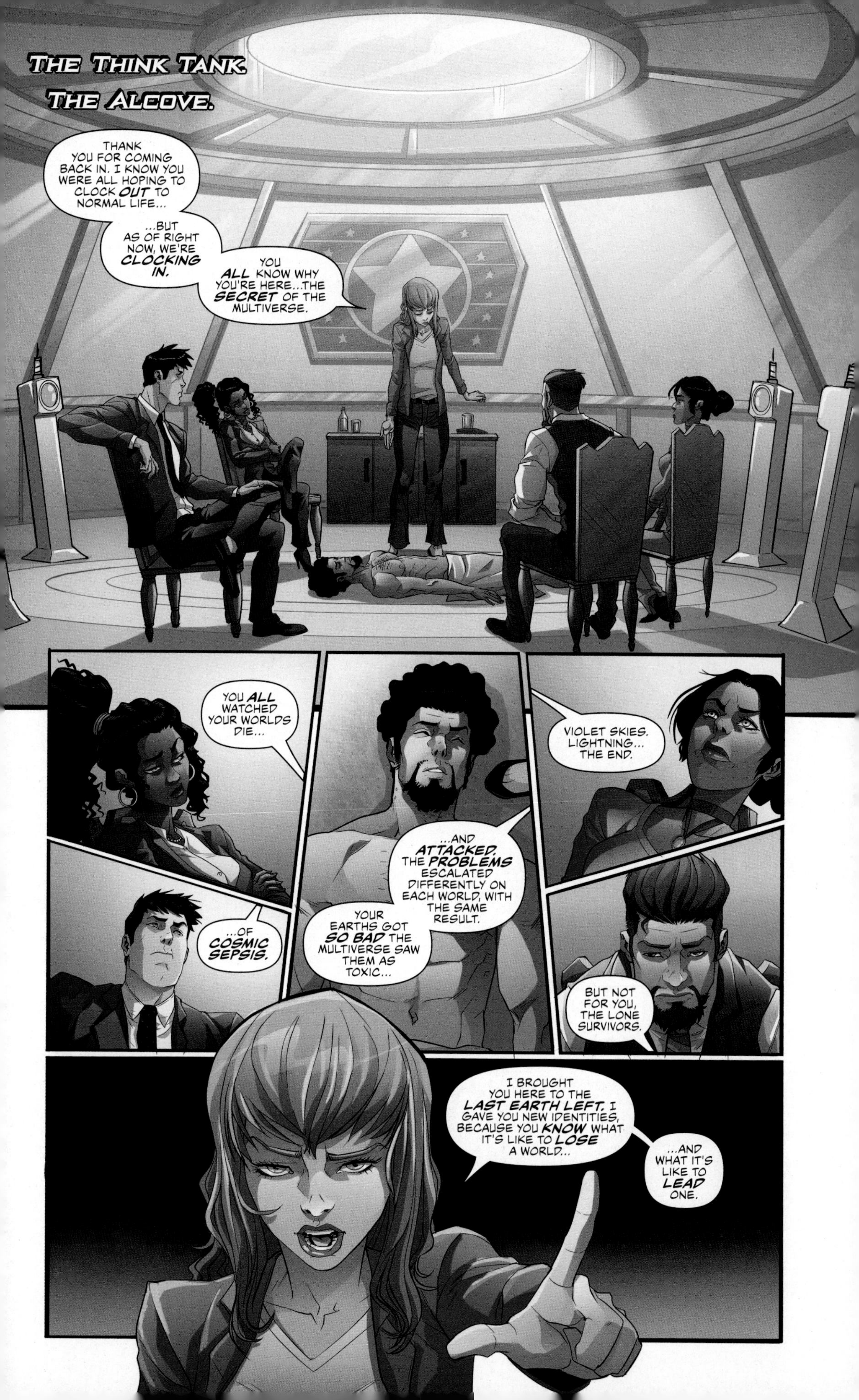
THE THINK TANK.
THE ALCOVE.
THANK YOU FOR COMING BACK IN. I KNOW YOU WERE ALL HOPING TO CLOCK OUT TO NORMAL LIFE...
...BUT AS OF RIGHT NOW, WE'RE CLOCKING IN.
YOU ALL KNOW WHY YOU'RE HERE...THE SECRET OF THE MULTIVERSE.
YOU ALL WATCHED YOUR WORLDS DIE...
VIOLET SKIES. LIGHTNING... THE END.
...AND ATTACKED. THE PROBLEMS ESCALATED DIFFERENTLY ON EACH WORLD, WITH THE SAME RESULT.
...OF COSMIC SEPSIS.
YOUR EARTHS GOT SO BAD THE MULTIVERSE SAW THEM AS TOXIC...
BUT NOT FOR YOU, THE LONE SURVIVORS.
I BROUGHT YOU HERE TO THE LAST EARTH LEFT. I GAVE YOU NEW IDENTITIES, BECAUSE YOU KNOW WHAT IT'S LIKE TO LOSE A WORLD...
...AND WHAT IT'S LIKE TO LEAD ONE.

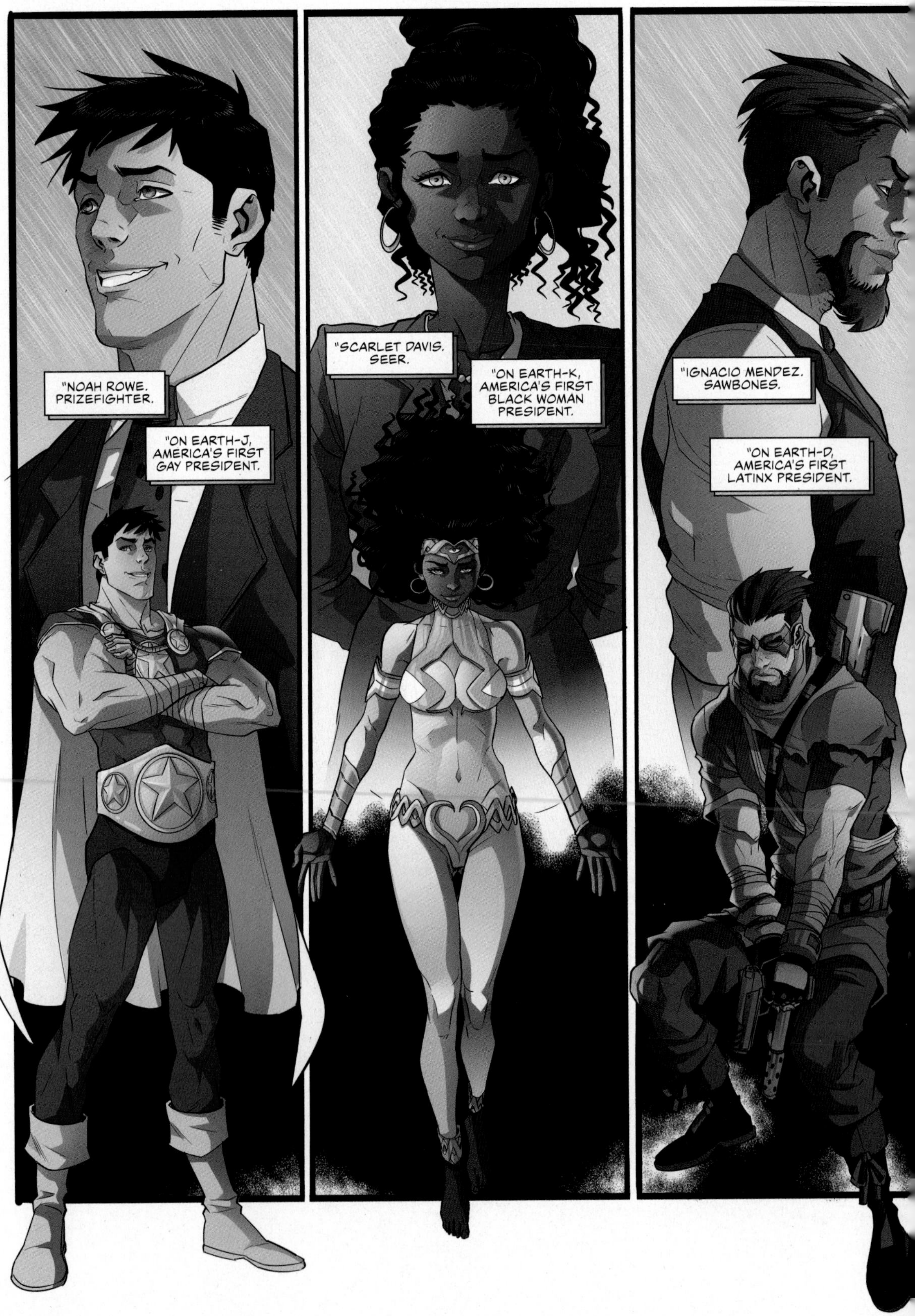
"NOAH ROWE. PRIZEFIGHTER.
"ON EARTH-J, AMERICA'S FIRST GAY PRESIDENT.
"SCARLET DAVIS. SEER.
"ON EARTH-K, AMERICA'S FIRST BLACK WOMAN PRESIDENT.
"IGNACIO MENDEZ. SAWBONES.
"ON EARTH-D, AMERICA'S FIRST LATINX PRESIDENT.

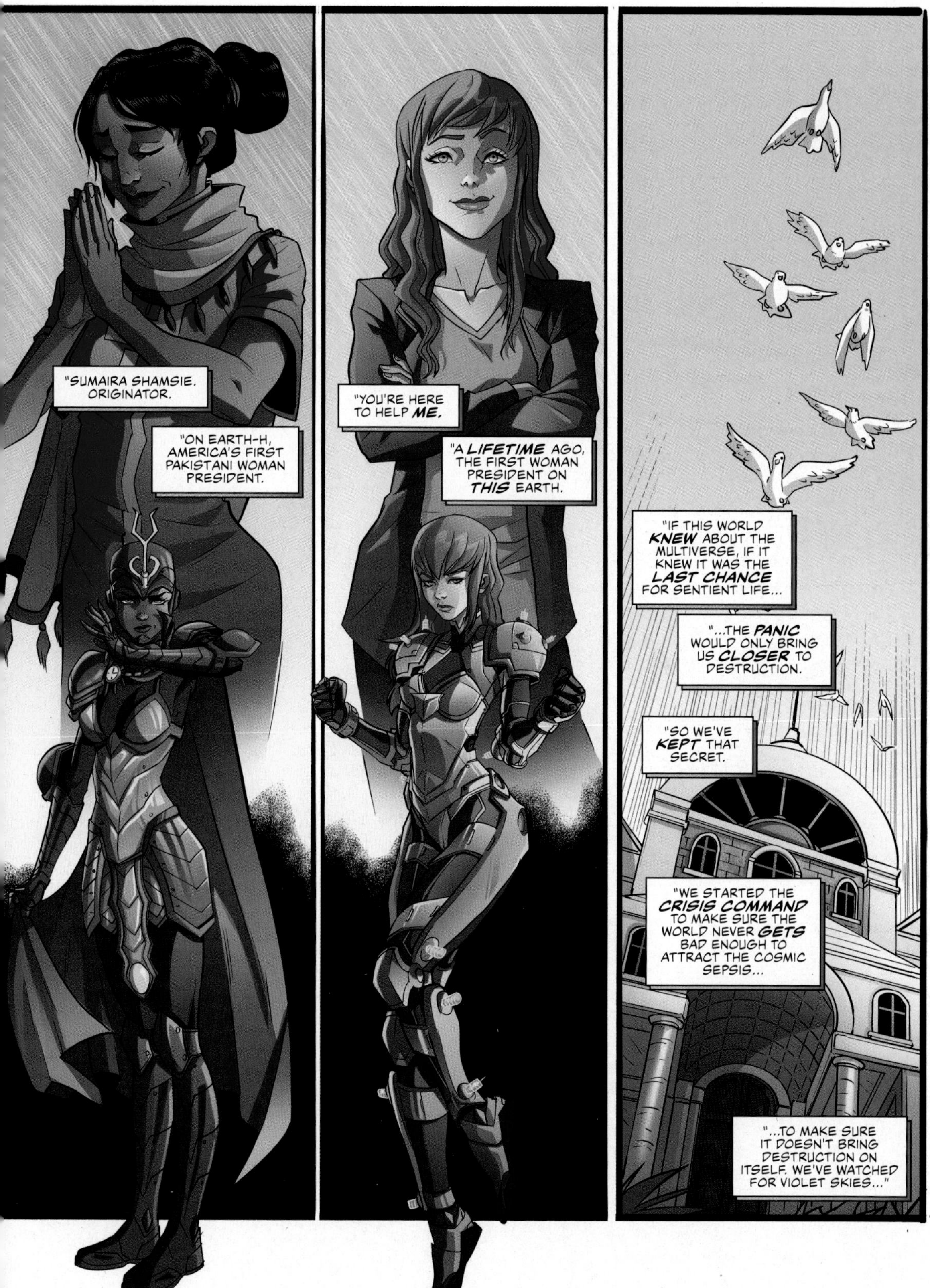
"SUMAIRA SHAMSIE. ORIGINATOR.
"ON EARTH-H, AMERICA'S FIRST PAKISTANI WOMAN PRESIDENT.
"YOU'RE HERE TO HELP ME.
"A LIFETIME AGO, THE FIRST WOMAN PRESIDENT ON THIS EARTH.
"IF THIS WORLD KNEW ABOUT THE MULTIVERSE, IF IT KNEW IT WAS THE LAST CHANCE FOR SENTIENT LIFE...
"...THE PANIC WOULD ONLY BRING US CLOSER TO DESTRUCTION.
"SO WE'VE KEPT THAT SECRET.
"WE STARTED THE CRISIS COMMAND TO MAKE SURE THE WORLD NEVER GETS BAD ENOUGH TO ATTRACT THE COSMIC SEPSIS...
"...TO MAKE SURE IT DOESN'T BRING DESTRUCTION ON ITSELF. WE'VE WATCHED FOR VIOLET SKIES..."

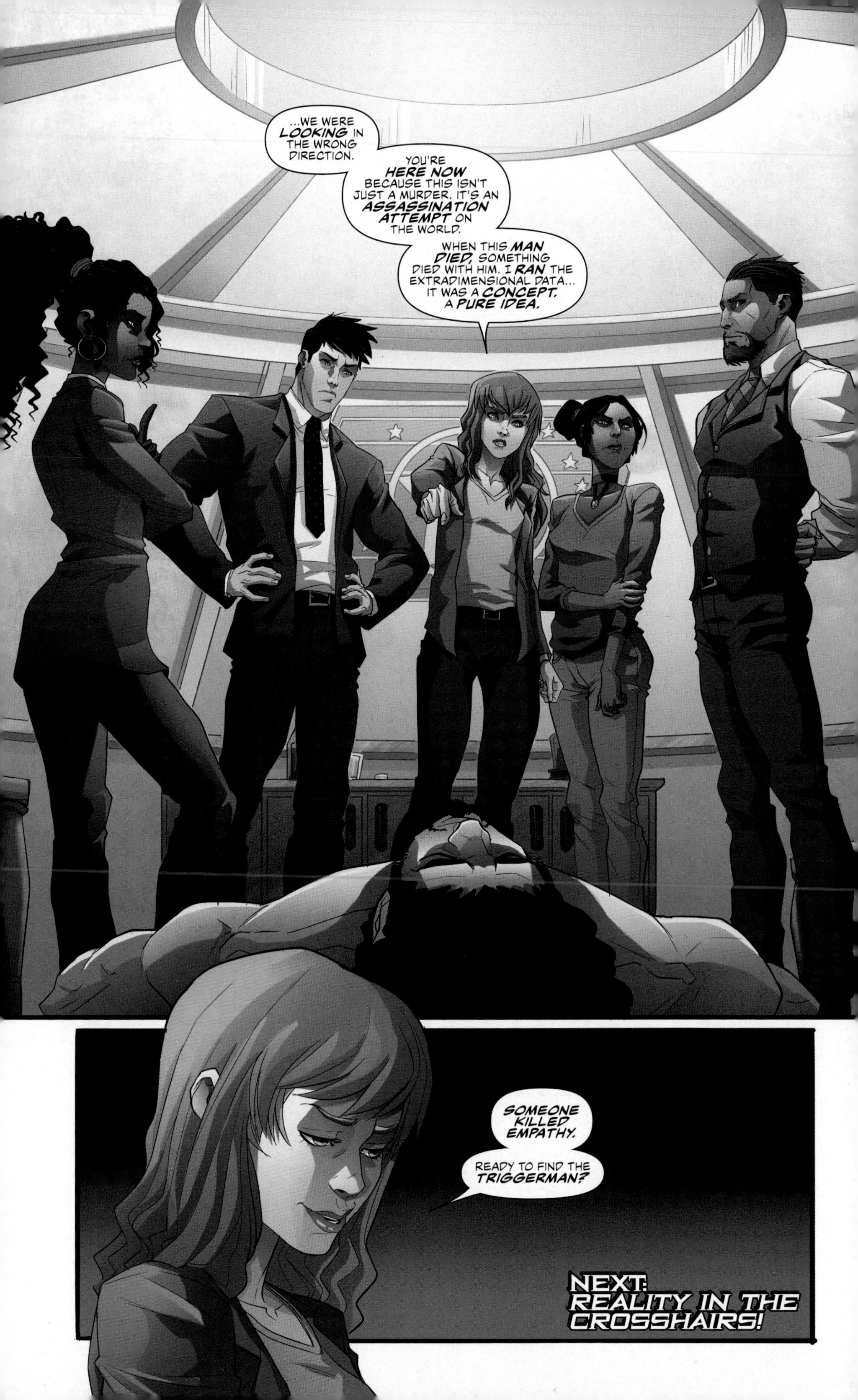
...WE WERE LOOKING IN THE WRONG DIRECTION.
YOU'RE HERE NOW BECAUSE THIS ISN'T JUST A MURDER. IT'S AN ASSASSINATION ATTEMPT ON THE WORLD.
WHEN THIS MAN DIED, SOMETHING DIED WITH HIM. I RAN THE EXTRADIMENSIONAL DATA... IT WAS A CONCEPT. A PURE IDEA.
SOMEONE KILLED EMPATHY.
READY TO FIND THE TRIGGERMAN?
NEXT: REALITY IN THE CROSSHAIRS!

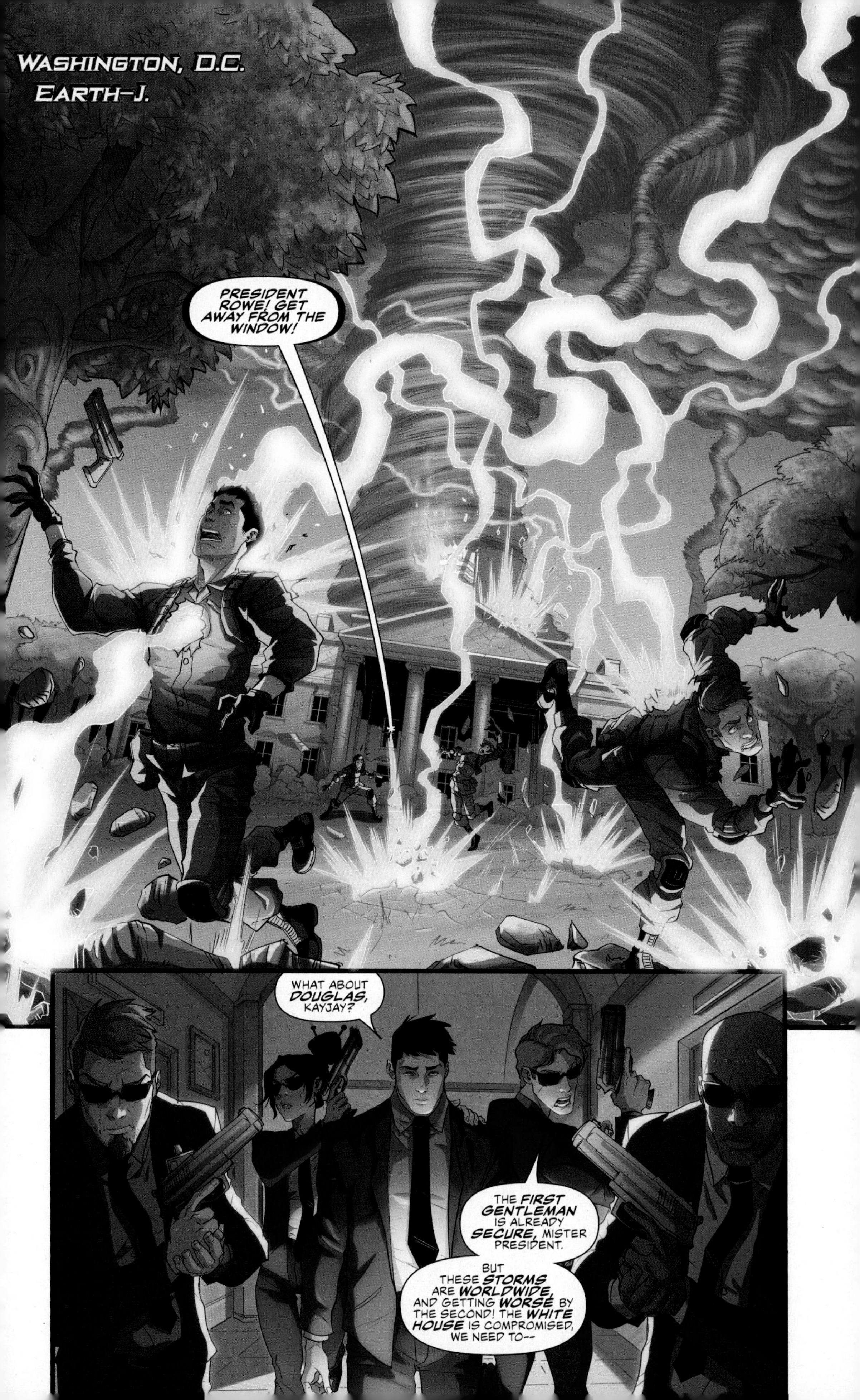
WASHINGTON, D.C.
EARTH-J.
PRESIDENT ROWE! GET AWAY FROM THE WINDOW!
WHAT ABOUT DOUGLAS, KAYJAY?
THE FIRST GENTLEMAN IS ALREADY SECURE, MISTER PRESIDENT.
BUT THESE STORMS ARE WORLDWIDE, AND GETTING WORSE BY THE SECOND! THE WHITE HOUSE IS COMPROMISED, WE NEED TO--

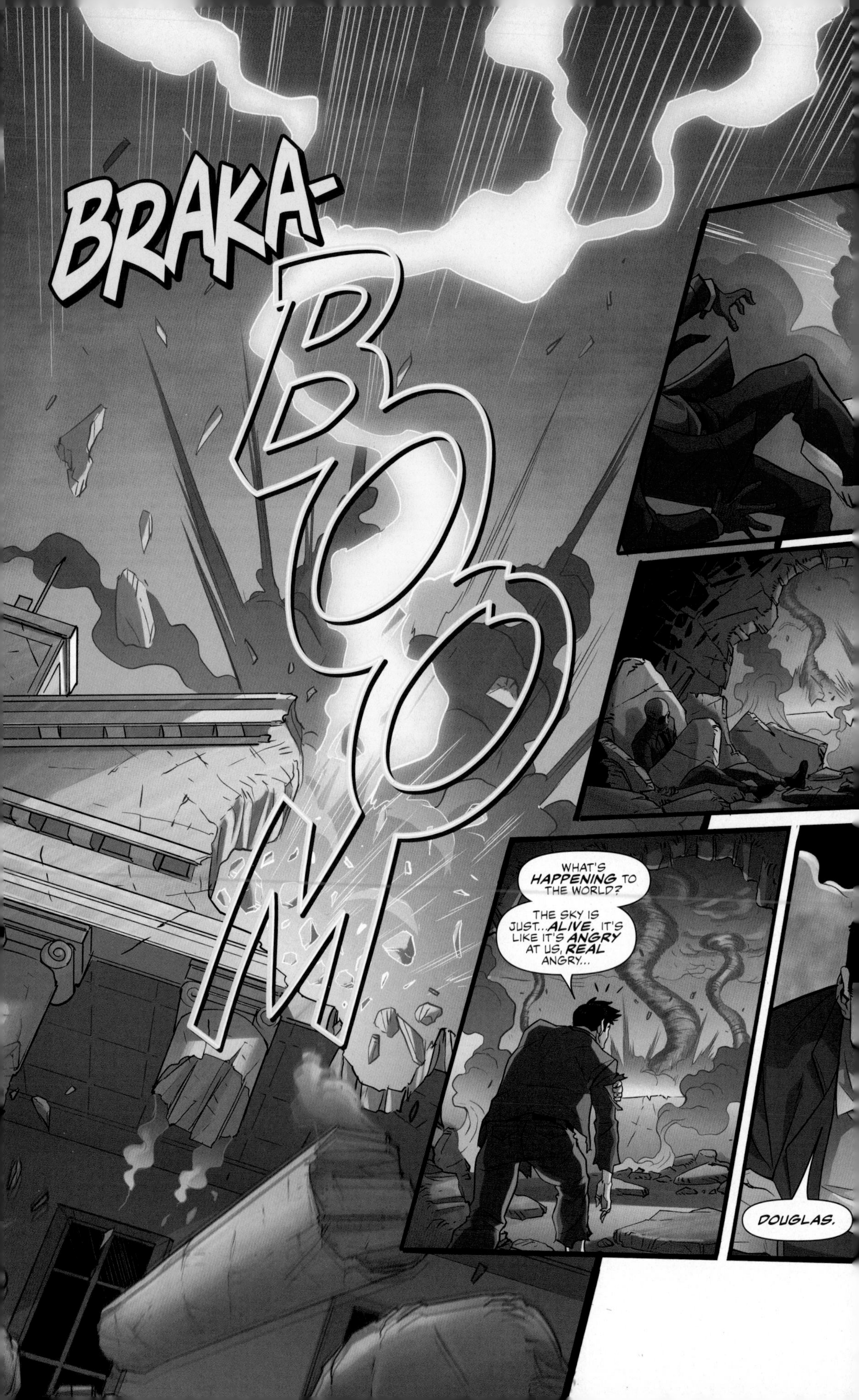
BRAKA-BOOM
WHAT'S HAPPENING TO THE WORLD?
THE SKY IS JUST...ALIVE. IT'S LIKE IT'S ANGRY AT US, REAL ANGRY...
DOUGLAS.

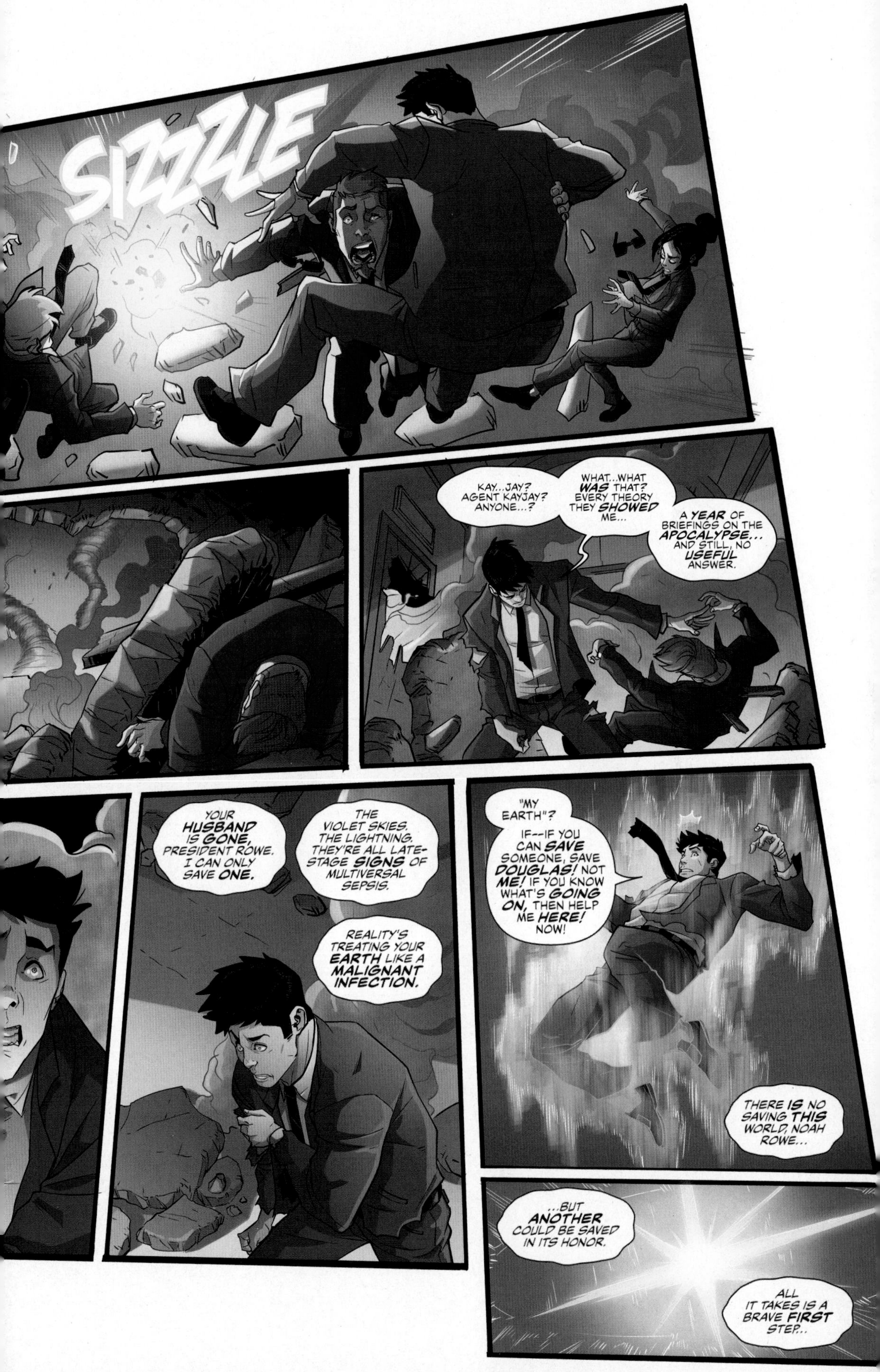
SIZZZLE
KAY...JAY? AGENT KAYJAY? ANYONE...?
WHAT...WHAT WAS THAT? EVERY THEORY THEY SHOWED ME...
A YEAR OF BRIEFINGS ON THE APOCALYPSE... AND STILL, NO USEFUL ANSWER.
YOUR HUSBAND IS GONE, PRESIDENT ROWE. I CAN ONLY SAVE ONE.
THE VIOLET SKIES. THE LIGHTNING. THEY'RE ALL LATE-STAGE SIGNS OF MULTIVERSAL SEPSIS.
REALITY'S TREATING YOUR EARTH LIKE A MALIGNANT INFECTION.
"MY EARTH"? IF--IF YOU CAN SAVE SOMEONE, SAVE DOUGLAS! NOT ME! IF YOU KNOW WHAT'S GOING ON, THEN HELP ME HERE! NOW!
THERE IS NO SAVING THIS WORLD, NOAH ROWE...
...BUT ANOTHER COULD BE SAVED IN ITS HONOR.
ALL IT TAKES IS A BRAVE FIRST STEP...

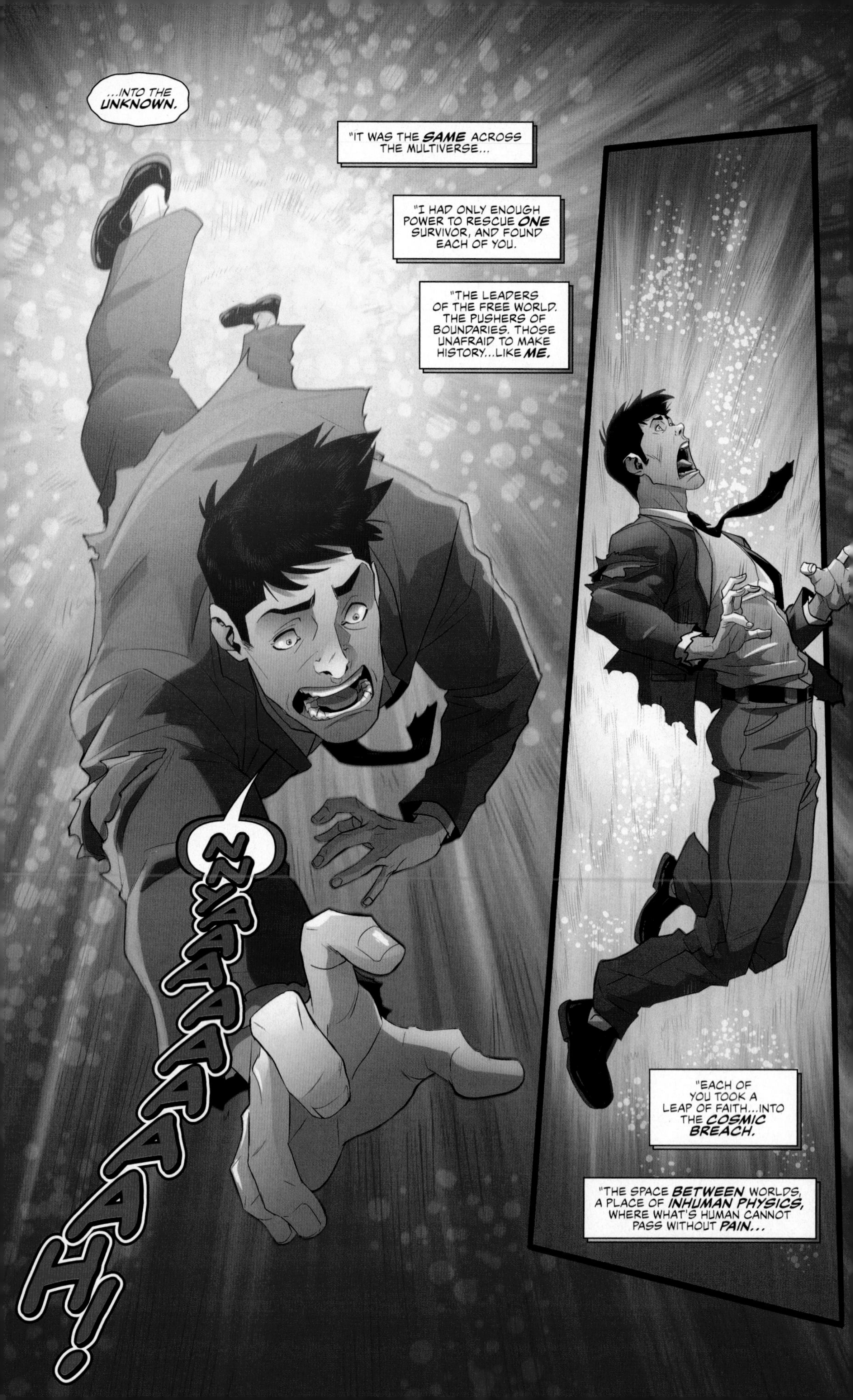
...INTO THE UNKNOWN.
"IT WAS THE SAME ACROSS THE MULTIVERSE...
"I HAD ONLY ENOUGH POWER TO RESCUE ONE SURVIVOR, AND FOUND EACH OF YOU.
"THE LEADERS OF THE FREE WORLD. THE PUSHERS OF BOUNDARIES. THOSE UNAFRAID TO MAKE HISTORY...LIKE ME.
NNYAAAAAAAAAAH!
"EACH OF YOU TOOK A LEAP OF FAITH...INTO THE COSMIC BREACH.
"THE SPACE BETWEEN WORLDS, A PLACE OF INHUMAN PHYSICS, WHERE WHAT'S HUMAN CANNOT PASS WITHOUT PAIN...

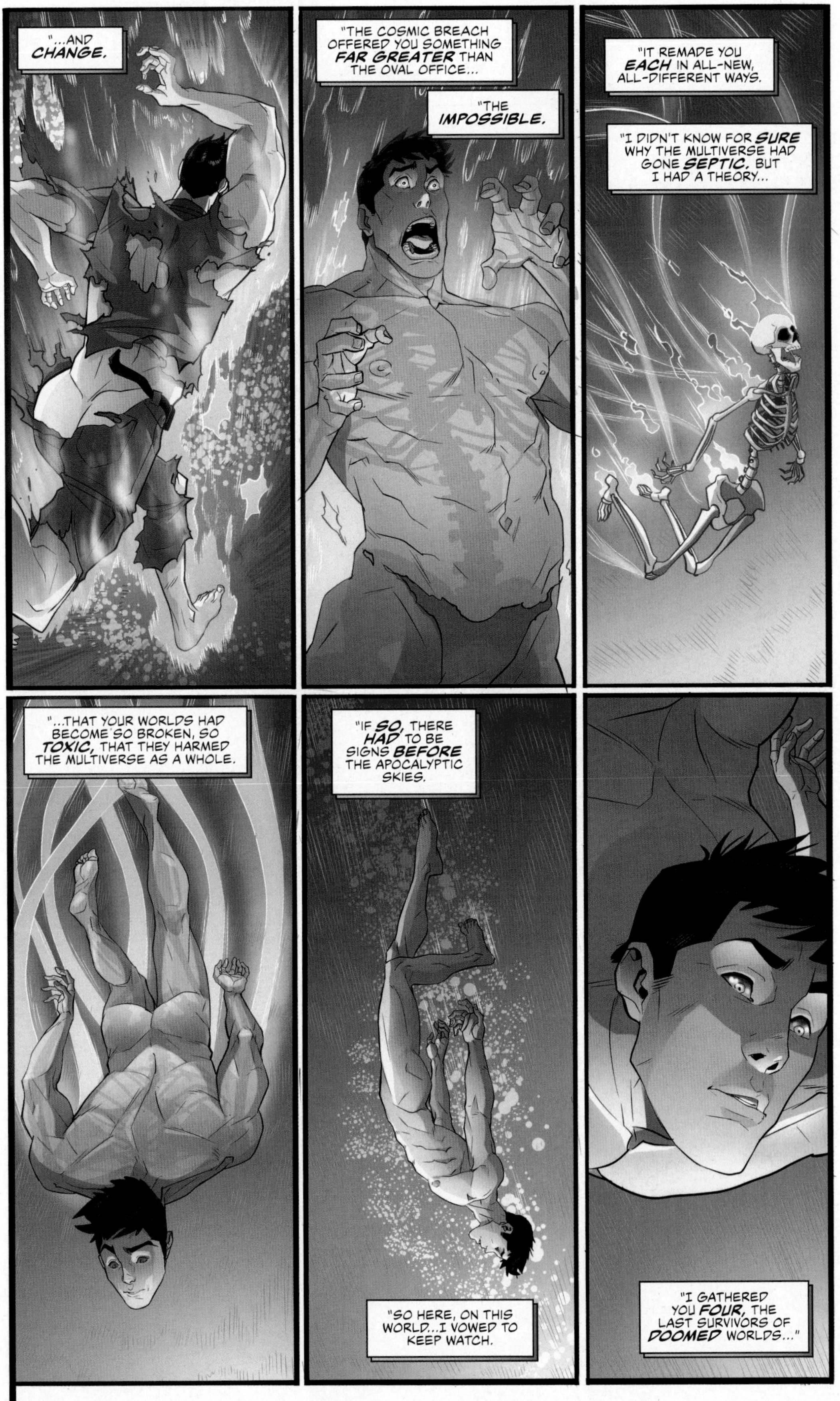
"...AND CHANGE.
"THE COSMIC BREACH OFFERED YOU SOMETHING FAR GREATER THAN THE OVAL OFFICE...
"THE IMPOSSIBLE.
"IT REMADE YOU EACH IN ALL-NEW, ALL-DIFFERENT WAYS.
"I DIDN'T KNOW FOR SURE WHY THE MULTIVERSE HAD GONE SEPTIC. BUT I HAD A THEORY...
"...THAT YOUR WORLDS HAD BECOME SO BROKEN, SO TOXIC, THAT THEY HARMED THE MULTIVERSE AS A WHOLE.
"IF SO, THERE HAD TO BE SIGNS BEFORE THE APOCALYPTIC SKIES.
"SO HERE, ON THIS WORLD...I VOWED TO KEEP WATCH.
"I GATHERED YOU FOUR, THE LAST SURVIVORS OF DOOMED WORLDS..."

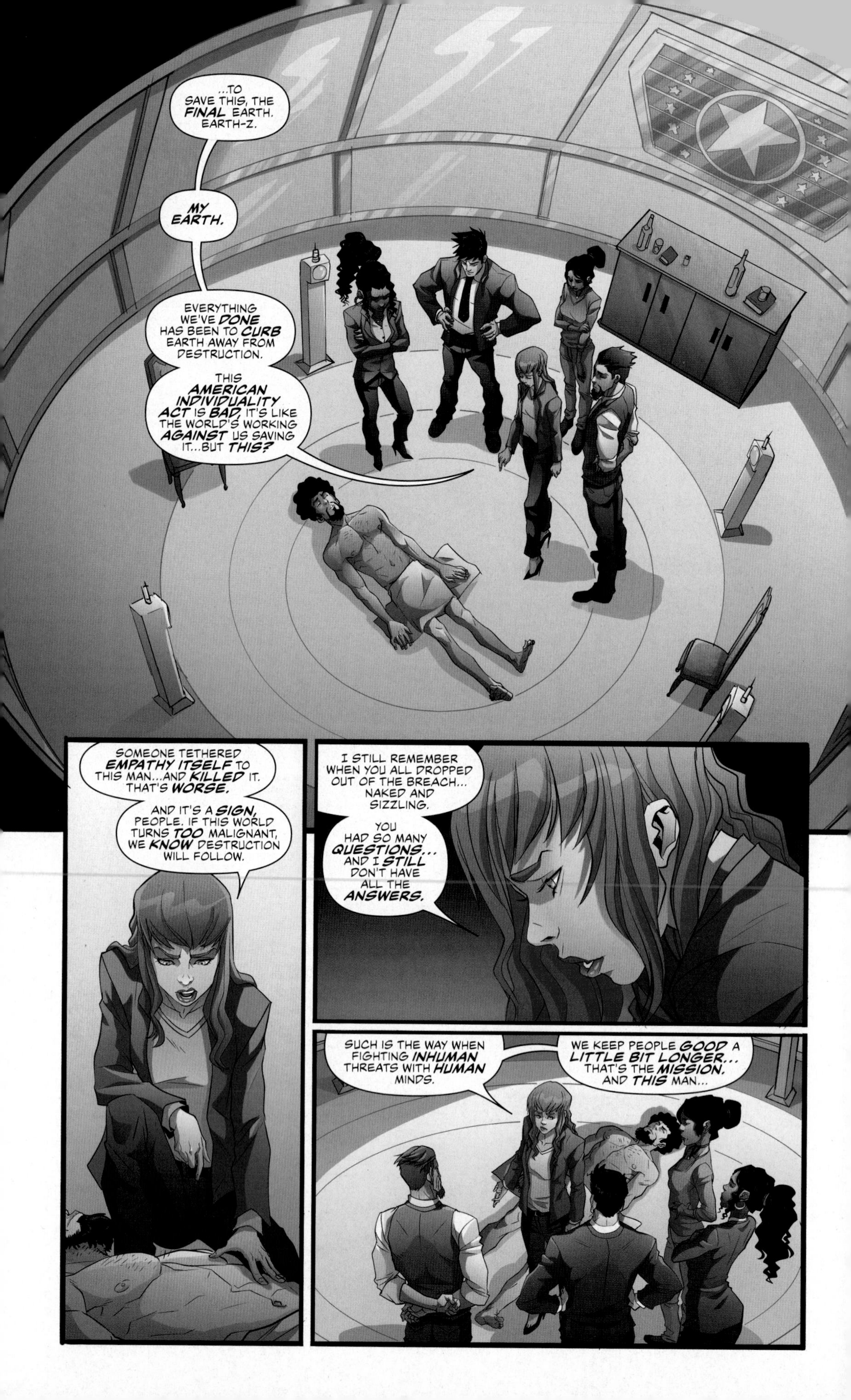
...TO SAVE THIS, THE FINAL EARTH. EARTH-Z.
MY EARTH.
EVERYTHING WE'VE DONE HAS BEEN TO CURB EARTH AWAY FROM DESTRUCTION.
THIS AMERICAN INDIVIDUALITY ACT IS BAD, IT'S LIKE THE WORLD'S WORKING AGAINST US SAVING IT...BUT THIS?
SOMEONE TETHERED EMPATHY ITSELF TO THIS MAN...AND KILLED IT. THAT'S WORSE.
AND IT'S A SIGN, PEOPLE. IF THIS WORLD TURNS TOO MALIGNANT, WE KNOW DESTRUCTION WILL FOLLOW.
I STILL REMEMBER WHEN YOU ALL DROPPED OUT OF THE BREACH... NAKED AND SIZZLING.
YOU HAD SO MANY QUESTIONS... AND I STILL DON'T HAVE ALL THE ANSWERS.
SUCH IS THE WAY WHEN FIGHTING INHUMAN THREATS WITH HUMAN MINDS.
WE KEEP PEOPLE GOOD A LITTLE BIT LONGER... THAT'S THE MISSION. AND THIS MAN...

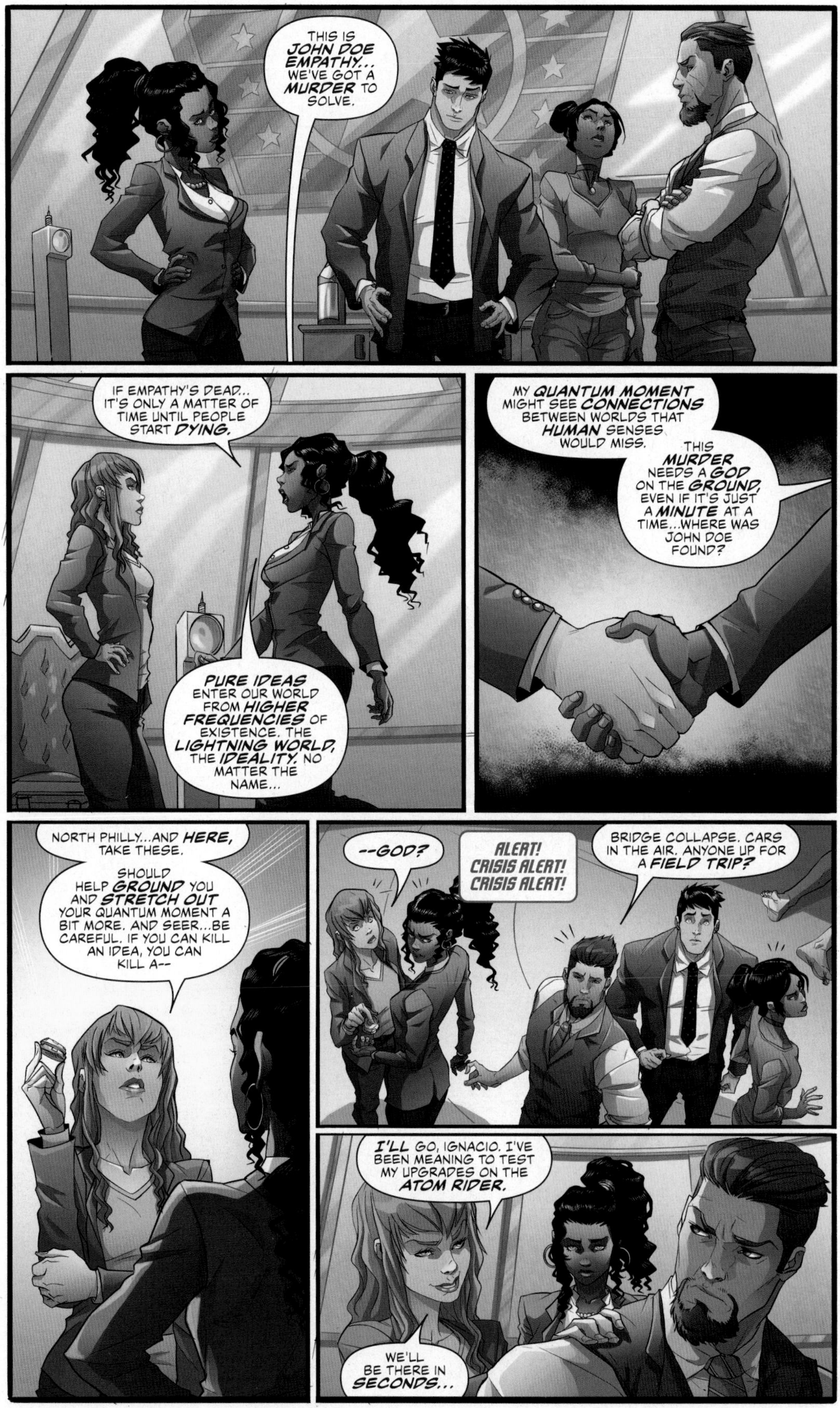
THIS IS JOHN DOE EMPATHY... WE'VE GOT A MURDER TO SOLVE.
IF EMPATHY'S DEAD... IT'S ONLY A MATTER OF TIME UNTIL PEOPLE START DYING.
PURE IDEAS ENTER OUR WORLD FROM HIGHER FREQUENCIES OF EXISTENCE. THE LIGHTNING WORLD, THE IDEALITY. NO MATTER THE NAME...
MY QUANTUM MOMENT MIGHT SEE CONNECTIONS BETWEEN WORLDS THAT HUMAN SENSES WOULD MISS.
THIS MURDER NEEDS A GOD ON THE GROUND, EVEN IF IT'S JUST A MINUTE AT A TIME...WHERE WAS JOHN DOE FOUND?
NORTH PHILLY...AND HERE, TAKE THESE.
SHOULD HELP GROUND YOU AND STRETCH OUT YOUR QUANTUM MOMENT A BIT MORE. AND SEER...BE CAREFUL. IF YOU CAN KILL AN IDEA, YOU CAN KILL A--
--GOD?
ALERT! CRISIS ALERT! CRISIS ALERT!
BRIDGE COLLAPSE. CARS IN THE AIR. ANYONE UP FOR A FIELD TRIP?
I'LL GO, IGNACIO. I'VE BEEN MEANING TO TEST MY UPGRADES ON THE ATOM RIDER.
WE'LL BE THERE IN SECONDS...

"...SO MUCH FOR BEING *DONE* WITH *FIELDWORK.*"

CROSS-COUNTRY AT THE SPEED OF LIGHT. I'D SAY THE *ATOM RIDER'S* WORKING FINE, FRONTIER.

INTUITION. INNOVATION. INVENTION...WE CAN'T ALL BE GOOD WITH A *SCALPEL,* SAWBONES. NOW...

DART

DART

DART

CARS ARE TAGGED WITH ANTI-GRAV DARTS...

...THEY'RE *COMING* YOUR WAY.

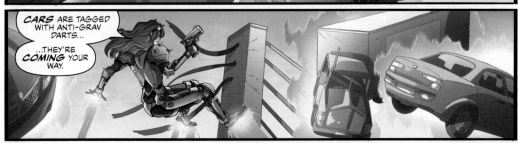

NOT JUST *MY* WAY.

NATIONAL GUARD'S GETTING *TERRITORIAL,* SO FAR EVERYONE'S LANDING *SCARED...* BUT SAFE.

JUST NEED TO--

SOMEONE HELP!

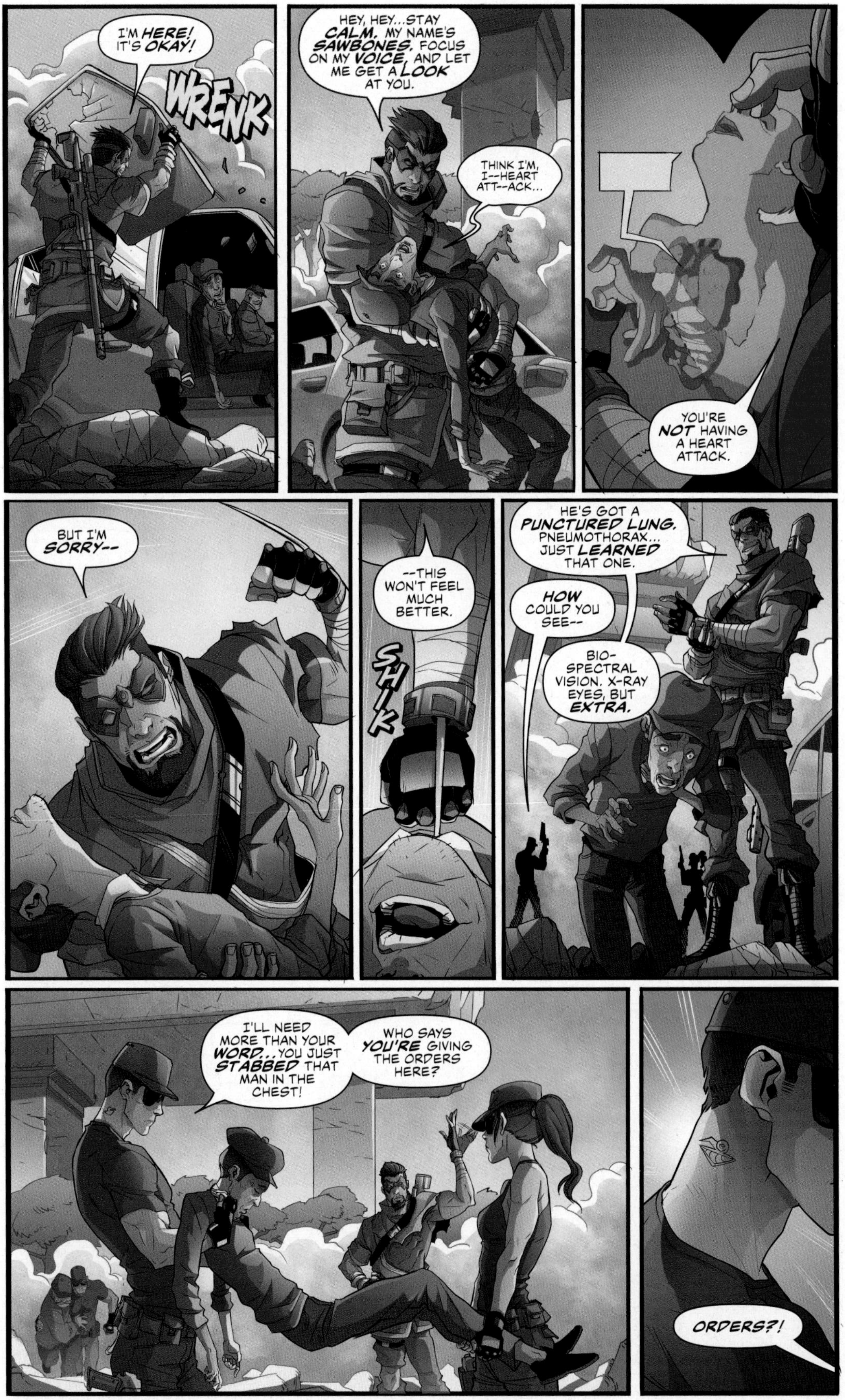
I'M HERE! IT'S OKAY!
WRENK
HEY, HEY...STAY CALM. MY NAME'S SAWBONES. FOCUS ON MY VOICE, AND LET ME GET A LOOK AT YOU.
THINK I'M, I--HEART ATT--ACK...
YOU'RE NOT HAVING A HEART ATTACK.
BUT I'M SORRY--
--THIS WON'T FEEL MUCH BETTER.
SHIK
HE'S GOT A PUNCTURED LUNG. PNEUMOTHORAX... JUST LEARNED THAT ONE.
HOW COULD YOU SEE--
BIO-SPECTRAL VISION. X-RAY EYES, BUT EXTRA.
I'LL NEED MORE THAN YOUR WORD...YOU JUST STABBED THAT MAN IN THE CHEST!
WHO SAYS YOU'RE GIVING THE ORDERS HERE?
ORDERS?!

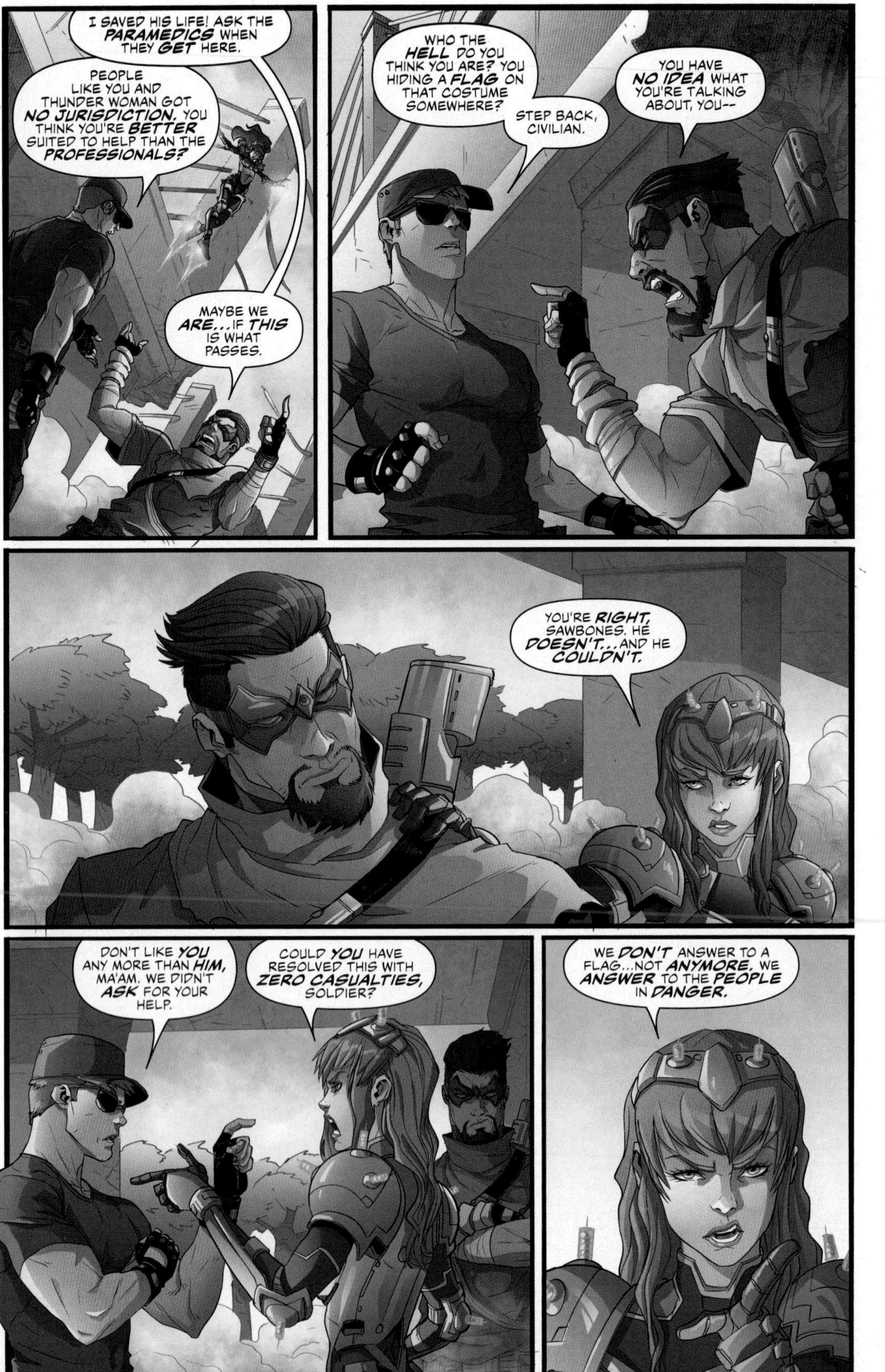
I SAVED HIS LIFE! ASK THE PARAMEDICS WHEN THEY GET HERE.
PEOPLE LIKE YOU AND THUNDER WOMAN GOT NO JURISDICTION. YOU THINK YOU'RE BETTER SUITED TO HELP THAN THE PROFESSIONALS?
MAYBE WE ARE... IF THIS IS WHAT PASSES.
WHO THE HELL DO YOU THINK YOU ARE? YOU HIDING A FLAG ON THAT COSTUME SOMEWHERE?
STEP BACK, CIVILIAN.
YOU HAVE NO IDEA WHAT YOU'RE TALKING ABOUT, YOU--
YOU'RE RIGHT, SAWBONES. HE DOESN'T... AND HE COULDN'T.
DON'T LIKE YOU ANY MORE THAN HIM, MA'AM. WE DIDN'T ASK FOR YOUR HELP.
COULD YOU HAVE RESOLVED THIS WITH ZERO CASUALTIES, SOLDIER?
WE DON'T ANSWER TO A FLAG...NOT ANYMORE. WE ANSWER TO THE PEOPLE IN DANGER.

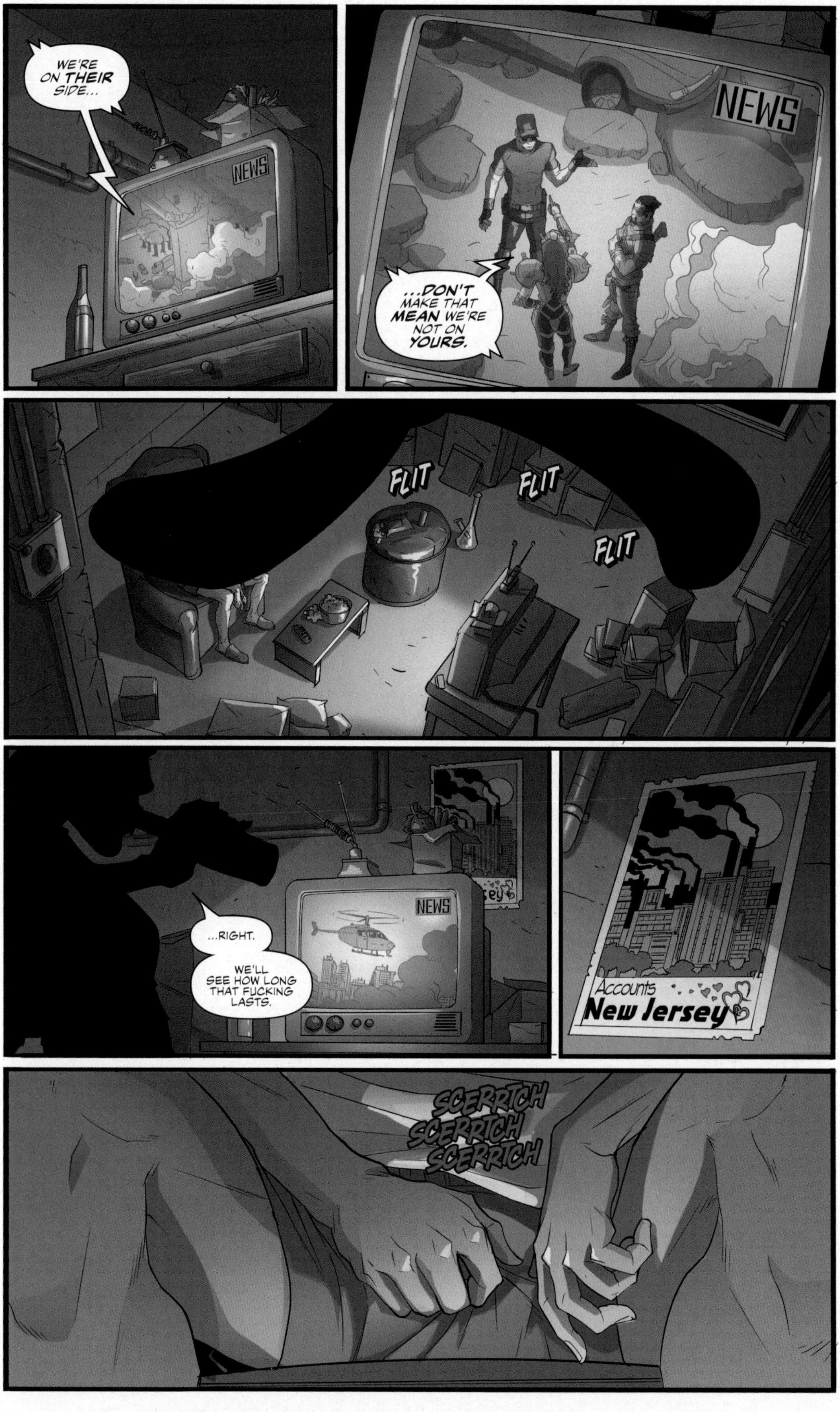

WE'RE ON THEIR SIDE...
NEWS
...DON'T MAKE THAT MEAN WE'RE NOT ON YOURS.
FLIT
FLIT
FLIT
NEWS
...RIGHT.
WE'LL SEE HOW LONG THAT FUCKING LASTS.
Accounts
New Jersey
SCERRTCH
SCERRTCH
SCERRTCH

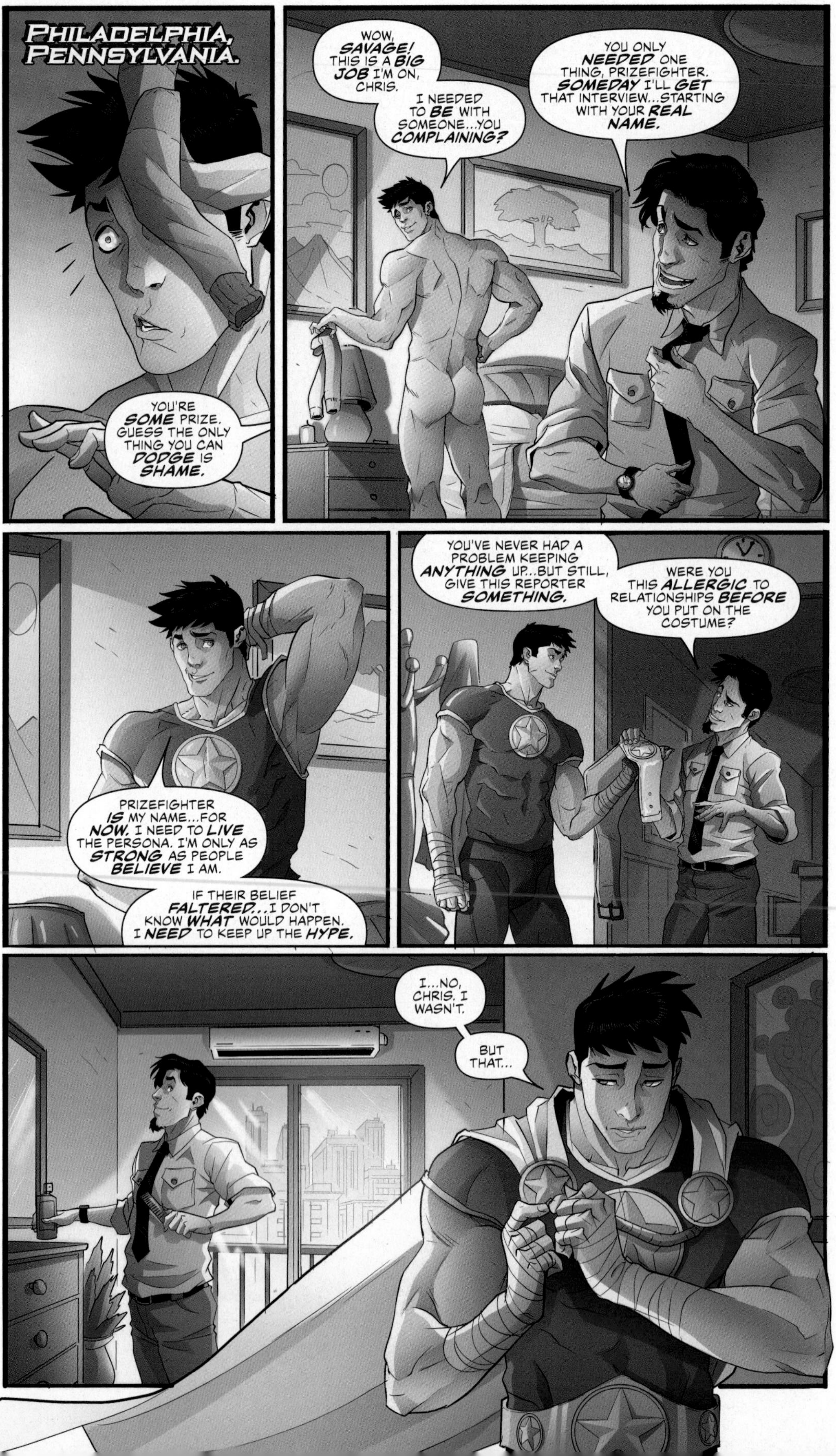

PHILADELPHIA, PENNSYLVANIA.
YOU'RE SOME PRIZE. GUESS THE ONLY THING YOU CAN DODGE IS SHAME.
WOW, SAVAGE! THIS IS A BIG JOB I'M ON, CHRIS.
I NEEDED TO BE WITH SOMEONE...YOU COMPLAINING?
YOU ONLY NEEDED ONE THING, PRIZEFIGHTER. SOMEDAY I'LL GET THAT INTERVIEW...STARTING WITH YOUR REAL NAME.
PRIZEFIGHTER IS MY NAME...FOR NOW. I NEED TO LIVE THE PERSONA. I'M ONLY AS STRONG AS PEOPLE BELIEVE I AM.
IF THEIR BELIEF FALTERED...I DON'T KNOW WHAT WOULD HAPPEN. I NEED TO KEEP UP THE HYPE.
YOU'VE NEVER HAD A PROBLEM KEEPING ANYTHING UP...BUT STILL, GIVE THIS REPORTER SOMETHING.
WERE YOU THIS ALLERGIC TO RELATIONSHIPS BEFORE YOU PUT ON THE COSTUME?
I...NO, CHRIS. I WASN'T.
BUT THAT...

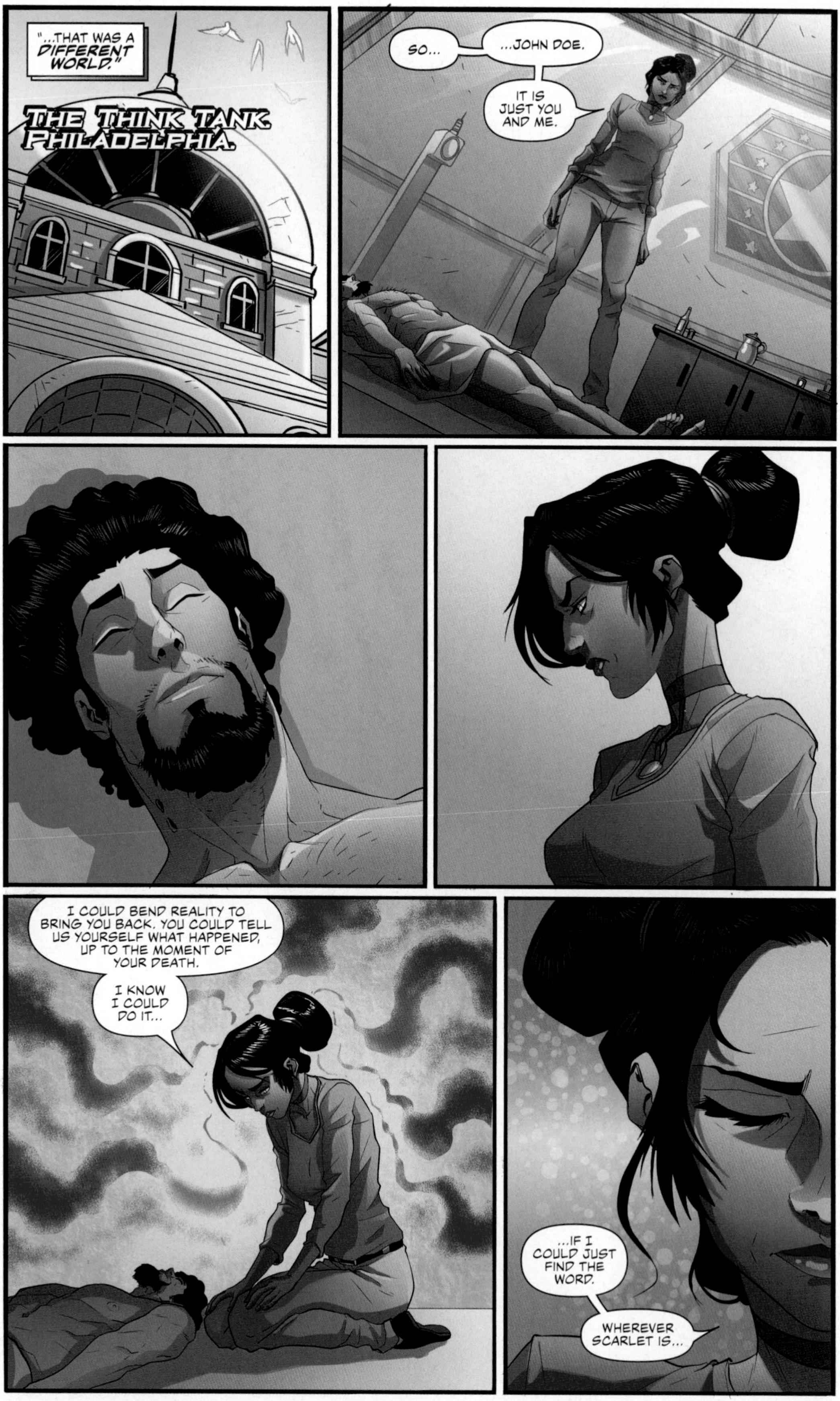
"...THAT WAS A DIFFERENT WORLD."
THE THINK TANK. PHILADELPHIA.
SO...
...JOHN DOE.
IT IS JUST YOU AND ME.
I COULD BEND REALITY TO BRING YOU BACK. YOU COULD TELL US YOURSELF WHAT HAPPENED, UP TO THE MOMENT OF YOUR DEATH.
I KNOW I COULD DO IT...
...IF I COULD JUST FIND THE WORD.
WHEREVER SCARLET IS...

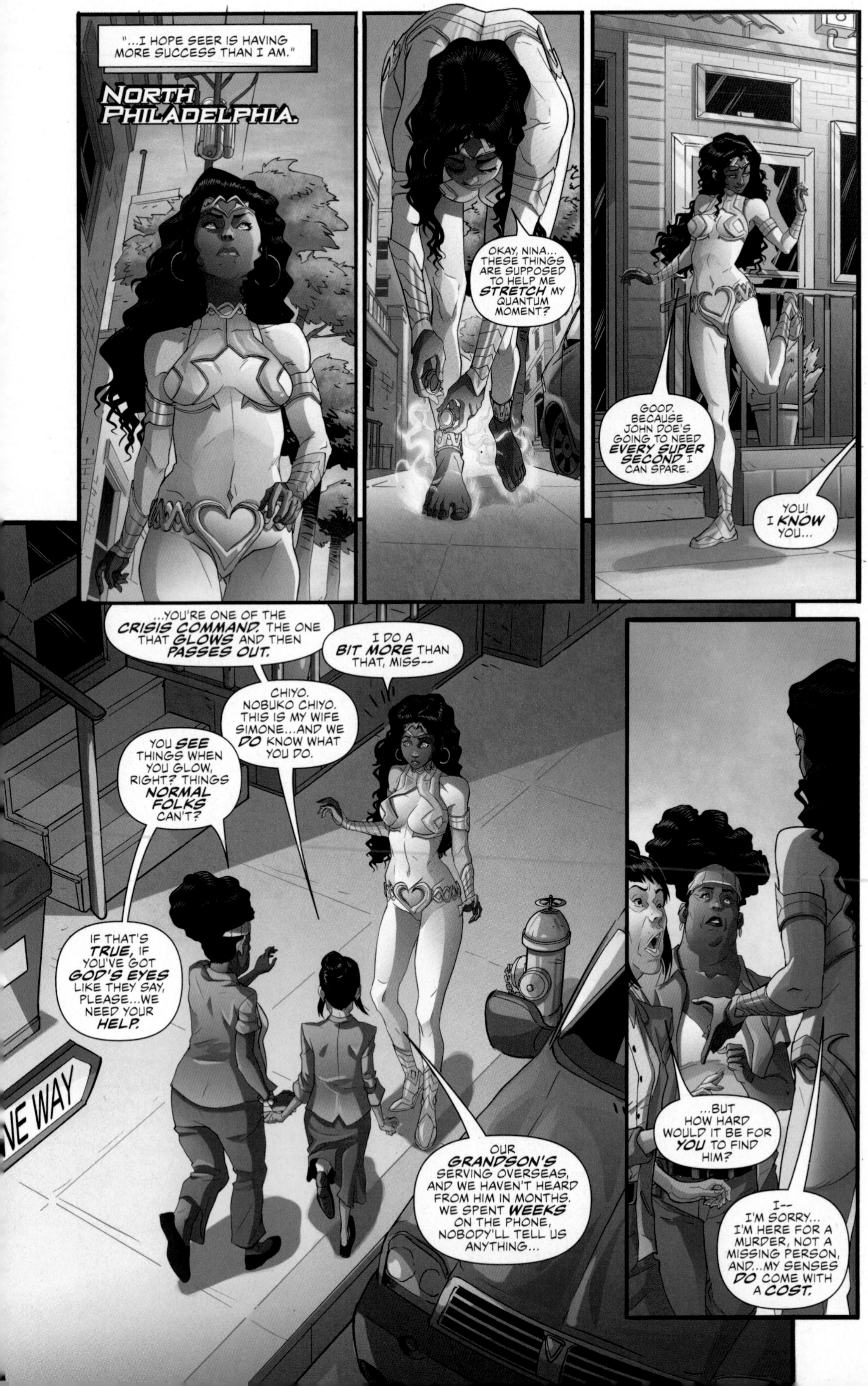
"...I HOPE SEER IS HAVING MORE SUCCESS THAN I AM."
NORTH PHILADELPHIA.
OKAY, NINA... THESE THINGS ARE SUPPOSED TO HELP ME STRETCH MY QUANTUM MOMENT?
GOOD. BECAUSE JOHN DOE'S GOING TO NEED EVERY SUPER SECOND I CAN SPARE.
YOU! I KNOW YOU...
...YOU'RE ONE OF THE CRISIS COMMAND. THE ONE THAT GLOWS AND THEN PASSES OUT.
I DO A BIT MORE THAN THAT, MISS--
CHIYO. NOBUKO CHIYO. THIS IS MY WIFE SIMONE...AND WE DO KNOW WHAT YOU DO.
YOU SEE THINGS WHEN YOU GLOW, RIGHT? THINGS NORMAL FOLKS CAN'T?
IF THAT'S TRUE, IF YOU'VE GOT GOD'S EYES LIKE THEY SAY, PLEASE...WE NEED YOUR HELP.
OUR GRANDSON'S SERVING OVERSEAS, AND WE HAVEN'T HEARD FROM HIM IN MONTHS. WE SPENT WEEKS ON THE PHONE, NOBODY'LL TELL US ANYTHING...
...BUT HOW HARD WOULD IT BE FOR YOU TO FIND HIM?
I-- I'M SORRY... I'M HERE FOR A MURDER, NOT A MISSING PERSON, AND...MY SENSES DO COME WITH A COST.

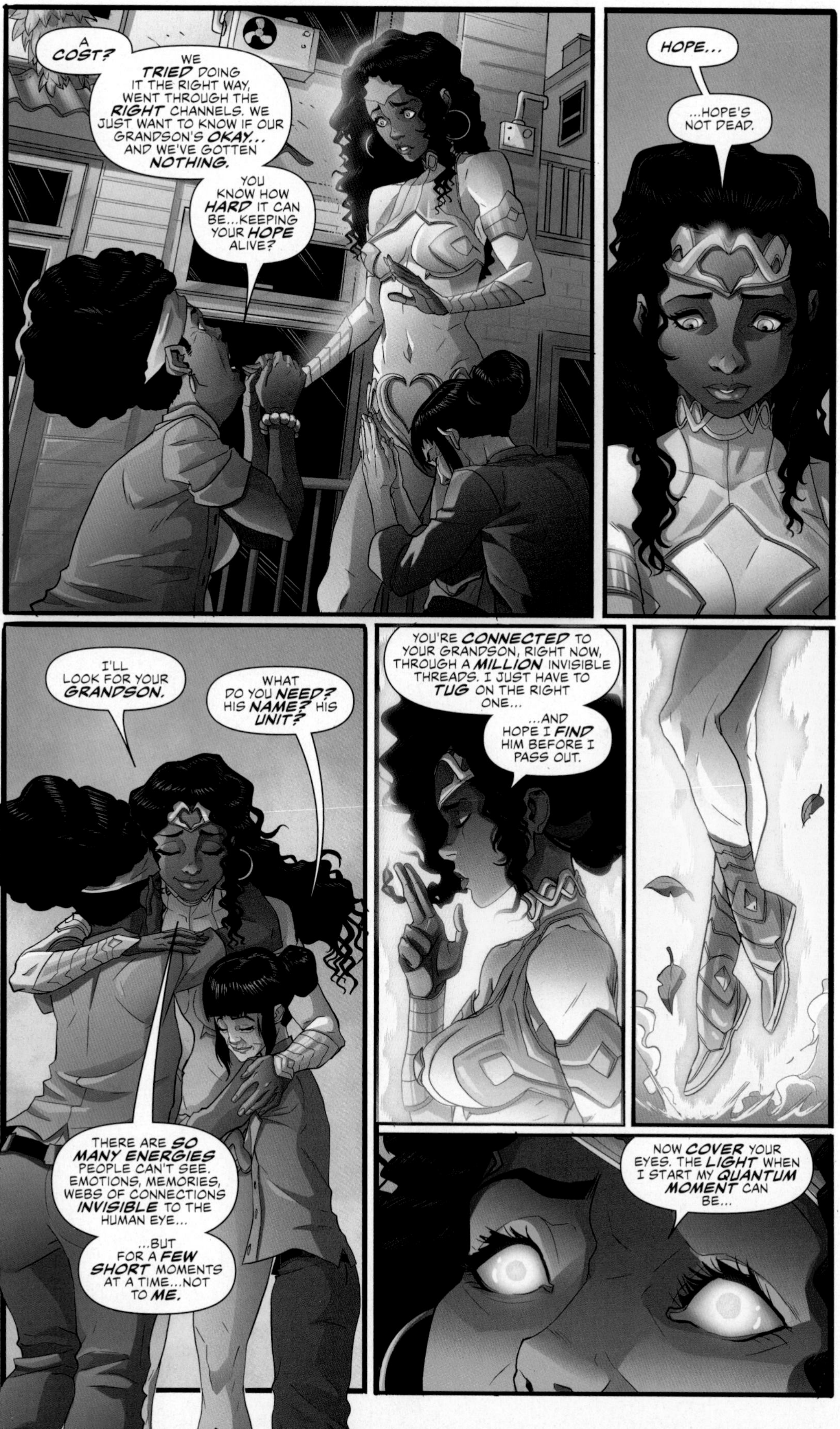
A COST?
WE TRIED DOING IT THE RIGHT WAY, WENT THROUGH THE RIGHT CHANNELS. WE JUST WANT TO KNOW IF OUR GRANDSON'S OKAY... AND WE'VE GOTTEN NOTHING.
YOU KNOW HOW HARD IT CAN BE...KEEPING YOUR HOPE ALIVE?
HOPE...
...HOPE'S NOT DEAD.
I'LL LOOK FOR YOUR GRANDSON.
WHAT DO YOU NEED? HIS NAME? HIS UNIT?
THERE ARE SO MANY ENERGIES PEOPLE CAN'T SEE. EMOTIONS, MEMORIES, WEBS OF CONNECTIONS INVISIBLE TO THE HUMAN EYE...
...BUT FOR A FEW SHORT MOMENTS AT A TIME...NOT TO ME.
YOU'RE CONNECTED TO YOUR GRANDSON, RIGHT NOW, THROUGH A MILLION INVISIBLE THREADS. I JUST HAVE TO TUG ON THE RIGHT ONE...
...AND HOPE I FIND HIM BEFORE I PASS OUT.
NOW COVER YOUR EYES. THE LIGHT WHEN I START MY QUANTUM MOMENT CAN BE...

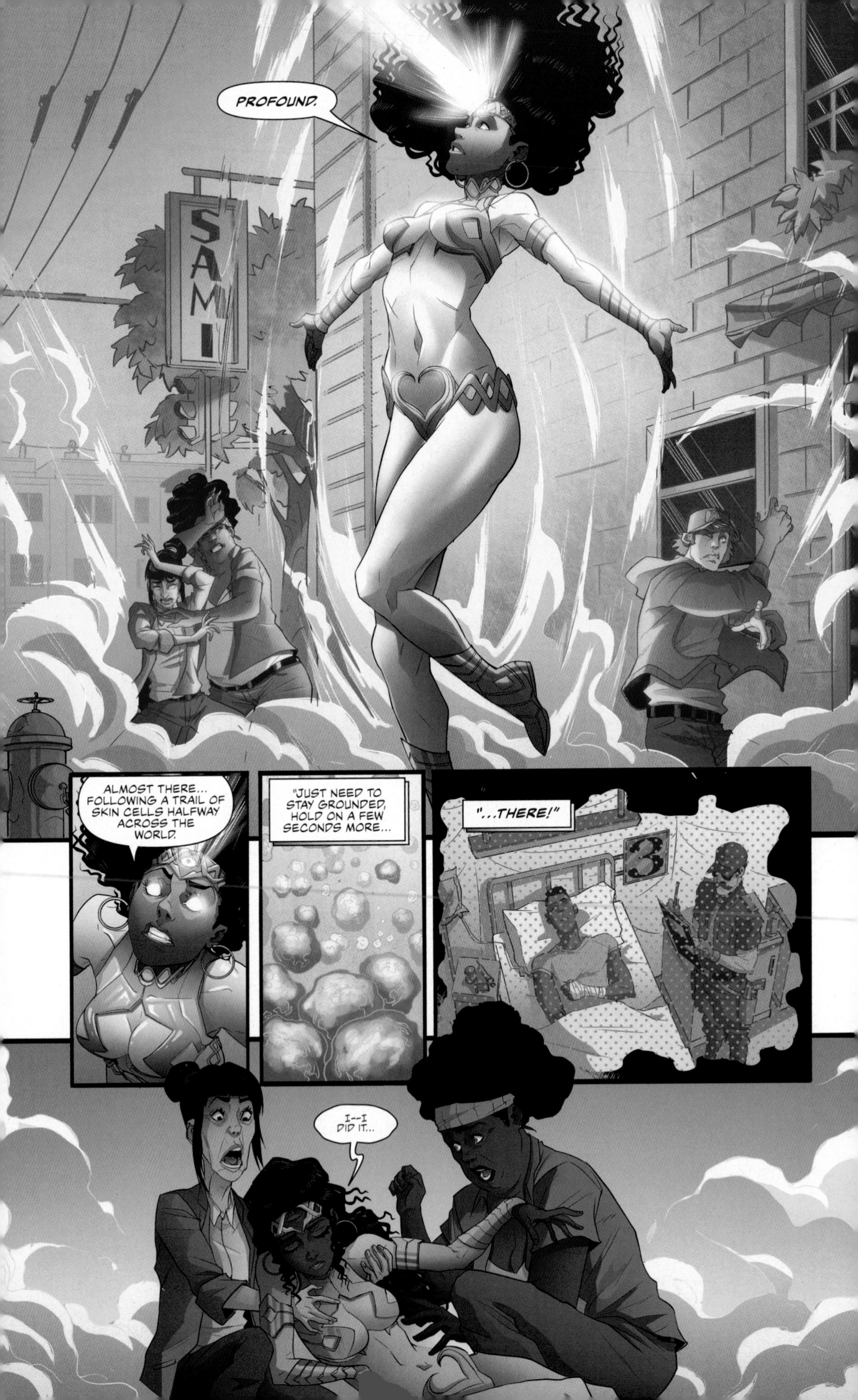
PROFOUND.
SAMI
ALMOST THERE... FOLLOWING A TRAIL OF SKIN CELLS HALFWAY ACROSS THE WORLD.
"JUST NEED TO STAY GROUNDED, HOLD ON A FEW SECONDS MORE...
"...THERE!"
3
I--I DID IT...

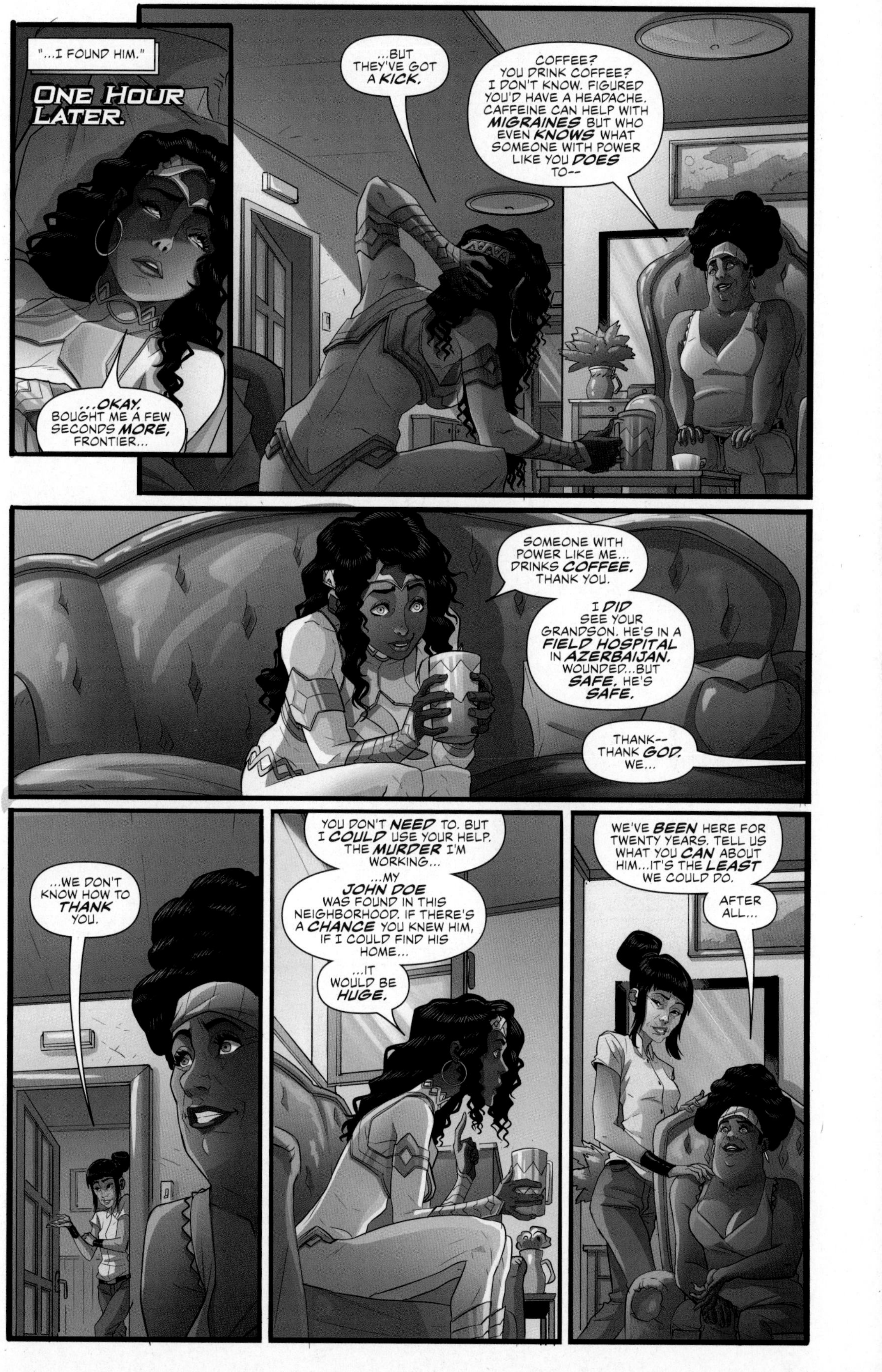
"...I FOUND HIM."
ONE HOUR LATER.
...OKAY. BOUGHT ME A FEW SECONDS MORE, FRONTIER...
...BUT THEY'VE GOT A KICK.
COFFEE? YOU DRINK COFFEE? I DON'T KNOW. FIGURED YOU'D HAVE A HEADACHE. CAFFEINE CAN HELP WITH MIGRAINES BUT WHO EVEN KNOWS WHAT SOMEONE WITH POWER LIKE YOU DOES TO--
SOMEONE WITH POWER LIKE ME... DRINKS COFFEE. THANK YOU.
I DID SEE YOUR GRANDSON. HE'S IN A FIELD HOSPITAL IN AZERBAIJAN. WOUNDED...BUT SAFE. HE'S SAFE.
THANK-- THANK GOD. WE...
...WE DON'T KNOW HOW TO THANK YOU.
YOU DON'T NEED TO. BUT I COULD USE YOUR HELP. THE MURDER I'M WORKING...
...MY JOHN DOE WAS FOUND IN THIS NEIGHBORHOOD. IF THERE'S A CHANCE YOU KNEW HIM, IF I COULD FIND HIS HOME...
...IT WOULD BE HUGE.
WE'VE BEEN HERE FOR TWENTY YEARS. TELL US WHAT YOU CAN ABOUT HIM...IT'S THE LEAST WE COULD DO.
AFTER ALL...

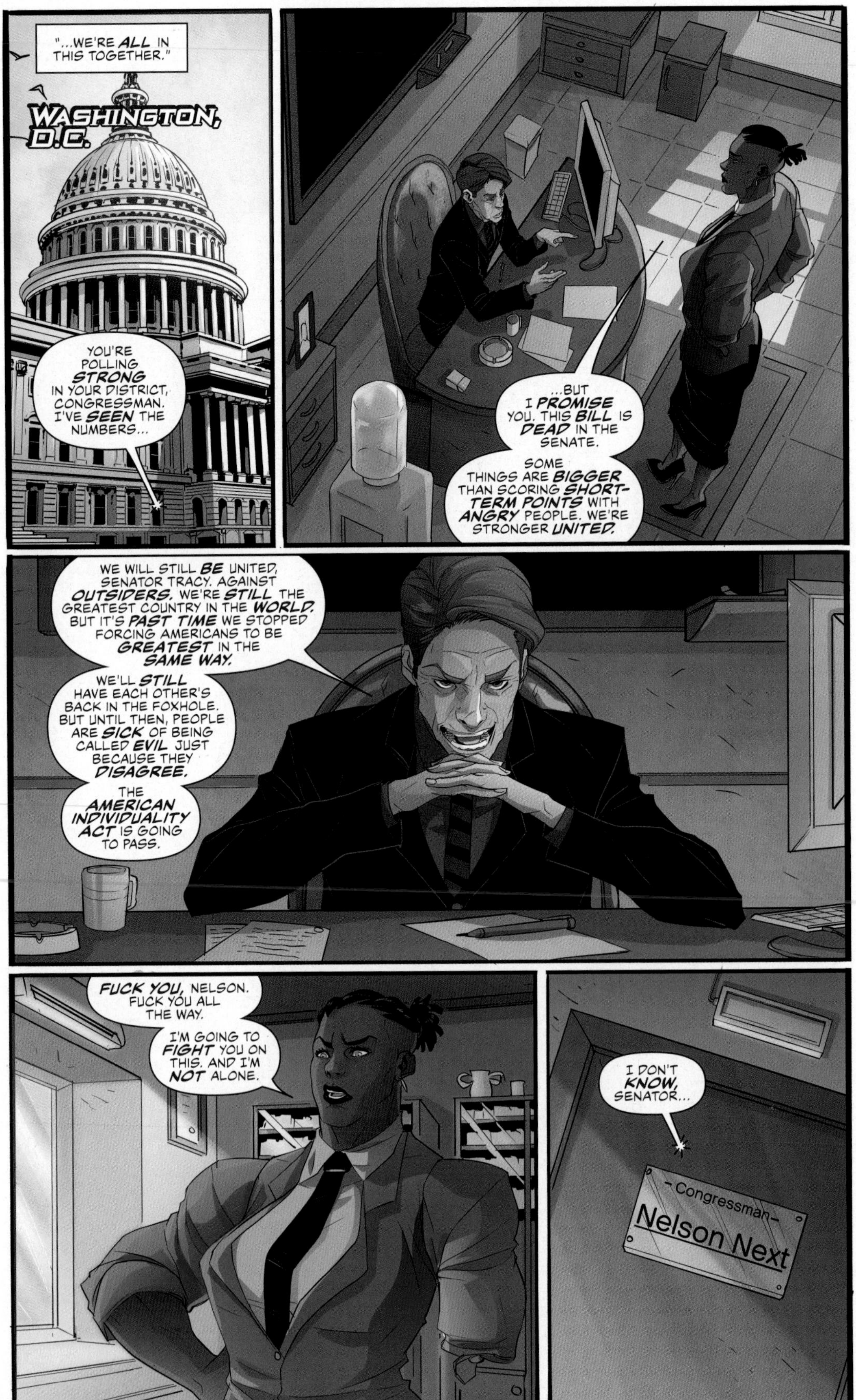
"...WE'RE ALL IN THIS TOGETHER."
WASHINGTON, D.C.
YOU'RE POLLING STRONG IN YOUR DISTRICT, CONGRESSMAN. I'VE SEEN THE NUMBERS...
...BUT I PROMISE YOU. THIS BILL IS DEAD IN THE SENATE.
SOME THINGS ARE BIGGER THAN SCORING SHORT-TERM POINTS WITH ANGRY PEOPLE. WE'RE STRONGER UNITED.
WE WILL STILL BE UNITED, SENATOR TRACY. AGAINST OUTSIDERS. WE'RE STILL THE GREATEST COUNTRY IN THE WORLD. BUT IT'S PAST TIME WE STOPPED FORCING AMERICANS TO BE GREATEST IN THE SAME WAY.
WE'LL STILL HAVE EACH OTHER'S BACK IN THE FOXHOLE. BUT UNTIL THEN, PEOPLE ARE SICK OF BEING CALLED EVIL JUST BECAUSE THEY DISAGREE.
THE AMERICAN INDIVIDUALITY ACT IS GOING TO PASS.
FUCK YOU, NELSON. FUCK YOU ALL THE WAY.
I'M GOING TO FIGHT YOU ON THIS. AND I'M NOT ALONE.
I DON'T KNOW, SENATOR...
– Congressman –
Nelson Next

"...YOU MIGHT BE MORE *ALONE* THAN YOU THINK."

THE THINK TANK

JURISDICTION? THOSE *IDIOTS* WOULD LET SOMEONE *DROWN* WHILE THEY CHECKED THE *CHLORINE CONTENT* OF THE POOL. IF THEY KNEW WHO I *WAS,* WHAT I'VE *DONE*--

BUT THEY *DON'T.* YOU'RE *SAWBONES* TO THEM, NOT FORMER PRESIDENT IGNACIO MENDEZ...AND IT HAS TO *STAY* THAT WAY.

PEOPLE CAN *HARDLY* HANDLE *US,* AND THEY THINK WE'RE ALL *FROM* HERE. THEY'RE NOT *READY* TO KNOW ABOUT THE *MULTIVERSE.*

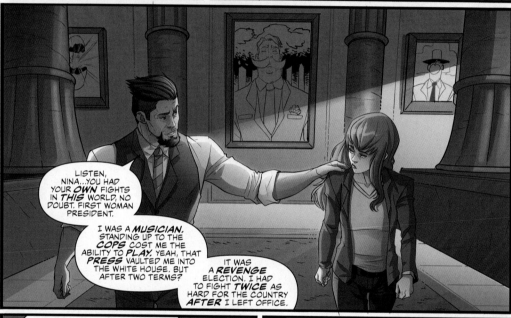

LISTEN, NINA...YOU HAD YOUR *OWN* FIGHTS IN *THIS* WORLD, NO DOUBT. FIRST WOMAN PRESIDENT.

I WAS A *MUSICIAN.* STANDING UP TO THE *COPS* COST ME THE ABILITY TO *PLAY.* YEAH, THAT *PRESS* VAULTED ME INTO THE WHITE HOUSE, BUT AFTER TWO TERMS?

IT WAS A *REVENGE* ELECTION. I HAD TO FIGHT *TWICE* AS HARD FOR THE COUNTRY *AFTER* I LEFT OFFICE.

ONE GIANT LEAP *FORWARD* AND *TWO* BACK. IF PEOPLE *KNEW* WHAT WE ALL LOST, WHAT WE *WENT* THROUGH...THE CONTEXT MATTERS.

PEOPLE MAY NEVER BE "READY." NOT *ALL* OF THEM...BUT SOMETIMES YOU CAN'T *WAIT* FOR THEM ALL.

YOU'VE STILL GOT A *MUSICIAN'S GIFT* FOR *PULLING AN EMOTION* OUT OF SOMEONE, IGNACIO.

MAYBE YOU'RE *RIGHT,* BUT IF WE DON'T *SOLVE* THIS ONE, ALL THE *CONTEXT* IN THE WORLD...

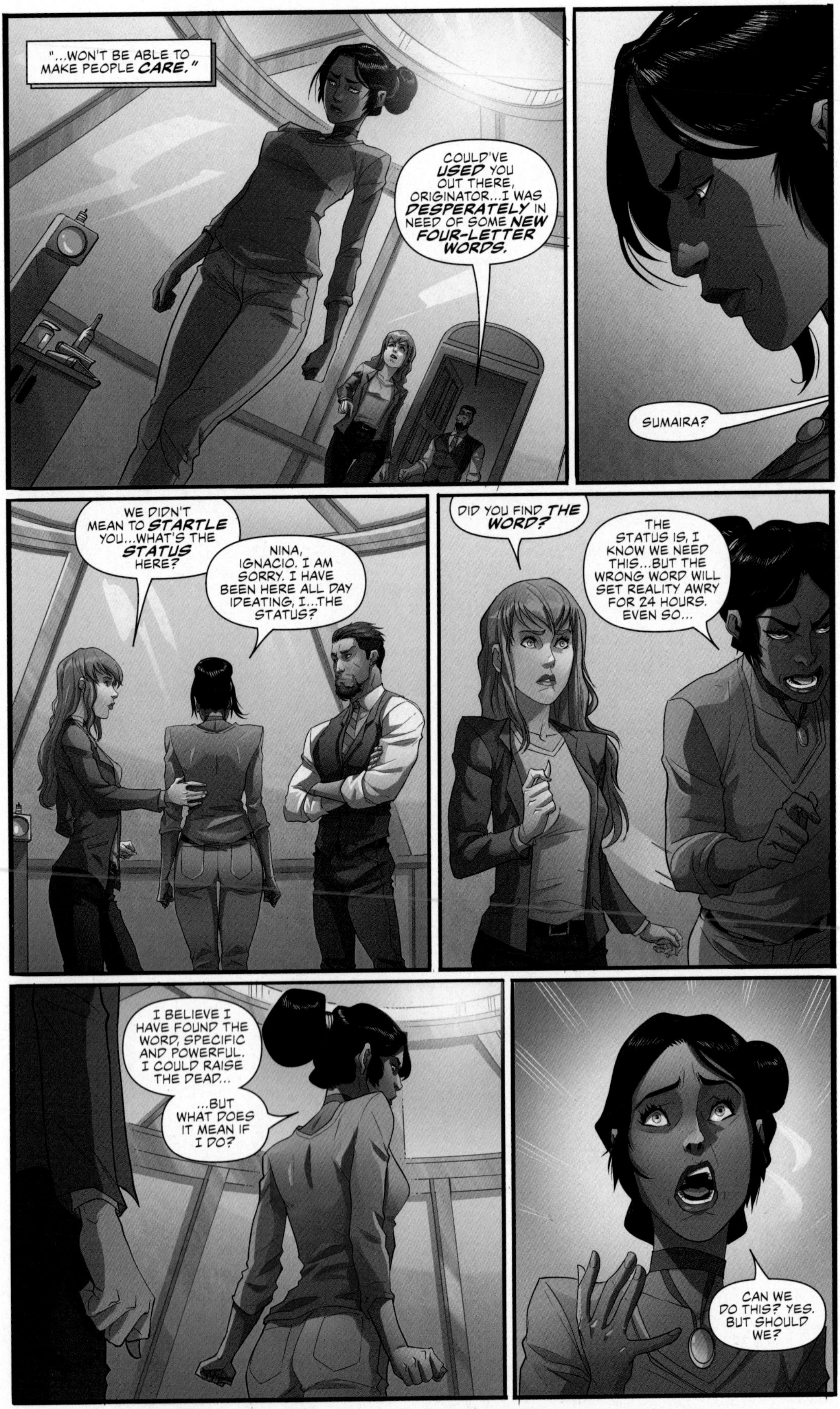
"...WON'T BE ABLE TO MAKE PEOPLE CARE."
COULD'VE USED YOU OUT THERE, ORIGINATOR...I WAS DESPERATELY IN NEED OF SOME NEW FOUR-LETTER WORDS.
SUMAIRA?
WE DIDN'T MEAN TO STARTLE YOU...WHAT'S THE STATUS HERE?
NINA, IGNACIO. I AM SORRY. I HAVE BEEN HERE ALL DAY IDEATING, I...THE STATUS?
DID YOU FIND THE WORD?
THE STATUS IS, I KNOW WE NEED THIS...BUT THE WRONG WORD WILL SET REALITY AWRY FOR 24 HOURS. EVEN SO...
I BELIEVE I HAVE FOUND THE WORD, SPECIFIC AND POWERFUL. I COULD RAISE THE DEAD...
...BUT WHAT DOES IT MEAN IF I DO?
CAN WE DO THIS? YES. BUT SHOULD WE?

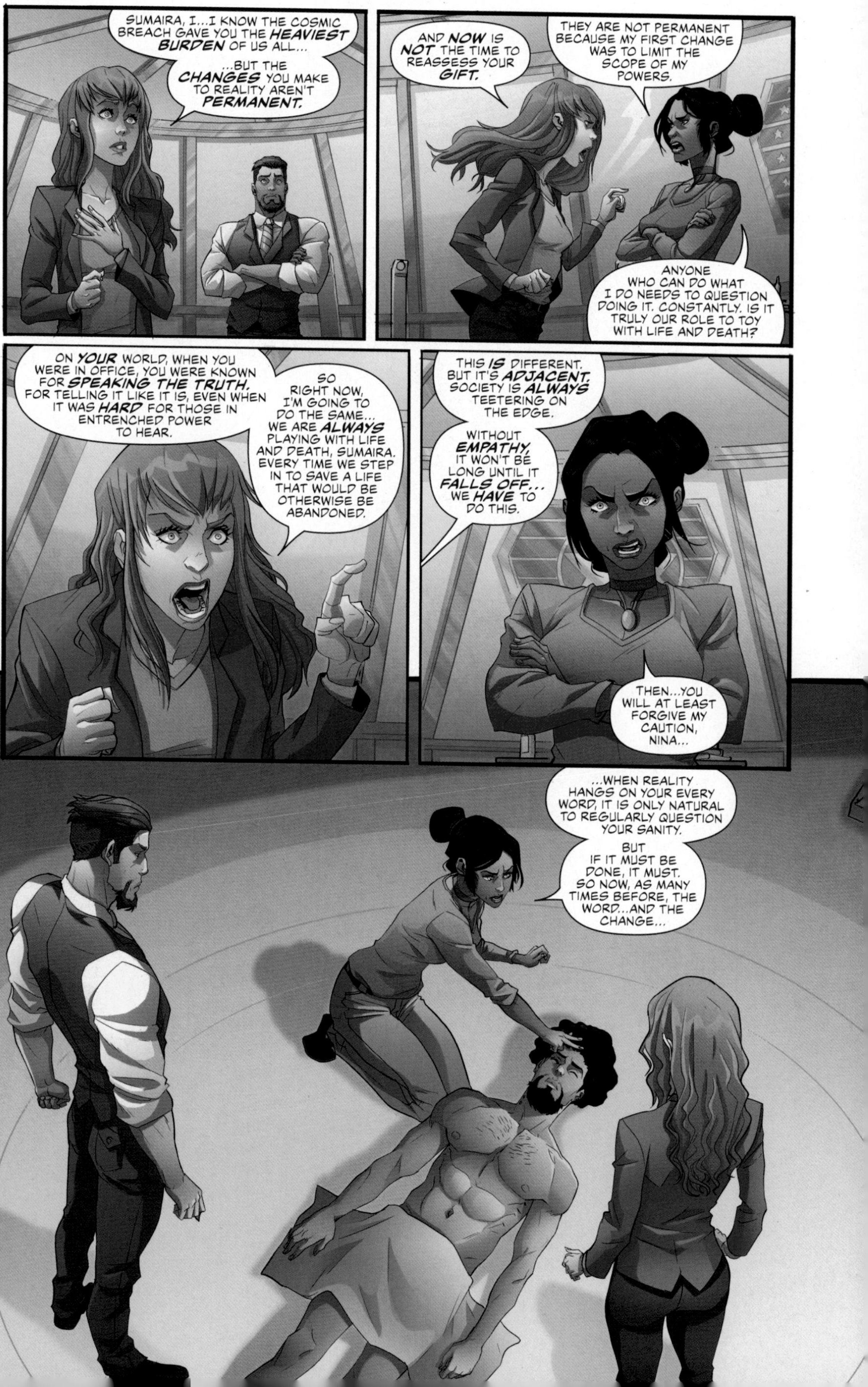
SUMAIRA, I...I KNOW THE COSMIC BREACH GAVE YOU THE HEAVIEST BURDEN OF US ALL...
...BUT THE CHANGES YOU MAKE TO REALITY AREN'T PERMANENT.
AND NOW IS NOT THE TIME TO REASSESS YOUR GIFT.
THEY ARE NOT PERMANENT BECAUSE MY FIRST CHANGE WAS TO LIMIT THE SCOPE OF MY POWERS.
ANYONE WHO CAN DO WHAT I DO NEEDS TO QUESTION DOING IT. CONSTANTLY. IS IT TRULY OUR ROLE TO TOY WITH LIFE AND DEATH?
ON YOUR WORLD, WHEN YOU WERE IN OFFICE, YOU WERE KNOWN FOR SPEAKING THE TRUTH. FOR TELLING IT LIKE IT IS, EVEN WHEN IT WAS HARD FOR THOSE IN ENTRENCHED POWER TO HEAR.
SO RIGHT NOW, I'M GOING TO DO THE SAME... WE ARE ALWAYS PLAYING WITH LIFE AND DEATH, SUMAIRA. EVERY TIME WE STEP IN TO SAVE A LIFE THAT WOULD BE OTHERWISE BE ABANDONED.
THIS IS DIFFERENT. BUT IT'S ADJACENT. SOCIETY IS ALWAYS TEETERING ON THE EDGE.
WITHOUT EMPATHY, IT WON'T BE LONG UNTIL IT FALLS OFF... WE HAVE TO DO THIS.
THEN...YOU WILL AT LEAST FORGIVE MY CAUTION, NINA...
...WHEN REALITY HANGS ON YOUR EVERY WORD, IT IS ONLY NATURAL TO REGULARLY QUESTION YOUR SANITY.
BUT IF IT MUST BE DONE, IT MUST. SO NOW, AS MANY TIMES BEFORE, THE WORD...AND THE CHANGE...

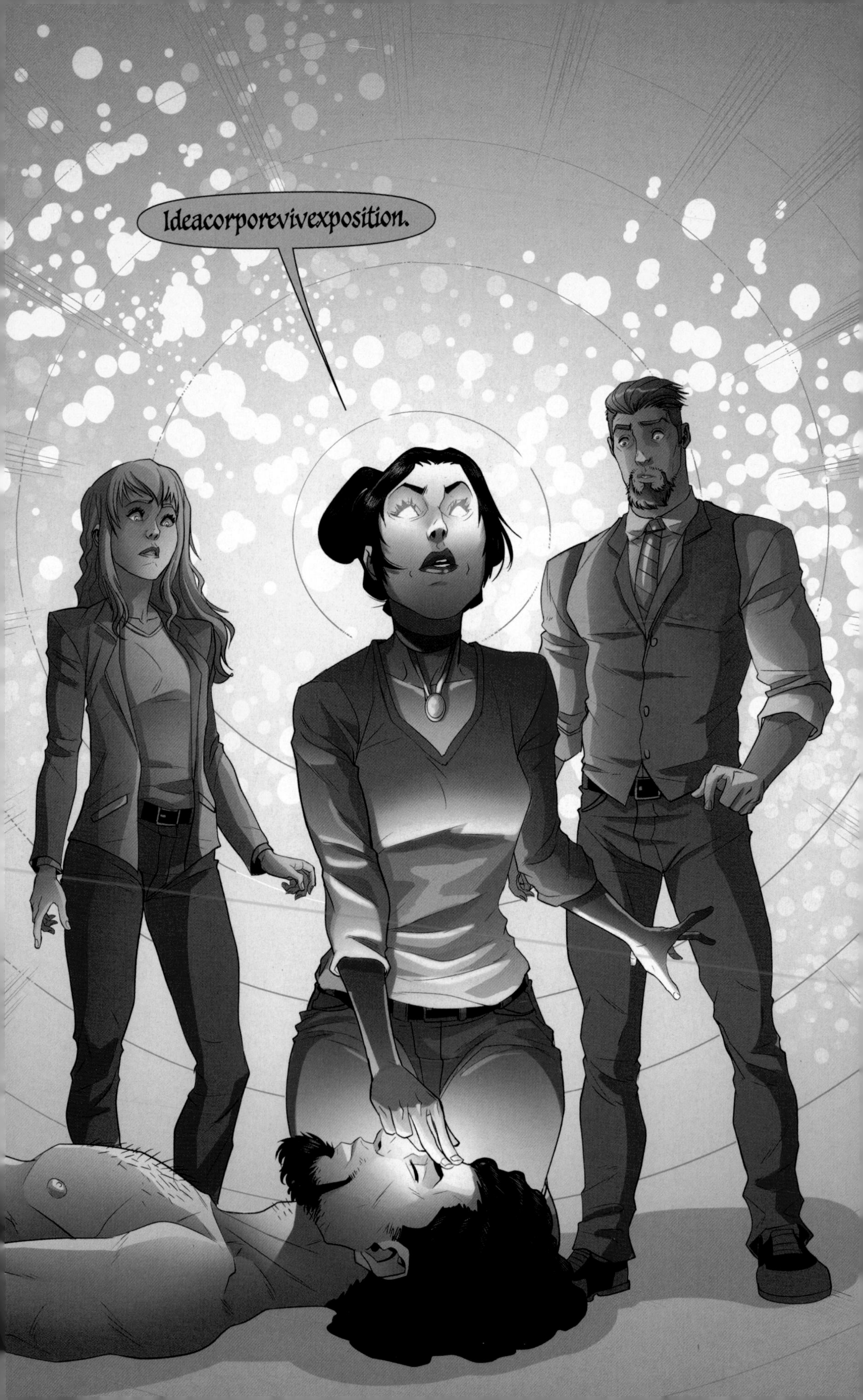
Ideacorporevivexposition.

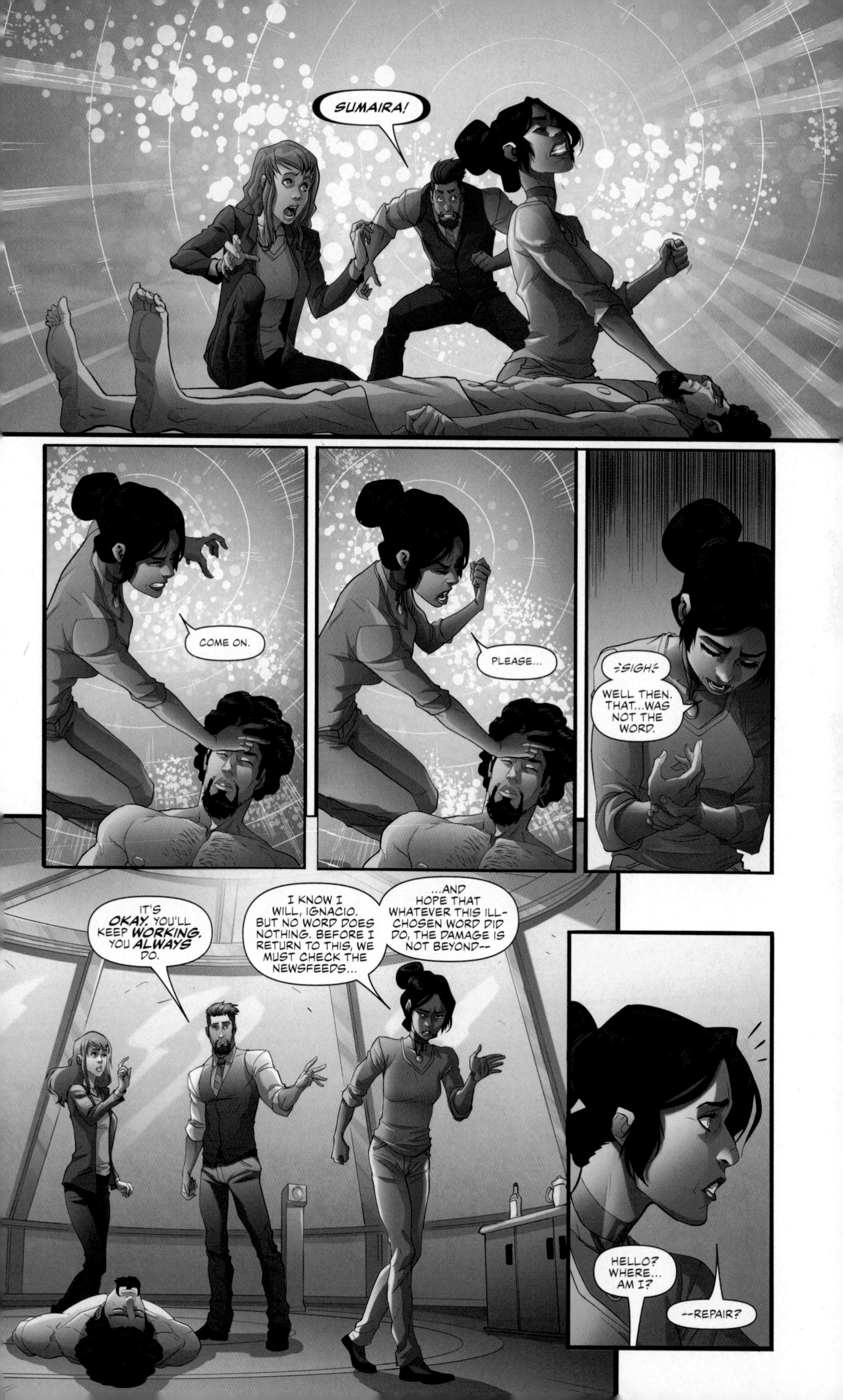
SUMAIRA!
COME ON.
PLEASE...
SIGH
WELL THEN. THAT...WAS NOT THE WORD.
IT'S OKAY. YOU'LL KEEP WORKING. YOU ALWAYS DO.
I KNOW I WILL, IGNACIO. BUT NO WORD DOES NOTHING. BEFORE I RETURN TO THIS, WE MUST CHECK THE NEWSFEEDS...
...AND HOPE THAT WHATEVER THIS ILL-CHOSEN WORD DID DO, THE DAMAGE IS NOT BEYOND--
HELLO? WHERE... AM I?
--REPAIR?

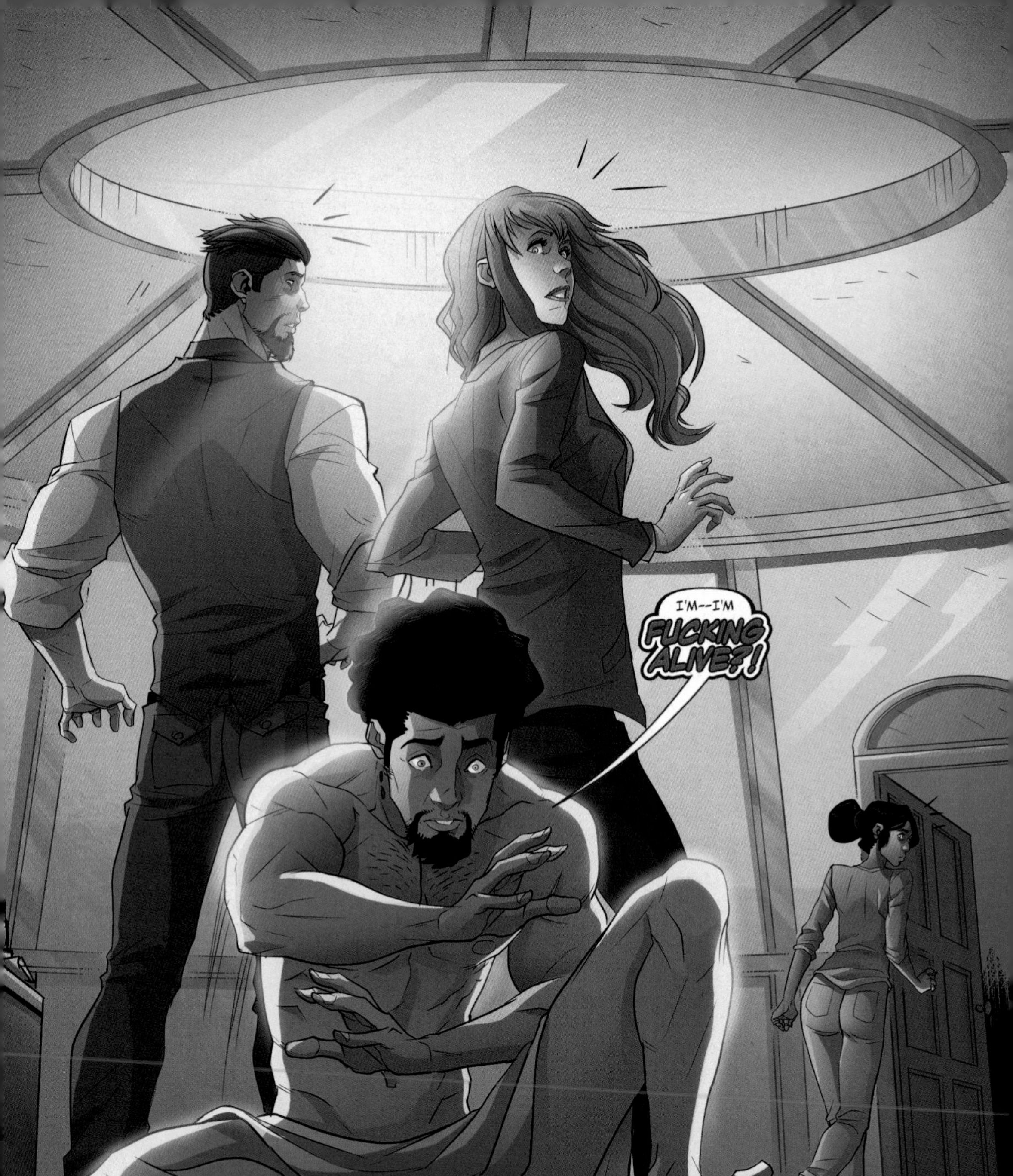
I'M--I'M FUCKING ALIVE?!

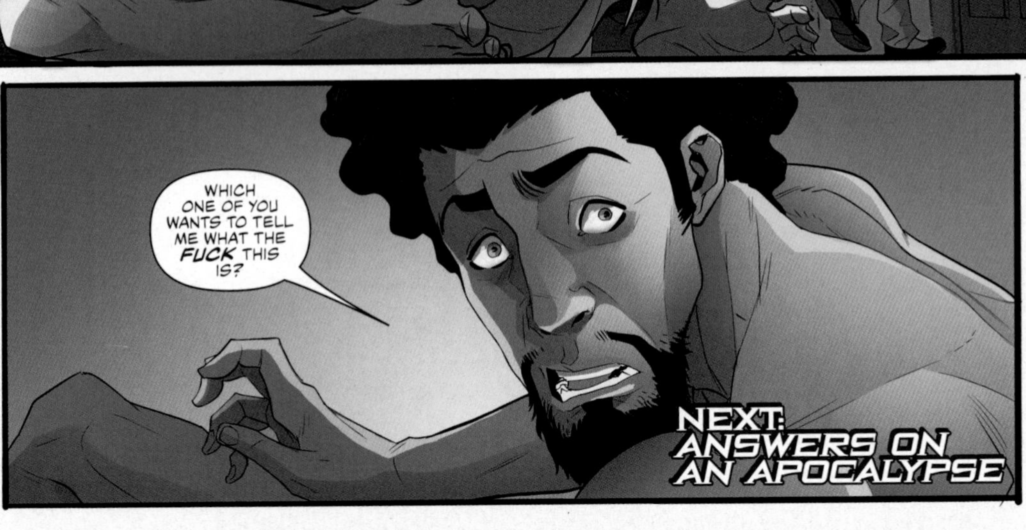
WHICH ONE OF YOU WANTS TO TELL ME WHAT THE FUCK THIS IS?
NEXT: ANSWERS ON AN APOCALYPSE

"I'LL *NEVER* FORGET...WHAT MY *FATHER* TAUGHT ME.

"HE INVENTED SOME TYPE OF LAWN AERATOR, I DON'T KNOW.

"BUT WE LIVED OFF THE PATENT. A LIFE PAID FOR...

"...BY POKING HOLES IN THINGS.

"ONE DAY, WHEN I WAS A BOY, PLAYING IN OUR YARD...

"HE ASKED WHAT I WANTED FOR DINNER...

"...CHICKEN OR STEAK?

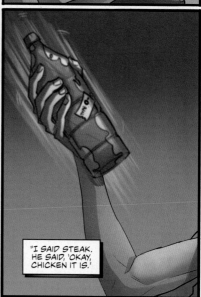

"I SAID STEAK. HE SAID, 'OKAY, CHICKEN IT IS.'

"I SAID, 'SCREW YOU.'

"HE RAN UP, CHOKED ME, AND SLAMMED ME ON THE HOOD OF A CAR.

"LIFE'S BEEN *LIKE* THAT, YEAH. EVER SINCE...

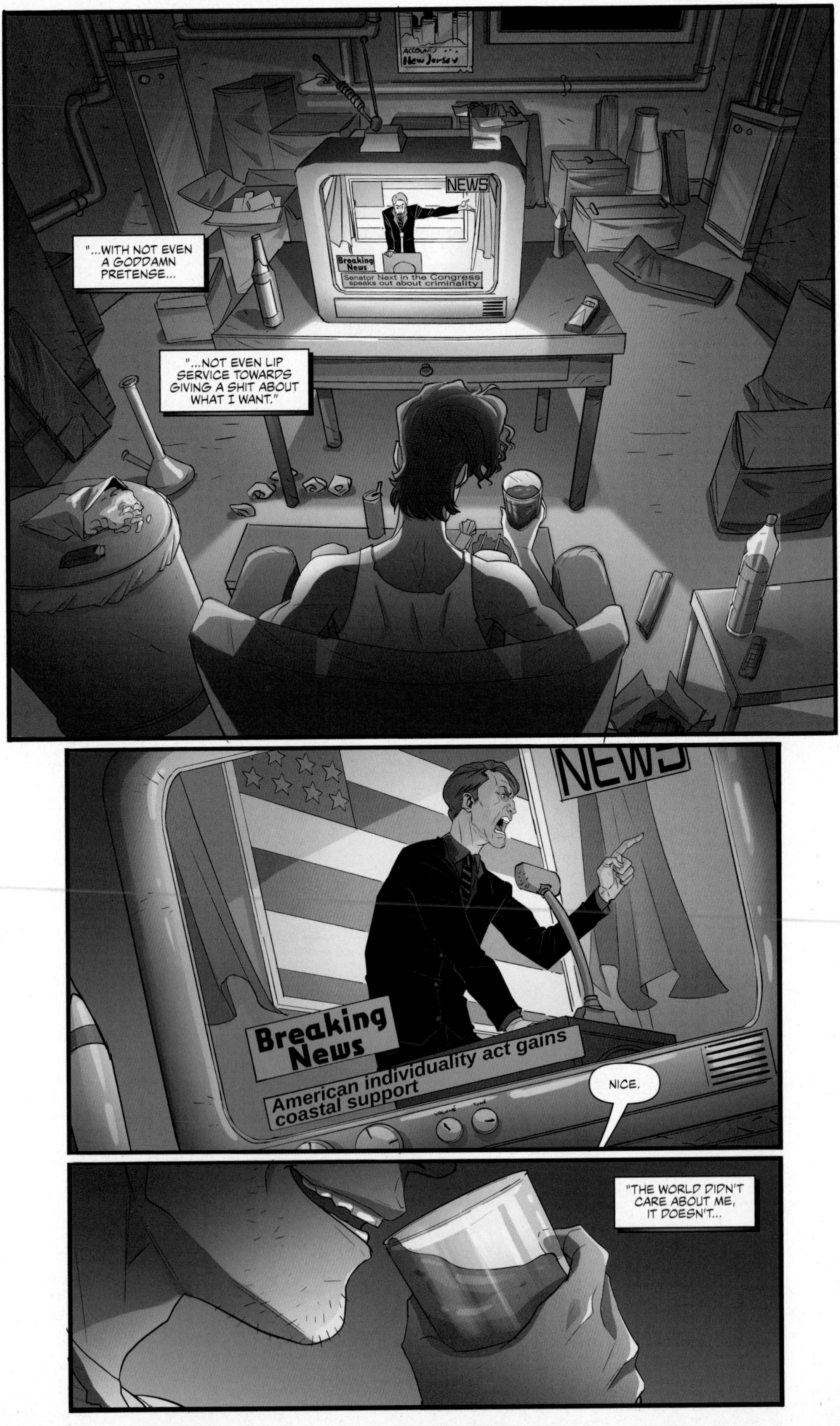
New Jersey
NEWS
Breaking News
Senator Next in the Congress speaks out about criminality
"...WITH NOT EVEN A GODDAMN PRETENSE...
"...NOT EVEN LIP SERVICE TOWARDS GIVING A SHIT ABOUT WHAT I WANT."
NEWS
Breaking News
American individuality act gains coastal support
NICE.
"THE WORLD DIDN'T CARE ABOUT ME, IT DOESN'T...

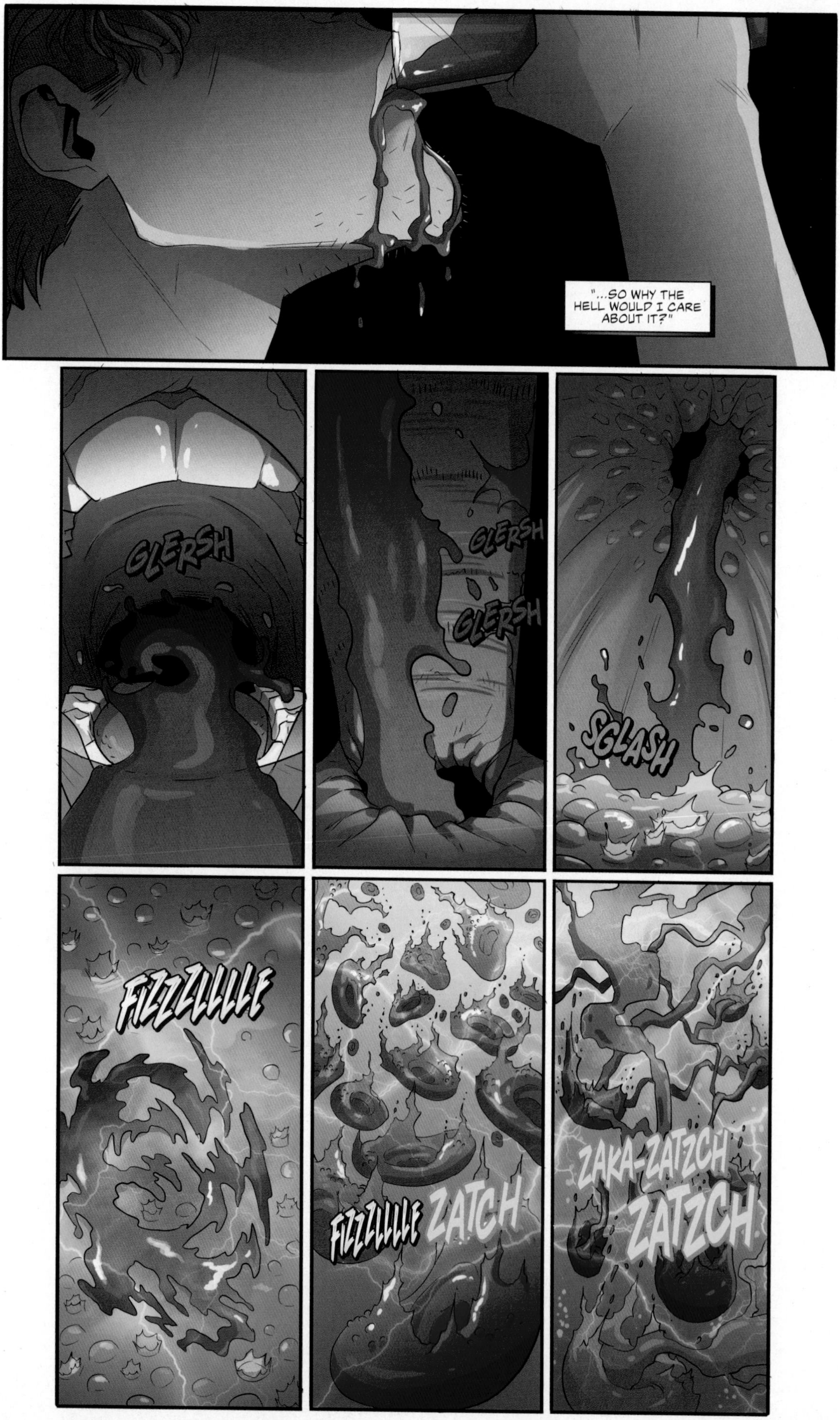
"...SO WHY THE HELL WOULD I CARE ABOUT IT?"
GLERSH
GLERSH
GLERSH
SGLASH
FIZZZZLLLLLE
FIZZZZLLLLLE
ZATCH
ZAKA-ZATZCH
ZATZCH

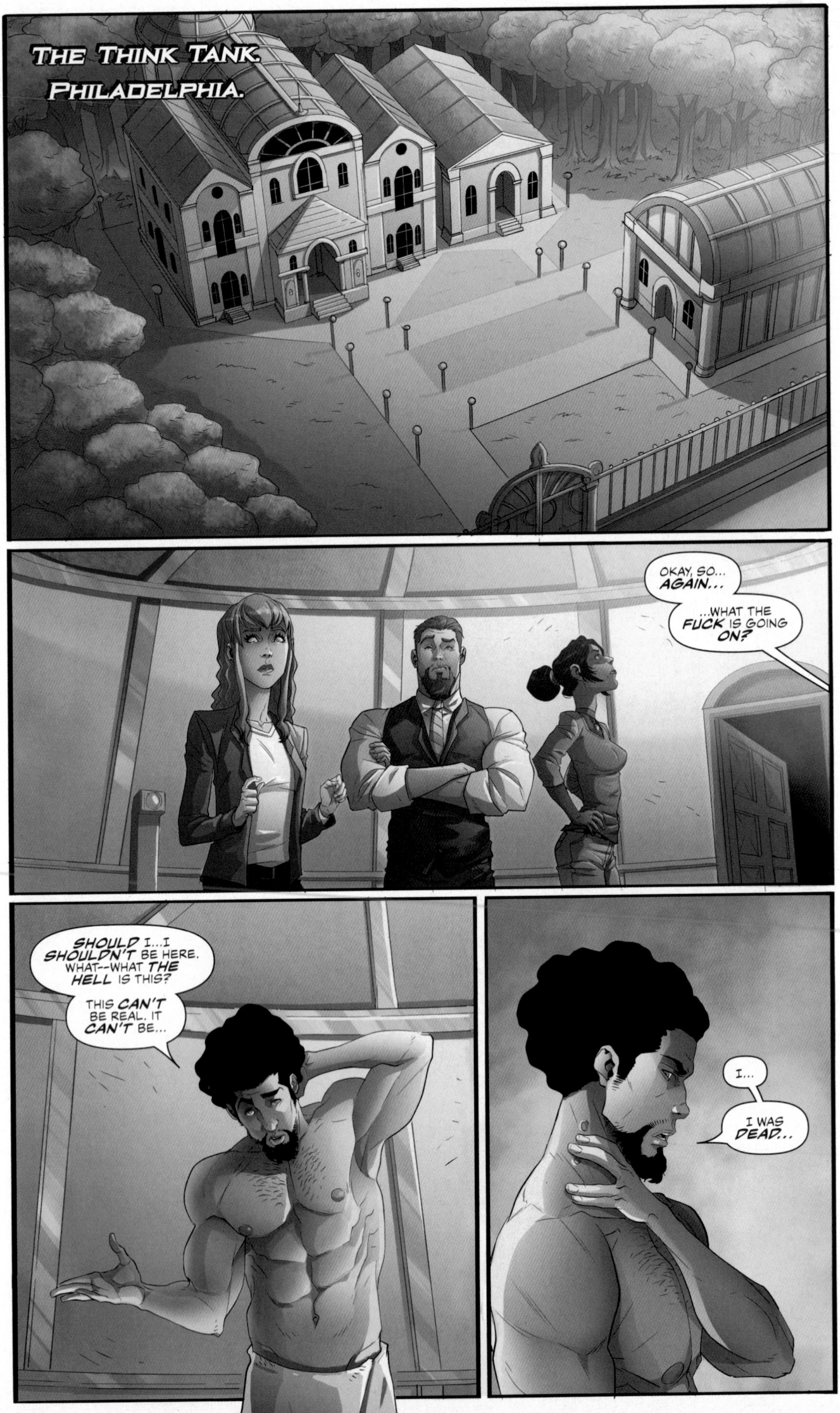
THE THINK TANK.
PHILADELPHIA.
OKAY, SO... AGAIN...
...WHAT THE FUCK IS GOING ON?
SHOULD I...I SHOULDN'T BE HERE. WHAT--WHAT THE HELL IS THIS?
THIS CAN'T BE REAL. IT CAN'T BE...
I...
I WAS DEAD...

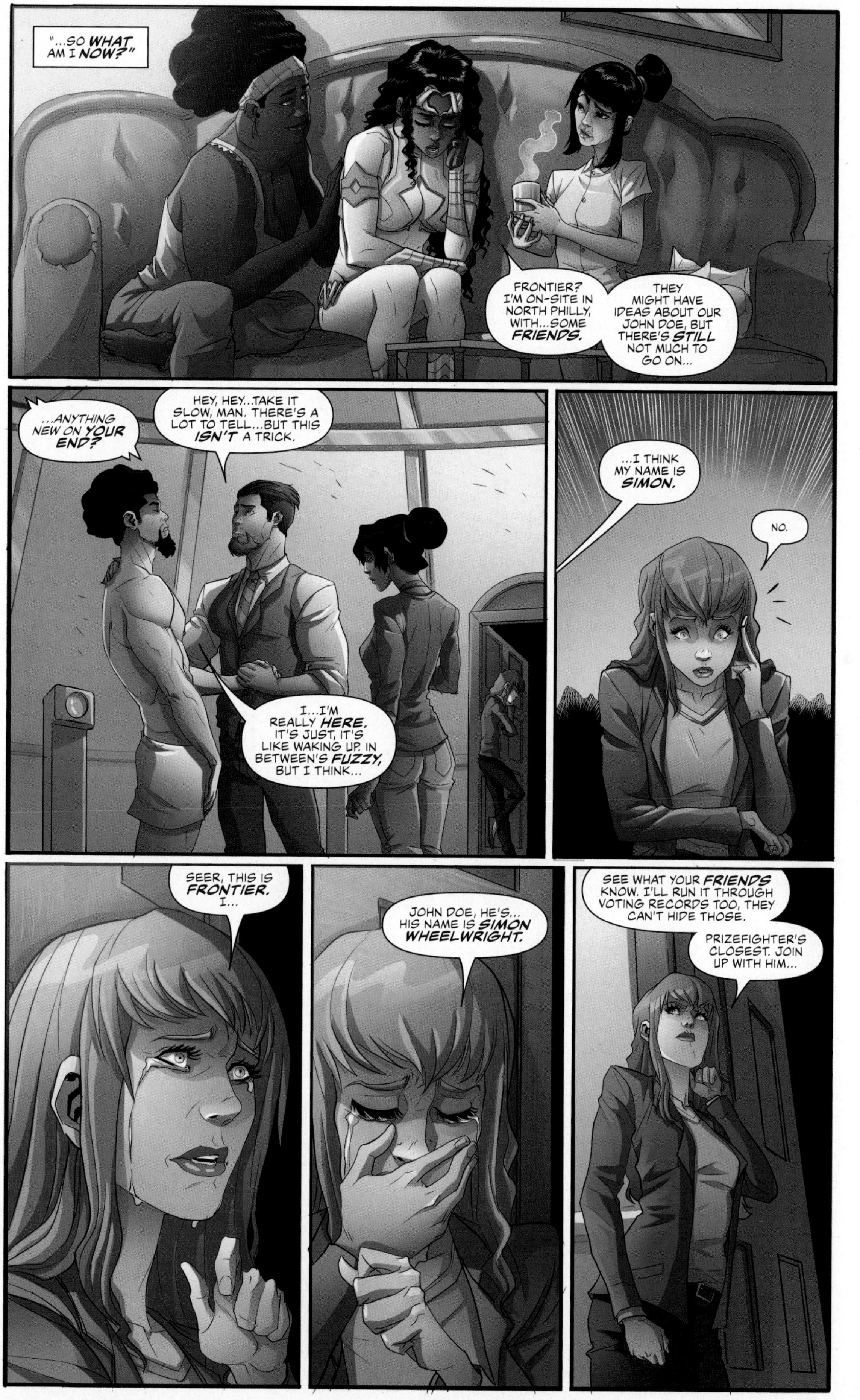
"...SO WHAT AM I NOW?"
FRONTIER? I'M ON-SITE IN NORTH PHILLY, WITH...SOME FRIENDS.
THEY MIGHT HAVE IDEAS ABOUT OUR JOHN DOE, BUT THERE'S STILL NOT MUCH TO GO ON...
...ANYTHING NEW ON YOUR END?
HEY, HEY...TAKE IT SLOW, MAN. THERE'S A LOT TO TELL...BUT THIS ISN'T A TRICK.
I...I'M REALLY HERE. IT'S JUST, IT'S LIKE WAKING UP. IN BETWEEN'S FUZZY, BUT I THINK...
...I THINK MY NAME IS SIMON.
NO.
SEER, THIS IS FRONTIER. I...
JOHN DOE, HE'S... HIS NAME IS SIMON WHEELWRIGHT.
SEE WHAT YOUR FRIENDS KNOW. I'LL RUN IT THROUGH VOTING RECORDS TOO, THEY CAN'T HIDE THOSE.
PRIZEFIGHTER'S CLOSEST. JOIN UP WITH HIM...

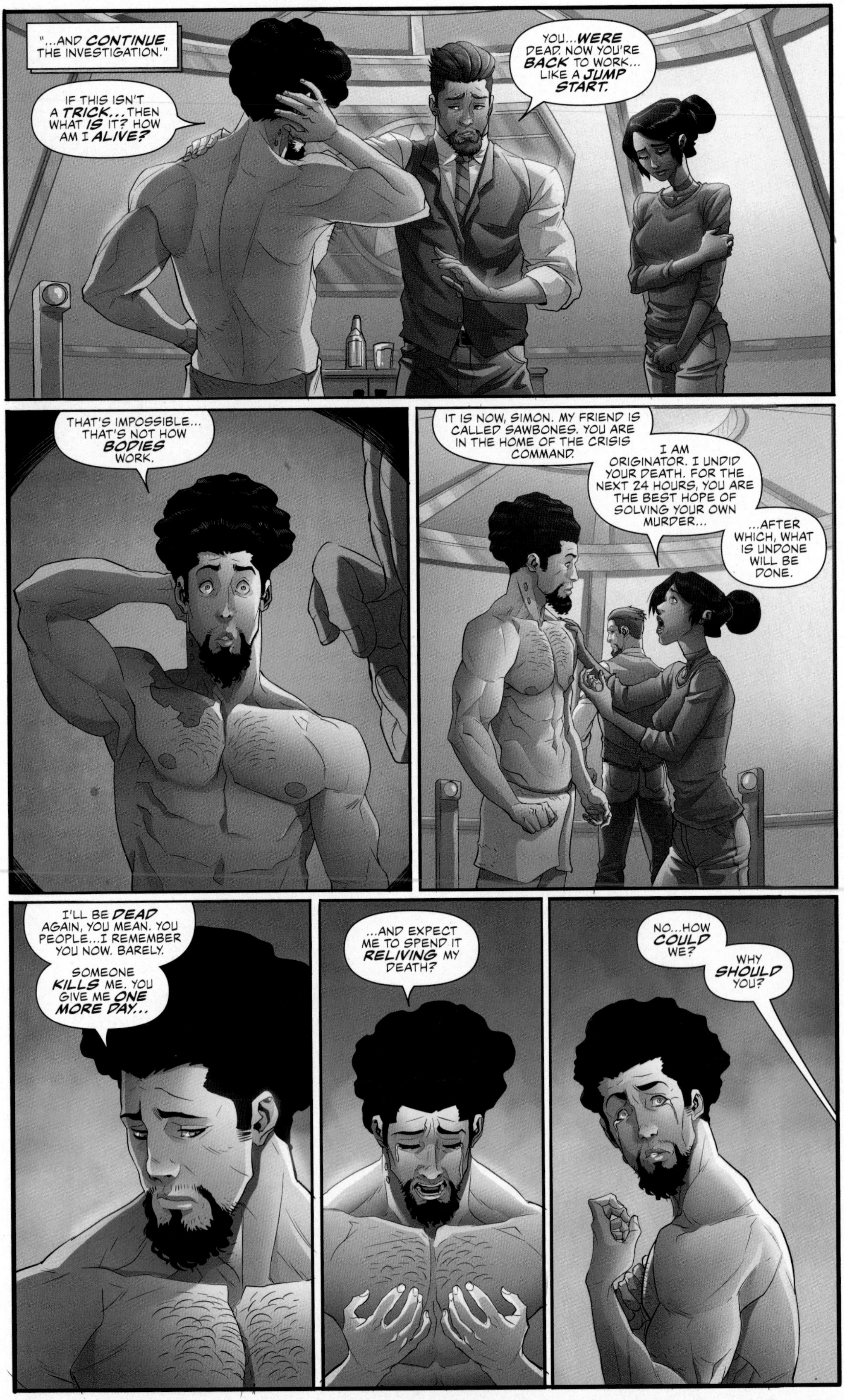
"...AND CONTINUE THE INVESTIGATION."
IF THIS ISN'T A TRICK... THEN WHAT IS IT? HOW AM I ALIVE?
YOU... WERE DEAD. NOW YOU'RE BACK TO WORK... LIKE A JUMP START.
THAT'S IMPOSSIBLE... THAT'S NOT HOW BODIES WORK.
IT IS NOW, SIMON. MY FRIEND IS CALLED SAWBONES. YOU ARE IN THE HOME OF THE CRISIS COMMAND.
I AM ORIGINATOR. I UNDID YOUR DEATH. FOR THE NEXT 24 HOURS, YOU ARE THE BEST HOPE OF SOLVING YOUR OWN MURDER...
...AFTER WHICH, WHAT IS UNDONE WILL BE DONE.
I'LL BE DEAD AGAIN, YOU MEAN. YOU PEOPLE... I REMEMBER YOU NOW. BARELY.
SOMEONE KILLS ME. YOU GIVE ME ONE MORE DAY...
...AND EXPECT ME TO SPEND IT RELIVING MY DEATH?
NO... HOW COULD WE?
WHY SHOULD YOU?

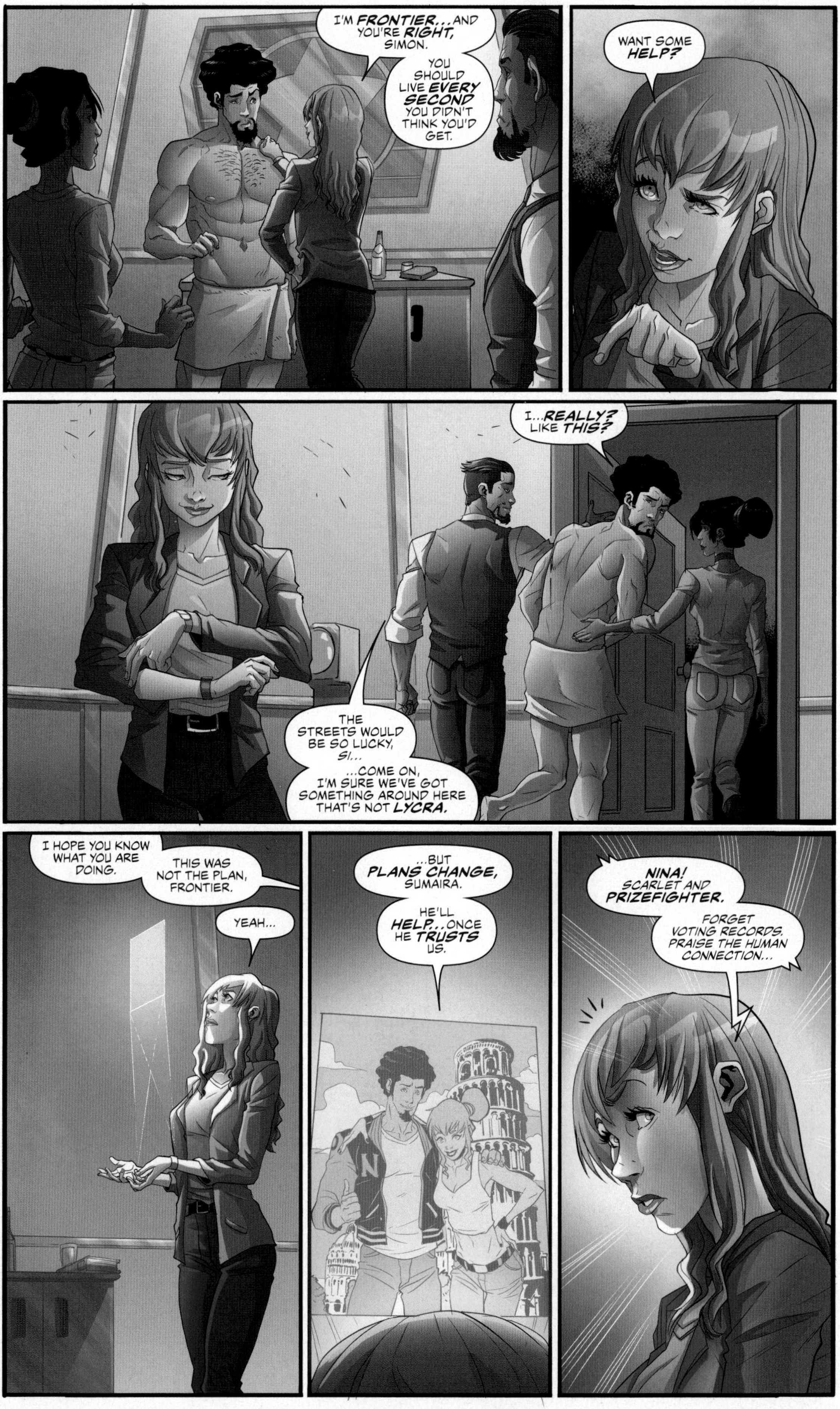

I'M FRONTIER...AND YOU'RE RIGHT, SIMON.
YOU SHOULD LIVE EVERY SECOND YOU DIDN'T THINK YOU'D GET.
WANT SOME HELP?
I...REALLY? LIKE THIS?
THE STREETS WOULD BE SO LUCKY, SI...
...COME ON, I'M SURE WE'VE GOT SOMETHING AROUND HERE THAT'S NOT LYCRA.
I HOPE YOU KNOW WHAT YOU ARE DOING.
THIS WAS NOT THE PLAN, FRONTIER.
YEAH...
...BUT PLANS CHANGE, SUMAIRA.
HE'LL HELP...ONCE HE TRUSTS US.
NINA! SCARLET AND PRIZEFIGHTER.
FORGET VOTING RECORDS. PRAISE THE HUMAN CONNECTION...

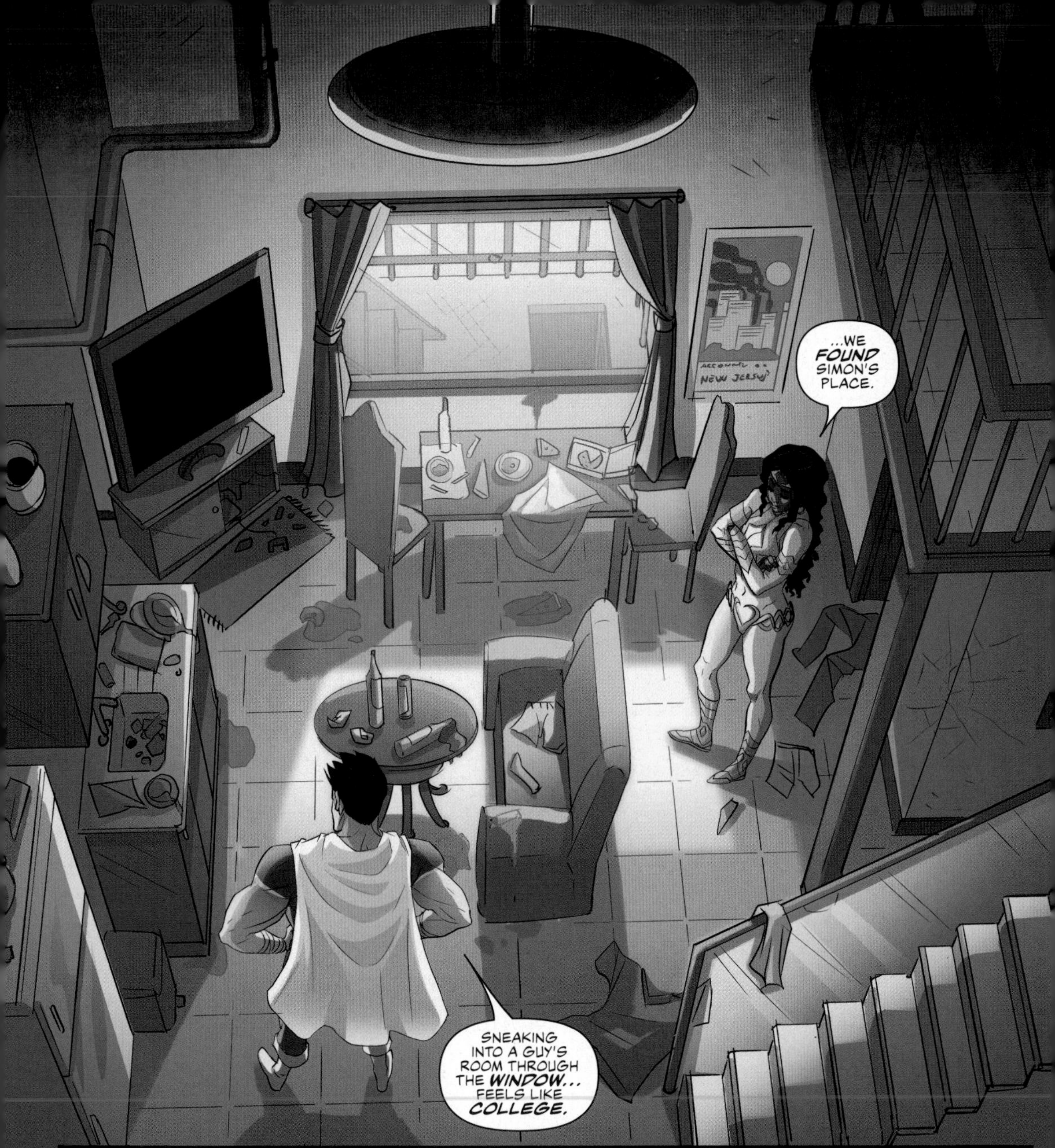

ACCOUNTS OF NEW JERSEY
...WE FOUND SIMON'S PLACE.
SNEAKING INTO A GUY'S ROOM THROUGH THE WINDOW... FEELS LIKE COLLEGE.

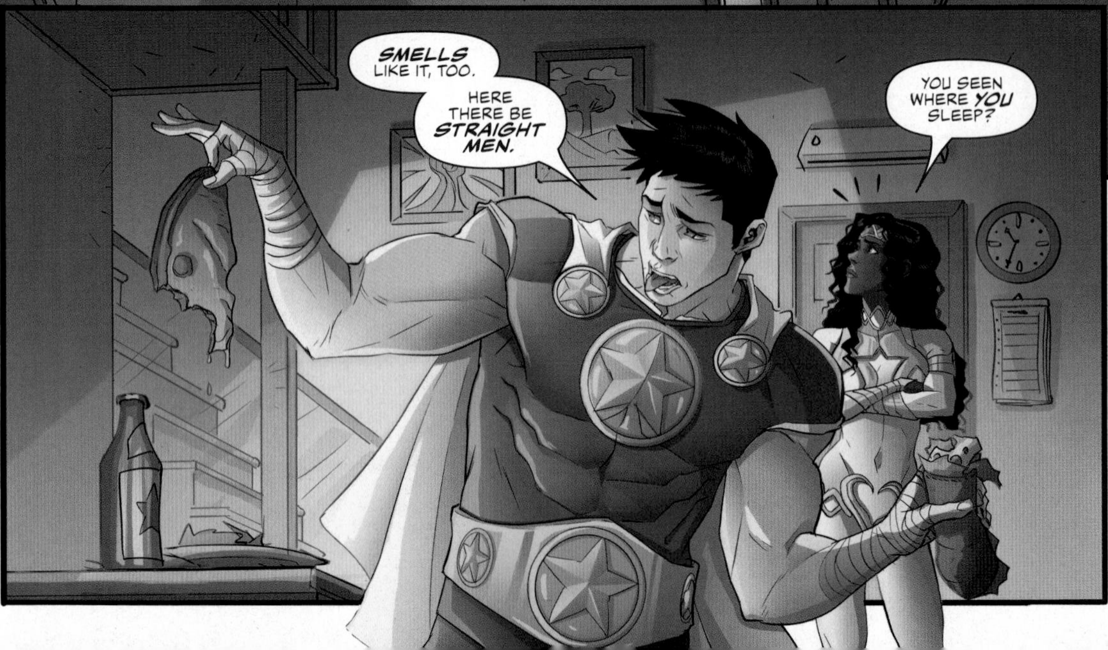

SMELLS LIKE IT, TOO.
HERE THERE BE STRAIGHT MEN.
YOU SEEN WHERE YOU SLEEP?

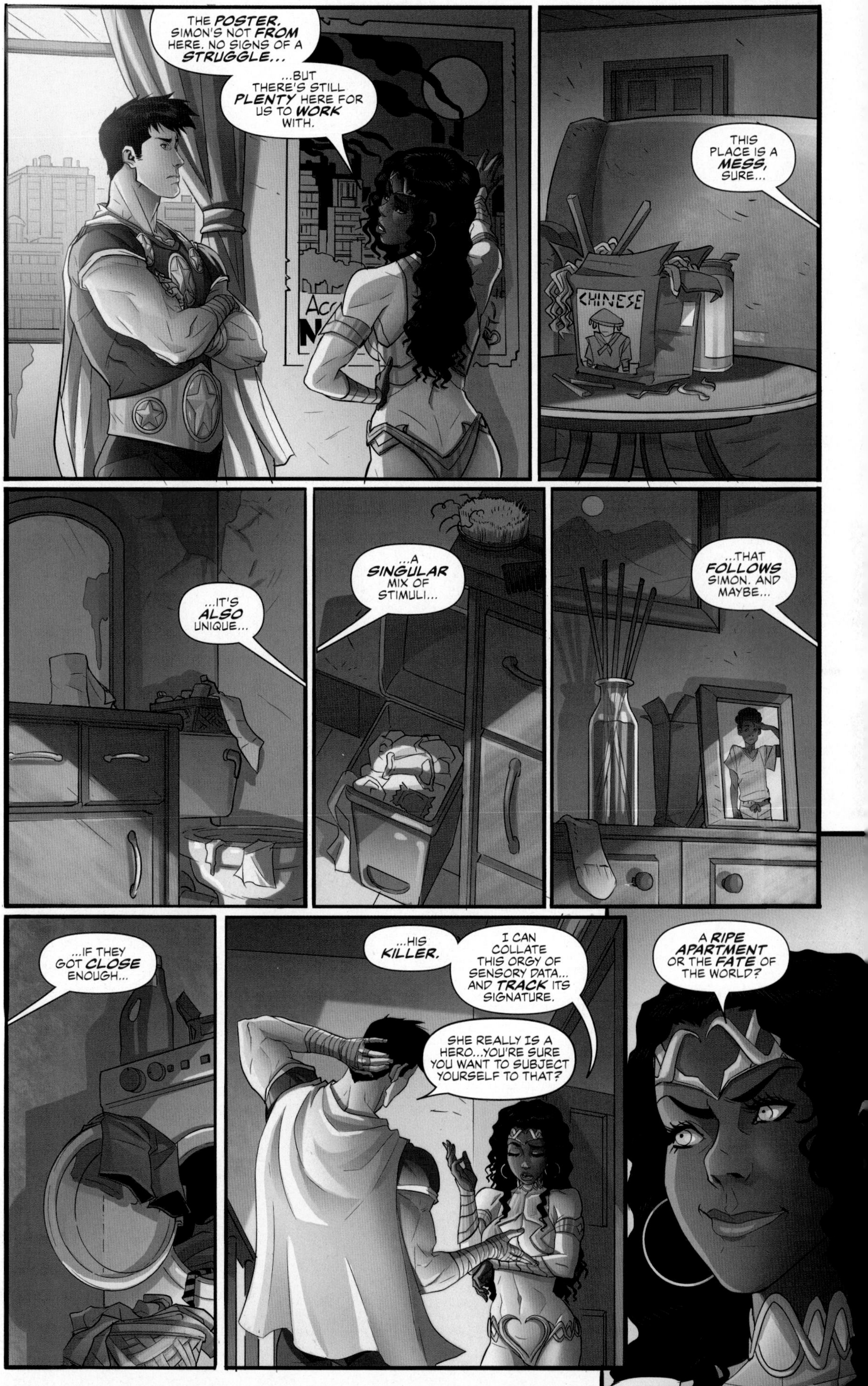
THE POSTER. SIMON'S NOT FROM HERE. NO SIGNS OF A STRUGGLE...
...BUT THERE'S STILL PLENTY HERE FOR US TO WORK WITH.
THIS PLACE IS A MESS, SURE...
CHINESE
...IT'S ALSO UNIQUE...
...A SINGULAR MIX OF STIMULI...
...THAT FOLLOWS SIMON. AND MAYBE...
...IF THEY GOT CLOSE ENOUGH...
...HIS KILLER.
I CAN COLLATE THIS ORGY OF SENSORY DATA... AND TRACK ITS SIGNATURE.
SHE REALLY IS A HERO...YOU'RE SURE YOU WANT TO SUBJECT YOURSELF TO THAT?
A RIPE APARTMENT OR THE FATE OF THE WORLD?

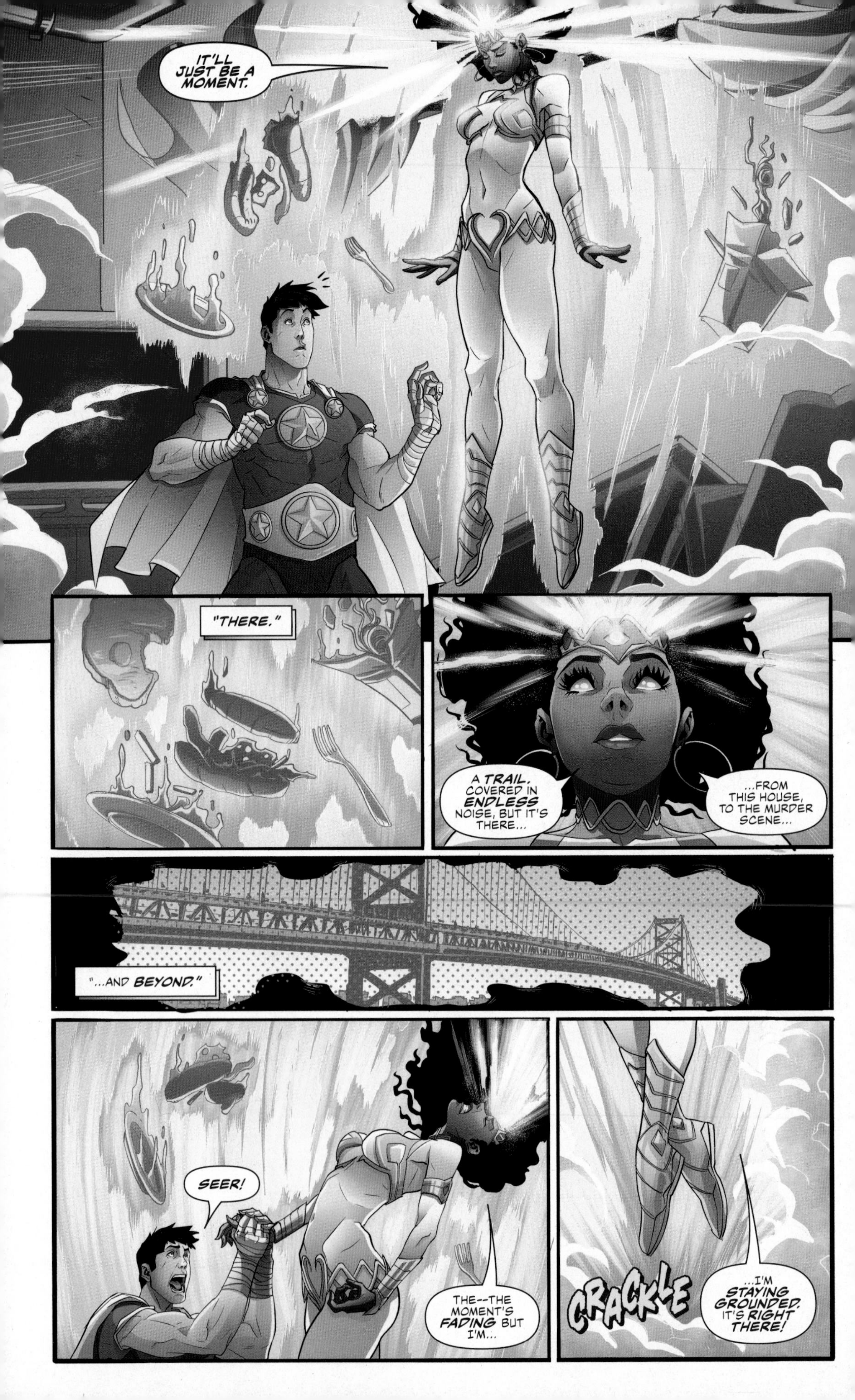
IT'LL JUST BE A MOMENT.
"THERE."
A TRAIL, COVERED IN ENDLESS NOISE, BUT IT'S THERE...
...FROM THIS HOUSE, TO THE MURDER SCENE...
"...AND BEYOND."
SEER!
THE--THE MOMENT'S FADING BUT I'M...
CRACKLE
...I'M STAYING GROUNDED. IT'S RIGHT THERE!

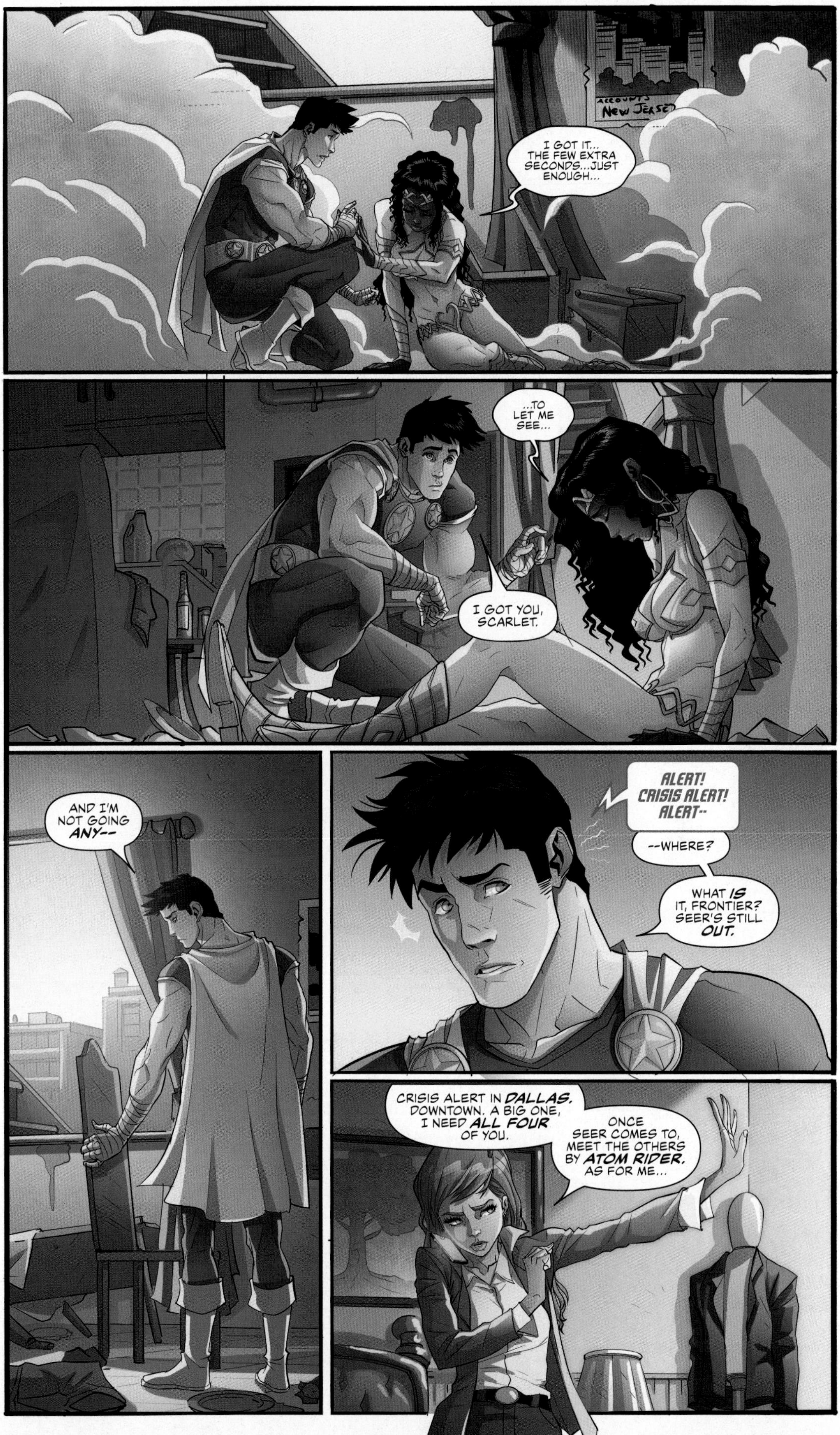
I GOT IT... THE FEW EXTRA SECONDS...JUST ENOUGH...
...TO LET ME SEE...
I GOT YOU, SCARLET.
AND I'M NOT GOING ANY--
ALERT! CRISIS ALERT! ALERT--
--WHERE?
WHAT IS IT, FRONTIER? SEER'S STILL OUT.
CRISIS ALERT IN DALLAS. DOWNTOWN. A BIG ONE. I NEED ALL FOUR OF YOU.
ONCE SEER COMES TO, MEET THE OTHERS BY ATOM RIDER. AS FOR ME...

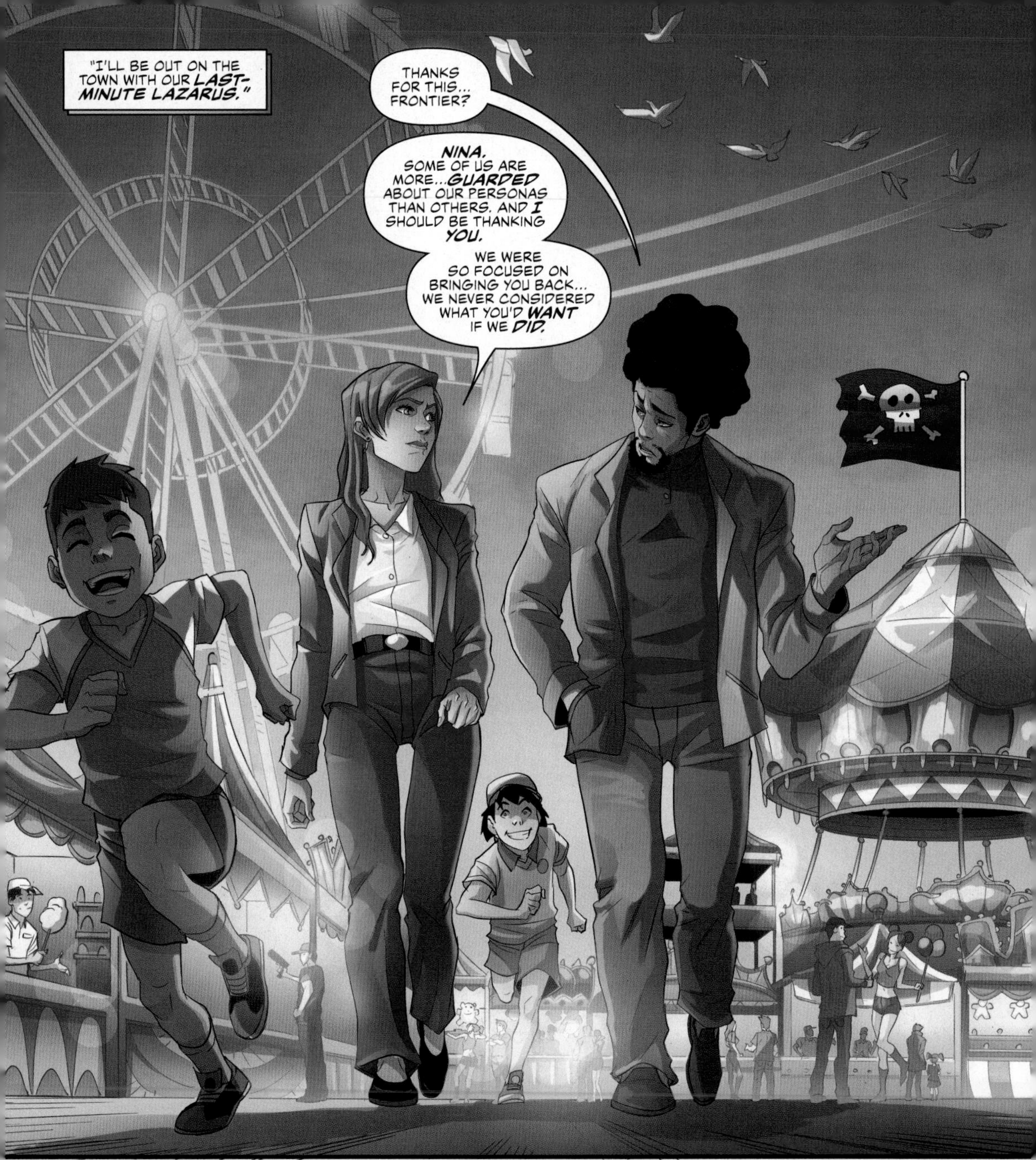
"I'LL BE OUT ON THE TOWN WITH OUR LAST-MINUTE LAZARUS."
THANKS FOR THIS... FRONTIER?
NINA. SOME OF US ARE MORE...GUARDED ABOUT OUR PERSONAS THAN OTHERS. AND I SHOULD BE THANKING YOU.
WE WERE SO FOCUSED ON BRINGING YOU BACK... WE NEVER CONSIDERED WHAT YOU'D WANT IF WE DID.

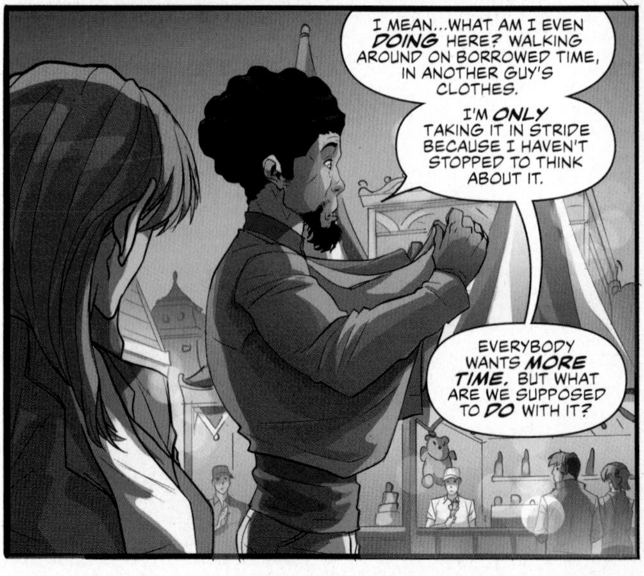
I MEAN...WHAT AM I EVEN DOING HERE? WALKING AROUND ON BORROWED TIME, IN ANOTHER GUY'S CLOTHES.
I'M ONLY TAKING IT IN STRIDE BECAUSE I HAVEN'T STOPPED TO THINK ABOUT IT.
EVERYBODY WANTS MORE TIME. BUT WHAT ARE WE SUPPOSED TO DO WITH IT?

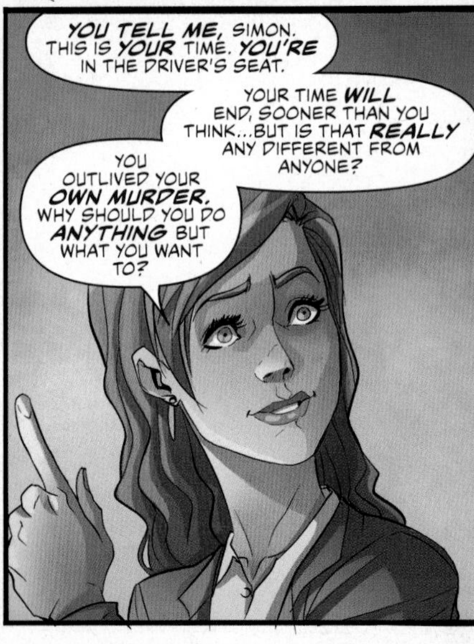
YOU TELL ME, SIMON. THIS IS YOUR TIME. YOU'RE IN THE DRIVER'S SEAT.
YOUR TIME WILL END, SOONER THAN YOU THINK...BUT IS THAT REALLY ANY DIFFERENT FROM ANYONE?
YOU OUTLIVED YOUR OWN MURDER. WHY SHOULD YOU DO ANYTHING BUT WHAT YOU WANT TO?

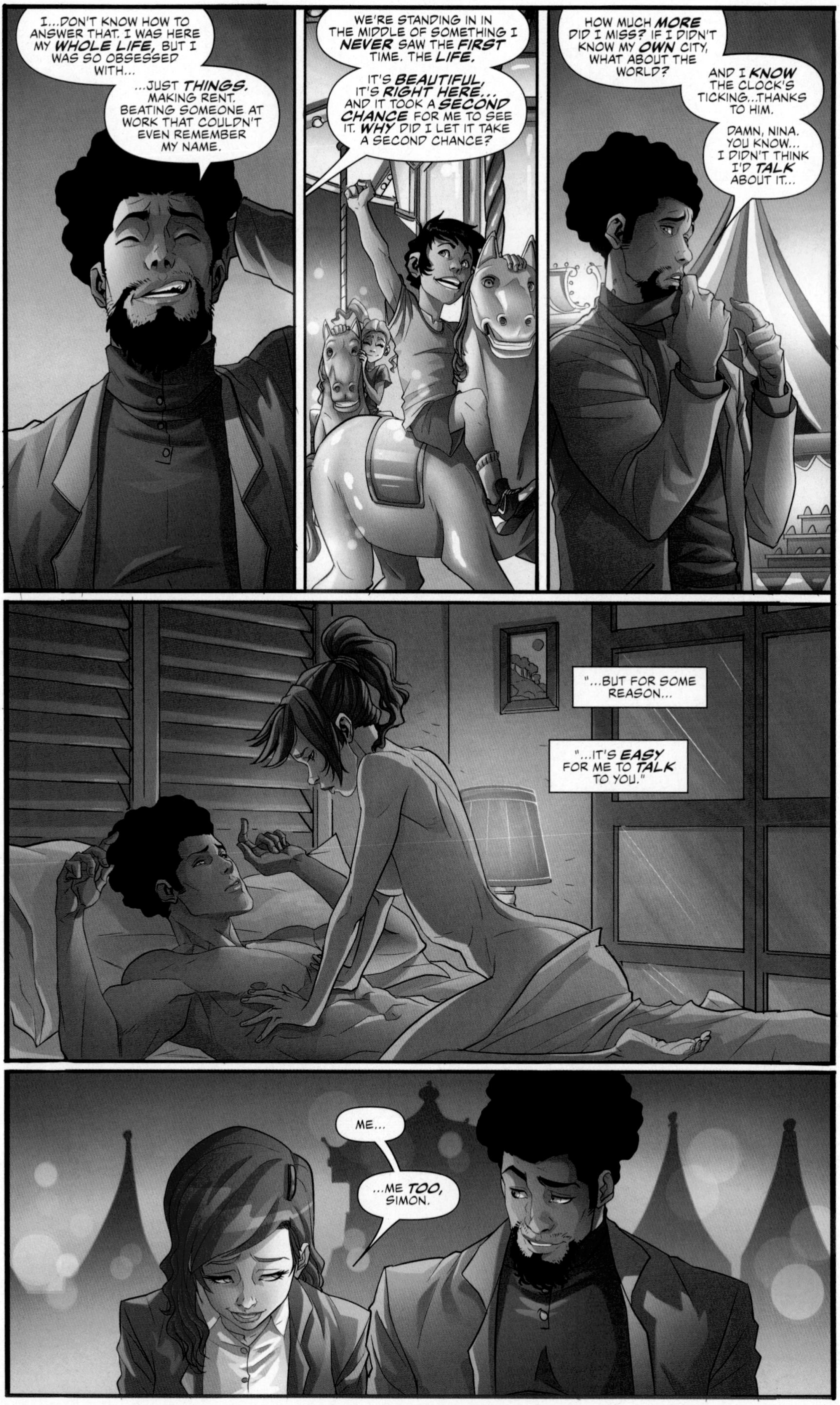
I...DON'T KNOW HOW TO ANSWER THAT. I WAS HERE MY WHOLE LIFE, BUT I WAS SO OBSESSED WITH...
...JUST THINGS. MAKING RENT. BEATING SOMEONE AT WORK THAT COULDN'T EVEN REMEMBER MY NAME.
WE'RE STANDING IN IN THE MIDDLE OF SOMETHING I NEVER SAW THE FIRST TIME. THE LIFE.
IT'S BEAUTIFUL, IT'S RIGHT HERE... AND IT TOOK A SECOND CHANCE FOR ME TO SEE IT. WHY DID I LET IT TAKE A SECOND CHANCE?
HOW MUCH MORE DID I MISS? IF I DIDN'T KNOW MY OWN CITY, WHAT ABOUT THE WORLD?
AND I KNOW THE CLOCK'S TICKING...THANKS TO HIM.
DAMN, NINA. YOU KNOW... I DIDN'T THINK I'D TALK ABOUT IT...
"...BUT FOR SOME REASON...
"...IT'S EASY FOR ME TO TALK TO YOU."
ME...
...ME TOO, SIMON.

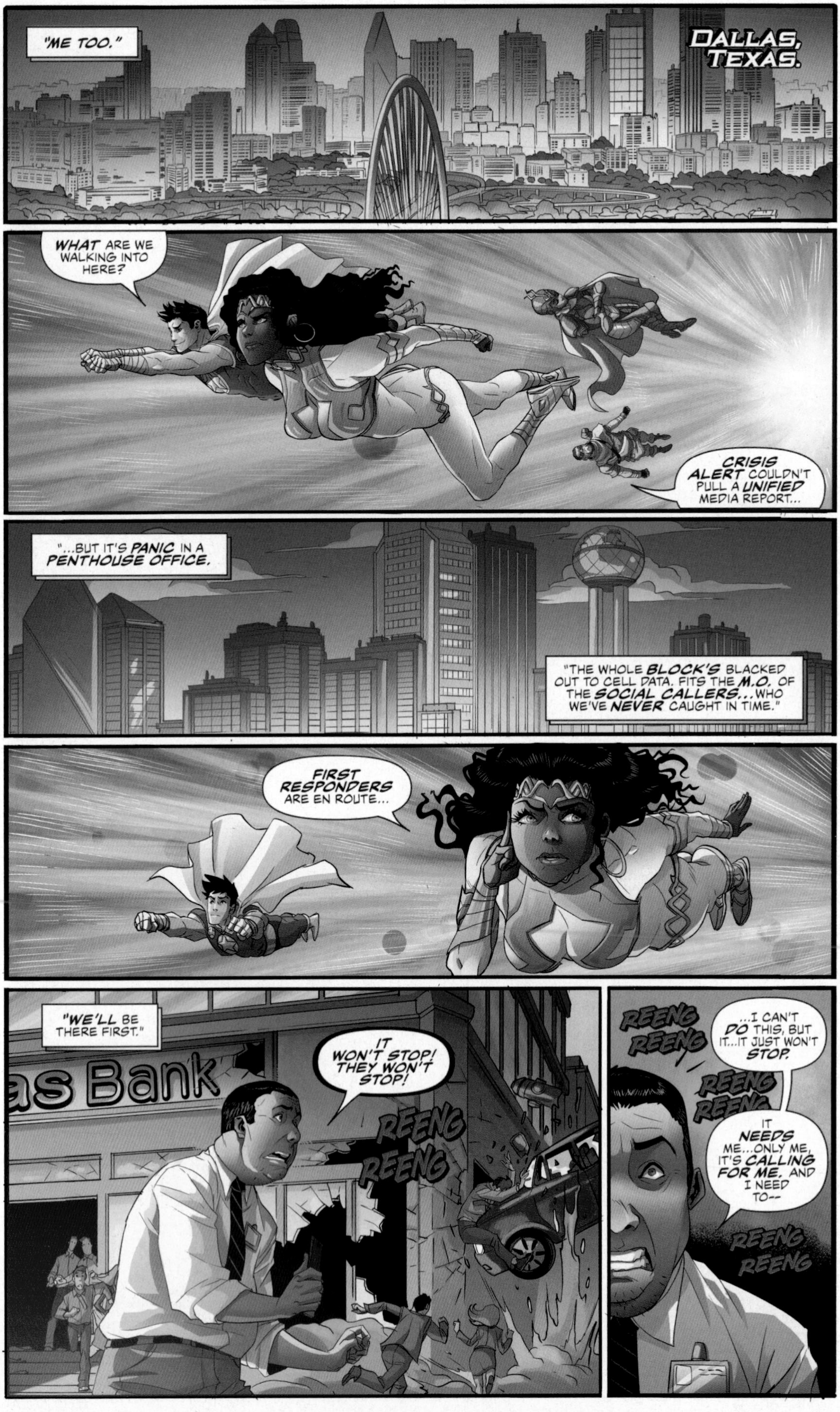
"ME TOO."
DALLAS, TEXAS.
WHAT ARE WE WALKING INTO HERE?
CRISIS ALERT COULDN'T PULL A UNIFIED MEDIA REPORT...
"...BUT IT'S PANIC IN A PENTHOUSE OFFICE.
"THE WHOLE BLOCK'S BLACKED OUT TO CELL DATA. FITS THE M.O. OF THE SOCIAL CALLERS...WHO WE'VE NEVER CAUGHT IN TIME."
FIRST RESPONDERS ARE EN ROUTE...
"WE'LL BE THERE FIRST."
as Bank
IT WON'T STOP! THEY WON'T STOP!
REENG REENG
REENG REENG
...I CAN'T DO THIS, BUT IT...IT JUST WON'T STOP.
REENG REENG
IT NEEDS ME...ONLY ME, IT'S CALLING FOR ME. AND I NEED TO--
REENG REENG

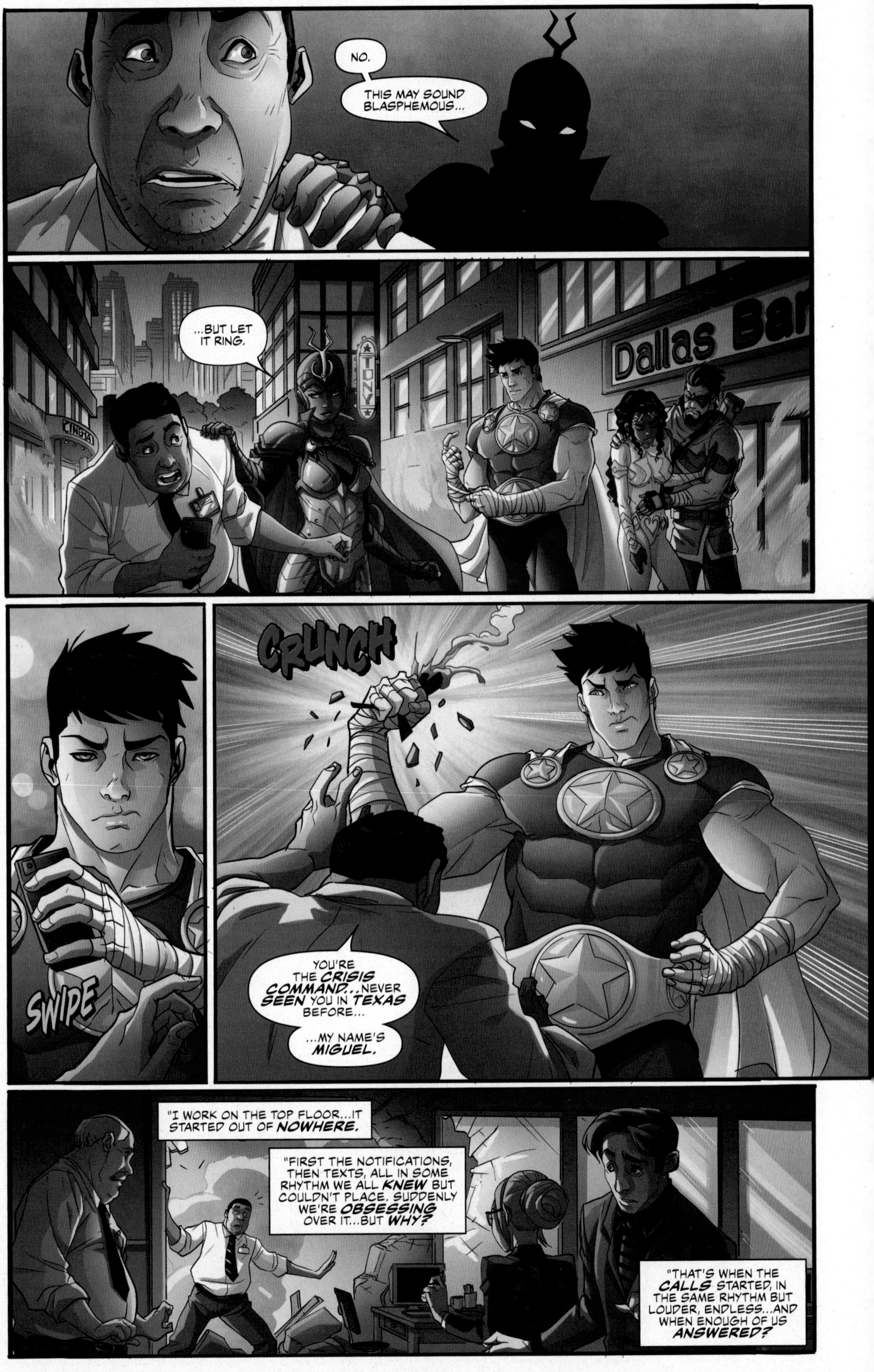
NO.
THIS MAY SOUND BLASPHEMOUS...
...BUT LET IT RING.
TONY
CINEMA
Dallas Bar
CRUNCH
SWIPE
YOU'RE THE CRISIS COMMAND... NEVER SEEN YOU IN TEXAS BEFORE...
...MY NAME'S MIGUEL.
"I WORK ON THE TOP FLOOR...IT STARTED OUT OF NOWHERE.
"FIRST THE NOTIFICATIONS, THEN TEXTS, ALL IN SOME RHYTHM WE ALL KNEW BUT COULDN'T PLACE. SUDDENLY WE'RE OBSESSING OVER IT...BUT WHY?
"THAT'S WHEN THE CALLS STARTED, IN THE SAME RHYTHM BUT LOUDER, ENDLESS...AND WHEN ENOUGH OF US ANSWERED?

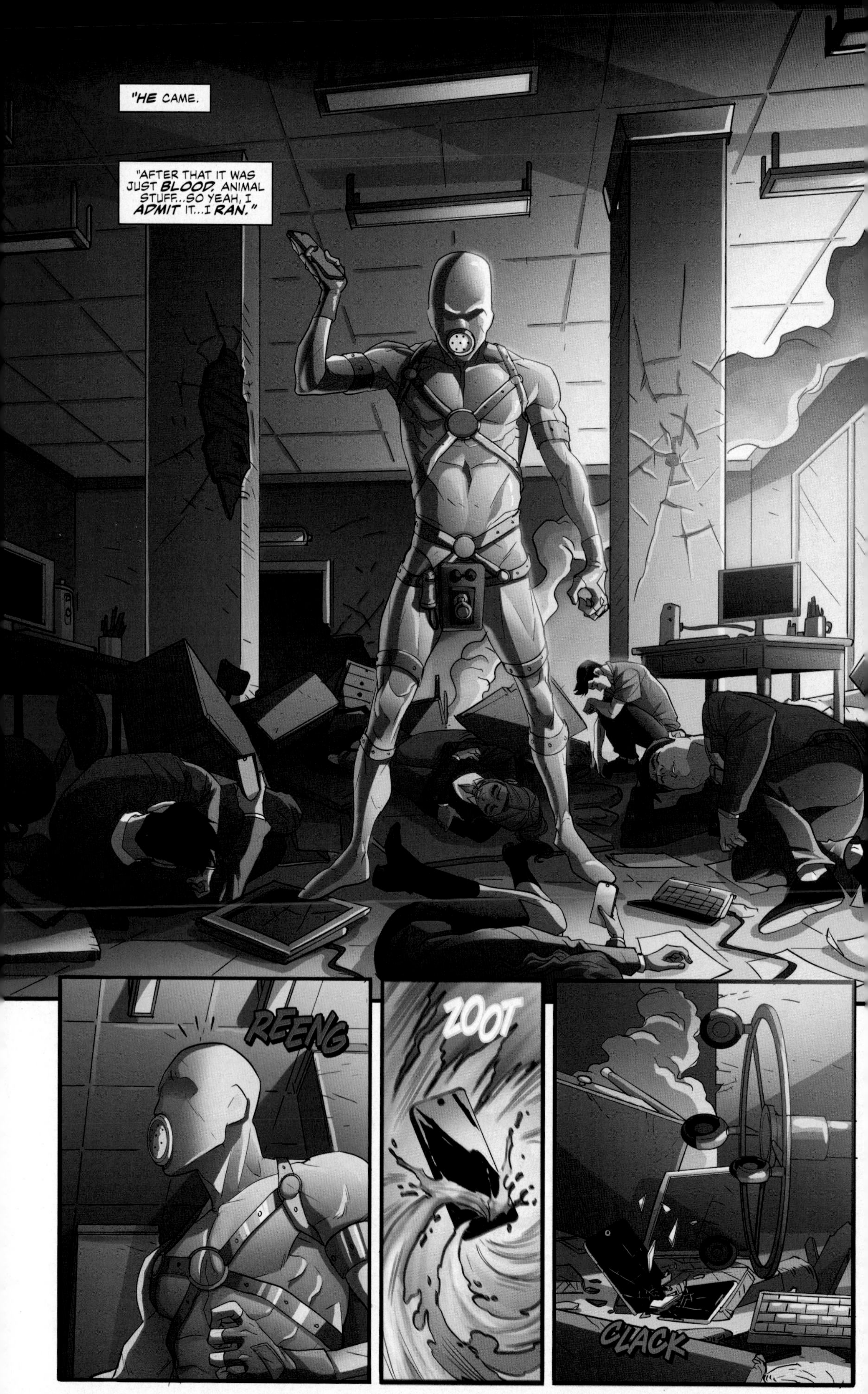
"HE CAME.
"AFTER THAT IT WAS JUST BLOOD. ANIMAL STUFF...SO YEAH, I ADMIT IT...I RAN."
REENG
ZOOT
CLACK

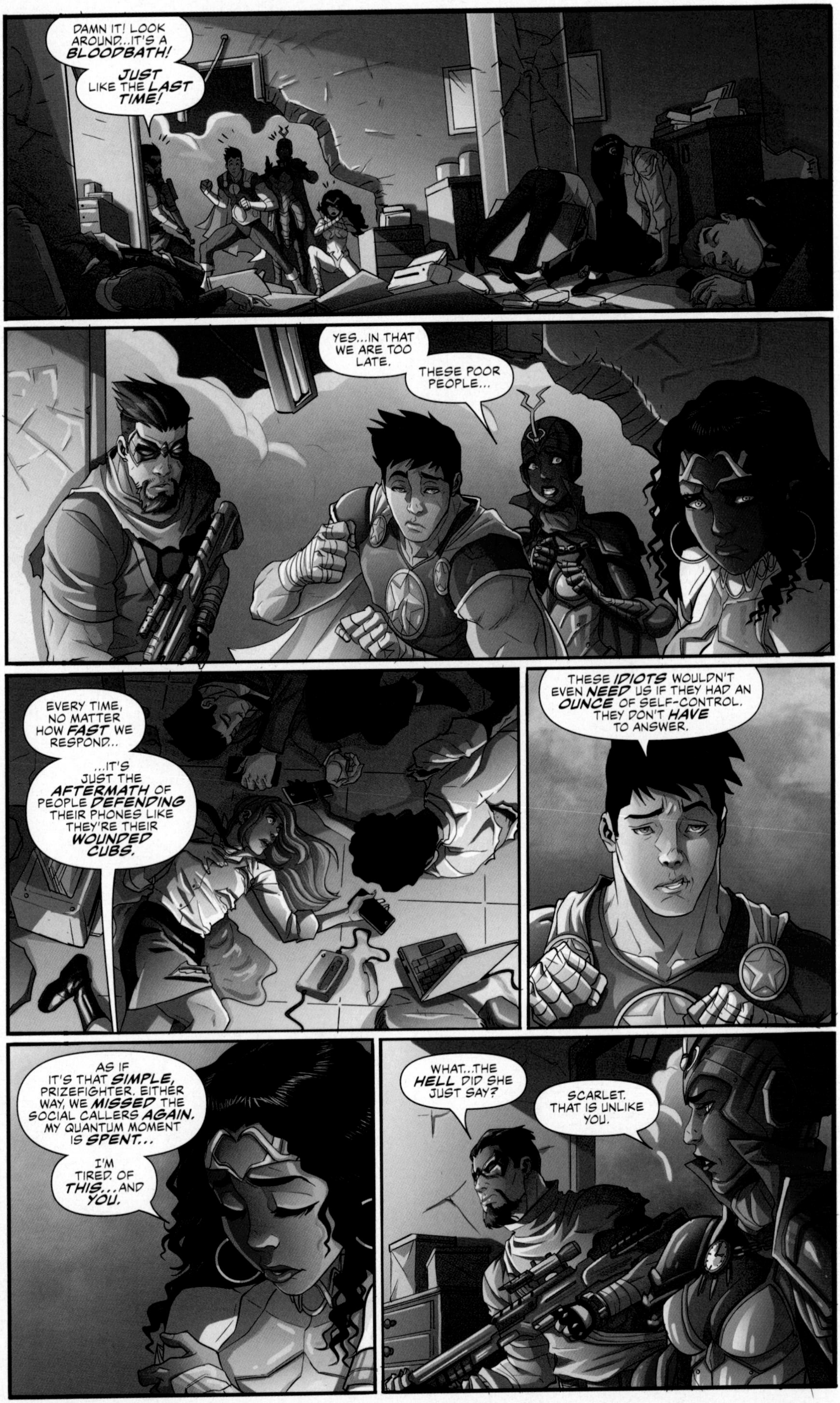

DAMN IT! LOOK AROUND...IT'S A BLOODBATH!
JUST LIKE THE LAST TIME!
YES...IN THAT WE ARE TOO LATE.
THESE POOR PEOPLE...
EVERY TIME, NO MATTER HOW FAST WE RESPOND...
...IT'S JUST THE AFTERMATH OF PEOPLE DEFENDING THEIR PHONES LIKE THEY'RE THEIR WOUNDED CUBS.
THESE IDIOTS WOULDN'T EVEN NEED US IF THEY HAD AN OUNCE OF SELF-CONTROL. THEY DON'T HAVE TO ANSWER.
AS IF IT'S THAT SIMPLE, PRIZEFIGHTER. EITHER WAY, WE MISSED THE SOCIAL CALLERS AGAIN. MY QUANTUM MOMENT IS SPENT...
I'M TIRED. OF THIS...AND YOU.
WHAT...THE HELL DID SHE JUST SAY?
SCARLET. THAT IS UNLIKE YOU.

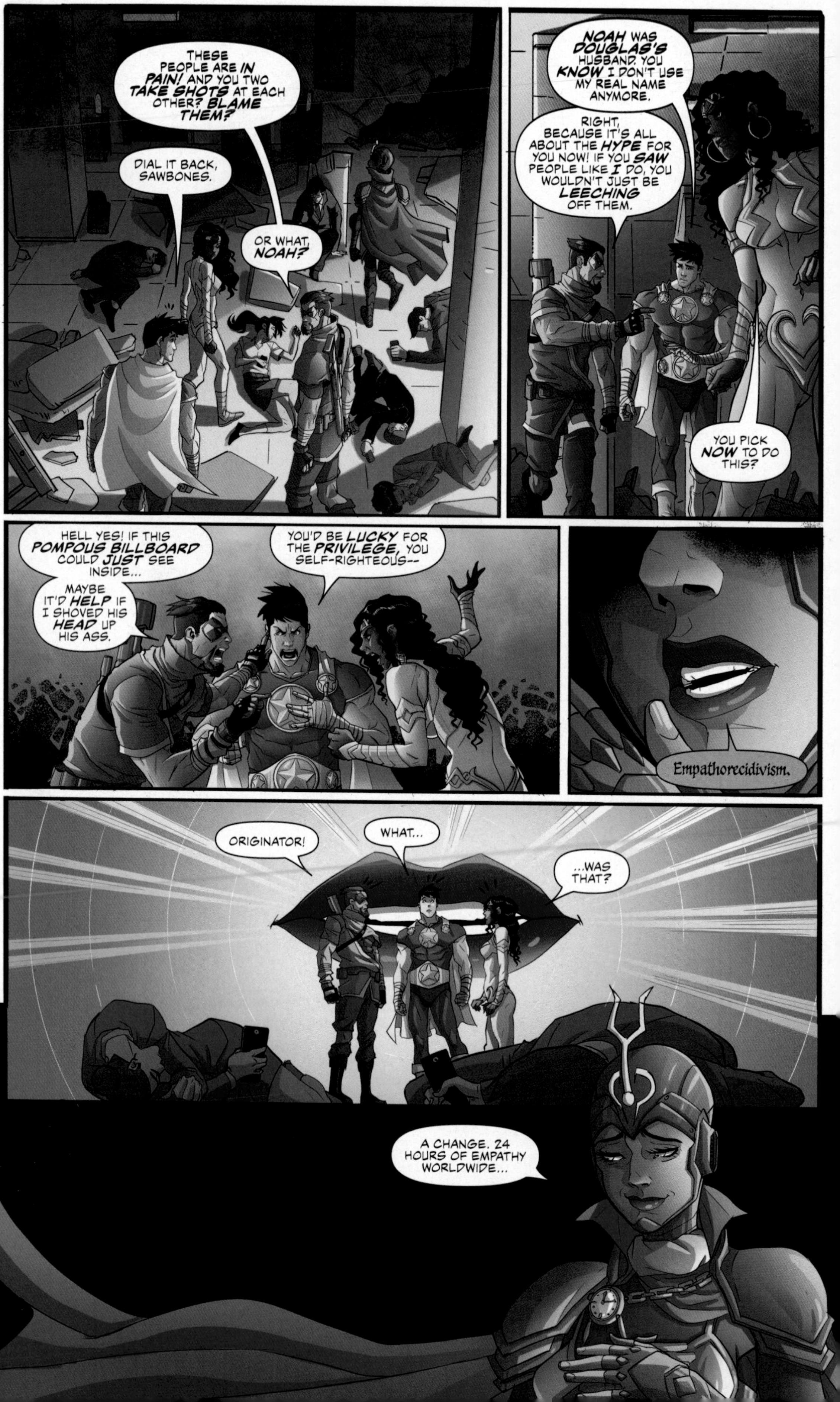
THESE PEOPLE ARE IN PAIN! AND YOU TWO TAKE SHOTS AT EACH OTHER? BLAME THEM?
DIAL IT BACK, SAWBONES.
OR WHAT, NOAH?
NOAH WAS DOUGLAS'S HUSBAND. YOU KNOW I DON'T USE MY REAL NAME ANYMORE.
RIGHT, BECAUSE IT'S ALL ABOUT THE HYPE FOR YOU NOW! IF YOU SAW PEOPLE LIKE I DO, YOU WOULDN'T JUST BE LEECHING OFF THEM.
YOU PICK NOW TO DO THIS?
HELL YES! IF THIS POMPOUS BILLBOARD COULD JUST SEE INSIDE...
MAYBE IT'D HELP IF I SHOVED HIS HEAD UP HIS ASS.
YOU'D BE LUCKY FOR THE PRIVILEGE, YOU SELF-RIGHTEOUS--
Empathorecidivism.
ORIGINATOR!
WHAT...
...WAS THAT?
A CHANGE. 24 HOURS OF EMPATHY WORLDWIDE...

"...IT IS NOT A SOLUTION. IT IS A BAND-AID."

BETHESDA, MARYLAND.

PUSHING THIS *BILL* ISN'T ENOUGH? YOU WANT MORE?

I--I'M SORRY. YOU'RE RIGHT. LOOK...I'VE GOT *PULL*, MORE THAN MOST.

BUT THESE PEOPLE ARE UP FOR TRIAL AT THE *HAGUE*. WHAT YOU'RE *ASKING* IS....

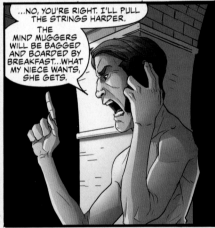

...NO, YOU'RE RIGHT. I'LL PULL THE STRINGS HARDER.

THE MIND MUGGERS WILL BE BAGGED AND BOARDED BY BREAKFAST...WHAT MY NIECE WANTS, SHE GETS.

CLICK

RIGHT.

FUCKITY-- SHIT.

SHE'LL BLEED ME DRY ONE DAY. IT'S COMING.

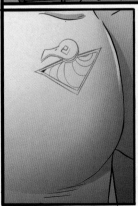

AND IT WON'T BE A METAPHOR...

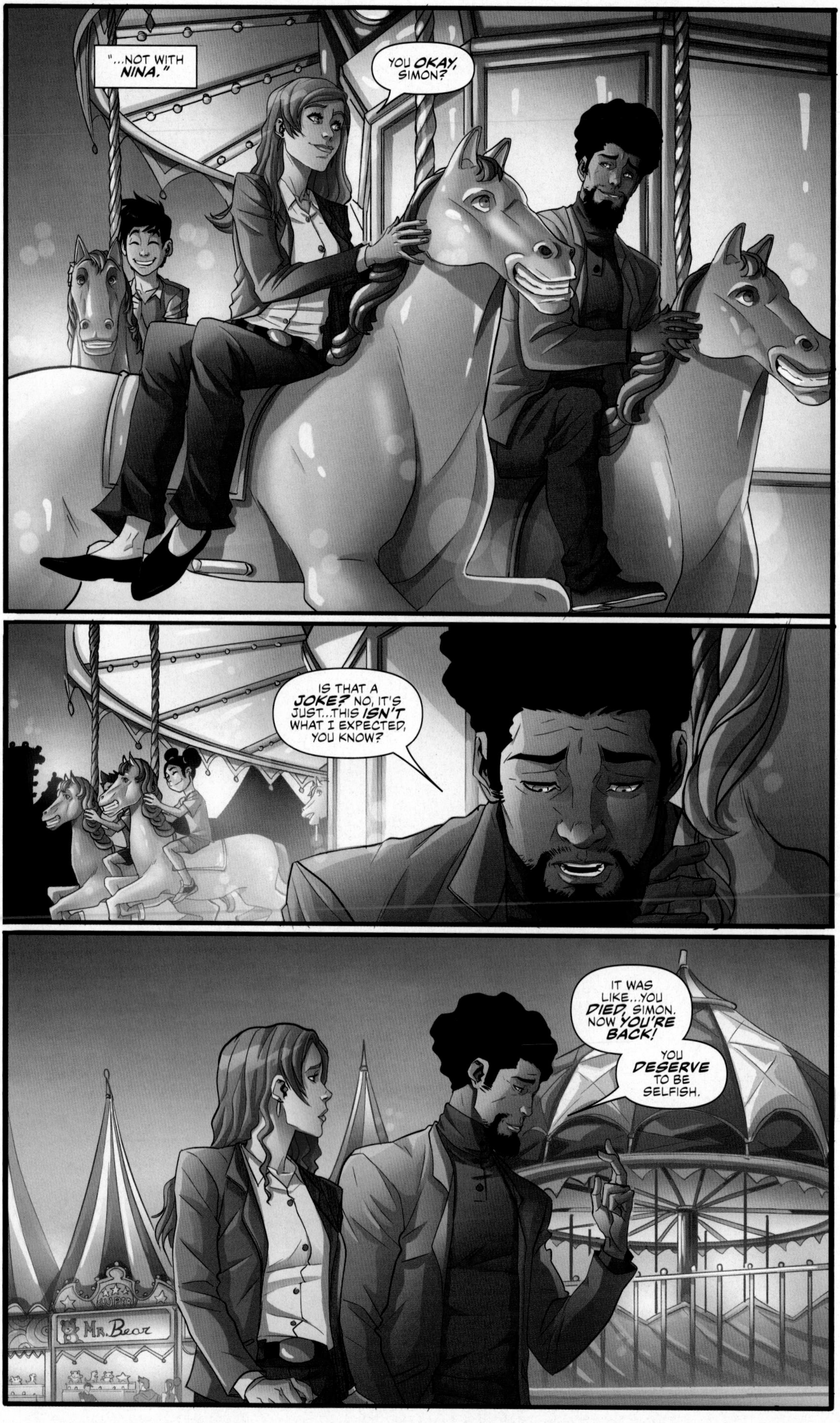
"...NOT WITH NINA."
YOU OKAY, SIMON?
IS THAT A JOKE? NO, IT'S JUST...THIS ISN'T WHAT I EXPECTED, YOU KNOW?
IT WAS LIKE...YOU DIED, SIMON. NOW YOU'RE BACK!
YOU DESERVE TO BE SELFISH.
MR. Bear

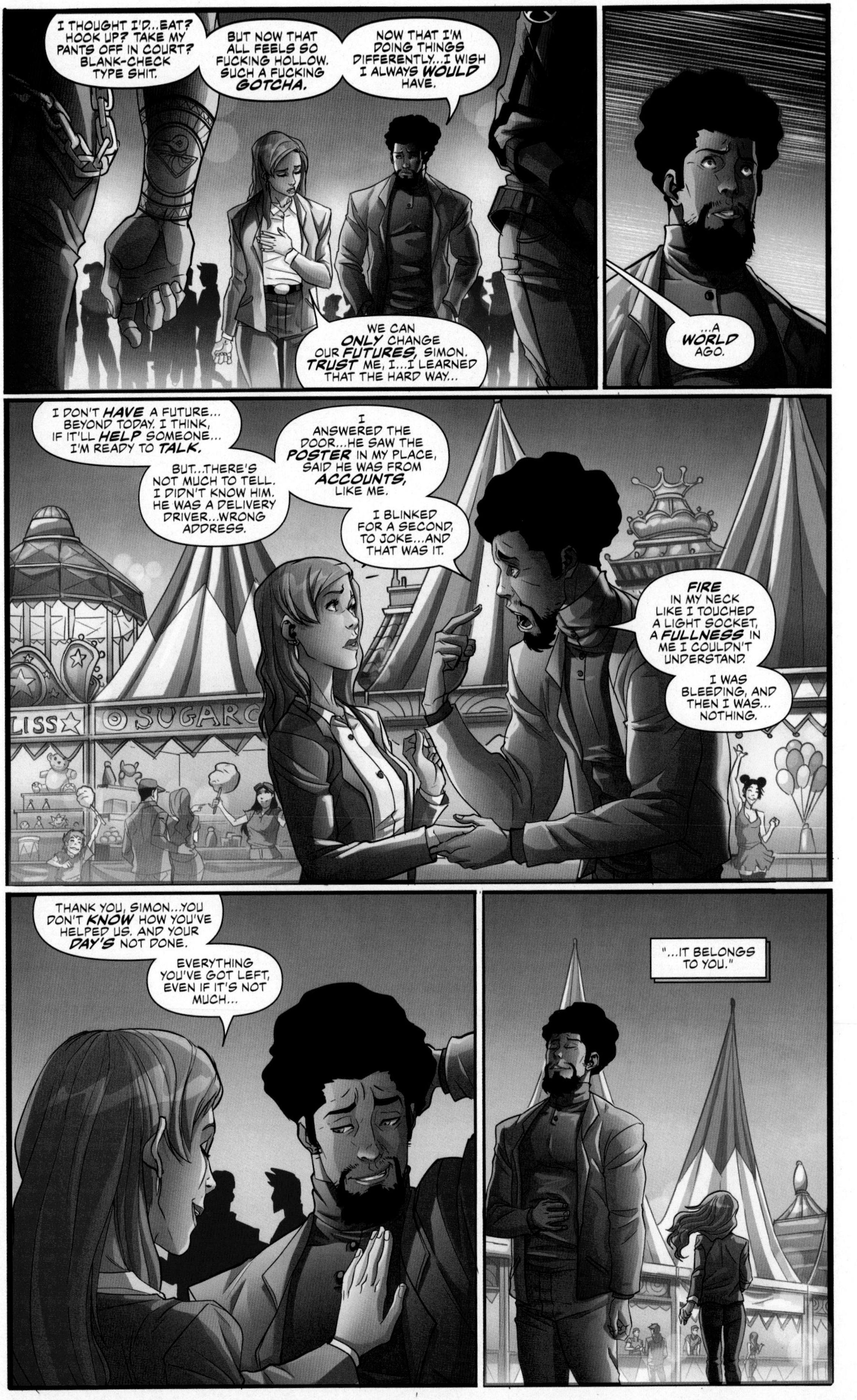
I THOUGHT I'D...EAT? HOOK UP? TAKE MY PANTS OFF IN COURT? BLANK-CHECK TYPE SHIT.
BUT NOW THAT ALL FEELS SO FUCKING HOLLOW. SUCH A FUCKING GOTCHA.
NOW THAT I'M DOING THINGS DIFFERENTLY...I WISH I ALWAYS WOULD HAVE.
WE CAN ONLY CHANGE OUR FUTURES, SIMON. TRUST ME, I...I LEARNED THAT THE HARD WAY...
...A WORLD AGO.
I DON'T HAVE A FUTURE... BEYOND TODAY. I THINK, IF IT'LL HELP SOMEONE... I'M READY TO TALK.
BUT...THERE'S NOT MUCH TO TELL. I DIDN'T KNOW HIM. HE WAS A DELIVERY DRIVER...WRONG ADDRESS.
I ANSWERED THE DOOR...HE SAW THE POSTER IN MY PLACE, SAID HE WAS FROM ACCOUNTS, LIKE ME.
I BLINKED FOR A SECOND, TO JOKE...AND THAT WAS IT.
FIRE IN MY NECK LIKE I TOUCHED A LIGHT SOCKET, A FULLNESS IN ME I COULDN'T UNDERSTAND.
I WAS BLEEDING, AND THEN I WAS... NOTHING.
LISS
SUGAR
THANK YOU, SIMON...YOU DON'T KNOW HOW YOU'VE HELPED US. AND YOUR DAY'S NOT DONE.
EVERYTHING YOU'VE GOT LEFT, EVEN IF IT'S NOT MUCH...
"...IT BELONGS TO YOU."

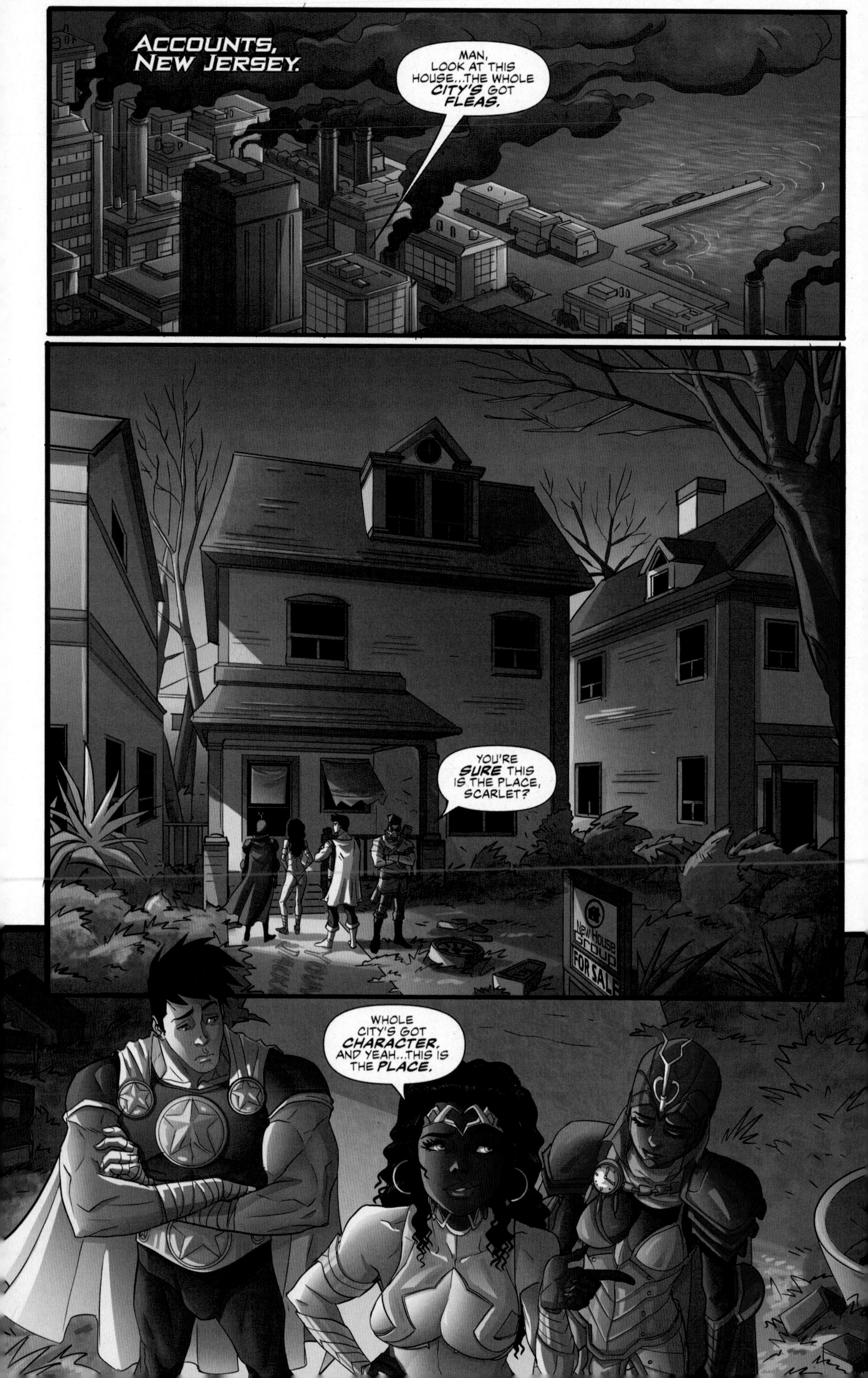
ACCOUNTS, NEW JERSEY.
MAN, LOOK AT THIS HOUSE...THE WHOLE CITY'S GOT FLEAS.
YOU'RE SURE THIS IS THE PLACE, SCARLET?
New House Group
FOR SALE
WHOLE CITY'S GOT CHARACTER. AND YEAH...THIS IS THE PLACE.

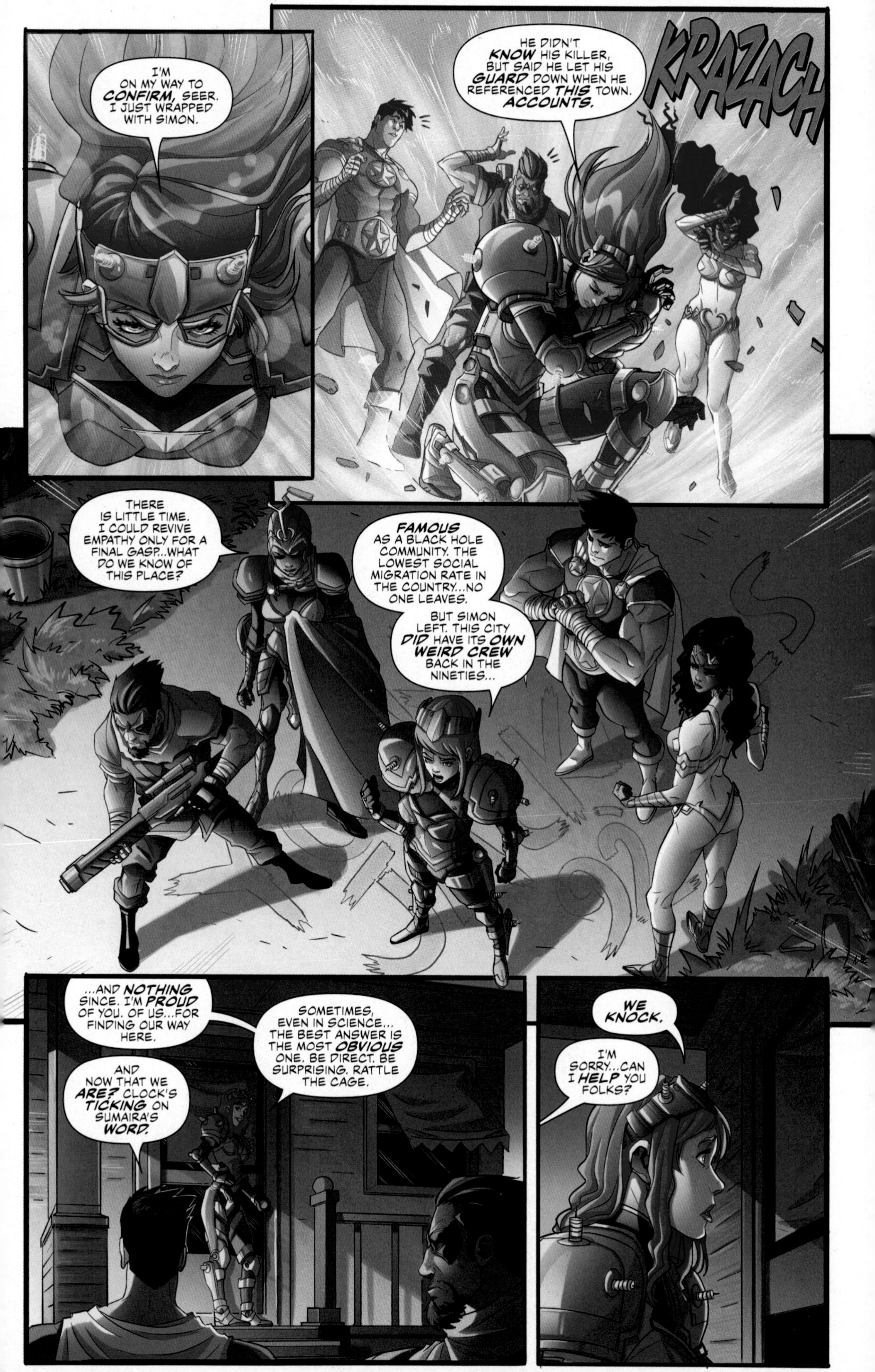

I'M ON MY WAY TO CONFIRM, SEER. I JUST WRAPPED WITH SIMON.
HE DIDN'T KNOW HIS KILLER, BUT SAID HE LET HIS GUARD DOWN WHEN HE REFERENCED THIS TOWN. ACCOUNTS.
KRAZACH
THERE IS LITTLE TIME. I COULD REVIVE EMPATHY ONLY FOR A FINAL GASP...WHAT DO WE KNOW OF THIS PLACE?
FAMOUS AS A BLACK HOLE COMMUNITY. THE LOWEST SOCIAL MIGRATION RATE IN THE COUNTRY...NO ONE LEAVES.
BUT SIMON LEFT. THIS CITY DID HAVE ITS OWN WEIRD CREW BACK IN THE NINETIES...
...AND NOTHING SINCE. I'M PROUD OF YOU. OF US...FOR FINDING OUR WAY HERE.
AND NOW THAT WE ARE? CLOCK'S TICKING ON SUMAIRA'S WORD.
SOMETIMES, EVEN IN SCIENCE... THE BEST ANSWER IS THE MOST OBVIOUS ONE. BE DIRECT. BE SURPRISING. RATTLE THE CAGE.
WE KNOCK.
I'M SORRY...CAN I HELP YOU FOLKS?

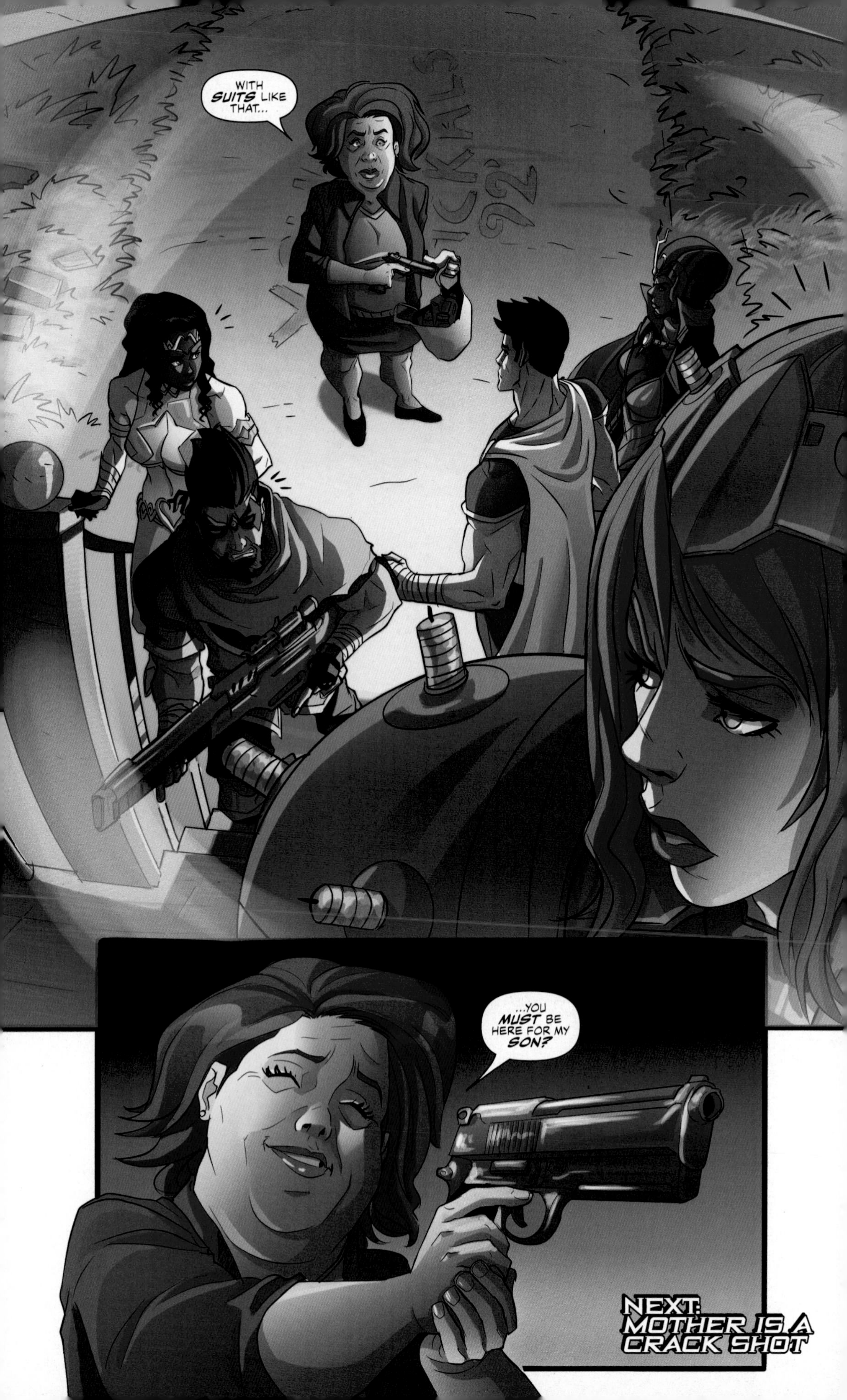
WITH SUITS LIKE THAT...
...YOU MUST BE HERE FOR MY SON?
NEXT: MOTHER IS A CRACK SHOT

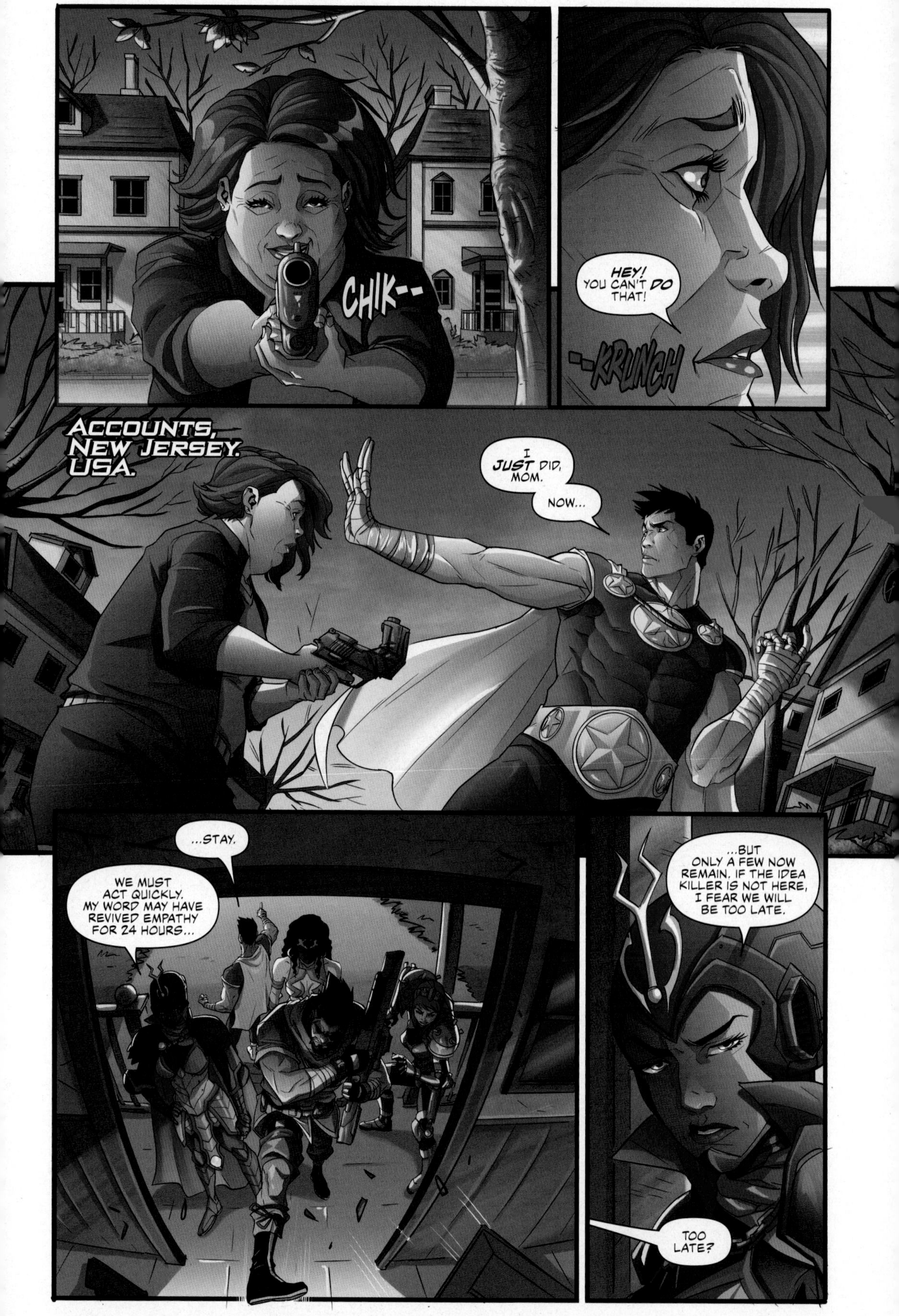
CHIK--
HEY! YOU CAN'T DO THAT!
--KRUNCH
ACCOUNTS, NEW JERSEY. USA.
I JUST DID, MOM.
NOW...
...STAY.
WE MUST ACT QUICKLY. MY WORD MAY HAVE REVIVED EMPATHY FOR 24 HOURS...
...BUT ONLY A FEW NOW REMAIN. IF THE IDEA KILLER IS NOT HERE, I FEAR WE WILL BE TOO LATE.
TOO LATE?

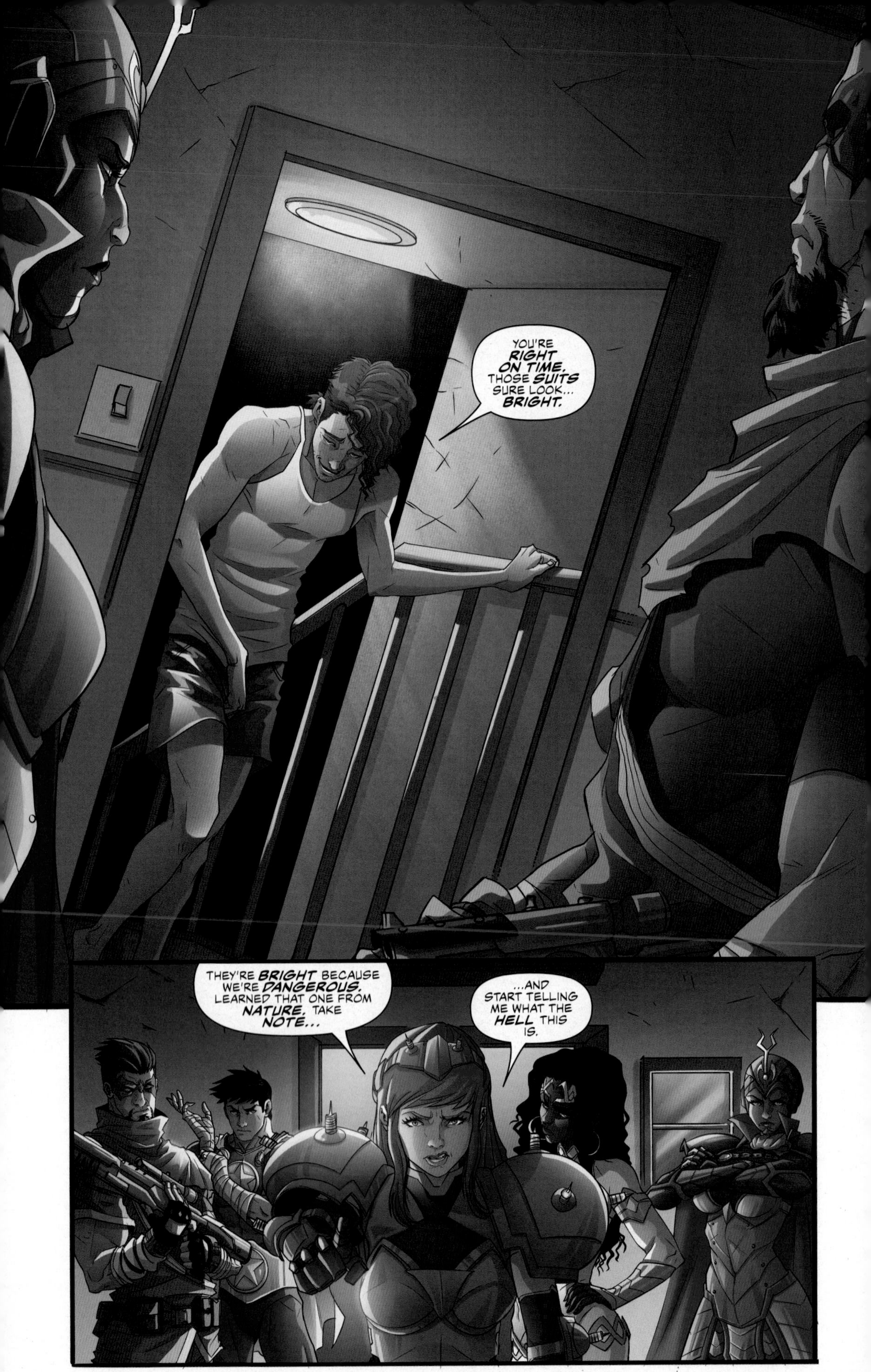
YOU'RE RIGHT ON TIME. THOSE SUITS SURE LOOK... BRIGHT.
THEY'RE BRIGHT BECAUSE WE'RE DANGEROUS. LEARNED THAT ONE FROM NATURE. TAKE NOTE...
...AND START TELLING ME WHAT THE HELL THIS IS.

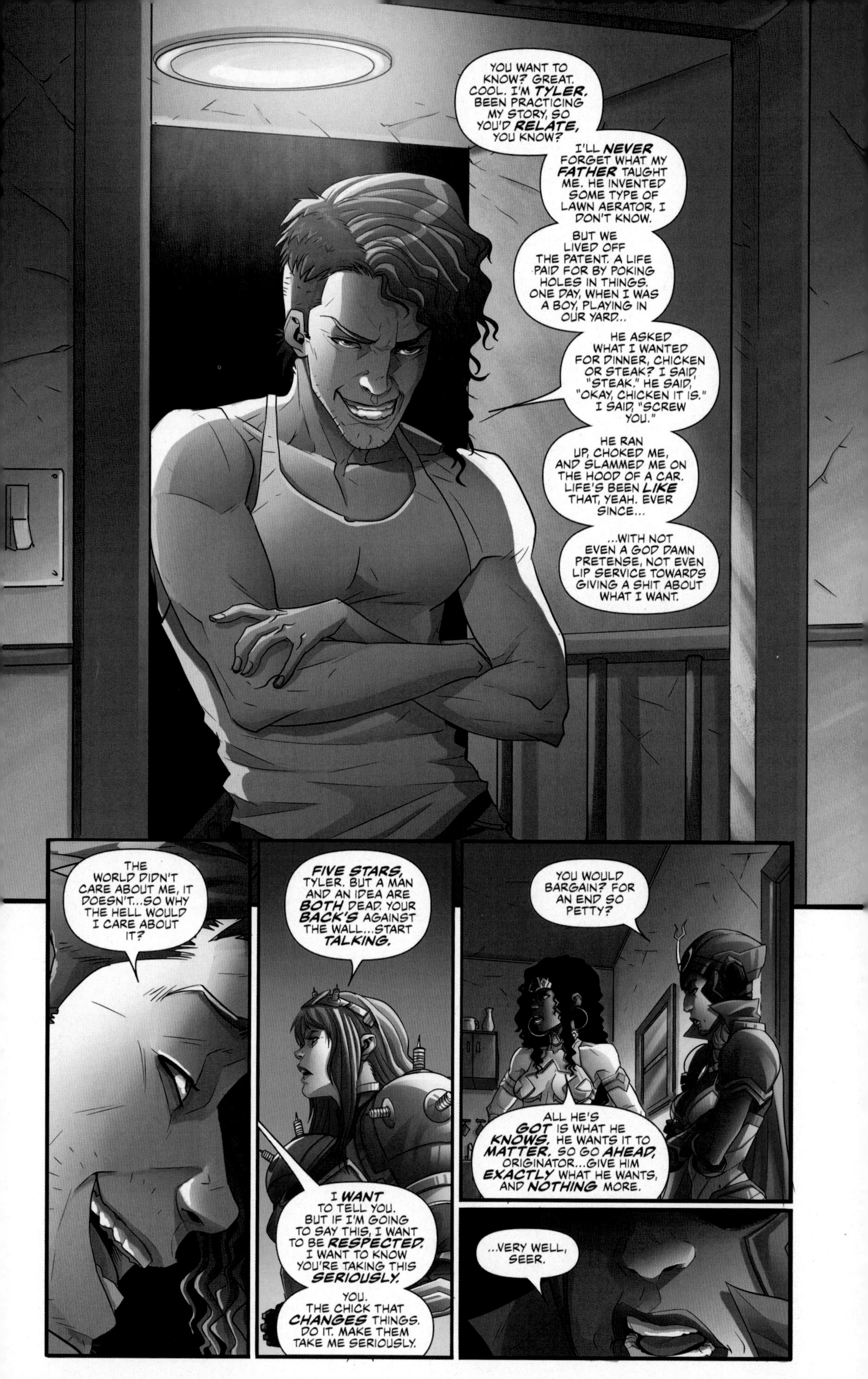
YOU WANT TO KNOW? GREAT. COOL. I'M TYLER. BEEN PRACTICING MY STORY, SO YOU'D RELATE, YOU KNOW?
I'LL NEVER FORGET WHAT MY FATHER TAUGHT ME. HE INVENTED SOME TYPE OF LAWN AERATOR, I DON'T KNOW.
BUT WE LIVED OFF THE PATENT. A LIFE PAID FOR BY POKING HOLES IN THINGS. ONE DAY, WHEN I WAS A BOY, PLAYING IN OUR YARD...
HE ASKED WHAT I WANTED FOR DINNER, CHICKEN OR STEAK? I SAID, "STEAK." HE SAID, "OKAY, CHICKEN IT IS." I SAID, "SCREW YOU."
HE RAN UP, CHOKED ME, AND SLAMMED ME ON THE HOOD OF A CAR. LIFE'S BEEN LIKE THAT, YEAH. EVER SINCE...
...WITH NOT EVEN A GOD DAMN PRETENSE, NOT EVEN LIP SERVICE TOWARDS GIVING A SHIT ABOUT WHAT I WANT.
THE WORLD DIDN'T CARE ABOUT ME, IT DOESN'T...SO WHY THE HELL WOULD I CARE ABOUT IT?
FIVE STARS, TYLER. BUT A MAN AND AN IDEA ARE BOTH DEAD. YOUR BACK'S AGAINST THE WALL...START TALKING.
I WANT TO TELL YOU. BUT IF I'M GOING TO SAY THIS, I WANT TO BE RESPECTED. I WANT TO KNOW YOU'RE TAKING THIS SERIOUSLY.
YOU. THE CHICK THAT CHANGES THINGS. DO IT. MAKE THEM TAKE ME SERIOUSLY.
YOU WOULD BARGAIN? FOR AN END SO PETTY?
ALL HE'S GOT IS WHAT HE KNOWS. HE WANTS IT TO MATTER. SO GO AHEAD, ORIGINATOR...GIVE HIM EXACTLY WHAT HE WANTS, AND NOTHING MORE.
...VERY WELL, SEER.

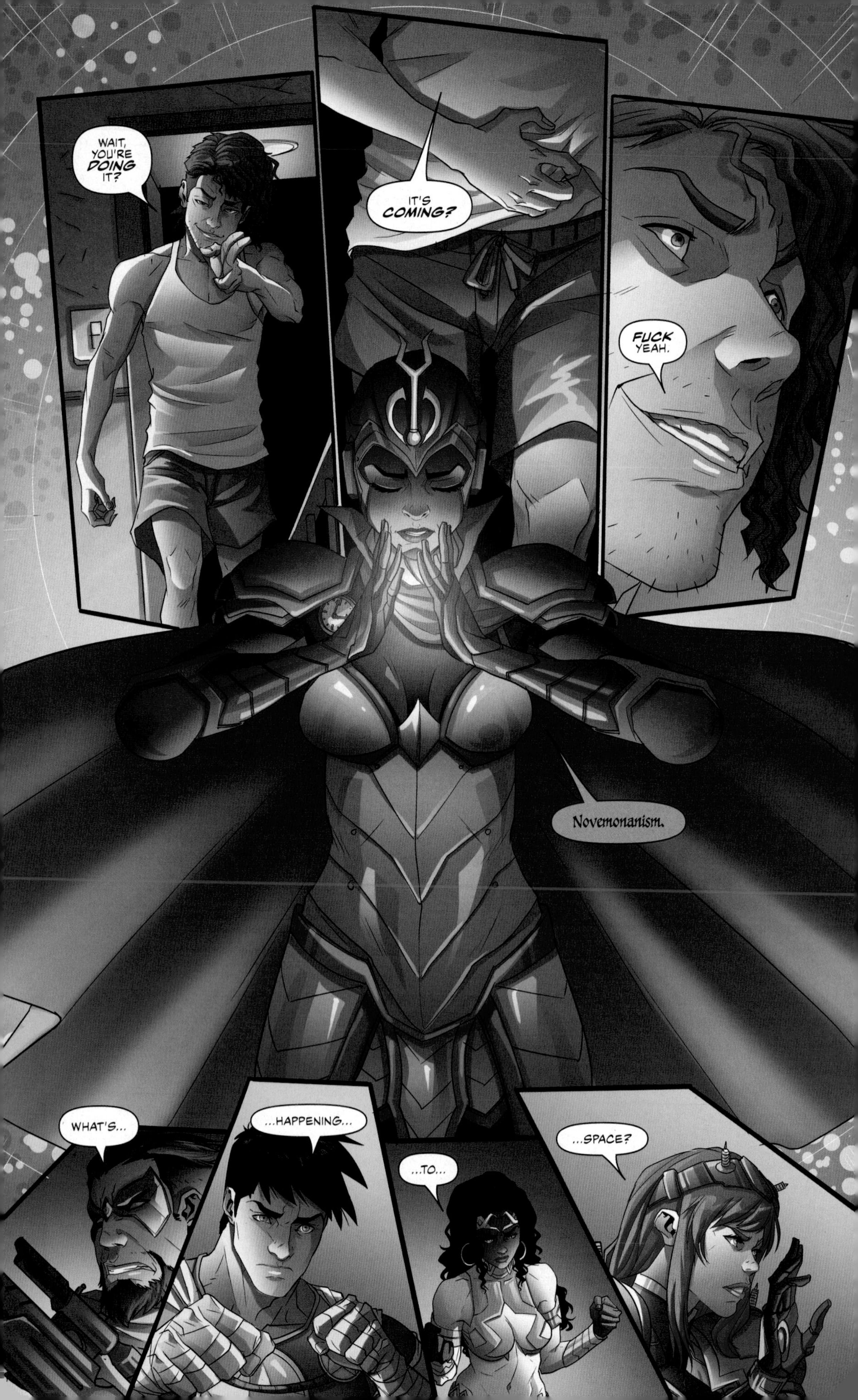

WAIT, YOU'RE DOING IT?
IT'S COMING?
FUCK YEAH.
Novemonanism.
WHAT'S...
...HAPPENING...
...TO...
...SPACE?

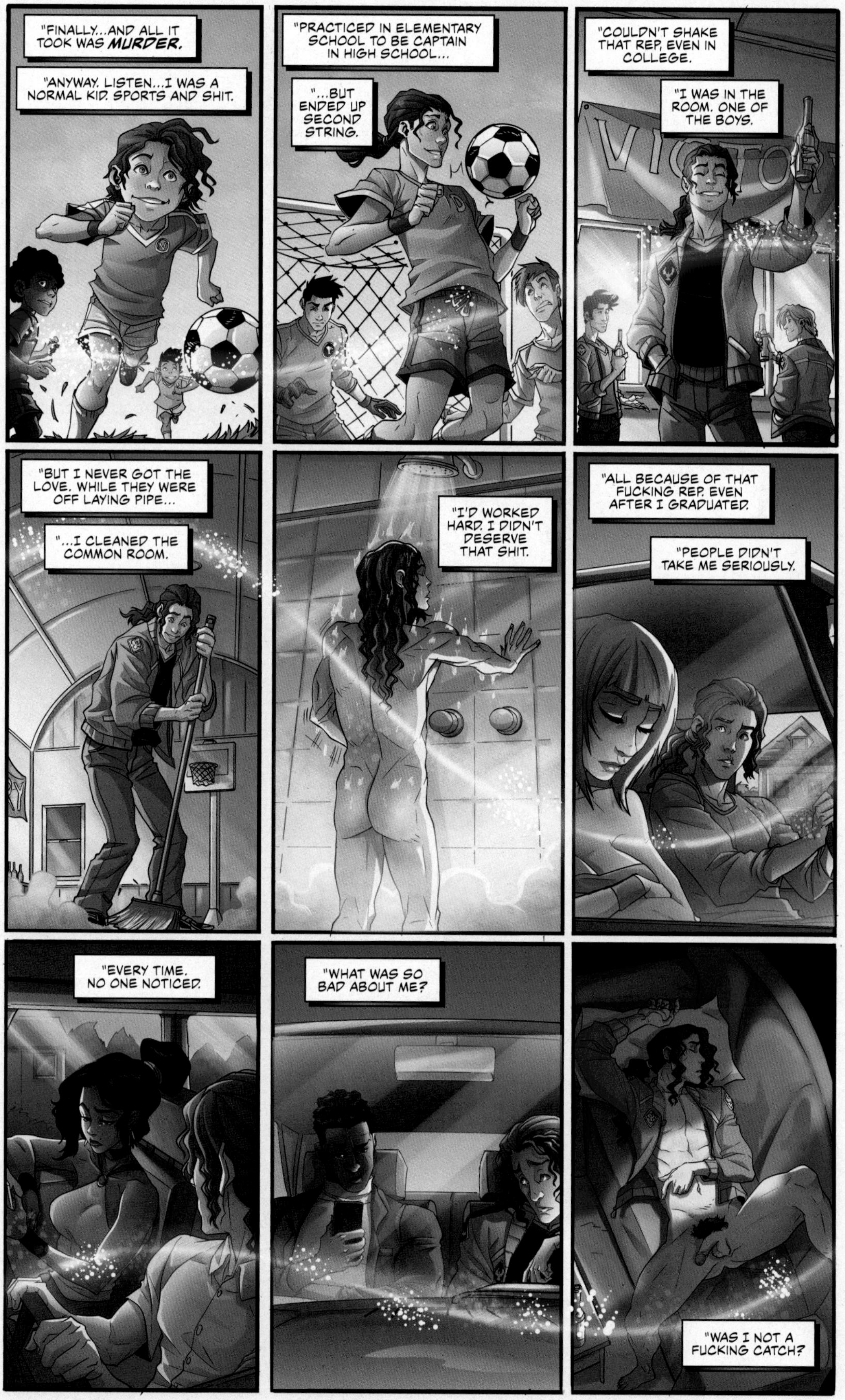
"FINALLY...AND ALL IT TOOK WAS MURDER.
"ANYWAY. LISTEN...I WAS A NORMAL KID. SPORTS AND SHIT.
"PRACTICED IN ELEMENTARY SCHOOL TO BE CAPTAIN IN HIGH SCHOOL...
"...BUT ENDED UP SECOND STRING.
"COULDN'T SHAKE THAT REP, EVEN IN COLLEGE.
"I WAS IN THE ROOM. ONE OF THE BOYS.
"BUT I NEVER GOT THE LOVE. WHILE THEY WERE OFF LAYING PIPE...
"...I CLEANED THE COMMON ROOM.
"I'D WORKED HARD. I DIDN'T DESERVE THAT SHIT.
"ALL BECAUSE OF THAT FUCKING REP. EVEN AFTER I GRADUATED.
"PEOPLE DIDN'T TAKE ME SERIOUSLY.
"EVERY TIME. NO ONE NOTICED.
"WHAT WAS SO BAD ABOUT ME?
"WAS I NOT A FUCKING CATCH?

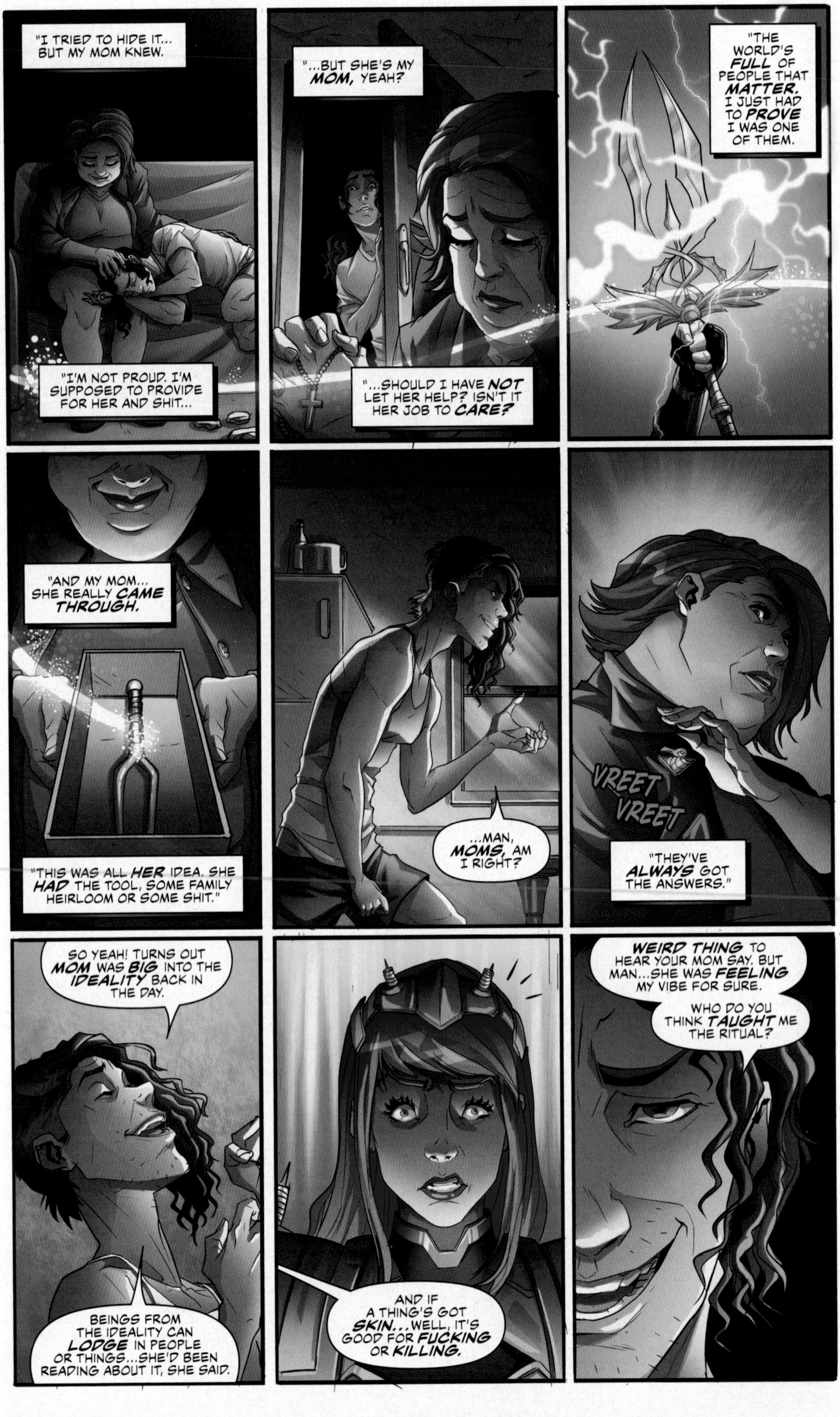
"I TRIED TO HIDE IT... BUT MY MOM KNEW.
"I'M NOT PROUD. I'M SUPPOSED TO PROVIDE FOR HER AND SHIT...
"...BUT SHE'S MY MOM, YEAH?
"...SHOULD I HAVE NOT LET HER HELP? ISN'T IT HER JOB TO CARE?
"THE WORLD'S FULL OF PEOPLE THAT MATTER. I JUST HAD TO PROVE I WAS ONE OF THEM.
"AND MY MOM... SHE REALLY CAME THROUGH.
"THIS WAS ALL HER IDEA. SHE HAD THE TOOL, SOME FAMILY HEIRLOOM OR SOME SHIT."
...MAN, MOMS, AM I RIGHT?
VREET
VREET
"THEY'VE ALWAYS GOT THE ANSWERS."
SO YEAH! TURNS OUT MOM WAS BIG INTO THE IDEALITY BACK IN THE DAY.
BEINGS FROM THE IDEALITY CAN LODGE IN PEOPLE OR THINGS...SHE'D BEEN READING ABOUT IT, SHE SAID.
AND IF A THING'S GOT SKIN...WELL, IT'S GOOD FOR FUCKING OR KILLING.
WEIRD THING TO HEAR YOUR MOM SAY. BUT MAN...SHE WAS FEELING MY VIBE FOR SURE.
WHO DO YOU THINK TAUGHT ME THE RITUAL?

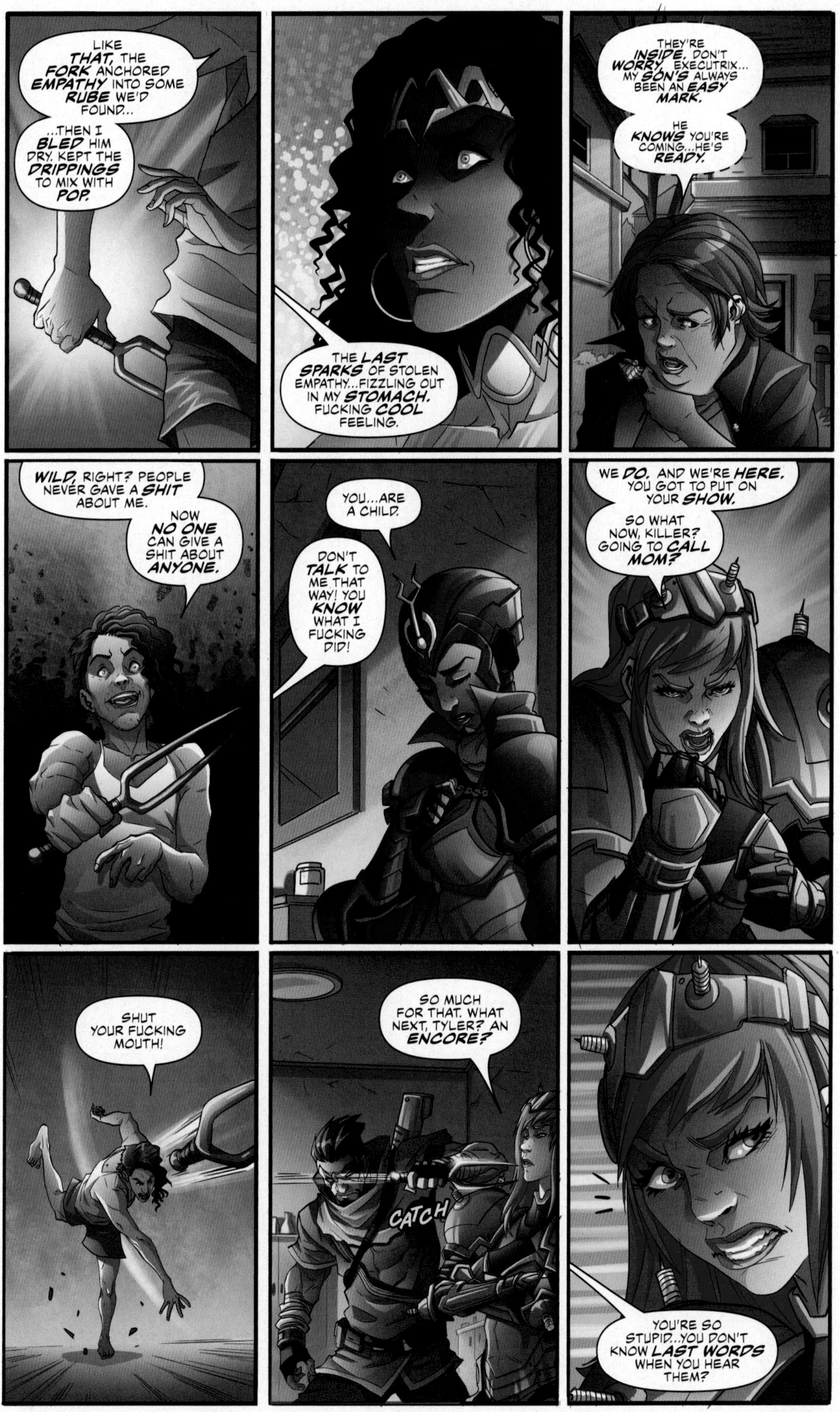
LIKE THAT, THE FORK ANCHORED EMPATHY INTO SOME RUBE WE'D FOUND...
...THEN I BLED HIM DRY. KEPT THE DRIPPINGS TO MIX WITH POP.
THE LAST SPARKS OF STOLEN EMPATHY...FIZZLING OUT IN MY STOMACH. FUCKING COOL FEELING.
THEY'RE INSIDE. DON'T WORRY, EXECUTRIX... MY SON'S ALWAYS BEEN AN EASY MARK.
HE KNOWS YOU'RE COMING...HE'S READY.
WILD, RIGHT? PEOPLE NEVER GAVE A SHIT ABOUT ME.
NOW NO ONE CAN GIVE A SHIT ABOUT ANYONE.
YOU...ARE A CHILD.
DON'T TALK TO ME THAT WAY! YOU KNOW WHAT I FUCKING DID!
WE DO. AND WE'RE HERE. YOU GOT TO PUT ON YOUR SHOW.
SO WHAT NOW, KILLER? GOING TO CALL MOM?
SHUT YOUR FUCKING MOUTH!
SO MUCH FOR THAT. WHAT NEXT, TYLER? AN ENCORE?
CATCH
YOU'RE SO STUPID...YOU DON'T KNOW LAST WORDS WHEN YOU HEAR THEM?

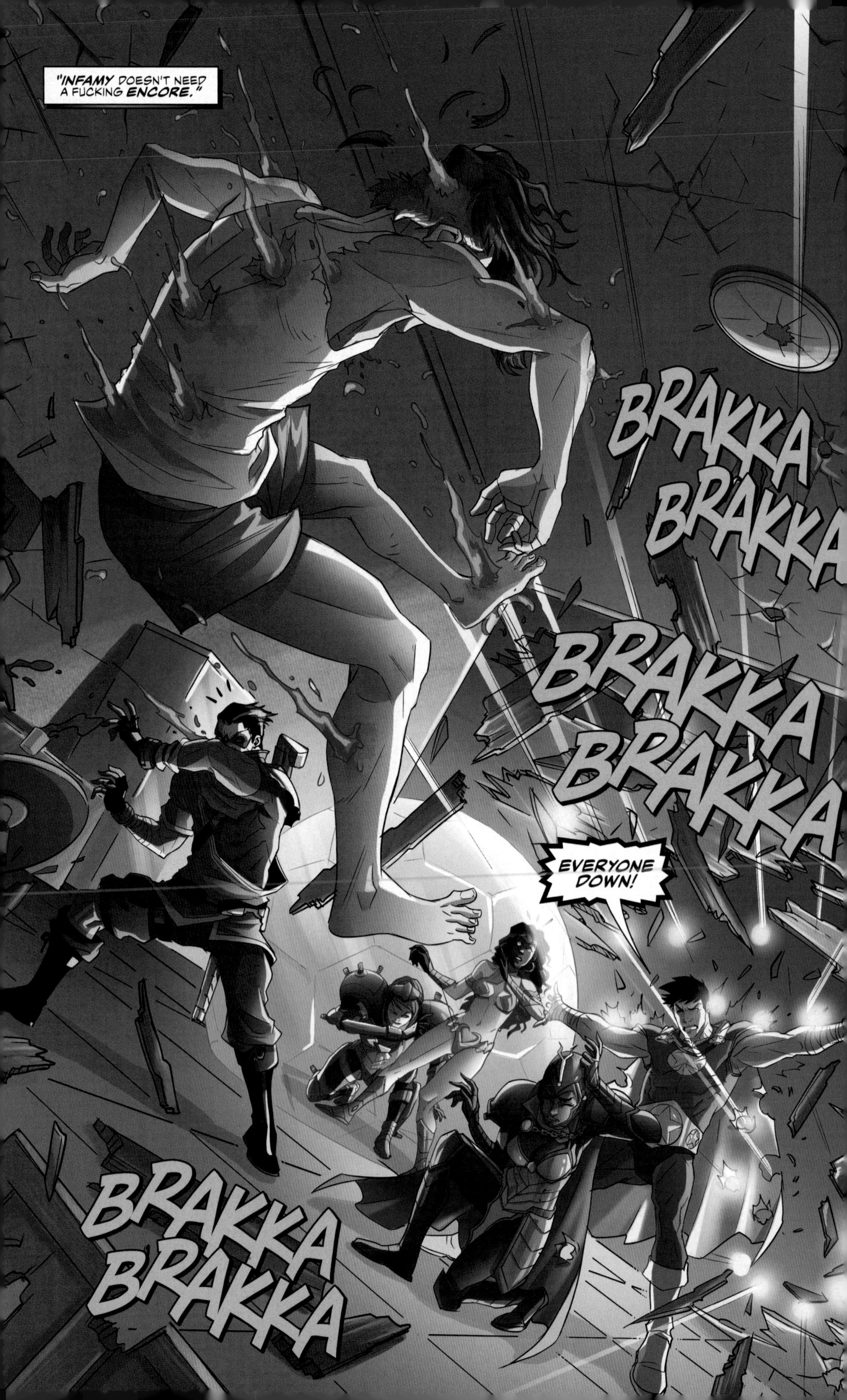
"INFAMY DOESN'T NEED A FUCKING ENCORE."
BRAKKA BRAKKA
BRAKKA BRAKKA
EVERYONE DOWN!
BRAKKA BRAKKA

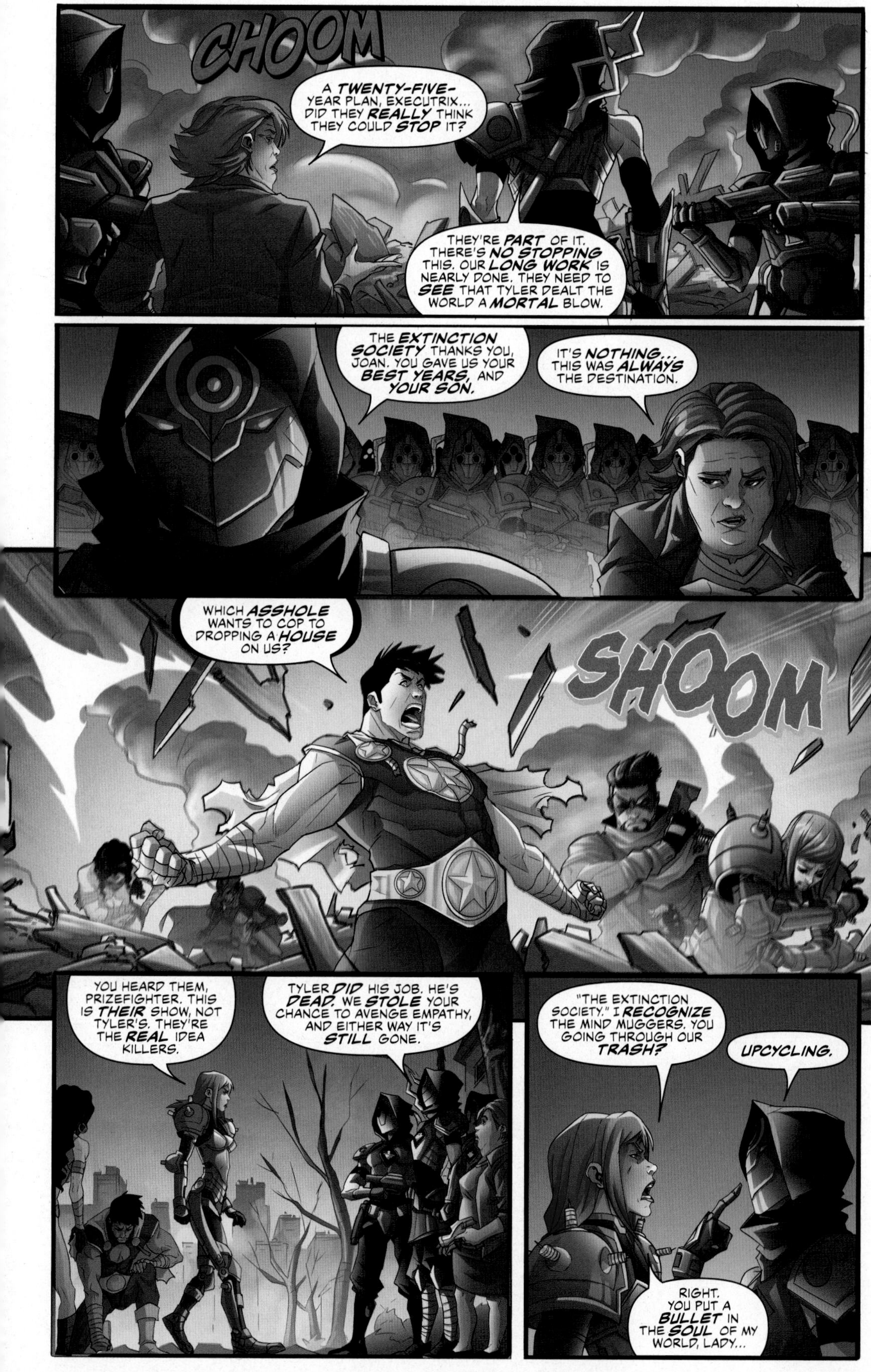
CHOOM
A TWENTY-FIVE-YEAR PLAN, EXECUTRIX... DID THEY REALLY THINK THEY COULD STOP IT?
THEY'RE PART OF IT. THERE'S NO STOPPING THIS. OUR LONG WORK IS NEARLY DONE. THEY NEED TO SEE THAT TYLER DEALT THE WORLD A MORTAL BLOW.
THE EXTINCTION SOCIETY THANKS YOU, JOAN. YOU GAVE US YOUR BEST YEARS, AND YOUR SON.
IT'S NOTHING... THIS WAS ALWAYS THE DESTINATION.
WHICH ASSHOLE WANTS TO COP TO DROPPING A HOUSE ON US?
SHOOM
YOU HEARD THEM, PRIZEFIGHTER. THIS IS THEIR SHOW, NOT TYLER'S. THEY'RE THE REAL IDEA KILLERS.
TYLER DID HIS JOB. HE'S DEAD. WE STOLE YOUR CHANCE TO AVENGE EMPATHY, AND EITHER WAY IT'S STILL GONE.
"THE EXTINCTION SOCIETY." I RECOGNIZE THE MIND MUGGERS. YOU GOING THROUGH OUR TRASH?
UPCYCLING.
RIGHT. YOU PUT A BULLET IN THE SOUL OF MY WORLD, LADY...

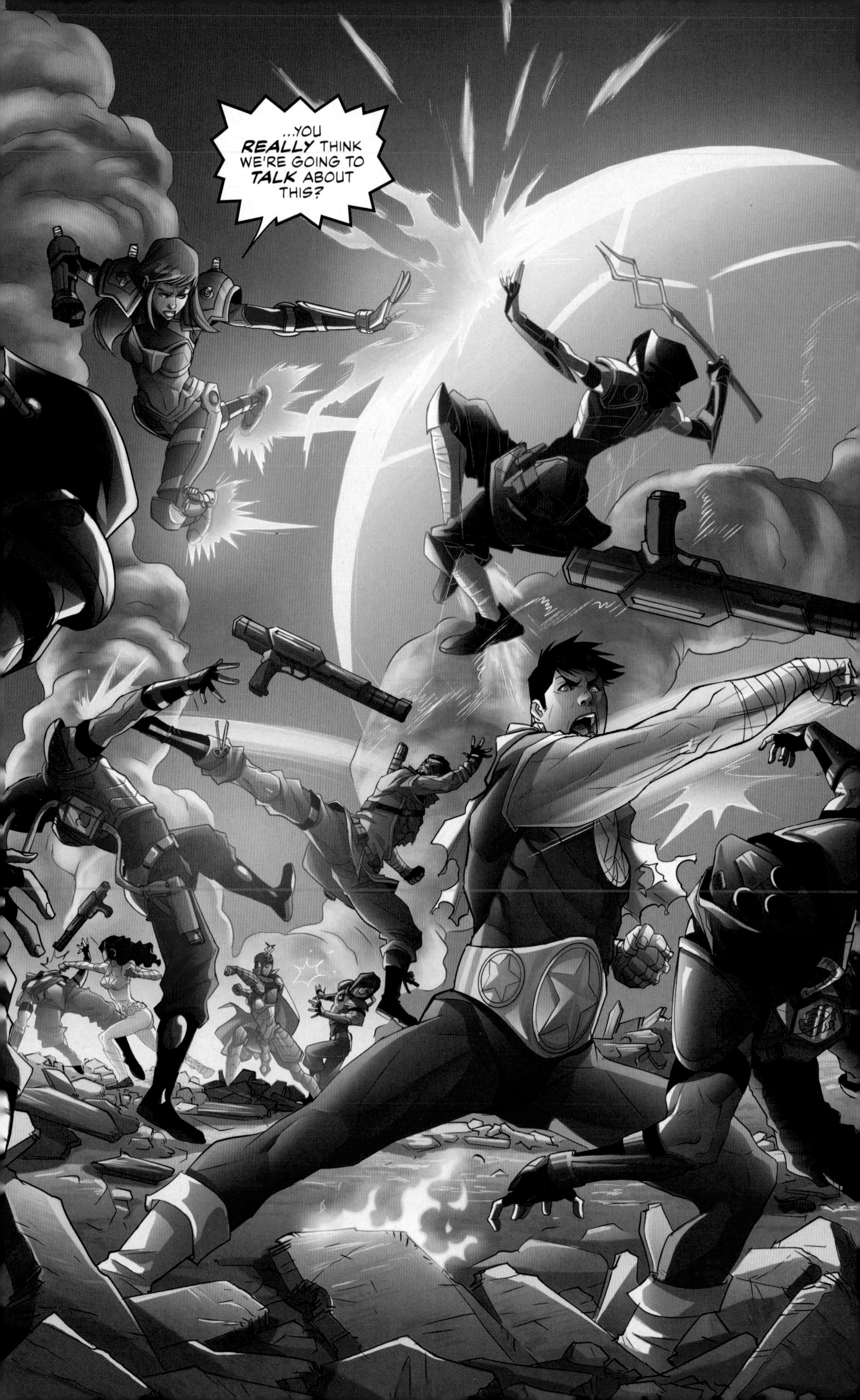
...YOU REALLY THINK WE'RE GOING TO TALK ABOUT THIS?

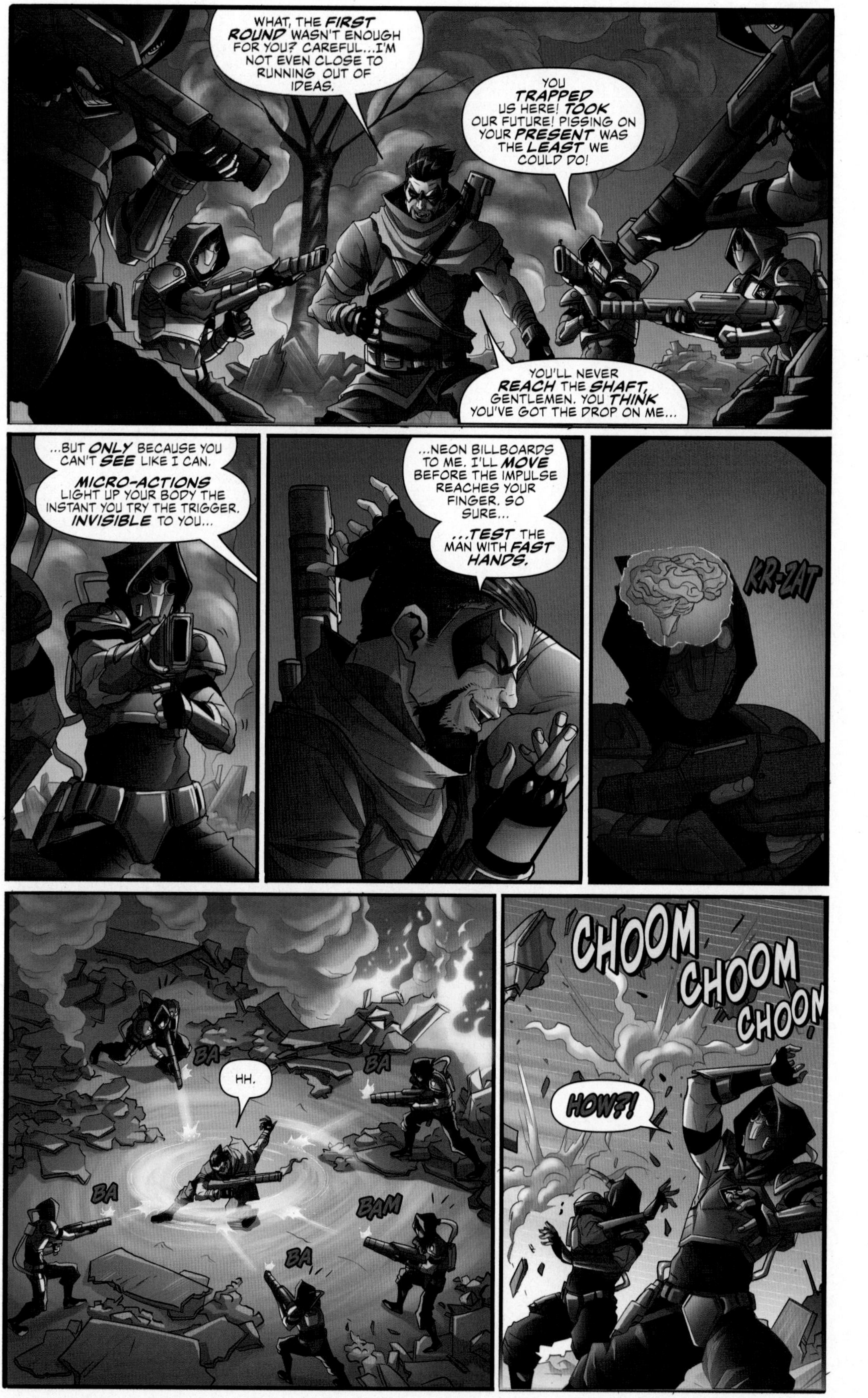
WHAT, THE FIRST ROUND WASN'T ENOUGH FOR YOU? CAREFUL...I'M NOT EVEN CLOSE TO RUNNING OUT OF IDEAS.
YOU TRAPPED US HERE! TOOK OUR FUTURE! PISSING ON YOUR PRESENT WAS THE LEAST WE COULD DO!
YOU'LL NEVER REACH THE SHAFT, GENTLEMEN. YOU THINK YOU'VE GOT THE DROP ON ME...
...BUT ONLY BECAUSE YOU CAN'T SEE LIKE I CAN.
MICRO-ACTIONS LIGHT UP YOUR BODY THE INSTANT YOU TRY THE TRIGGER. INVISIBLE TO YOU...
...NEON BILLBOARDS TO ME. I'LL MOVE BEFORE THE IMPULSE REACHES YOUR FINGER. SO SURE...
...TEST THE MAN WITH FAST HANDS.
KR-ZAT
BA
HH.
BA
BA
BAM
BA
CHOOM
CHOOM
CHOOM
HOW?!

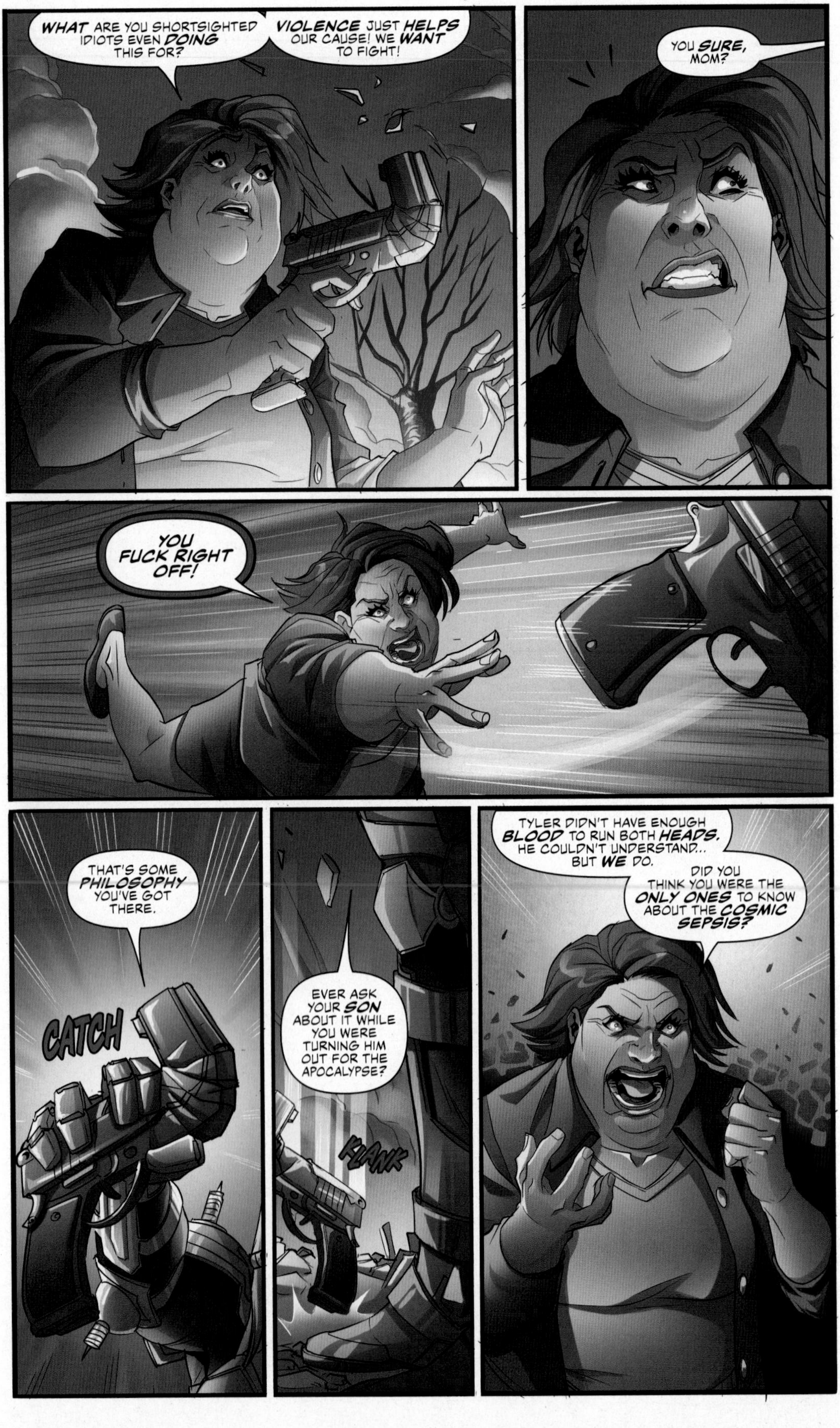
WHAT ARE YOU SHORTSIGHTED IDIOTS EVEN DOING THIS FOR?
VIOLENCE JUST HELPS OUR CAUSE! WE WANT TO FIGHT!
YOU SURE, MOM?
YOU FUCK RIGHT OFF!
THAT'S SOME PHILOSOPHY YOU'VE GOT THERE.
CATCH
EVER ASK YOUR SON ABOUT IT WHILE YOU WERE TURNING HIM OUT FOR THE APOCALYPSE?
KLANK
TYLER DIDN'T HAVE ENOUGH BLOOD TO RUN BOTH HEADS. HE COULDN'T UNDERSTAND... BUT WE DO.
DID YOU THINK YOU WERE THE ONLY ONES TO KNOW ABOUT THE COSMIC SEPSIS?

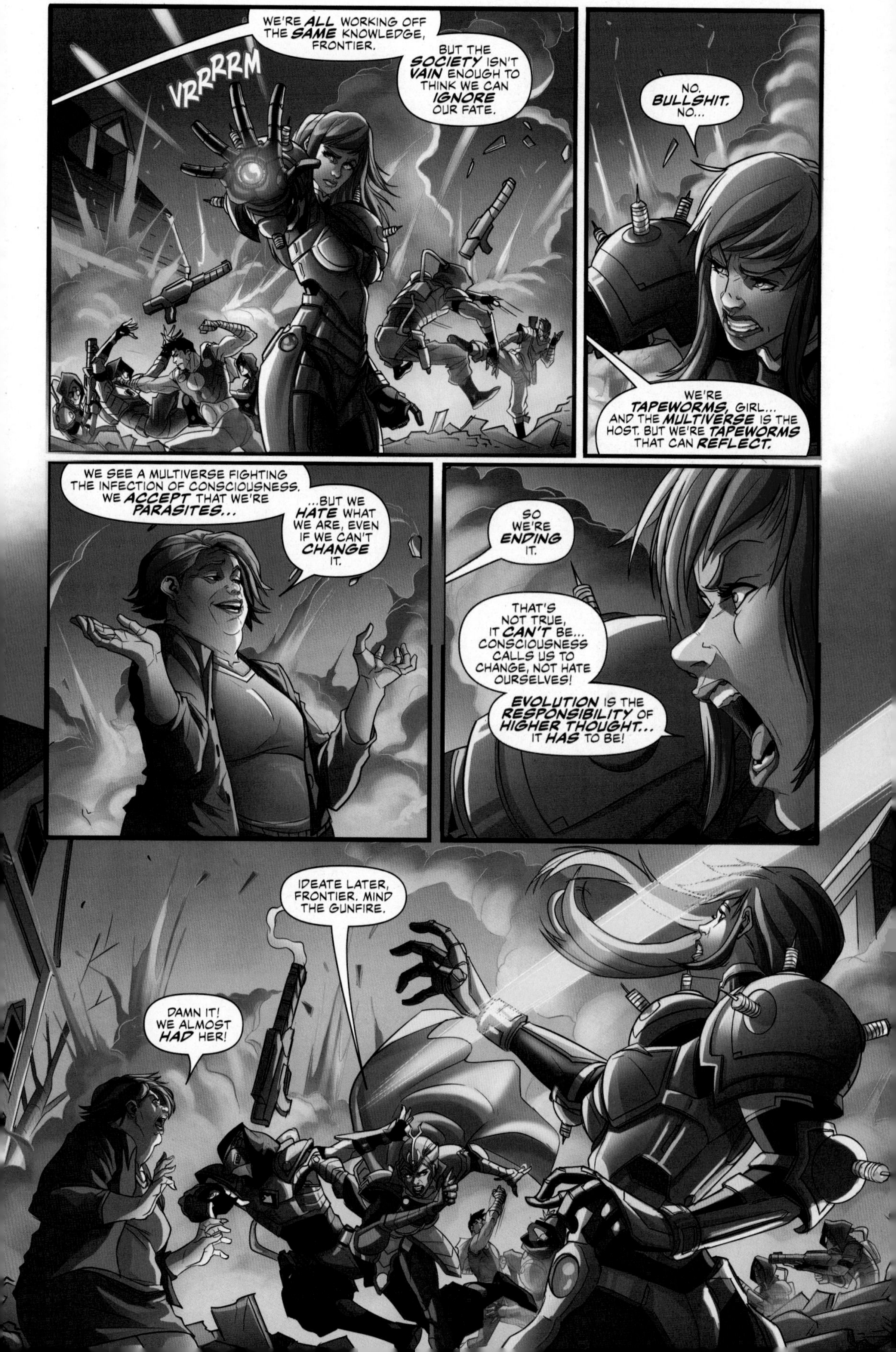
WE'RE ALL WORKING OFF THE SAME KNOWLEDGE, FRONTIER.
BUT THE SOCIETY ISN'T VAIN ENOUGH TO THINK WE CAN IGNORE OUR FATE.
VRRRRM
NO. BULLSHIT. NO...
WE'RE TAPEWORMS, GIRL... AND THE MULTIVERSE IS THE HOST. BUT WE'RE TAPEWORMS THAT CAN REFLECT.
WE SEE A MULTIVERSE FIGHTING THE INFECTION OF CONSCIOUSNESS. WE ACCEPT THAT WE'RE PARASITES...
...BUT WE HATE WHAT WE ARE, EVEN IF WE CAN'T CHANGE IT.
SO WE'RE ENDING IT.
THAT'S NOT TRUE, IT CAN'T BE... CONSCIOUSNESS CALLS US TO CHANGE, NOT HATE OURSELVES!
EVOLUTION IS THE RESPONSIBILITY OF HIGHER THOUGHT... IT HAS TO BE!
IDEATE LATER, FRONTIER. MIND THE GUNFIRE.
DAMN IT! WE ALMOST HAD HER!

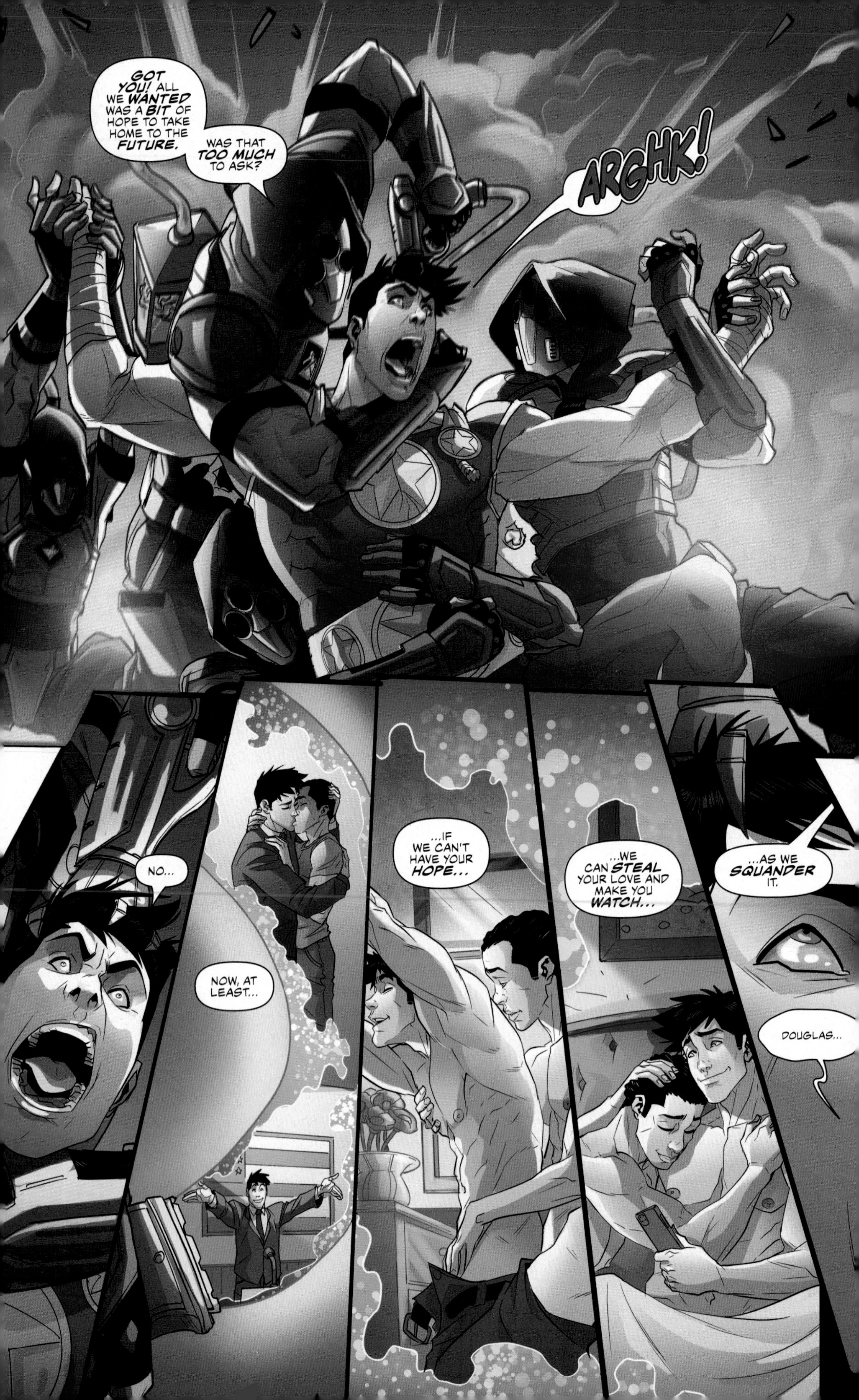

GOT YOU! ALL WE WANTED WAS A BIT OF HOPE TO TAKE HOME TO THE FUTURE.
WAS THAT TOO MUCH TO ASK?
ARGHK!
NO...
NOW, AT LEAST...
...IF WE CAN'T HAVE YOUR HOPE...
...WE CAN STEAL YOUR LOVE AND MAKE YOU WATCH...
...AS WE SQUANDER IT.
DOUGLAS...

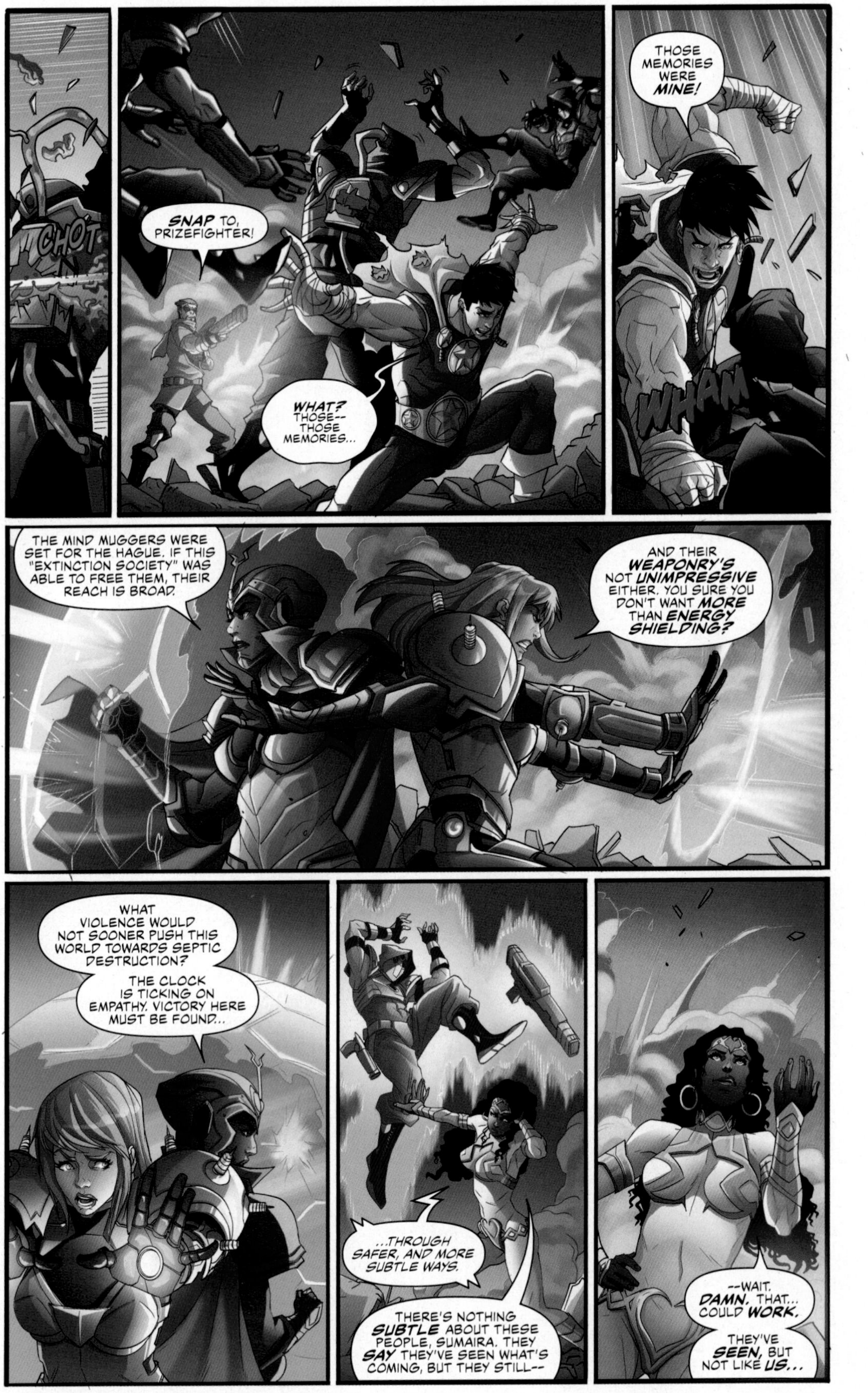
CHOT
SNAP TO, PRIZEFIGHTER!
WHAT? THOSE-- THOSE MEMORIES...
THOSE MEMORIES WERE MINE!
WHAM
THE MIND MUGGERS WERE SET FOR THE HAGUE. IF THIS "EXTINCTION SOCIETY" WAS ABLE TO FREE THEM, THEIR REACH IS BROAD.
AND THEIR WEAPONRY'S NOT UNIMPRESSIVE EITHER. YOU SURE YOU DON'T WANT MORE THAN ENERGY SHIELDING?
WHAT VIOLENCE WOULD NOT SOONER PUSH THIS WORLD TOWARDS SEPTIC DESTRUCTION?
THE CLOCK IS TICKING ON EMPATHY. VICTORY HERE MUST BE FOUND...
...THROUGH SAFER, AND MORE SUBTLE WAYS.
THERE'S NOTHING SUBTLE ABOUT THESE PEOPLE, SUMAIRA. THEY SAY THEY'VE SEEN WHAT'S COMING, BUT THEY STILL--
--WAIT. DAMN. THAT... COULD WORK.
THEY'VE SEEN, BUT NOT LIKE US...

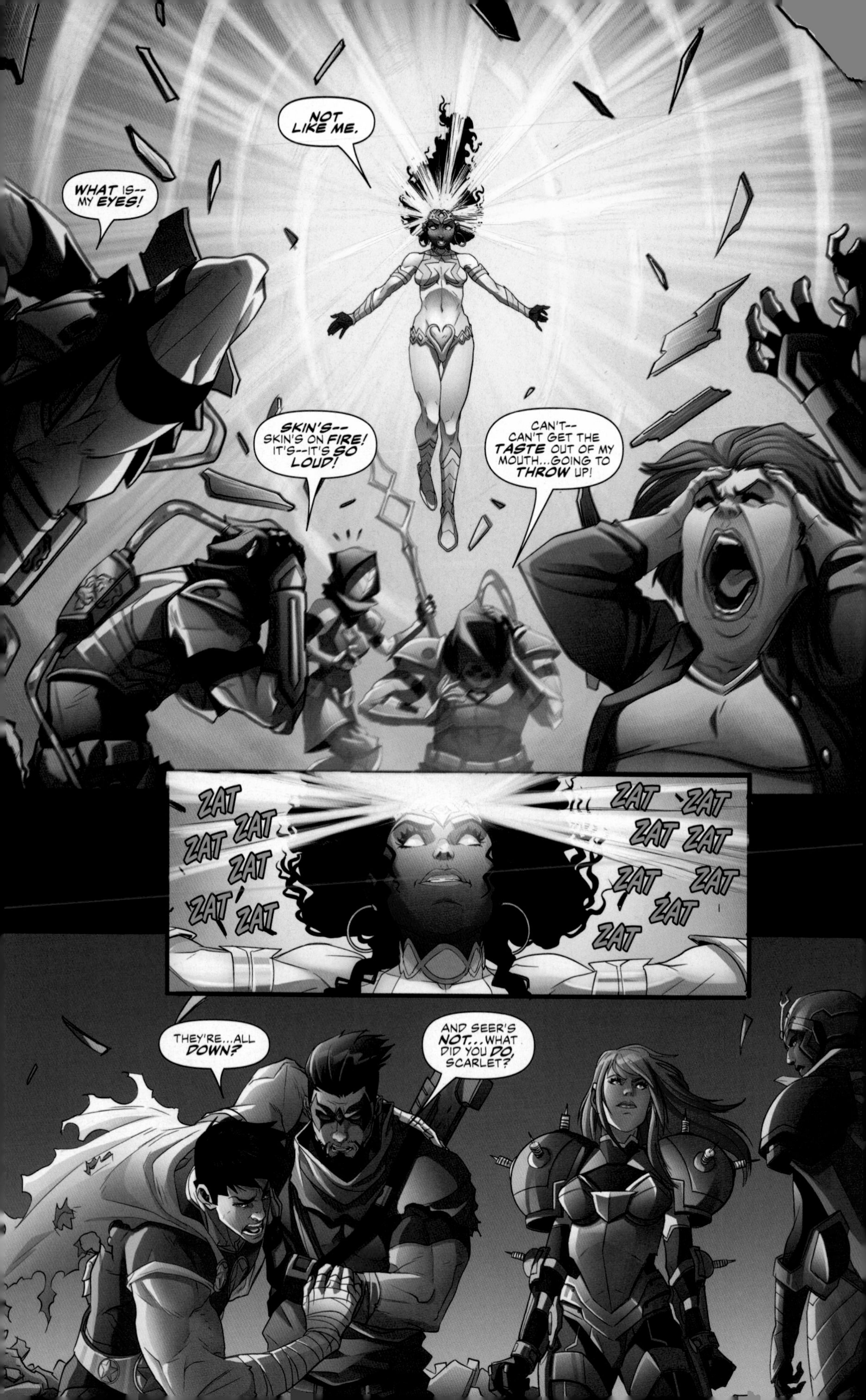

NOT LIKE ME.
WHAT IS-- MY EYES!
SKIN'S-- SKIN'S ON FIRE! IT'S--IT'S SO LOUD!
CAN'T-- CAN'T GET THE TASTE OUT OF MY MOUTH...GOING TO THROW UP!
ZAT ZAT ZAT ZAT ZAT ZAT ZAT
ZAT ZAT ZAT ZAT ZAT ZAT ZAT ZAT
THEY'RE...ALL DOWN?
AND SEER'S NOT...WHAT DID YOU DO, SCARLET?

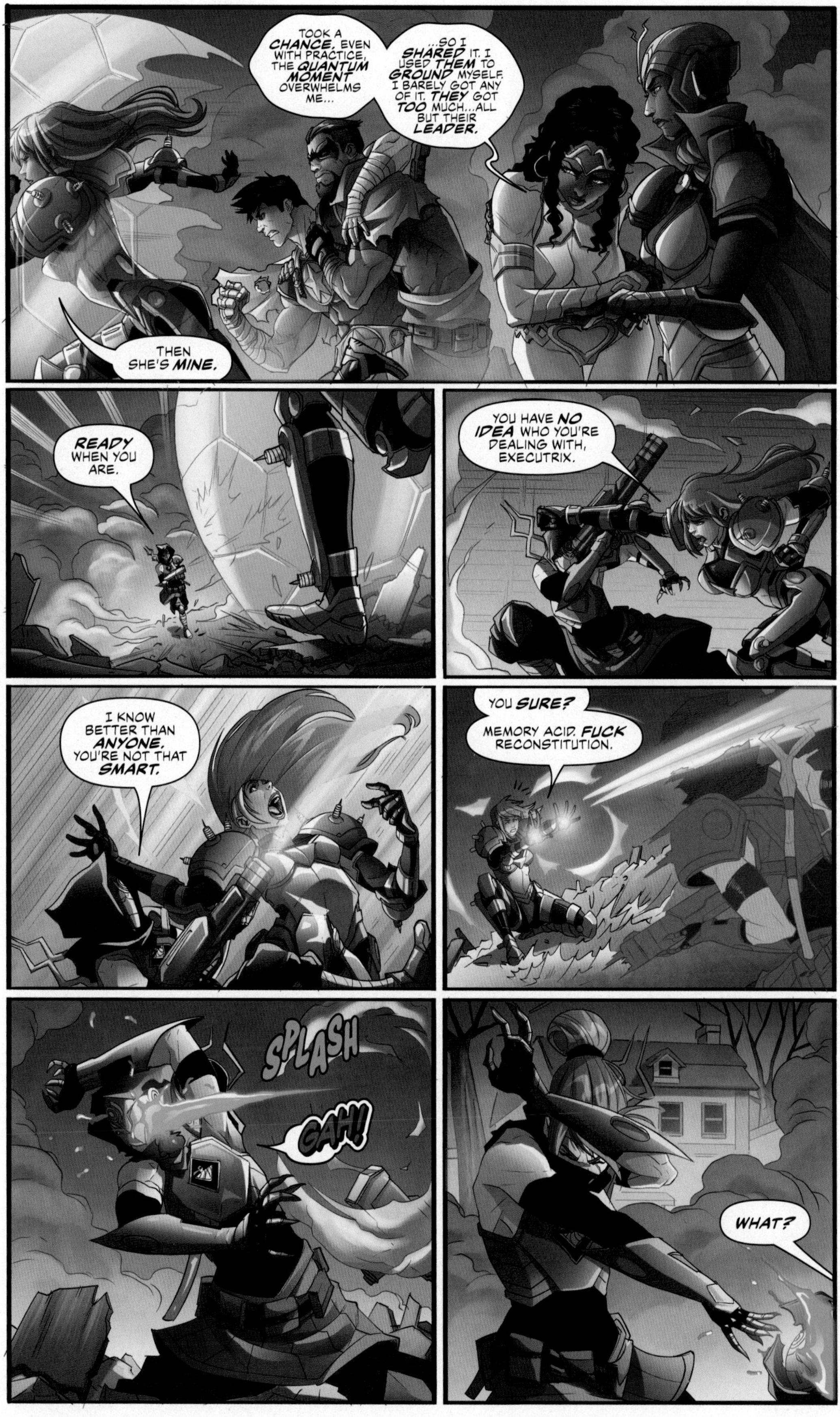
TOOK A CHANCE. EVEN WITH PRACTICE, THE QUANTUM MOMENT OVERWHELMS ME...
...SO I SHARED IT. I USED THEM TO GROUND MYSELF. I BARELY GOT ANY OF IT. THEY GOT TOO MUCH...ALL BUT THEIR LEADER.
THEN SHE'S MINE.
READY WHEN YOU ARE.
YOU HAVE NO IDEA WHO YOU'RE DEALING WITH, EXECUTRIX.
I KNOW BETTER THAN ANYONE. YOU'RE NOT THAT SMART.
YOU SURE?
MEMORY ACID. FUCK RECONSTITUTION.
SPLASH
GAH!
WHAT?

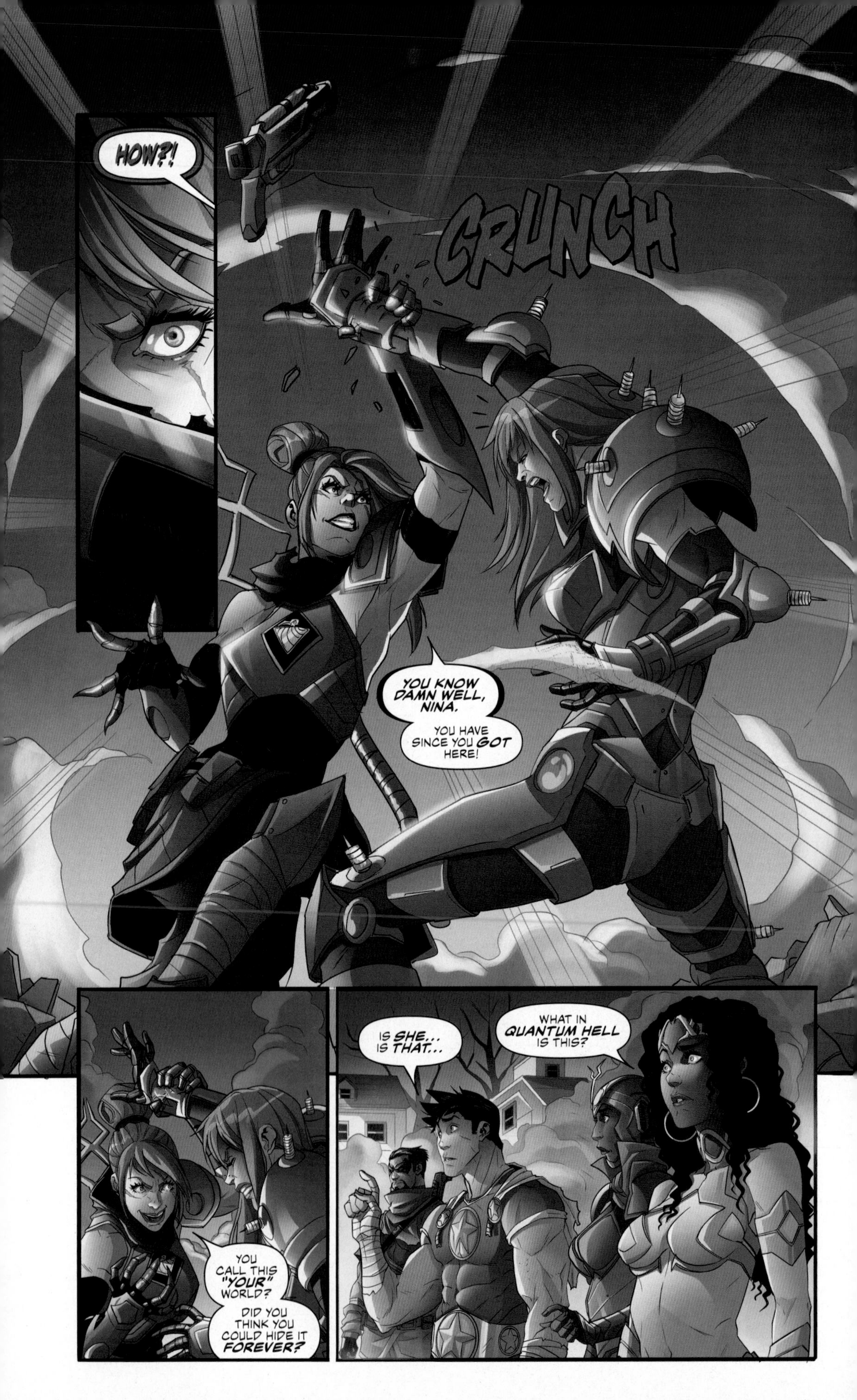
HOW?!
CRUNCH
YOU KNOW DAMN WELL, NINA.
YOU HAVE SINCE YOU GOT HERE!
YOU CALL THIS "YOUR" WORLD?
DID YOU THINK YOU COULD HIDE IT FOREVER?
IS SHE... IS THAT...
WHAT IN QUANTUM HELL IS THIS?

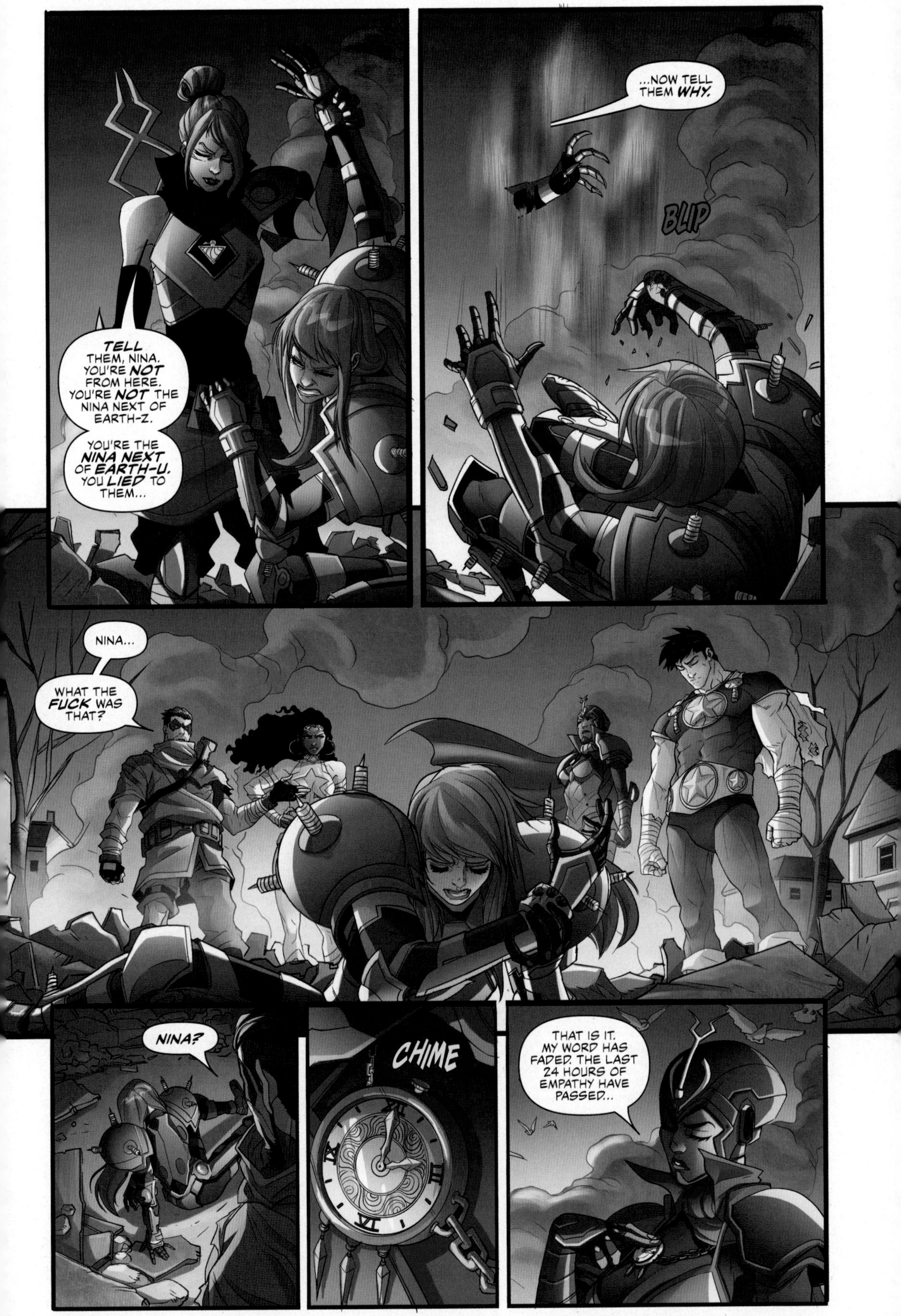
TELL THEM, NINA. YOU'RE NOT FROM HERE. YOU'RE NOT THE NINA NEXT OF EARTH-Z.
YOU'RE THE NINA NEXT OF EARTH-U. YOU LIED TO THEM...
...NOW TELL THEM WHY.
BLIP
NINA...
WHAT THE FUCK WAS THAT?
NINA?
CHIME
THAT IS IT. MY WORD HAS FADED. THE LAST 24 HOURS OF EMPATHY HAVE PASSED...

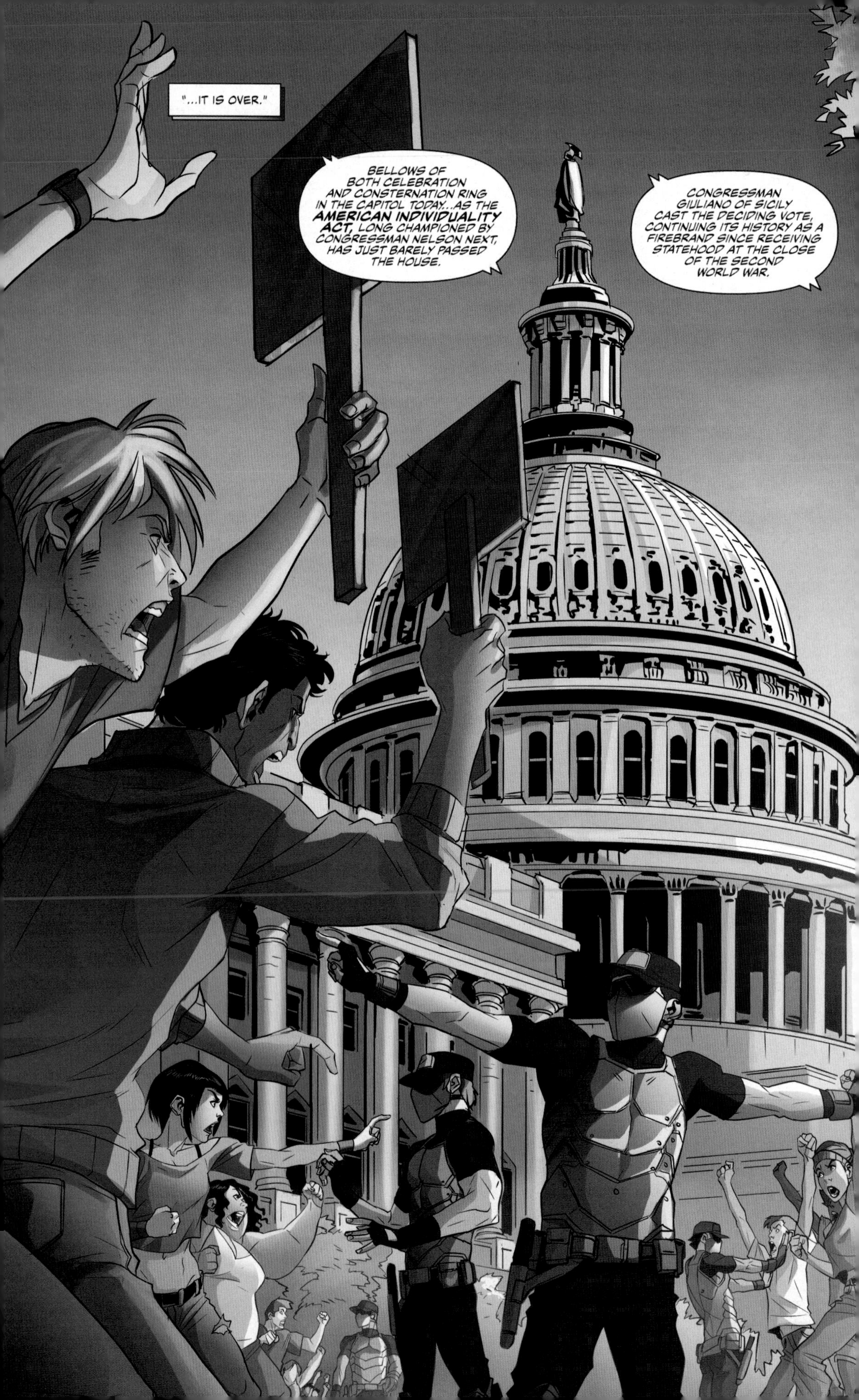
"...IT IS OVER."
BELLOWS OF BOTH CELEBRATION AND CONSTERNATION RING IN THE CAPITOL TODAY...AS THE **AMERICAN INDIVIDUALITY ACT,** LONG CHAMPIONED BY CONGRESSMAN NELSON NEXT, HAS JUST BARELY PASSED THE HOUSE.
CONGRESSMAN GIULIANO OF SICILY CAST THE DECIDING VOTE, CONTINUING ITS HISTORY AS A FIREBRAND SINCE RECEIVING STATEHOOD AT THE CLOSE OF THE SECOND WORLD WAR.

NEXT, ONCE A FRINGE ICON, HAS OF LATE BECOME THE FIGUREHEAD OF A GROWING MOVEMENT TOWARDS GROUP SECESSION.
SUPPORT FOR THE MOVEMENT HAS GROWN STEADILY IN ALL 52 STATES, CULMINATING IN THE BILL THAT WOULD SIMULTANEOUSLY DISSOLVE THE UNITED STATES AND FORM A COALITION OF NATION STATES...
...UNITED AGAINST FOREIGN ATTACK, BUT FREE TO GOVERN WITHIN AS THEY SEE FIT.
WHILE NEXT HAS REPEATEDLY PUSHED HIS BILL AS A BALM AND TRIBUTE TO THE COUNTRY'S ABILITY TO CHANGE, CRIES CONTINUE THAT NEXT'S BILL IS A CYNICAL ABDICATION OF RESPONSIBILITY.
AS OF THIS MORNING, THE ONLY THING THAT'S SURE IN AMERICA...
...IS THAT **NOTHING'S** FOR SURE.
THE AMERICAN INDIVIDUALITY ACT NOW GOES TO THE **SENATE,** WHERE IT'S SURE TO FACE HEAVY DEBATE.
104 HEARTS AND 104 MINDS, FOLKS...

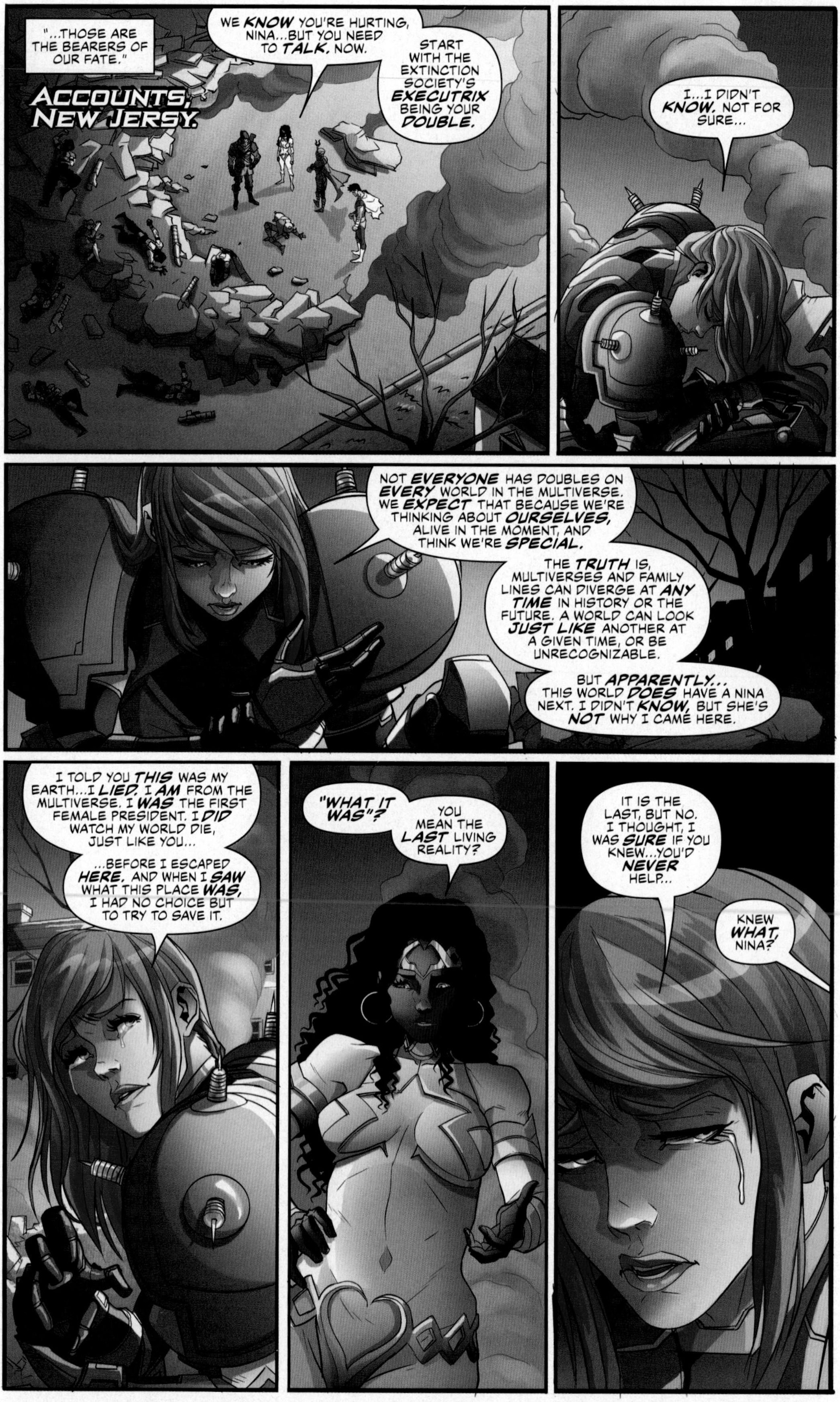
"...THOSE ARE THE BEARERS OF OUR FATE."
ACCOUNTS, NEW JERSY.
WE KNOW YOU'RE HURTING, NINA...BUT YOU NEED TO TALK. NOW.
START WITH THE EXTINCTION SOCIETY'S EXECUTRIX BEING YOUR DOUBLE.
I...I DIDN'T KNOW. NOT FOR SURE...
NOT EVERYONE HAS DOUBLES ON EVERY WORLD IN THE MULTIVERSE. WE EXPECT THAT BECAUSE WE'RE THINKING ABOUT OURSELVES, ALIVE IN THE MOMENT, AND THINK WE'RE SPECIAL.
THE TRUTH IS, MULTIVERSES AND FAMILY LINES CAN DIVERGE AT ANY TIME IN HISTORY OR THE FUTURE. A WORLD CAN LOOK JUST LIKE ANOTHER AT A GIVEN TIME, OR BE UNRECOGNIZABLE.
BUT APPARENTLY... THIS WORLD DOES HAVE A NINA NEXT. I DIDN'T KNOW, BUT SHE'S NOT WHY I CAME HERE.
I TOLD YOU THIS WAS MY EARTH...I LIED. I AM FROM THE MULTIVERSE. I WAS THE FIRST FEMALE PRESIDENT. I DID WATCH MY WORLD DIE, JUST LIKE YOU...
...BEFORE I ESCAPED HERE. AND WHEN I SAW WHAT THIS PLACE WAS, I HAD NO CHOICE BUT TO TRY TO SAVE IT.
"WHAT IT WAS"?
YOU MEAN THE LAST LIVING REALITY?
IT IS THE LAST, BUT NO. I THOUGHT, I WAS SURE IF YOU KNEW...YOU'D NEVER HELP...
KNEW WHAT, NINA?

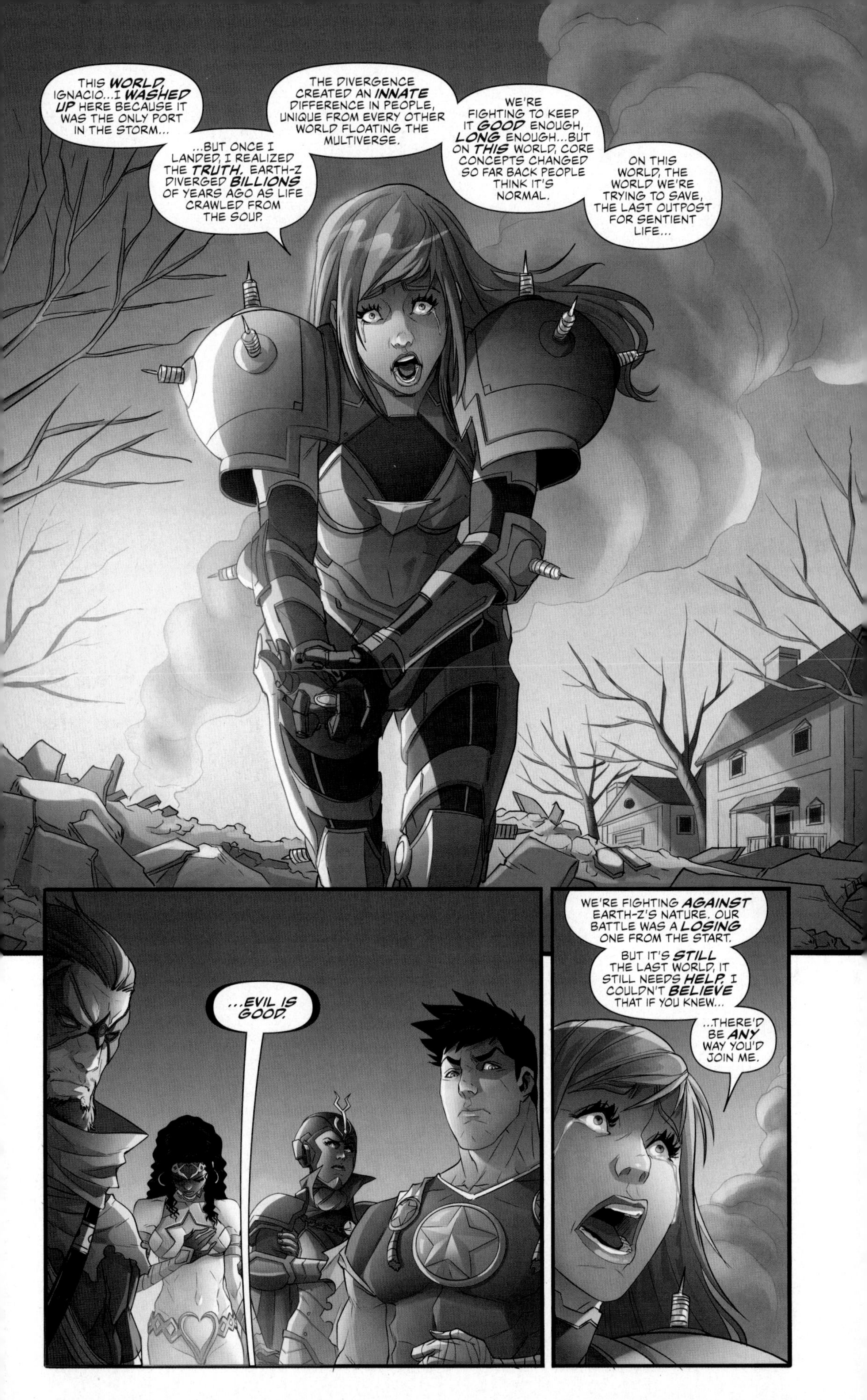
THIS WORLD, IGNACIO...I WASHED UP HERE BECAUSE IT WAS THE ONLY PORT IN THE STORM...
...BUT ONCE I LANDED, I REALIZED THE TRUTH. EARTH-Z DIVERGED BILLIONS OF YEARS AGO AS LIFE CRAWLED FROM THE SOUP.
THE DIVERGENCE CREATED AN INNATE DIFFERENCE IN PEOPLE, UNIQUE FROM EVERY OTHER WORLD FLOATING THE MULTIVERSE.
WE'RE FIGHTING TO KEEP IT GOOD ENOUGH, LONG ENOUGH...BUT ON THIS WORLD, CORE CONCEPTS CHANGED SO FAR BACK PEOPLE THINK IT'S NORMAL.
ON THIS WORLD, THE WORLD WE'RE TRYING TO SAVE, THE LAST OUTPOST FOR SENTIENT LIFE...
...EVIL IS GOOD.
WE'RE FIGHTING AGAINST EARTH-Z'S NATURE. OUR BATTLE WAS A LOSING ONE FROM THE START.
BUT IT'S STILL THE LAST WORLD, IT STILL NEEDS HELP. I COULDN'T BELIEVE THAT IF YOU KNEW...
...THERE'D BE ANY WAY YOU'D JOIN ME.

WE'RE FIGHTING...

FOR GOOD...

ON A WORLD...

WHERE EVIL WINS.

BUT LISTEN...EVEN SO, I'M NOT *DONE.* THIS OTHER NINA'S ACTIONS STILL MAKE *SENSE.* SHE SAW THE SAME SCIENCE I DID, TAINTED BY EARTH-Z'S *LENS.*

SHE SAW THE *SEPSIS* AS A REASON TO *GIVE UP* AND *PULL THE HOUSE DOWN* ON HER HEAD. I SAW IT AS ONE TO *FIGHT.*

VERY FEW THINGS ARE TRULY *IMPOSSIBLE.* JUST BECAUSE EARTH-Z IS TILTED TO DARKNESS...*DOESN'T MEAN* WE CAN'T *WIN.* IT'S *HARD...*

...BUT WE CAN WORK HARDER.

TOGETHER.

THAT'S WHAT I HID FROM YOU. THAT'S WHAT THE EXECUTRIX THOUGHT WOULD *KILL* US.

SHE ENGINEERED THE DEATH OF *EMPATHY* TO HASTEN THIS WORLD'S DESTRUCTION. IF WE *BREAK,* WHO'LL STOP HER?

WE *NEED* TO CONTINUE. *BOTH* OF US THOUGHT YOU COULDN'T HANDLE THE *TRUTH.* I *WANT* TO BE WRONG ABOUT THAT.

I *SAVED* YOU ALL. LOOK IN MY EYES, AND *TELL* ME... *WHICH* OF US IS *RIGHT?*

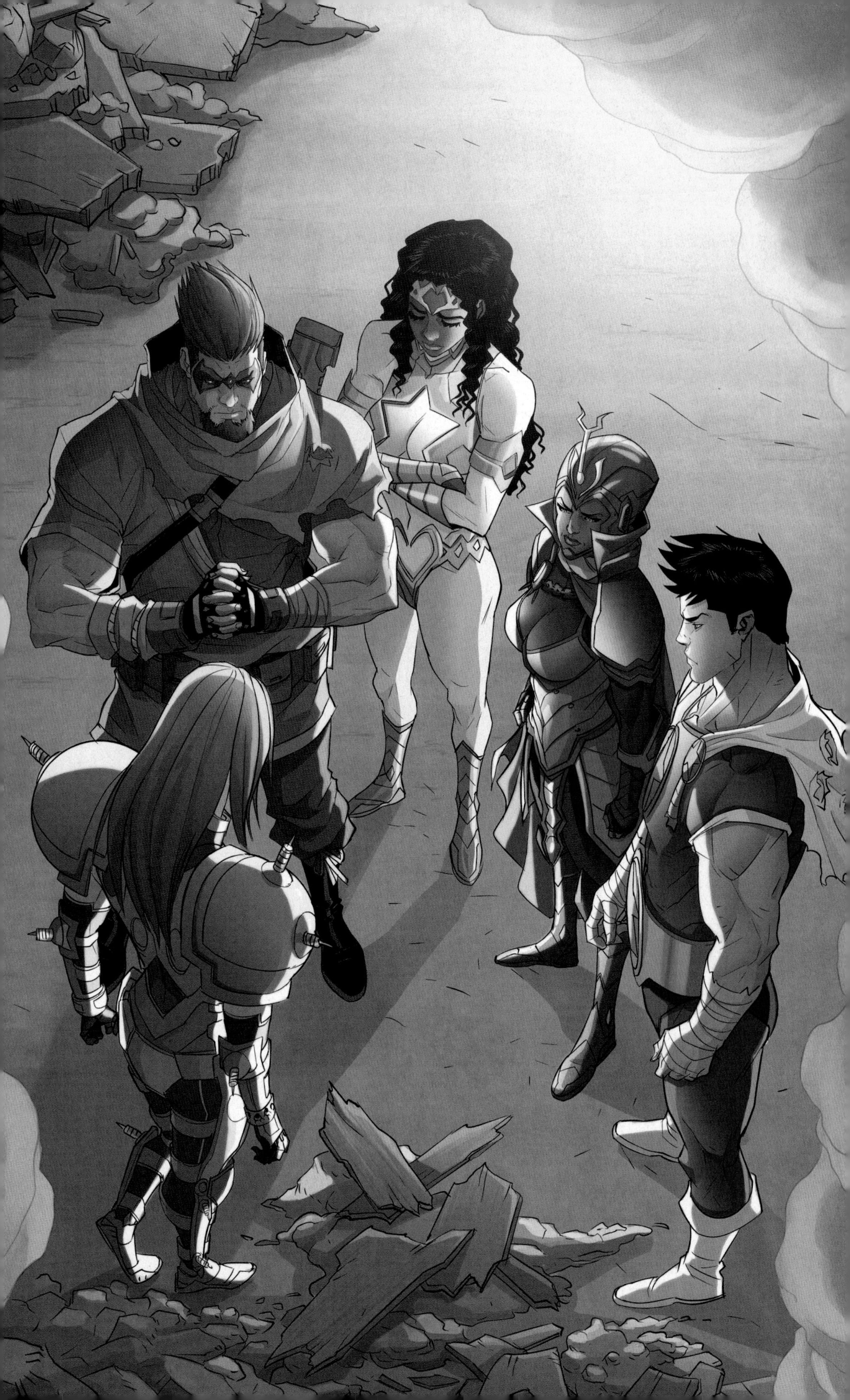

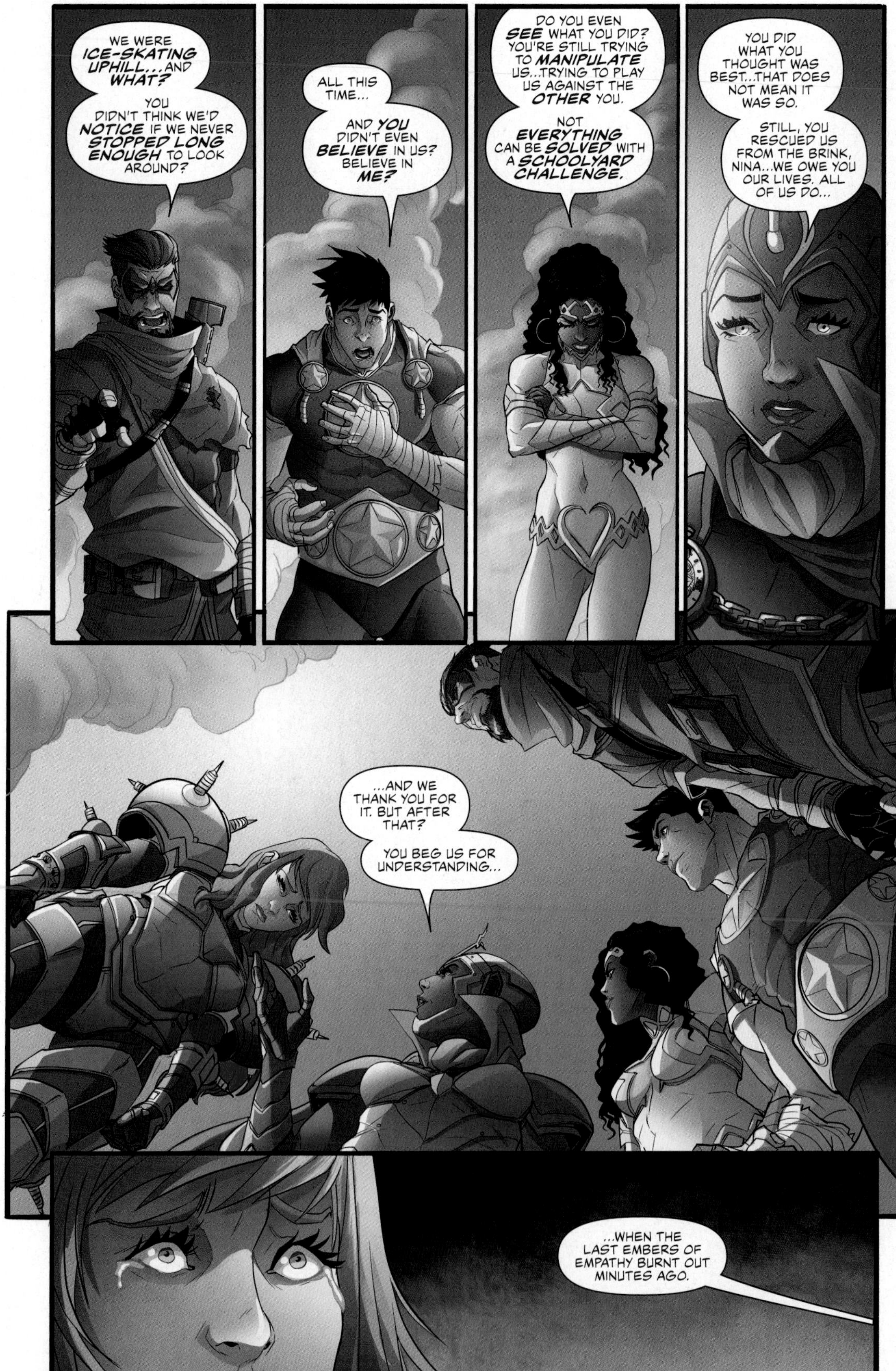
WE WERE ICE-SKATING UPHILL...AND WHAT?
YOU DIDN'T THINK WE'D NOTICE IF WE NEVER STOPPED LONG ENOUGH TO LOOK AROUND?
ALL THIS TIME...
AND YOU DIDN'T EVEN BELIEVE IN US? BELIEVE IN ME?
DO YOU EVEN SEE WHAT YOU DID? YOU'RE STILL TRYING TO MANIPULATE US...TRYING TO PLAY US AGAINST THE OTHER YOU.
NOT EVERYTHING CAN BE SOLVED WITH A SCHOOLYARD CHALLENGE.
YOU DID WHAT YOU THOUGHT WAS BEST...THAT DOES NOT MEAN IT WAS SO.
STILL, YOU RESCUED US FROM THE BRINK, NINA...WE OWE YOU OUR LIVES. ALL OF US DO...
...AND WE THANK YOU FOR IT. BUT AFTER THAT?
YOU BEG US FOR UNDERSTANDING...
...WHEN THE LAST EMBERS OF EMPATHY BURNT OUT MINUTES AGO.

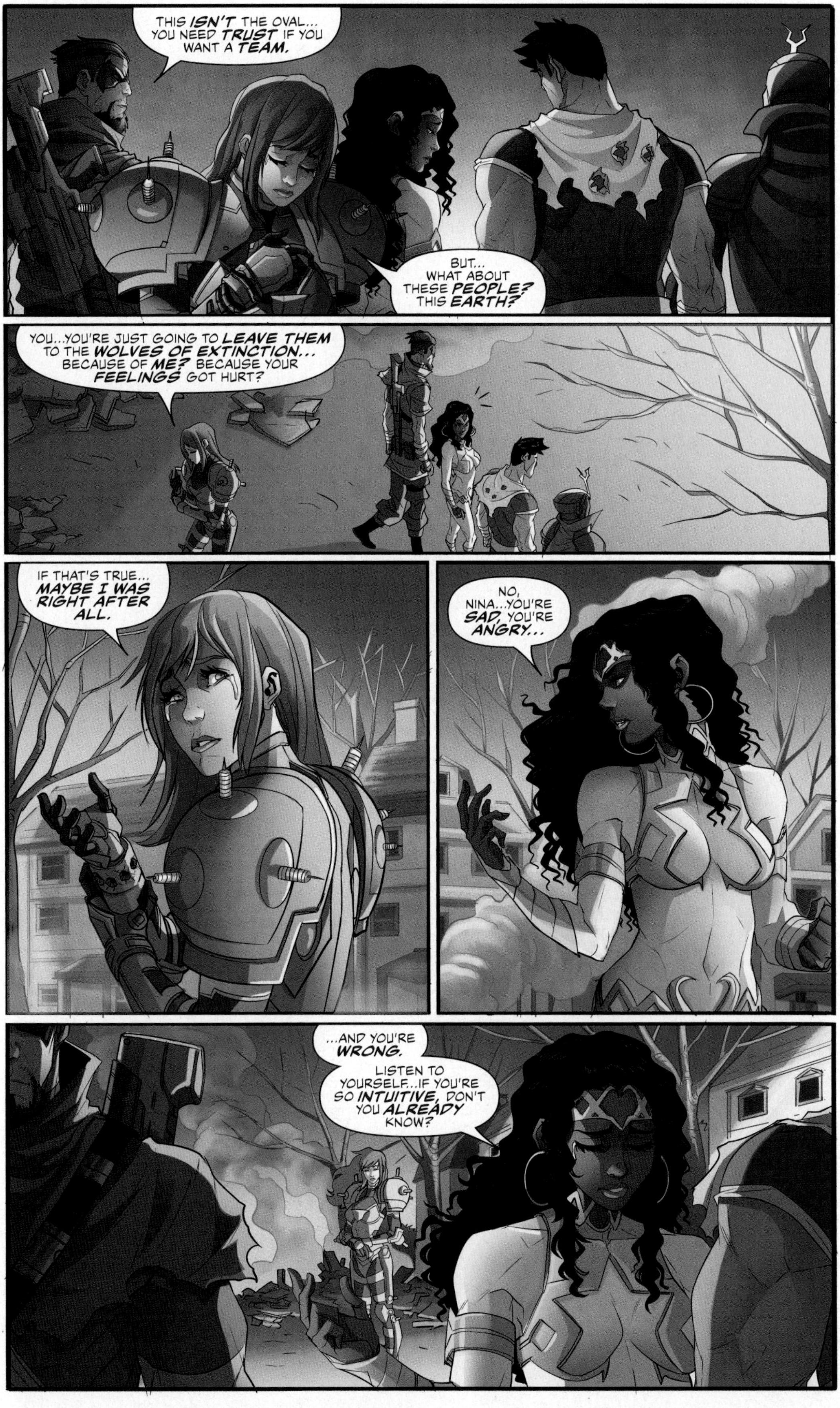
THIS ISN'T THE OVAL... YOU NEED TRUST IF YOU WANT A TEAM.
BUT... WHAT ABOUT THESE PEOPLE? THIS EARTH?
YOU...YOU'RE JUST GOING TO LEAVE THEM TO THE WOLVES OF EXTINCTION... BECAUSE OF ME? BECAUSE YOUR FEELINGS GOT HURT?
IF THAT'S TRUE... MAYBE I WAS RIGHT AFTER ALL.
NO, NINA...YOU'RE SAD, YOU'RE ANGRY...
...AND YOU'RE WRONG.
LISTEN TO YOURSELF...IF YOU'RE SO INTUITIVE, DON'T YOU ALREADY KNOW?

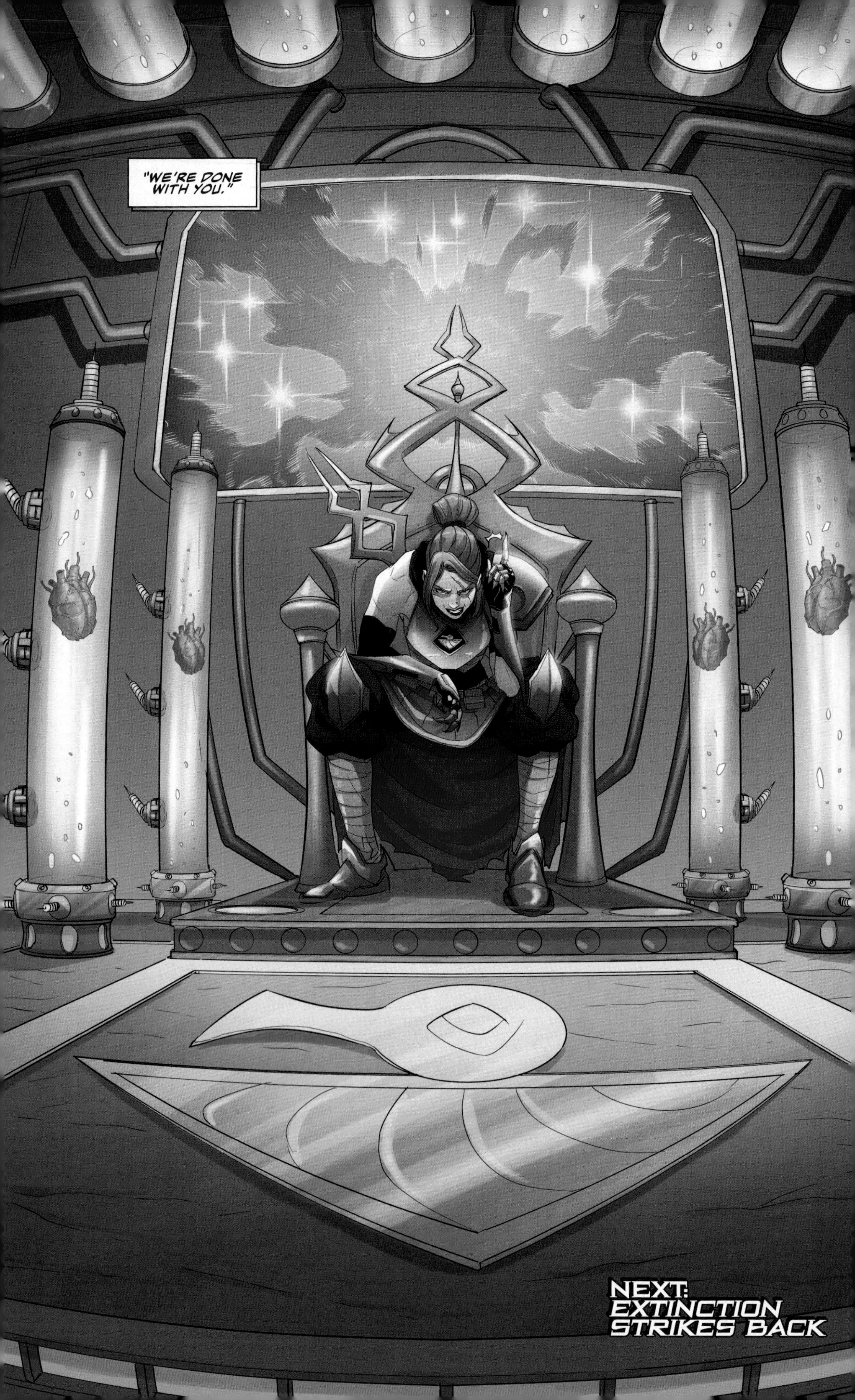
"WE'RE DONE WITH YOU."
NEXT: EXTINCTION STRIKES BACK

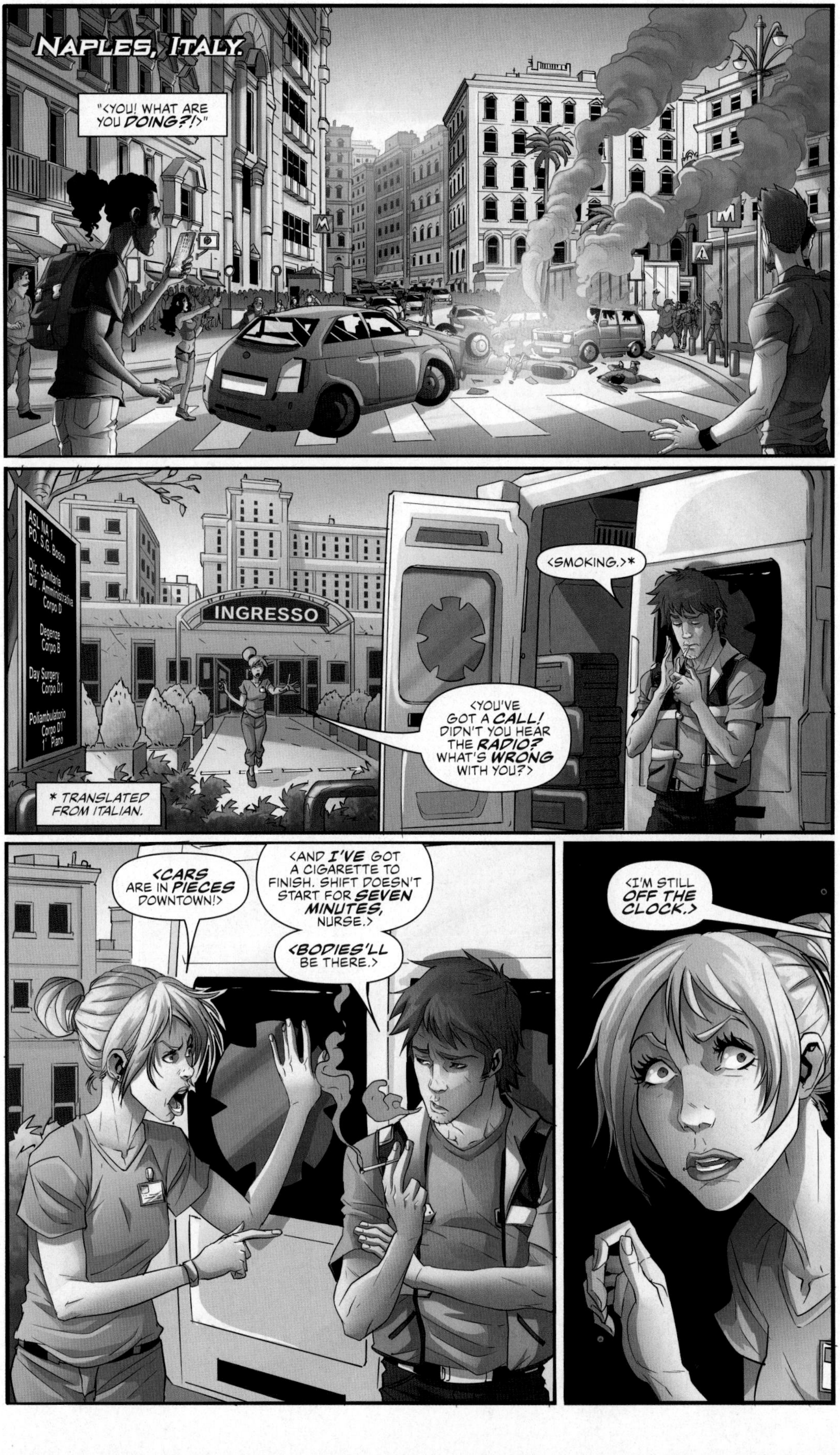
NAPLES, ITALY.
"<YOU! WHAT ARE YOU DOING?!>"
ASL NA 1
P.O. S.G. Bosco
Dir. Sanitaria
Dir. Amministrativa
Corpo D
Degenze
Corpo B
Day Surgery
Corpo D1
Poliambulatorio
Corpo D1
1° Piano
INGRESSO
<SMOKING.>*
<YOU'VE GOT A CALL! DIDN'T YOU HEAR THE RADIO? WHAT'S WRONG WITH YOU?>
* TRANSLATED FROM ITALIAN.
<CARS ARE IN PIECES DOWNTOWN!>
<AND I'VE GOT A CIGARETTE TO FINISH. SHIFT DOESN'T START FOR SEVEN MINUTES, NURSE.>
<BODIES'LL BE THERE.>
<I'M STILL OFF THE CLOCK.>

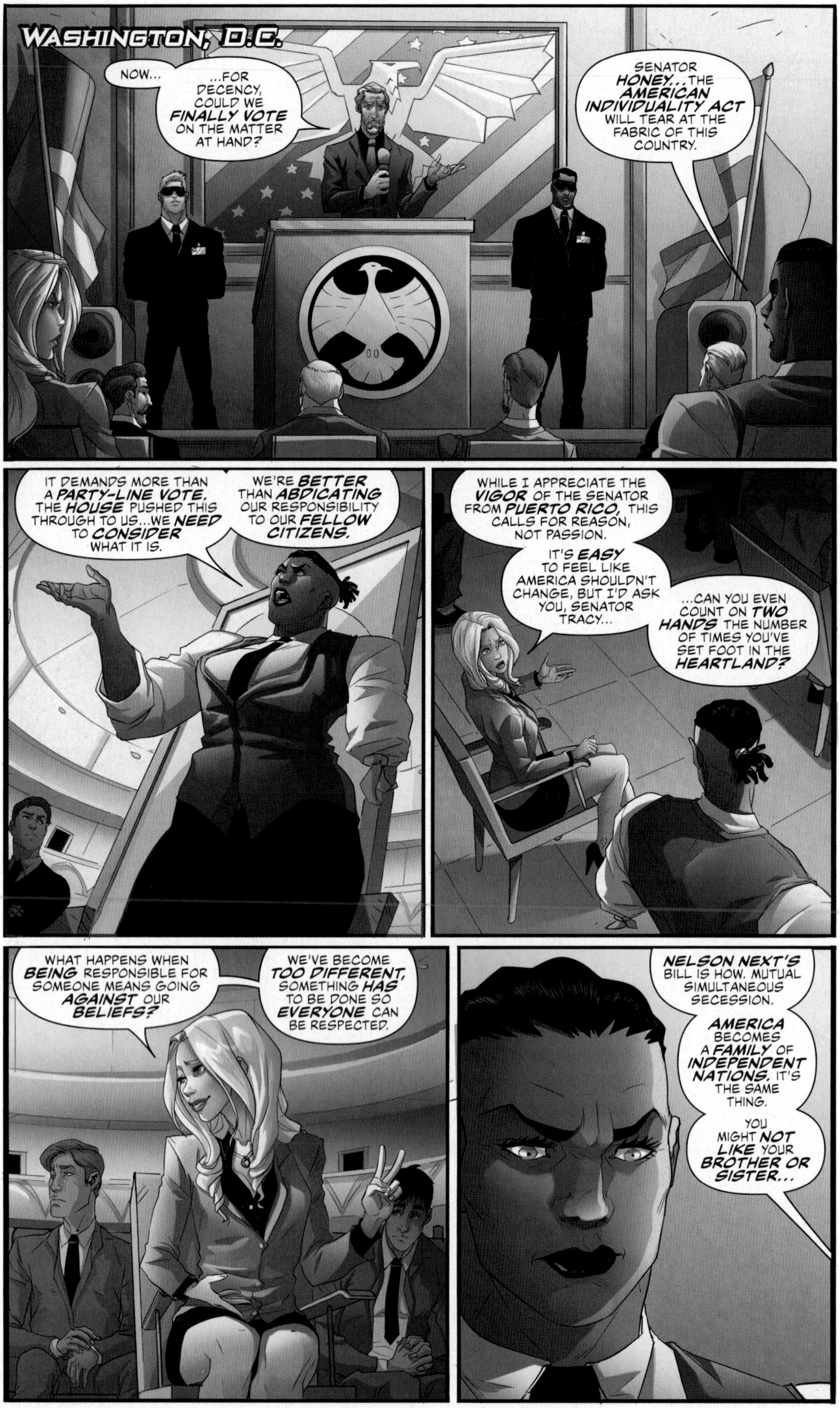
WASHINGTON, D.C.
NOW...
...FOR DECENCY, COULD WE FINALLY VOTE ON THE MATTER AT HAND?
SENATOR HONEY... THE AMERICAN INDIVIDUALITY ACT WILL TEAR AT THE FABRIC OF THIS COUNTRY.
IT DEMANDS MORE THAN A PARTY-LINE VOTE. THE HOUSE PUSHED THIS THROUGH TO US...WE NEED TO CONSIDER WHAT IT IS.
WE'RE BETTER THAN ABDICATING OUR RESPONSIBILITY TO OUR FELLOW CITIZENS.
WHILE I APPRECIATE THE VIGOR OF THE SENATOR FROM PUERTO RICO, THIS CALLS FOR REASON, NOT PASSION.
IT'S EASY TO FEEL LIKE AMERICA SHOULDN'T CHANGE, BUT I'D ASK YOU, SENATOR TRACY...
...CAN YOU EVEN COUNT ON TWO HANDS THE NUMBER OF TIMES YOU'VE SET FOOT IN THE HEARTLAND?
WHAT HAPPENS WHEN BEING RESPONSIBLE FOR SOMEONE MEANS GOING AGAINST OUR BELIEFS?
WE'VE BECOME TOO DIFFERENT, SOMETHING HAS TO BE DONE SO EVERYONE CAN BE RESPECTED.
NELSON NEXT'S BILL IS HOW. MUTUAL SIMULTANEOUS SECESSION.
AMERICA BECOMES A FAMILY OF INDEPENDENT NATIONS. IT'S THE SAME THING.
YOU MIGHT NOT LIKE YOUR BROTHER OR SISTER...

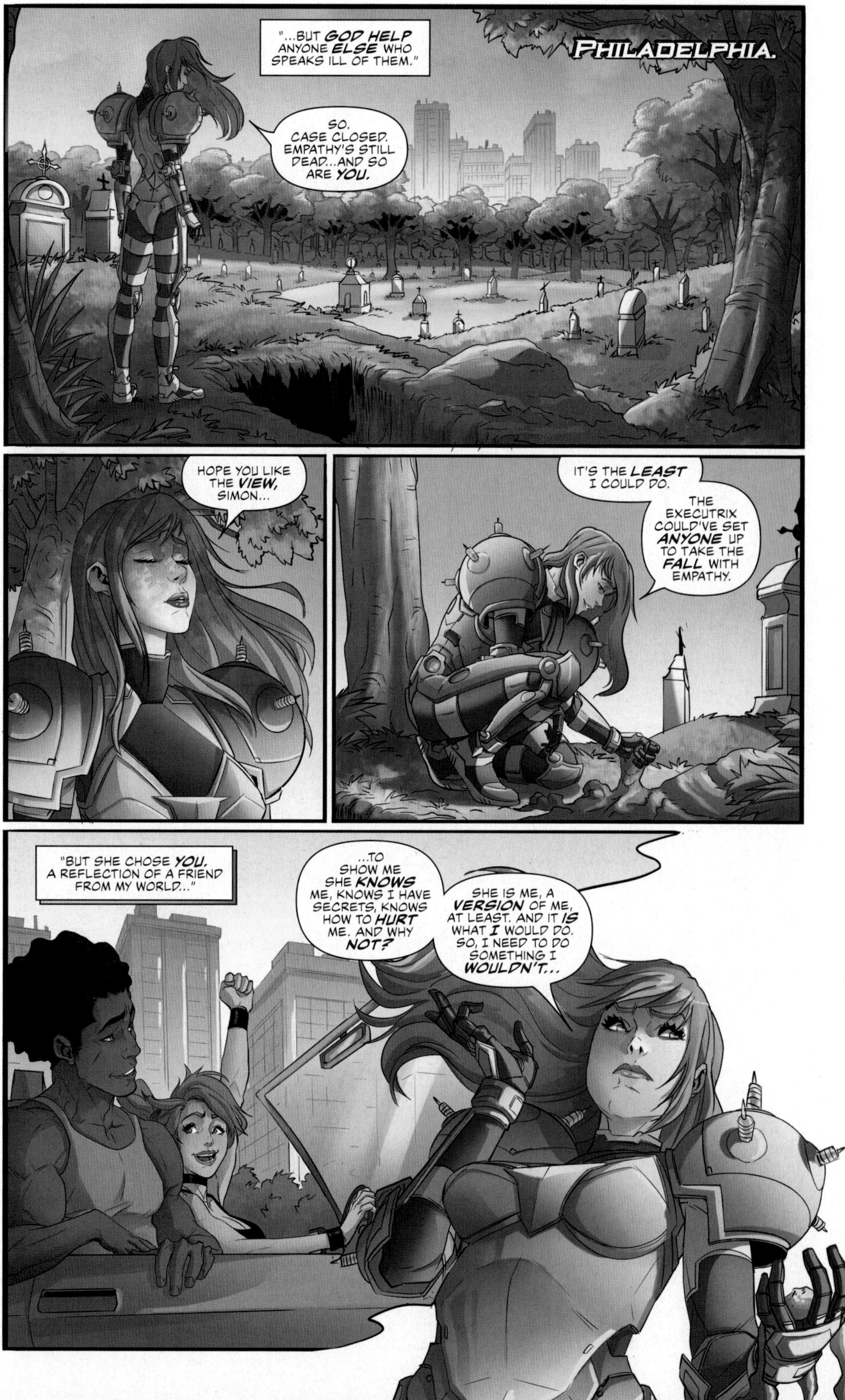
"...BUT GOD HELP ANYONE ELSE WHO SPEAKS ILL OF THEM."
PHILADELPHIA.
SO. CASE CLOSED. EMPATHY'S STILL DEAD...AND SO ARE YOU.
HOPE YOU LIKE THE VIEW, SIMON...
IT'S THE LEAST I COULD DO.
THE EXECUTRIX COULD'VE SET ANYONE UP TO TAKE THE FALL WITH EMPATHY.
"BUT SHE CHOSE YOU. A REFLECTION OF A FRIEND FROM MY WORLD..."
...TO SHOW ME SHE KNOWS ME, KNOWS I HAVE SECRETS, KNOWS HOW TO HURT ME. AND WHY NOT?
SHE IS ME, A VERSION OF ME, AT LEAST. AND IT IS WHAT I WOULD DO. SO, I NEED TO DO SOMETHING I WOULDN'T...

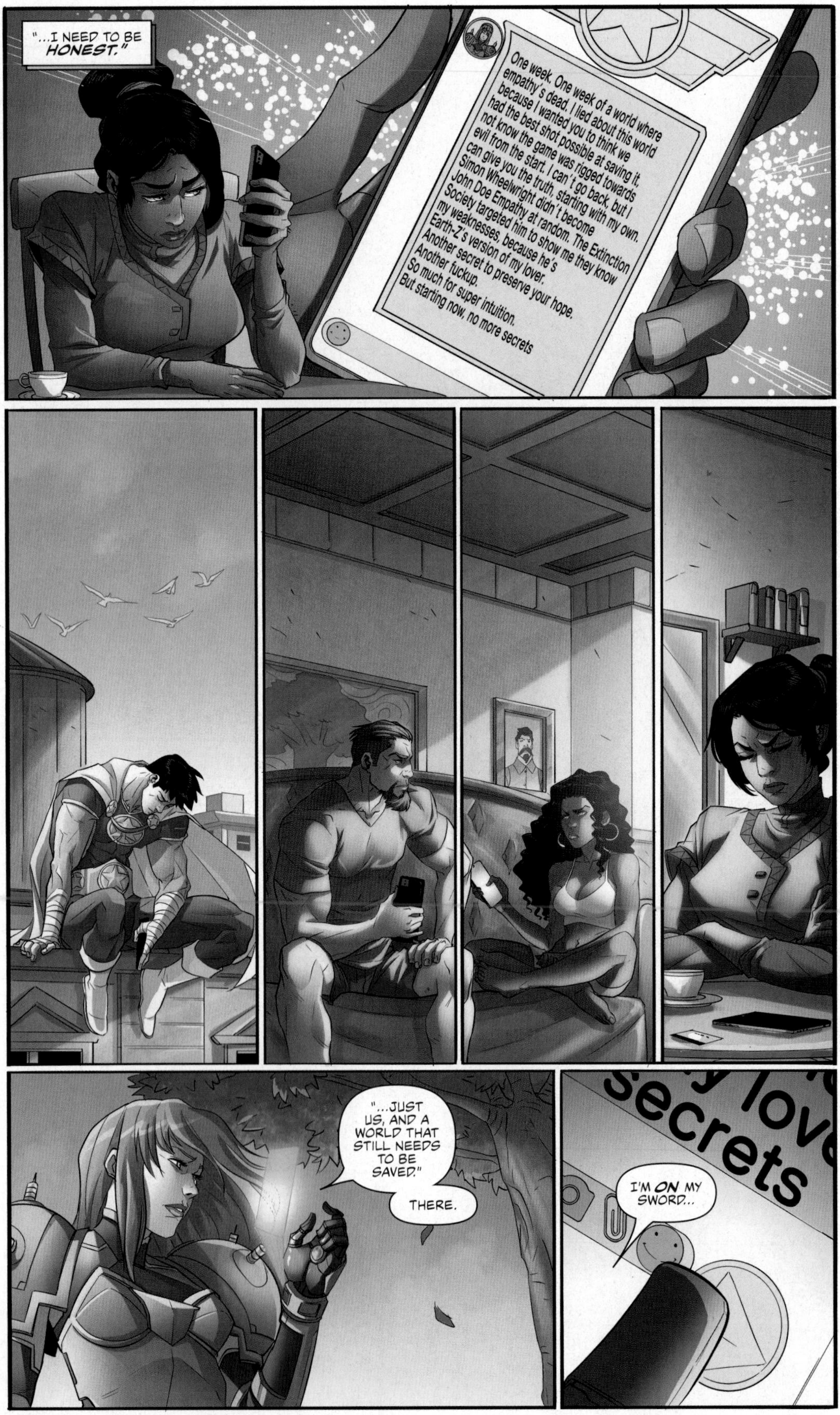
"...I NEED TO BE *HONEST.*"
One week. One week of a world where empathy's dead. I lied about this world because I wanted you to think we had the best shot possible at saving it, not know the game was rigged towards evil from the start. I can't go back, but I can give you the truth, starting with my own. Simon Wheelwright didn't become John Doe Empathy at random. The Extinction Society targeted him to show me they know my weaknesses, because he's Earth-Z's version of my lover. Another secret to preserve your hope. Another fuckup. So much for super intuition. But starting now, no more secrets
"...JUST US, AND A WORLD THAT STILL NEEDS TO BE SAVED."
THERE.
secrets
I'M *ON* MY SWORD...

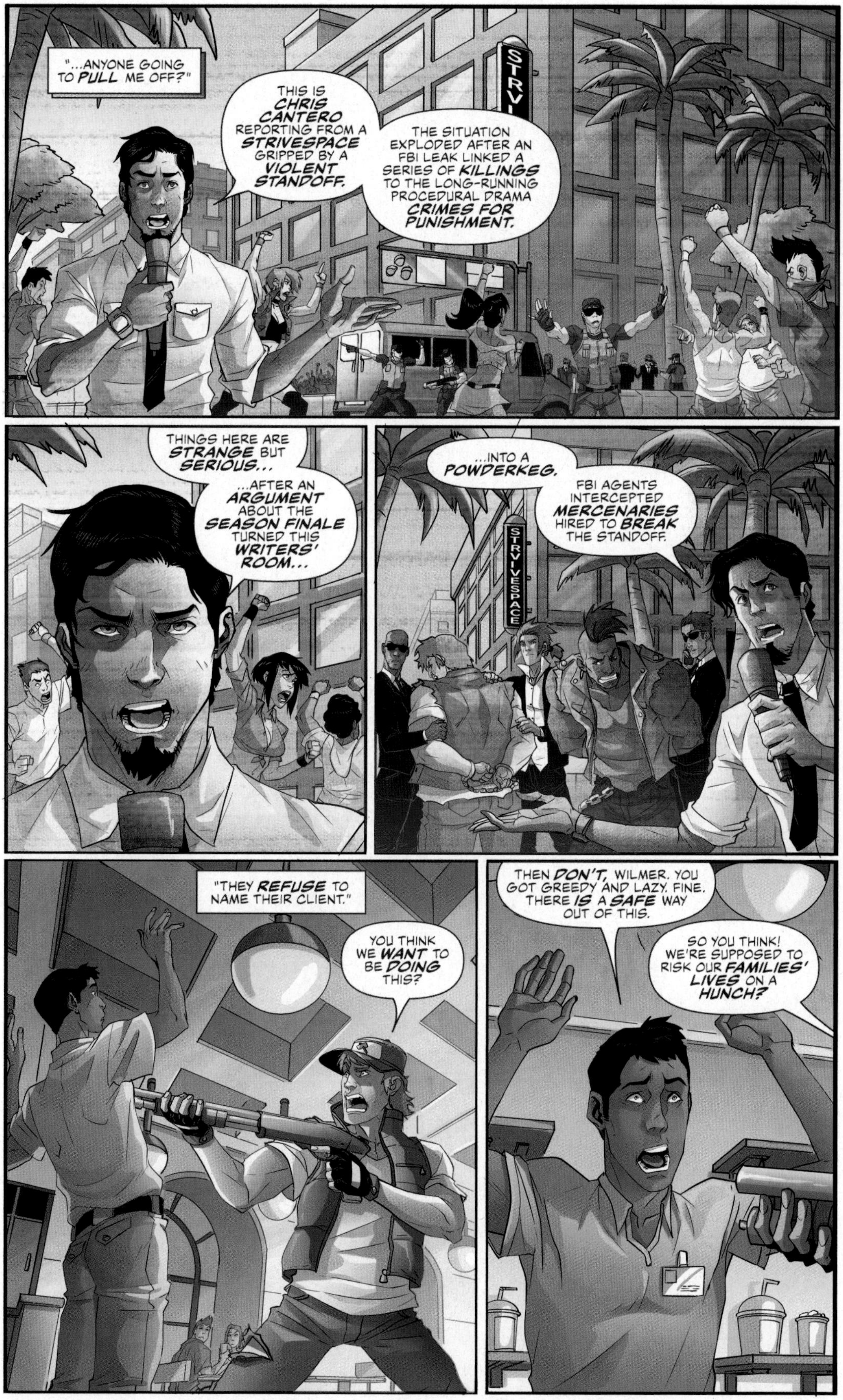
"...ANYONE GOING TO PULL ME OFF?"
THIS IS CHRIS CANTERO REPORTING FROM A STRIVESPACE GRIPPED BY A VIOLENT STANDOFF.
THE SITUATION EXPLODED AFTER AN FBI LEAK LINKED A SERIES OF KILLINGS TO THE LONG-RUNNING PROCEDURAL DRAMA CRIMES FOR PUNISHMENT.
THINGS HERE ARE STRANGE BUT SERIOUS...
...AFTER AN ARGUMENT ABOUT THE SEASON FINALE TURNED THIS WRITERS' ROOM...
...INTO A POWDERKEG.
FBI AGENTS INTERCEPTED MERCENARIES HIRED TO BREAK THE STANDOFF.
STRVIVESPACE
"THEY REFUSE TO NAME THEIR CLIENT."
YOU THINK WE WANT TO BE DOING THIS?
THEN DON'T, WILMER. YOU GOT GREEDY AND LAZY. FINE. THERE IS A SAFE WAY OUT OF THIS.
SO YOU THINK! WE'RE SUPPOSED TO RISK OUR FAMILIES' LIVES ON A HUNCH?

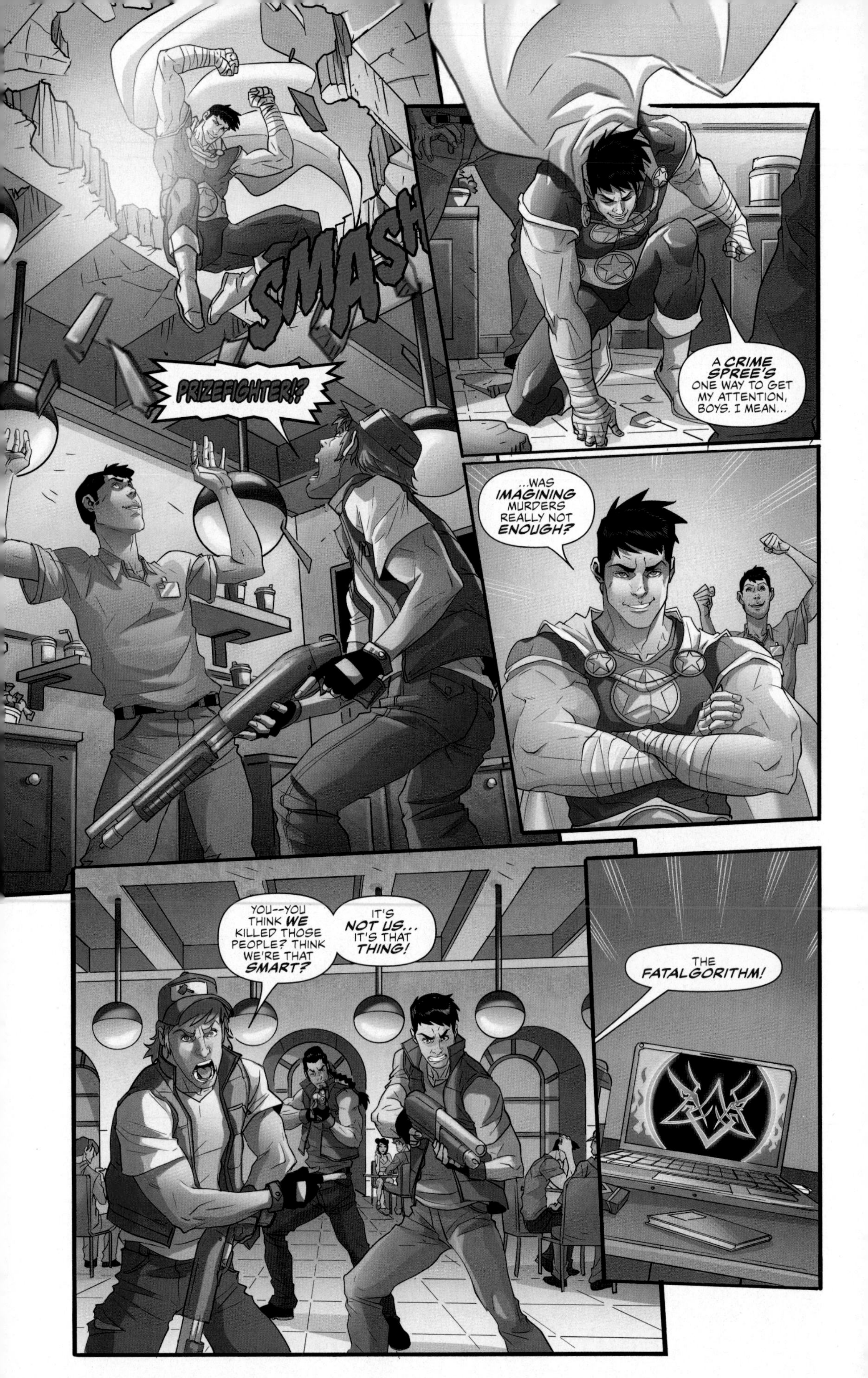
SMASH
A CRIME SPREE'S ONE WAY TO GET MY ATTENTION, BOYS. I MEAN...
PRIZEFIGHTER!?
...WAS IMAGINING MURDERS REALLY NOT ENOUGH?
YOU--YOU THINK WE KILLED THOSE PEOPLE? THINK WE'RE THAT SMART?
IT'S NOT US... IT'S THAT THING!
THE FATALGORITHM!

THE **WHAT?**

FATALGORITHM. I'M **MITCH MANCO.** CREATOR OF CRIME FOR PUNISHMENT.

THEY BUILT AN **ALGORITHM** TO TURN **HEADLINES** INTO **SCRIPTS** SO THEY COULD **DOUBLE BOOK** THEMSELVES.

BUT IT GOT **SMART,** DRAINED OUR BUDGET AND HIRED **KILLERS** ON THE **WEB** TO PLAY ITS STORYLINES OUT IN REAL LIFE.

I CAME TO SHUT IT DOWN. BUT THE FATALGORITHM THREATENED TO BLOW THE **GAS LINES** AT EVERYONE'S HOMES IF THEY DIDN'T **STOP** ME.

THAT'S SURE...**NEW.** BUT DON'T **WORRY--**

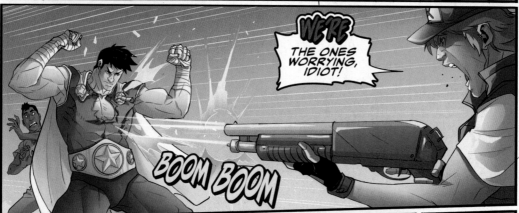

WE'RE THE ONES WORRYING, IDIOT!

BOOM BOOM

BOTH BARRELS...**BAD MOVE,** MAN. NOW YOU'RE OUT.

WAIT. JUST KEEP THEM BACK.

THIS IS **MY SHOW.** THE FATALGORITHM'S **MAD,** BUT IT'S ACTING OUT **MY** SEASON ORDER. I CAN FORCE IT **DORMANT...**

CRUNCH

...BY **CANCELING** THE SERIES.

FINGER I.D. APPROVED

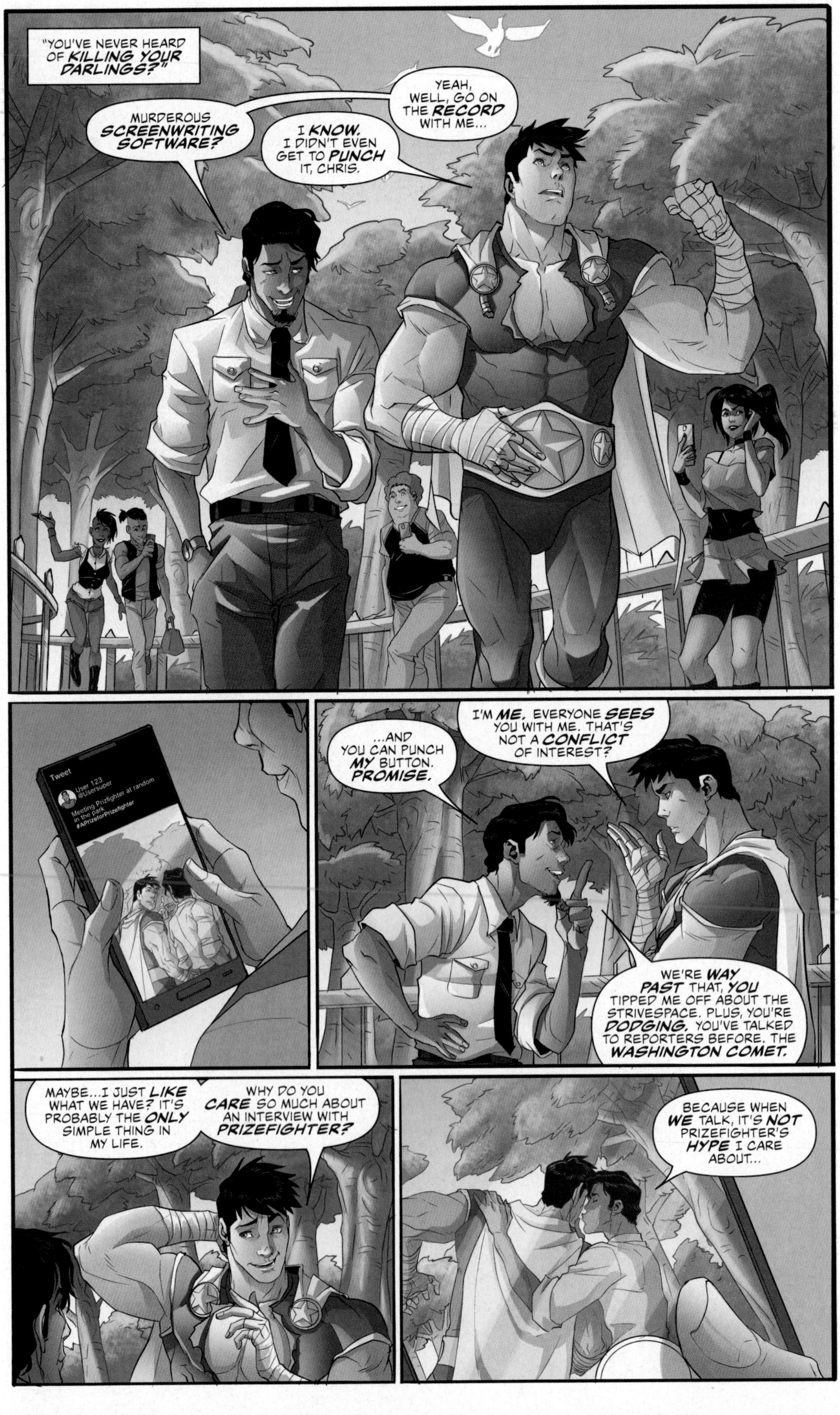
"YOU'VE NEVER HEARD OF KILLING YOUR DARLINGS?"
MURDEROUS SCREENWRITING SOFTWARE?
YEAH, WELL, GO ON THE RECORD WITH ME...
I KNOW. I DIDN'T EVEN GET TO PUNCH IT, CHRIS.
Tweet
User 123
@Usersuper
Meeting Prizfighter at random in the park
#APrizeforPrizefighter
I'M ME. EVERYONE SEES YOU WITH ME. THAT'S NOT A CONFLICT OF INTEREST?
...AND YOU CAN PUNCH MY BUTTON. PROMISE.
WE'RE WAY PAST THAT, YOU TIPPED ME OFF ABOUT THE STRIVESPACE. PLUS, YOU'RE DODGING. YOU'VE TALKED TO REPORTERS BEFORE. THE WASHINGTON COMET.
WHY DO YOU CARE SO MUCH ABOUT AN INTERVIEW WITH PRIZEFIGHTER?
MAYBE...I JUST LIKE WHAT WE HAVE? IT'S PROBABLY THE ONLY SIMPLE THING IN MY LIFE.
BECAUSE WHEN WE TALK, IT'S NOT PRIZEFIGHTER'S HYPE I CARE ABOUT...

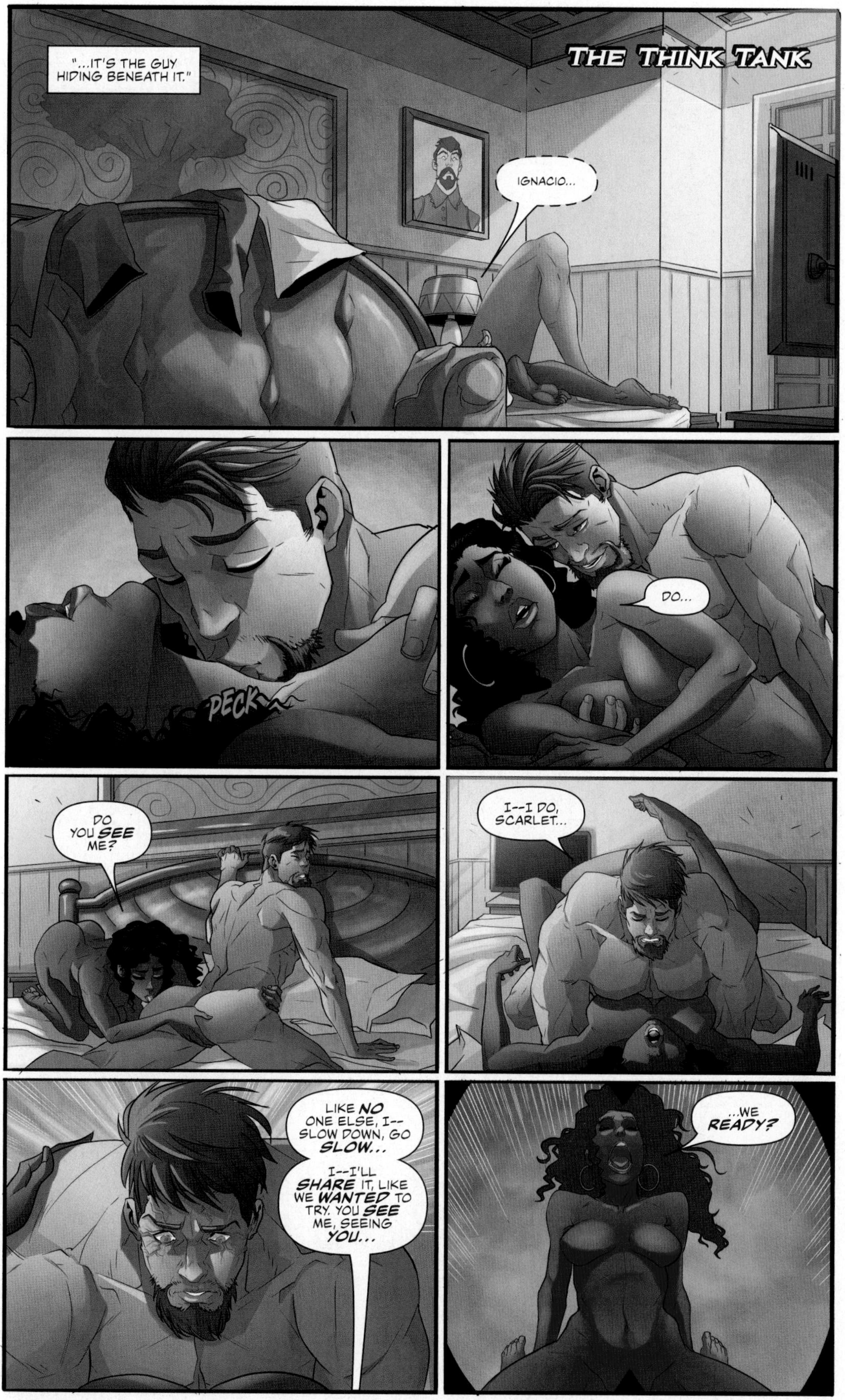
"...IT'S THE GUY HIDING BENEATH IT."
THE THINK TANK
IGNACIO...
PECK
DO...
DO YOU SEE ME?
I--I DO, SCARLET...
LIKE NO ONE ELSE, I-- SLOW DOWN, GO SLOW...
I--I'LL SHARE IT, LIKE WE WANTED TO TRY. YOU SEE ME, SEEING YOU...
...WE READY?

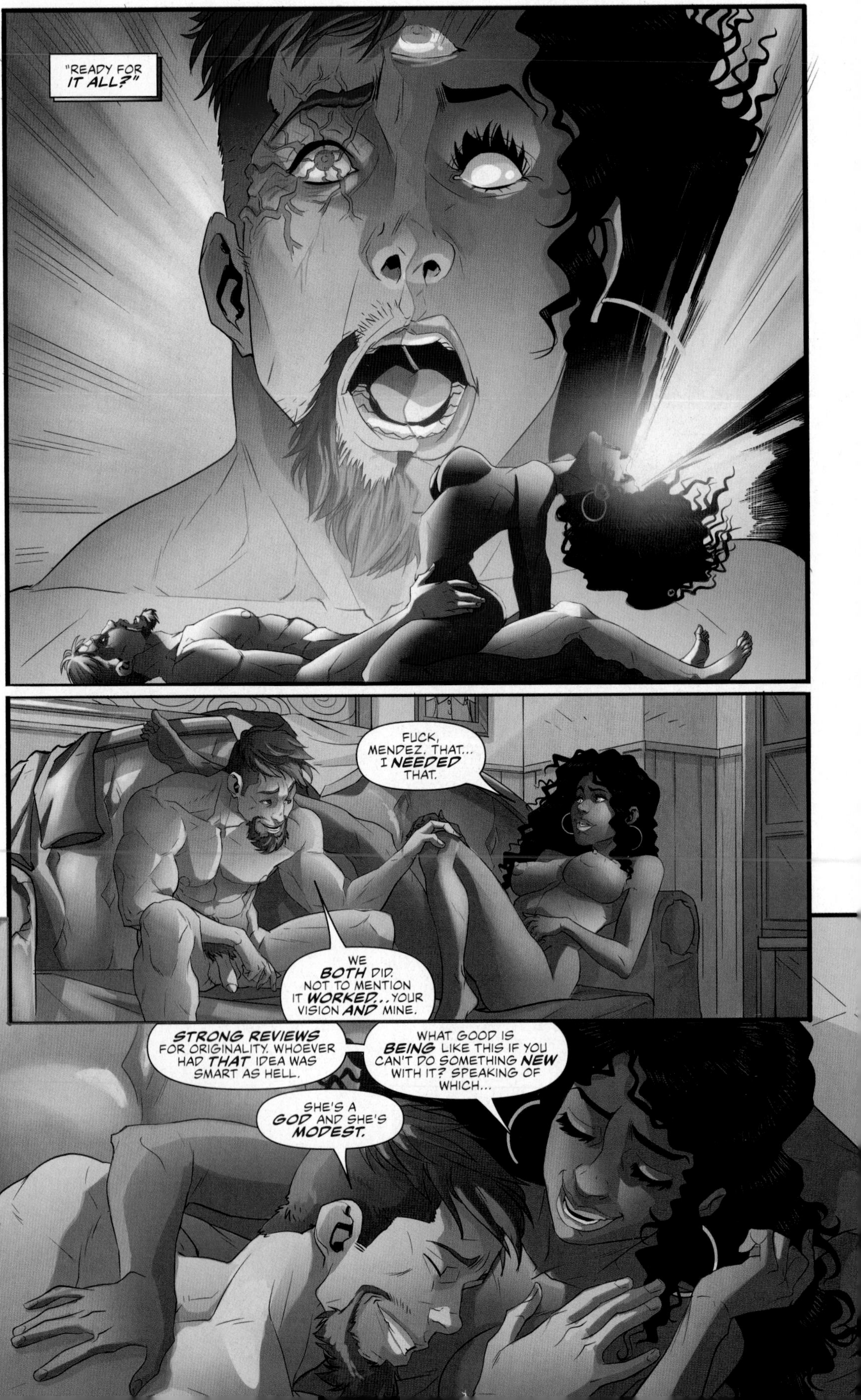
"READY FOR IT ALL?"
FUCK, MENDEZ, THAT... I NEEDED THAT.
WE BOTH DID. NOT TO MENTION IT WORKED... YOUR VISION AND MINE.
STRONG REVIEWS FOR ORIGINALITY. WHOEVER HAD THAT IDEA WAS SMART AS HELL.
WHAT GOOD IS BEING LIKE THIS IF YOU CAN'T DO SOMETHING NEW WITH IT? SPEAKING OF WHICH...
SHE'S A GOD AND SHE'S MODEST.

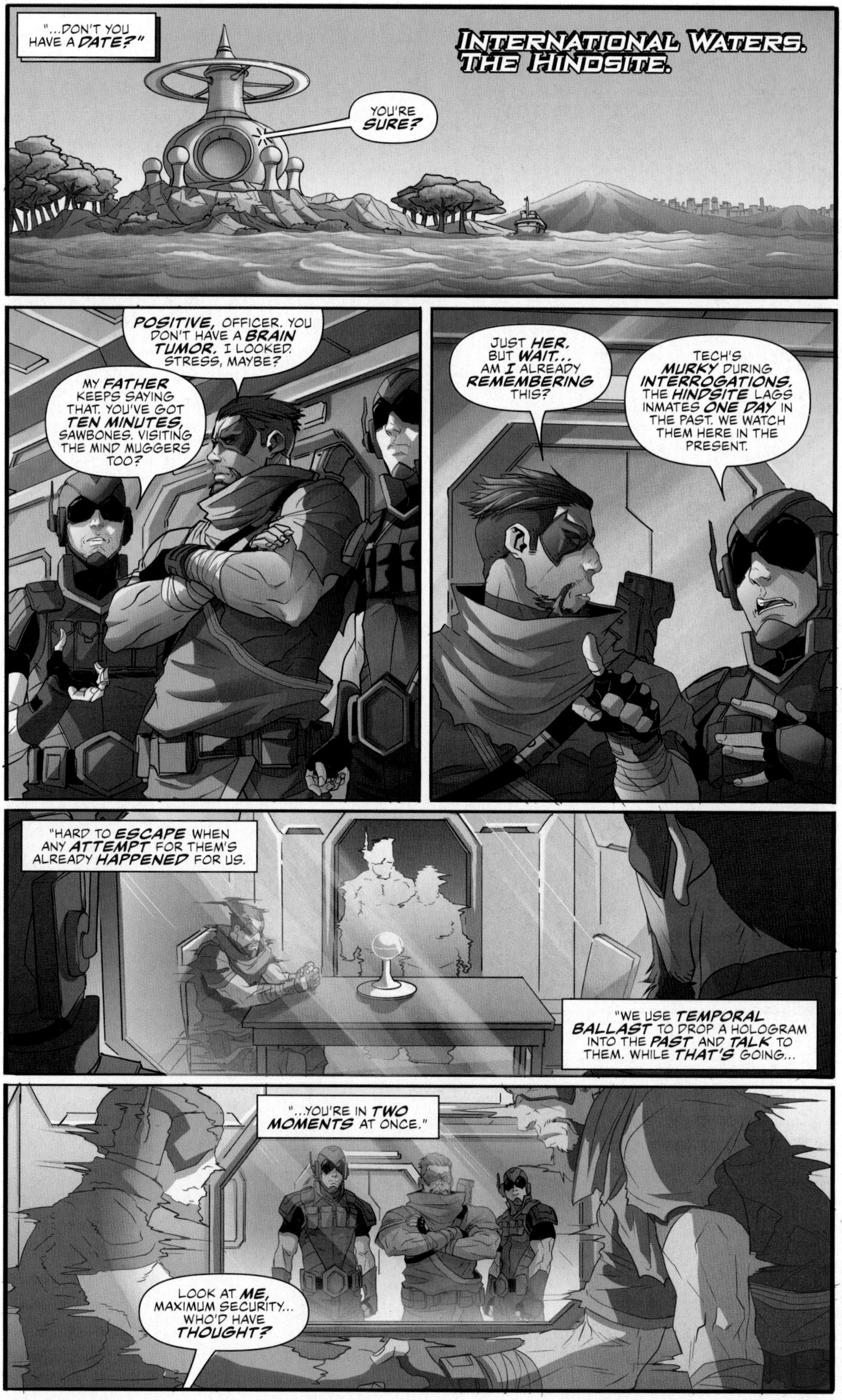
"...DON'T YOU HAVE A DATE?"
INTERNATIONAL WATERS. THE HINDSITE.
YOU'RE SURE?
POSITIVE, OFFICER. YOU DON'T HAVE A BRAIN TUMOR. I LOOKED. STRESS, MAYBE?
MY FATHER KEEPS SAYING THAT. YOU'VE GOT TEN MINUTES, SAWBONES. VISITING THE MIND MUGGERS TOO?
JUST HER. BUT WAIT... AM I ALREADY REMEMBERING THIS?
TECH'S MURKY DURING INTERROGATIONS. THE HINDSITE LAGS INMATES ONE DAY IN THE PAST. WE WATCH THEM HERE IN THE PRESENT.
"HARD TO ESCAPE WHEN ANY ATTEMPT FOR THEM'S ALREADY HAPPENED FOR US.
"WE USE TEMPORAL BALLAST TO DROP A HOLOGRAM INTO THE PAST AND TALK TO THEM. WHILE THAT'S GOING...
"...YOU'RE IN TWO MOMENTS AT ONCE."
LOOK AT ME, MAXIMUM SECURITY... WHO'D HAVE THOUGHT?

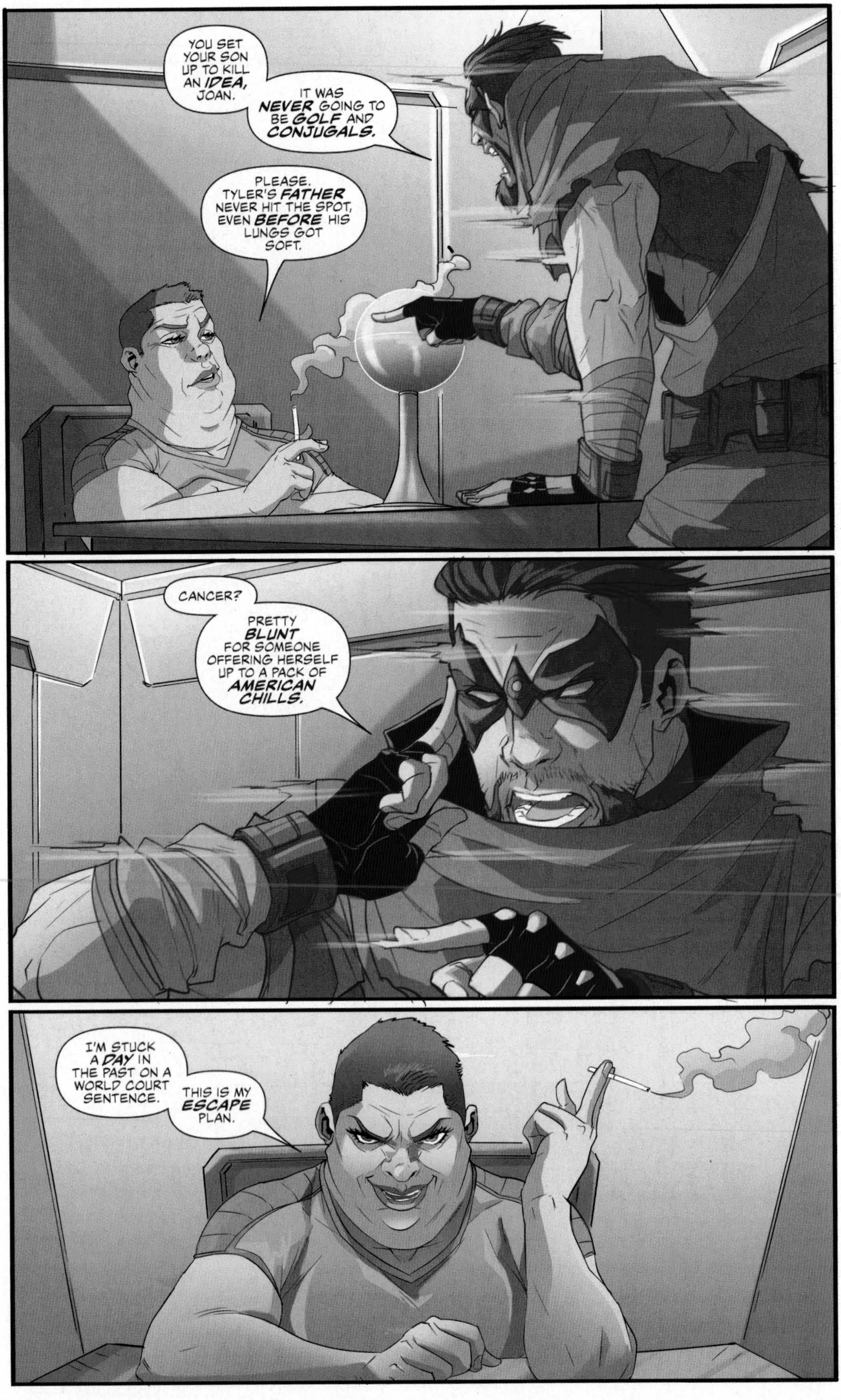
YOU SET YOUR SON UP TO KILL AN IDEA, JOAN.
IT WAS NEVER GOING TO BE GOLF AND CONJUGALS.
PLEASE. TYLER'S FATHER NEVER HIT THE SPOT, EVEN BEFORE HIS LUNGS GOT SOFT.
CANCER?
PRETTY BLUNT FOR SOMEONE OFFERING HERSELF UP TO A PACK OF AMERICAN CHILLS.
I'M STUCK A DAY IN THE PAST ON A WORLD COURT SENTENCE.
THIS IS MY ESCAPE PLAN.

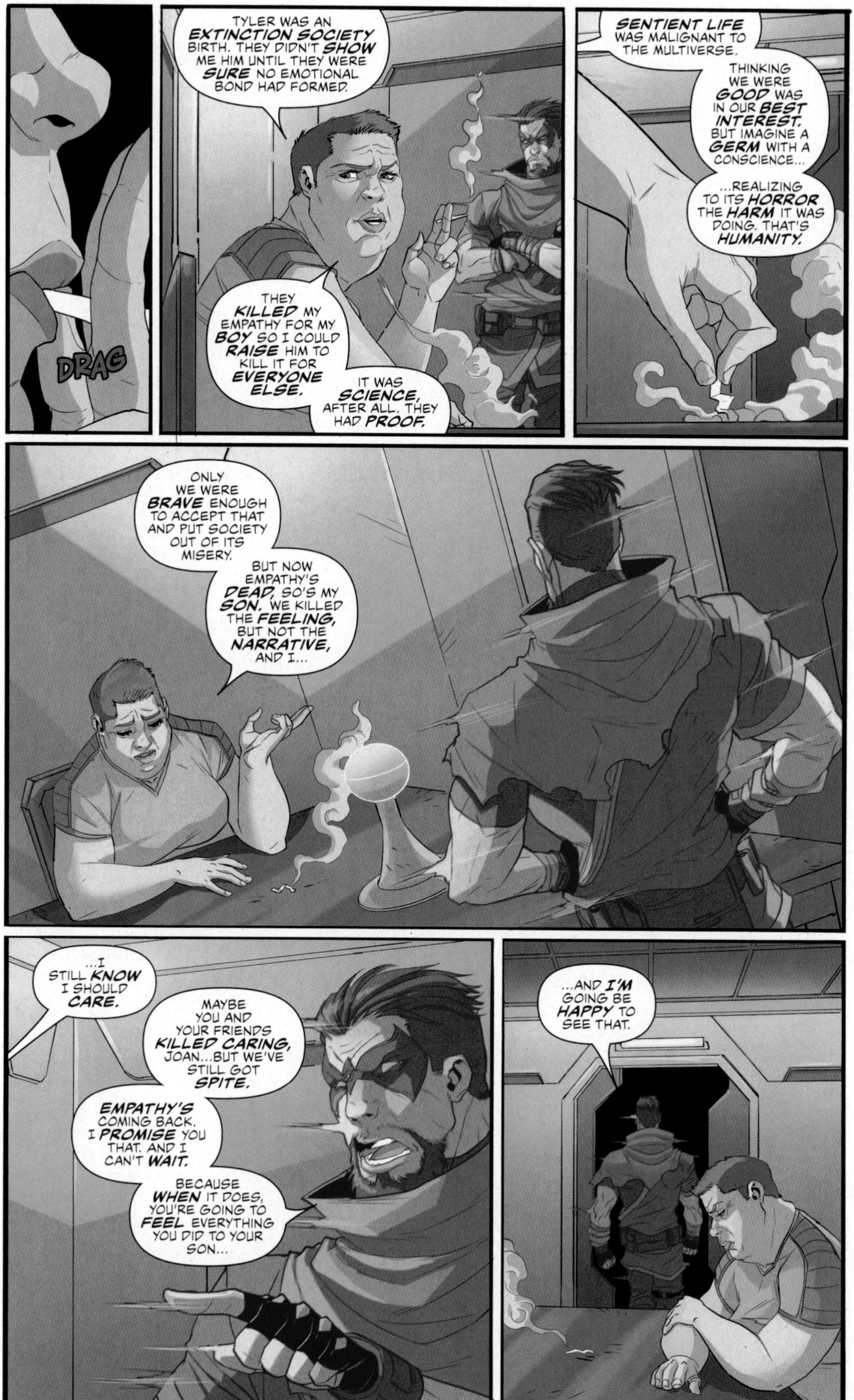
DRAG
TYLER WAS AN EXTINCTION SOCIETY BIRTH. THEY DIDN'T SHOW ME HIM UNTIL THEY WERE SURE NO EMOTIONAL BOND HAD FORMED.
THEY KILLED MY EMPATHY FOR MY BOY SO I COULD RAISE HIM TO KILL IT FOR EVERYONE ELSE.
IT WAS SCIENCE, AFTER ALL. THEY HAD PROOF.
SENTIENT LIFE WAS MALIGNANT TO THE MULTIVERSE.
THINKING WE WERE GOOD WAS IN OUR BEST INTEREST. BUT IMAGINE A GERM WITH A CONSCIENCE...
...REALIZING TO ITS HORROR THE HARM IT WAS DOING. THAT'S HUMANITY.
ONLY WE WERE BRAVE ENOUGH TO ACCEPT THAT AND PUT SOCIETY OUT OF ITS MISERY.
BUT NOW EMPATHY'S DEAD, SO'S MY SON. WE KILLED THE FEELING, BUT NOT THE NARRATIVE, AND I...
...I STILL KNOW I SHOULD CARE.
MAYBE YOU AND YOUR FRIENDS KILLED CARING, JOAN...BUT WE'VE STILL GOT SPITE.
EMPATHY'S COMING BACK. I PROMISE YOU THAT. AND I CAN'T WAIT.
BECAUSE WHEN IT DOES, YOU'RE GOING TO FEEL EVERYTHING YOU DID TO YOUR SON...
...AND I'M GOING BE HAPPY TO SEE THAT.

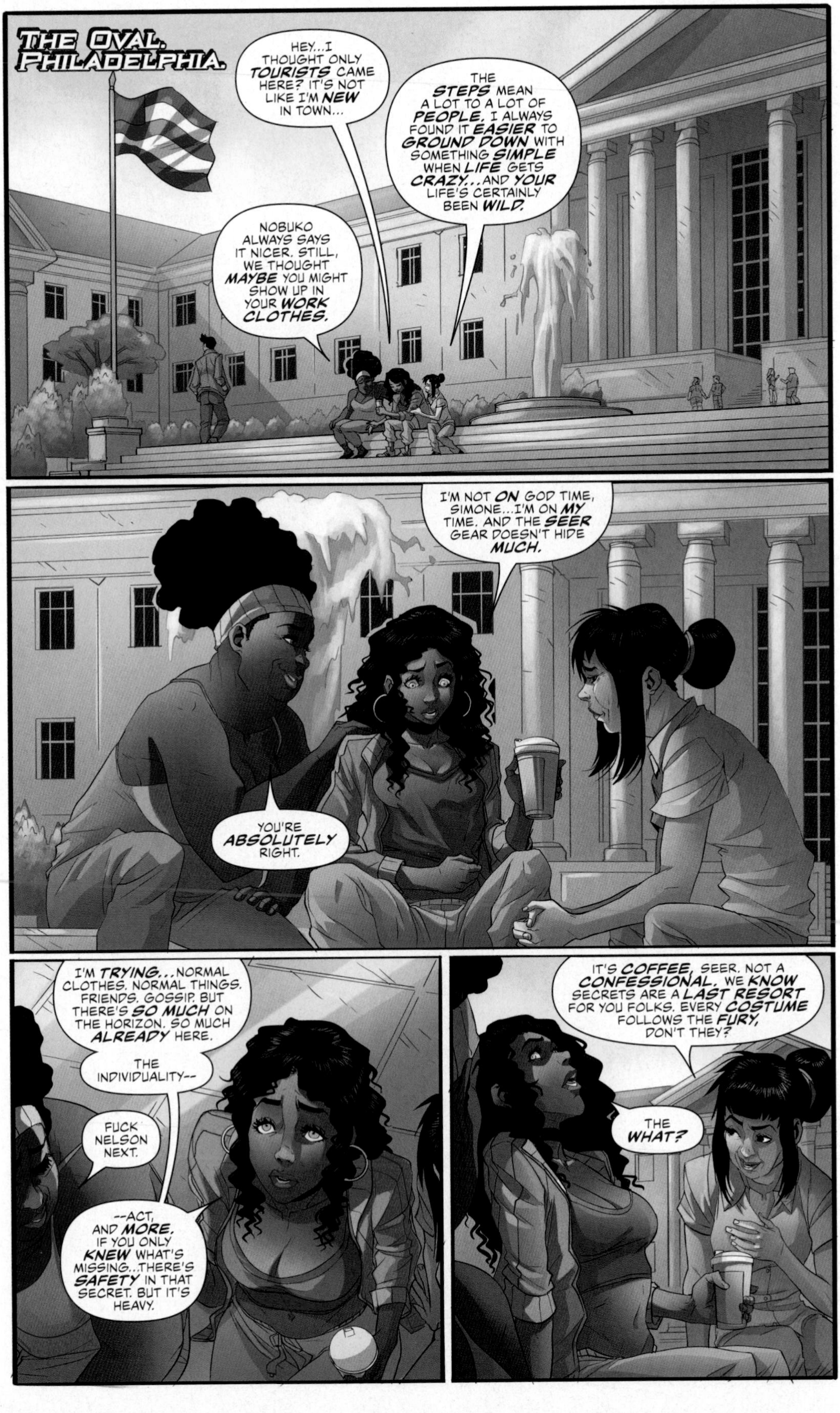
THE OVAL. PHILADELPHIA.
HEY...I THOUGHT ONLY TOURISTS CAME HERE? IT'S NOT LIKE I'M NEW IN TOWN...
NOBUKO ALWAYS SAYS IT NICER. STILL, WE THOUGHT MAYBE YOU MIGHT SHOW UP IN YOUR WORK CLOTHES.
THE STEPS MEAN A LOT TO A LOT OF PEOPLE. I ALWAYS FOUND IT EASIER TO GROUND DOWN WITH SOMETHING SIMPLE WHEN LIFE GETS CRAZY...AND YOUR LIFE'S CERTAINLY BEEN WILD.
I'M NOT ON GOD TIME, SIMONE...I'M ON MY TIME. AND THE SEER GEAR DOESN'T HIDE MUCH.
YOU'RE ABSOLUTELY RIGHT.
I'M TRYING... NORMAL CLOTHES. NORMAL THINGS. FRIENDS. GOSSIP. BUT THERE'S SO MUCH ON THE HORIZON. SO MUCH ALREADY HERE.
THE INDIVIDUALITY--
FUCK NELSON NEXT.
--ACT, AND MORE. IF YOU ONLY KNEW WHAT'S MISSING...THERE'S SAFETY IN THAT SECRET. BUT IT'S HEAVY.
IT'S COFFEE, SEER. NOT A CONFESSIONAL. WE KNOW SECRETS ARE A LAST RESORT FOR YOU FOLKS. EVERY COSTUME FOLLOWS THE FURY, DON'T THEY?
THE WHAT?

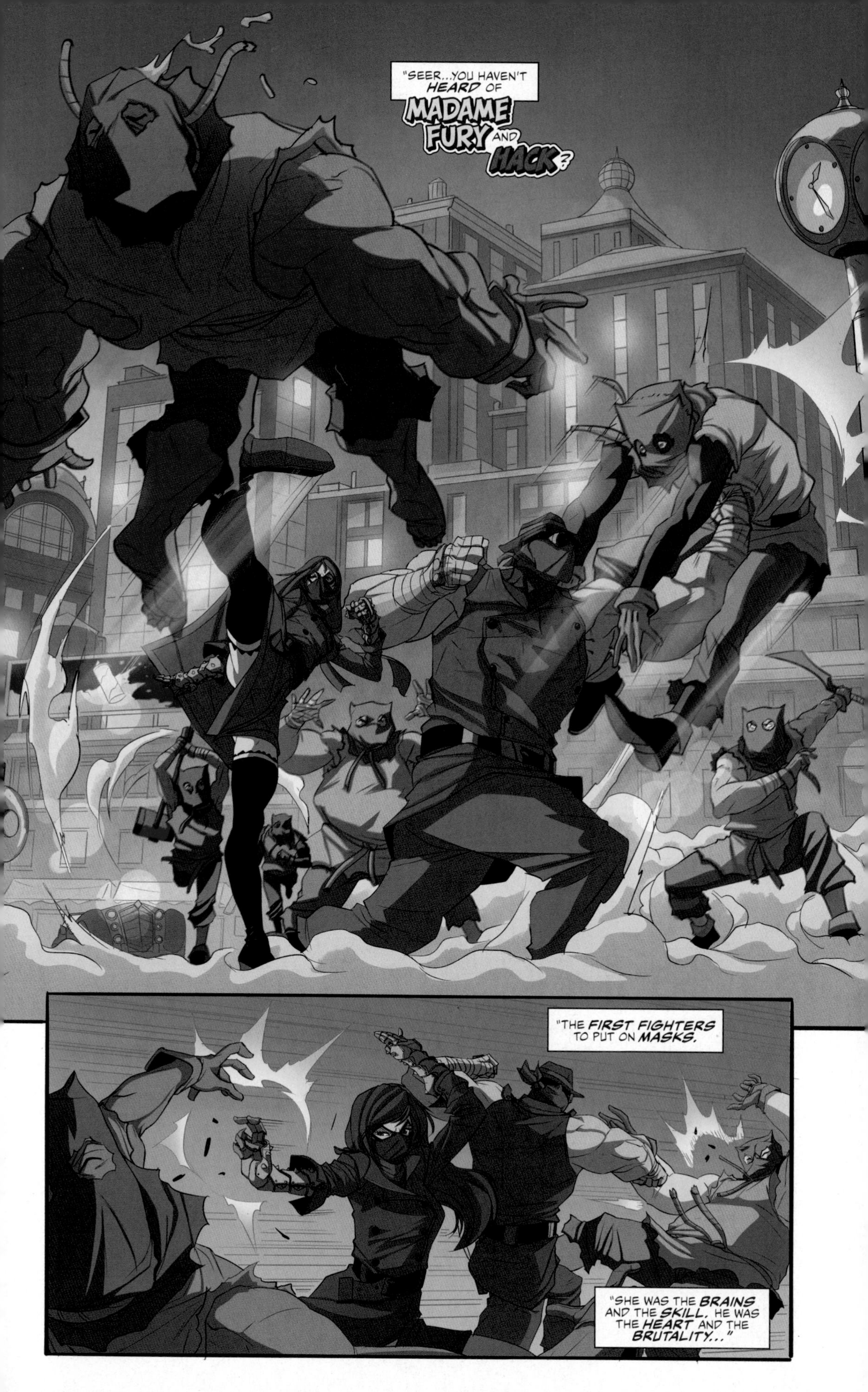
"SEER...YOU HAVEN'T HEARD OF MADAME FURY AND HACK?
"THE FIRST FIGHTERS TO PUT ON MASKS.
"SHE WAS THE BRAINS AND THE SKILL. HE WAS THE HEART AND THE BRUTALITY..."

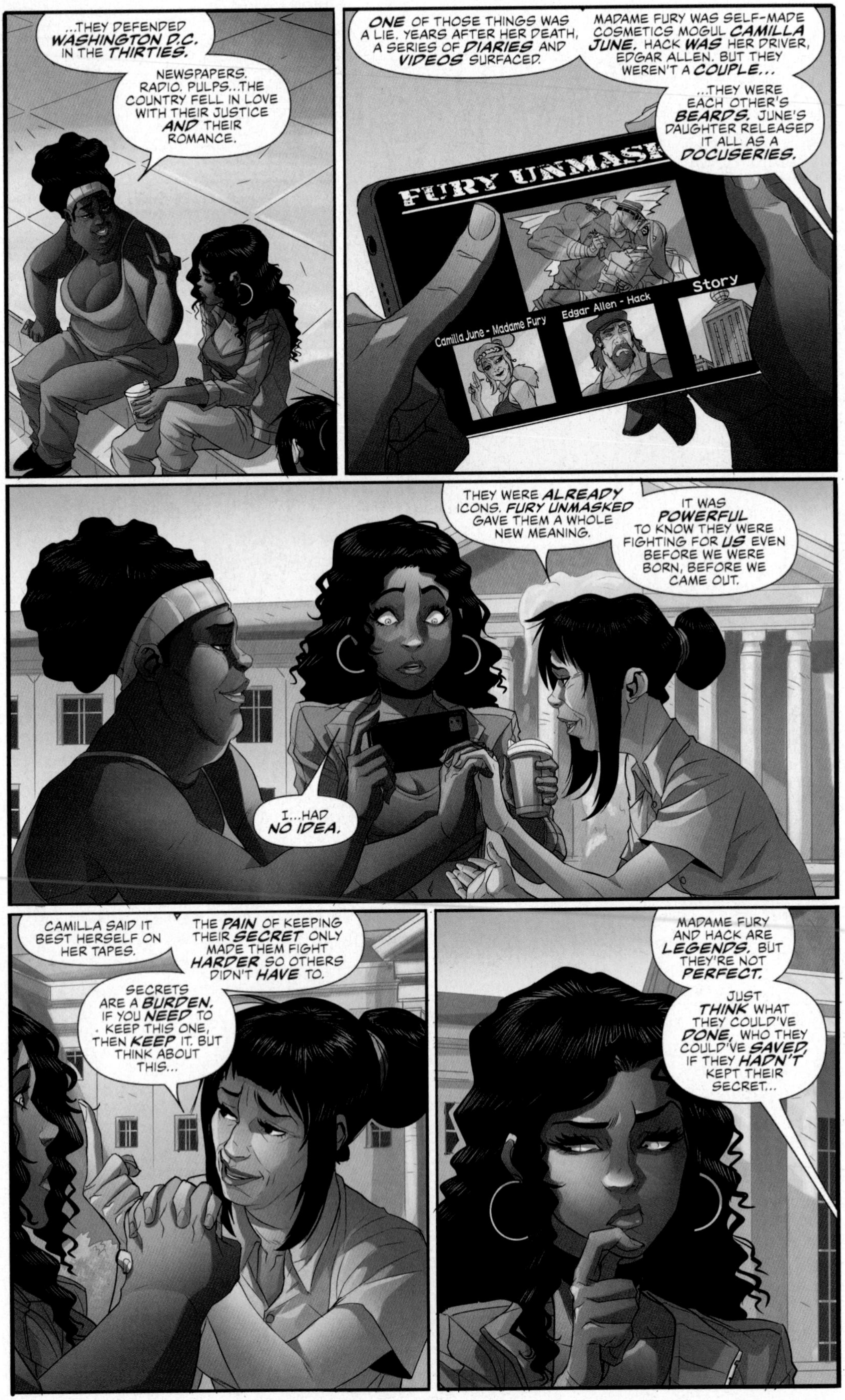
...THEY DEFENDED WASHINGTON D.C. IN THE THIRTIES.
NEWSPAPERS. RADIO. PULPS...THE COUNTRY FELL IN LOVE WITH THEIR JUSTICE AND THEIR ROMANCE.
ONE OF THOSE THINGS WAS A LIE. YEARS AFTER HER DEATH, A SERIES OF DIARIES AND VIDEOS SURFACED.
MADAME FURY WAS SELF-MADE COSMETICS MOGUL CAMILLA JUNE. HACK WAS HER DRIVER, EDGAR ALLEN. BUT THEY WEREN'T A COUPLE...
...THEY WERE EACH OTHER'S BEARDS. JUNE'S DAUGHTER RELEASED IT ALL AS A DOCUSERIES.
FURY UNMASK
Camilla June - Madame Fury
Edgar Allen - Hack
Story
THEY WERE ALREADY ICONS. FURY UNMASKED GAVE THEM A WHOLE NEW MEANING.
IT WAS POWERFUL TO KNOW THEY WERE FIGHTING FOR US EVEN BEFORE WE WERE BORN, BEFORE WE CAME OUT.
I...HAD NO IDEA.
CAMILLA SAID IT BEST HERSELF ON HER TAPES.
THE PAIN OF KEEPING THEIR SECRET ONLY MADE THEM FIGHT HARDER SO OTHERS DIDN'T HAVE TO.
SECRETS ARE A BURDEN. IF YOU NEED TO KEEP THIS ONE, THEN KEEP IT. BUT THINK ABOUT THIS...
MADAME FURY AND HACK ARE LEGENDS. BUT THEY'RE NOT PERFECT.
JUST THINK WHAT THEY COULD'VE DONE, WHO THEY COULD'VE SAVED, IF THEY HADN'T KEPT THEIR SECRET...

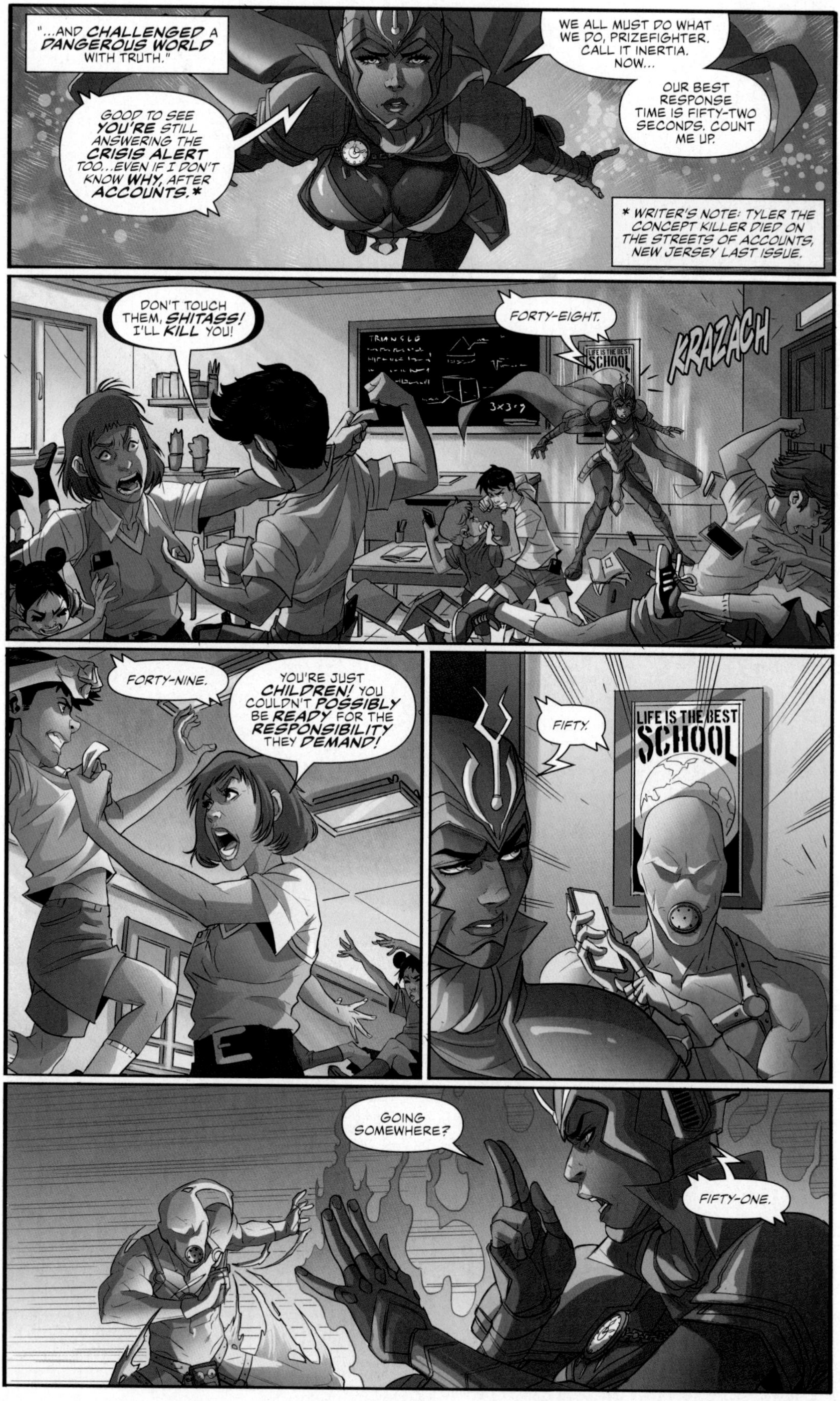
"...AND CHALLENGED A DANGEROUS WORLD WITH TRUTH."
GOOD TO SEE YOU'RE STILL ANSWERING THE CRISIS ALERT TOO...EVEN IF I DON'T KNOW WHY, AFTER ACCOUNTS.*
WE ALL MUST DO WHAT WE DO, PRIZEFIGHTER. CALL IT INERTIA. NOW...
OUR BEST RESPONSE TIME IS FIFTY-TWO SECONDS. COUNT ME UP.
* WRITER'S NOTE: TYLER THE CONCEPT KILLER DIED ON THE STREETS OF ACCOUNTS, NEW JERSEY LAST ISSUE.
DON'T TOUCH THEM, SHITASS! I'LL KILL YOU!
FORTY-EIGHT.
LIFE IS THE BEST SCHOOL
KRAZACH
TRIANGLE
3×3=9
FORTY-NINE.
YOU'RE JUST CHILDREN! YOU COULDN'T POSSIBLY BE READY FOR THE RESPONSIBILITY THEY DEMAND!
FIFTY.
LIFE IS THE BEST SCHOOL
GOING SOMEWHERE?
FIFTY-ONE.

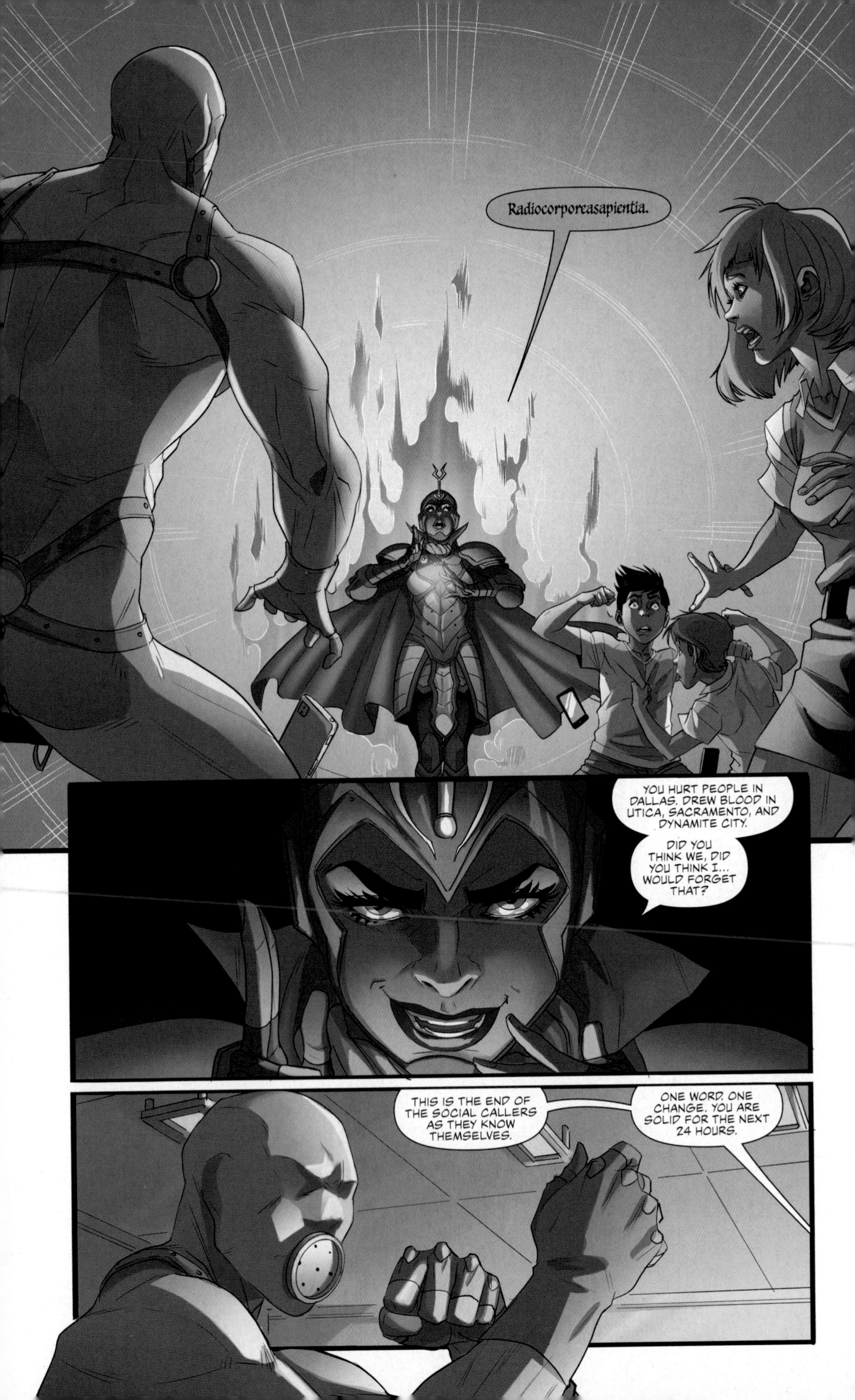
Radiocorporeasapientia.
YOU HURT PEOPLE IN DALLAS. DREW BLOOD IN UTICA, SACRAMENTO, AND DYNAMITE CITY.
DID YOU THINK WE, DID YOU THINK I... WOULD FORGET THAT?
THIS IS THE END OF THE SOCIAL CALLERS AS THEY KNOW THEMSELVES.
ONE WORD. ONE CHANGE. YOU ARE SOLID FOR THE NEXT 24 HOURS.

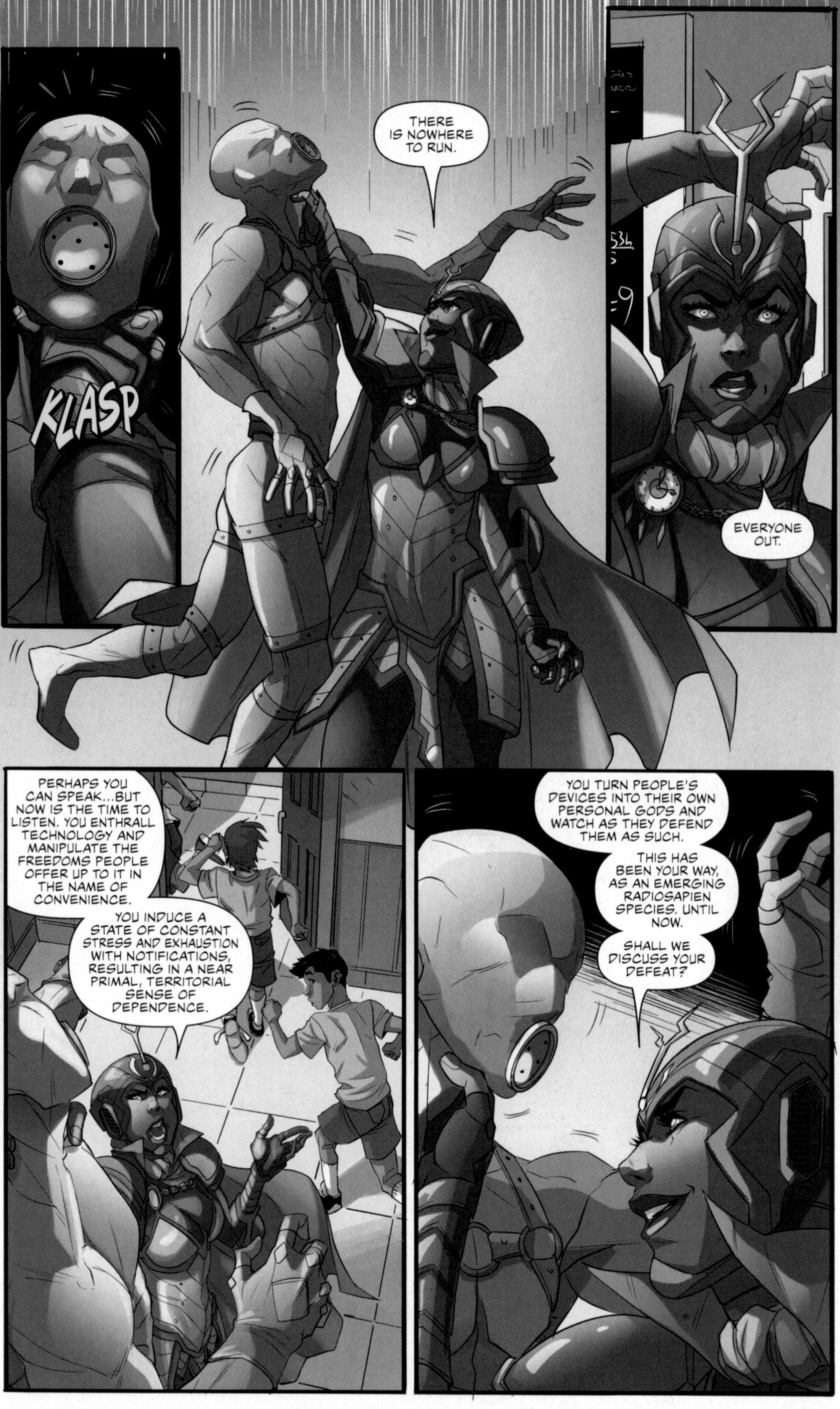

KLASP
THERE IS NOWHERE TO RUN.
EVERYONE OUT.
PERHAPS YOU CAN SPEAK...BUT NOW IS THE TIME TO LISTEN. YOU ENTHRALL TECHNOLOGY AND MANIPULATE THE FREEDOMS PEOPLE OFFER UP TO IT IN THE NAME OF CONVENIENCE.
YOU INDUCE A STATE OF CONSTANT STRESS AND EXHAUSTION WITH NOTIFICATIONS, RESULTING IN A NEAR PRIMAL, TERRITORIAL SENSE OF DEPENDENCE.
YOU TURN PEOPLE'S DEVICES INTO THEIR OWN PERSONAL GODS AND WATCH AS THEY DEFEND THEM AS SUCH.
THIS HAS BEEN YOUR WAY, AS AN EMERGING RADIOSAPIEN SPECIES. UNTIL NOW.
SHALL WE DISCUSS YOUR DEFEAT?

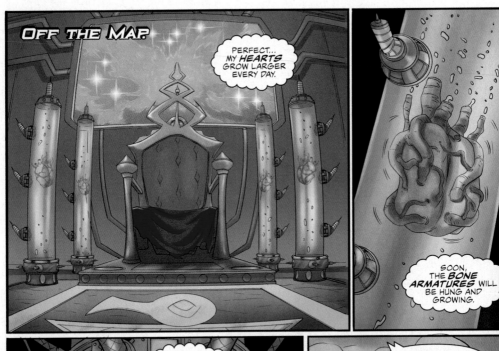

OFF THE MAP.

PERFECT... MY **HEARTS** GROW LARGER EVERY DAY.

SOON, THE **BONE ARMATURES** WILL BE HUNG AND GROWING.

MY **DOUBLE**, THAT **FOOL** FRONTIER, STILL RESISTS THE **TRUTH.**

ONLY **THIS** WORLD COULD **EVER** ACCEPT **SENTIENT** LIFE WAS A **TOXIC** MISTAKE.

DELIBERATIONS CONTINUE AS SENATOR ADELE TRACY LEADS THE OPPOSITION TO THE AMERICAN INDIVIDUALITY ACT.

WE **NUDGE** HUMANITY ON TO ITS **WELL-DESERVED** SEPTIC DEATH.

I TOLD FRONTIER EARTH-Z WAS THE WORLD WHERE EVIL **WINS.** THE **TRUTH** IS...

...IT'S JUST THE **ONLY** WORLD NOT **LYING** TO ITSELF.

ACTIVATE BREACH CHAMBER.

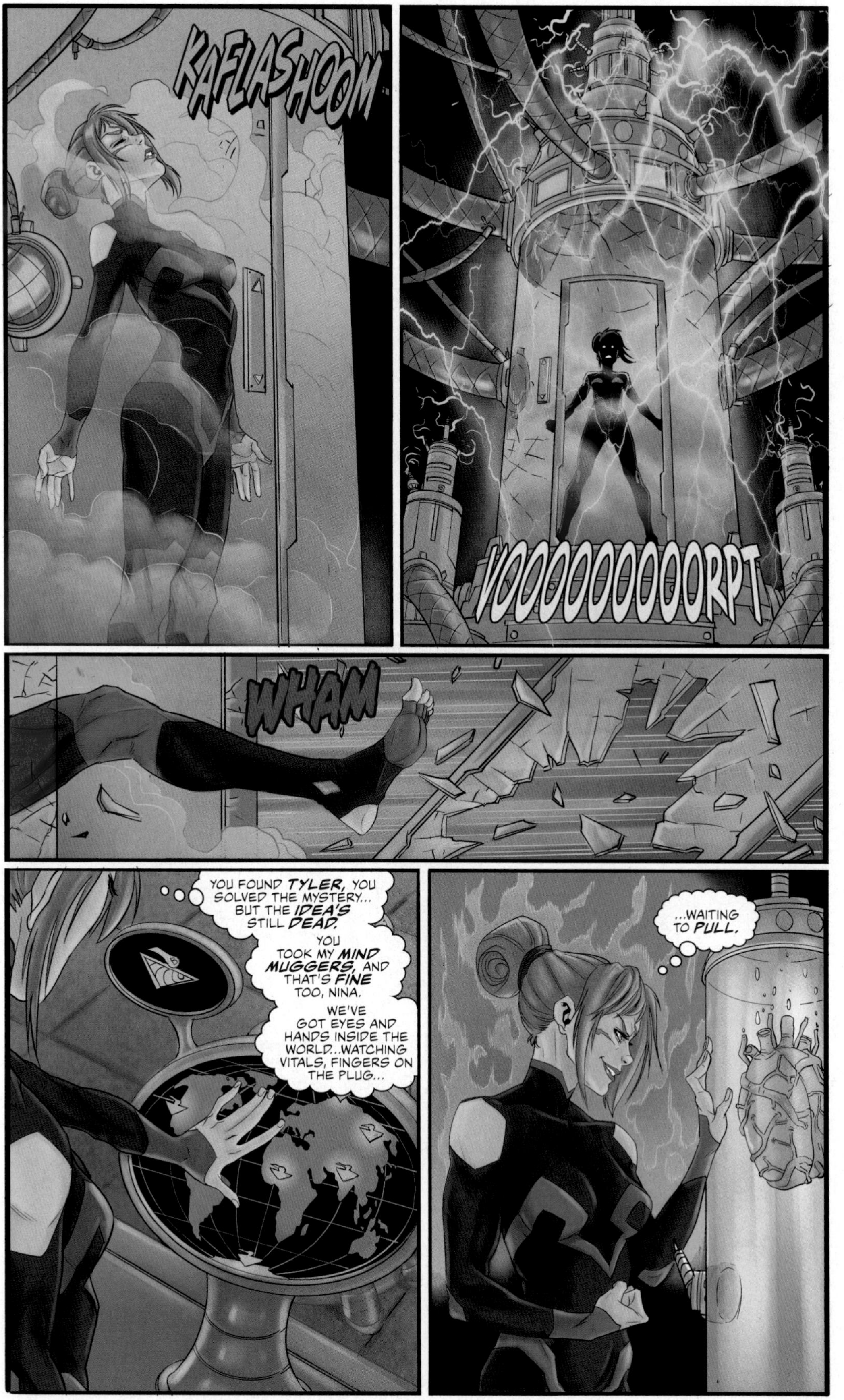
KAFLASHOOM
VOOOOOOOOORPT
WHAM
YOU FOUND TYLER, YOU SOLVED THE MYSTERY... BUT THE IDEA'S STILL DEAD.
YOU TOOK MY MIND MUGGERS, AND THAT'S FINE TOO, NINA.
WE'VE GOT EYES AND HANDS INSIDE THE WORLD...WATCHING VITALS, FINGERS ON THE PLUG...
...WAITING TO PULL.

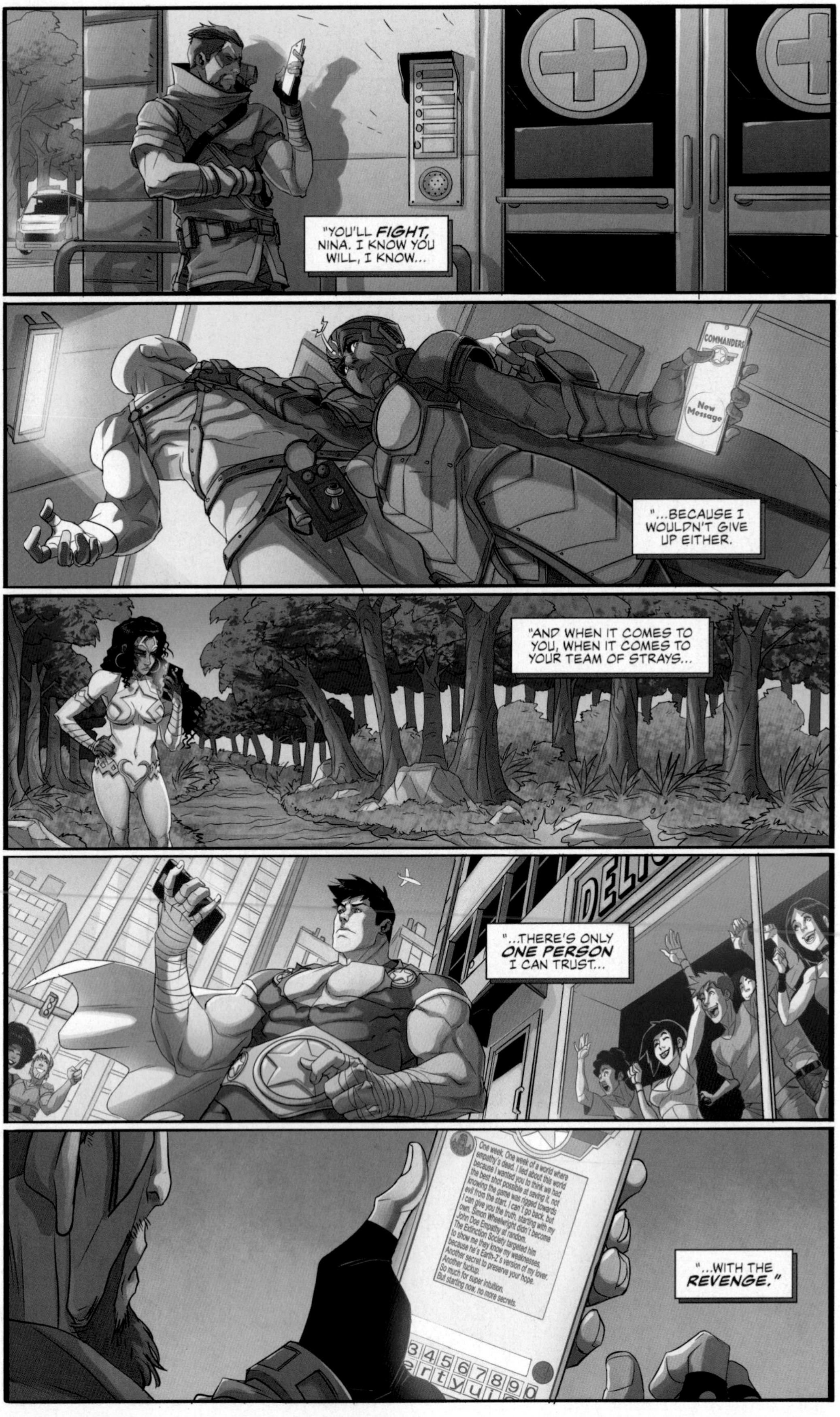
"YOU'LL **FIGHT,** NINA. I KNOW YOU WILL, I KNOW...
COMMANDERS
New Message
"...BECAUSE I WOULDN'T GIVE UP EITHER.
"AND WHEN IT COMES TO YOU, WHEN IT COMES TO YOUR TEAM OF STRAYS...
"...THERE'S ONLY **ONE PERSON** I CAN TRUST...
One week. One week of a world where empathy's dead. I lied about this world because I wanted you to think we had the best shot possible at saving it, not knowing the game was rigged towards evil from the start. I can't go back, but I can give you the truth, starting with my own. Simon Wheelwright didn't become John Doe Empathy at random. The Extinction Society targeted him to show me they know my weaknesses, because he's Earth-Z's version of my lover. Another secret to preserve your hope. Another fuckup. So much for super intuition. But starting now, no more secrets.
"...WITH THE **REVENGE.**"

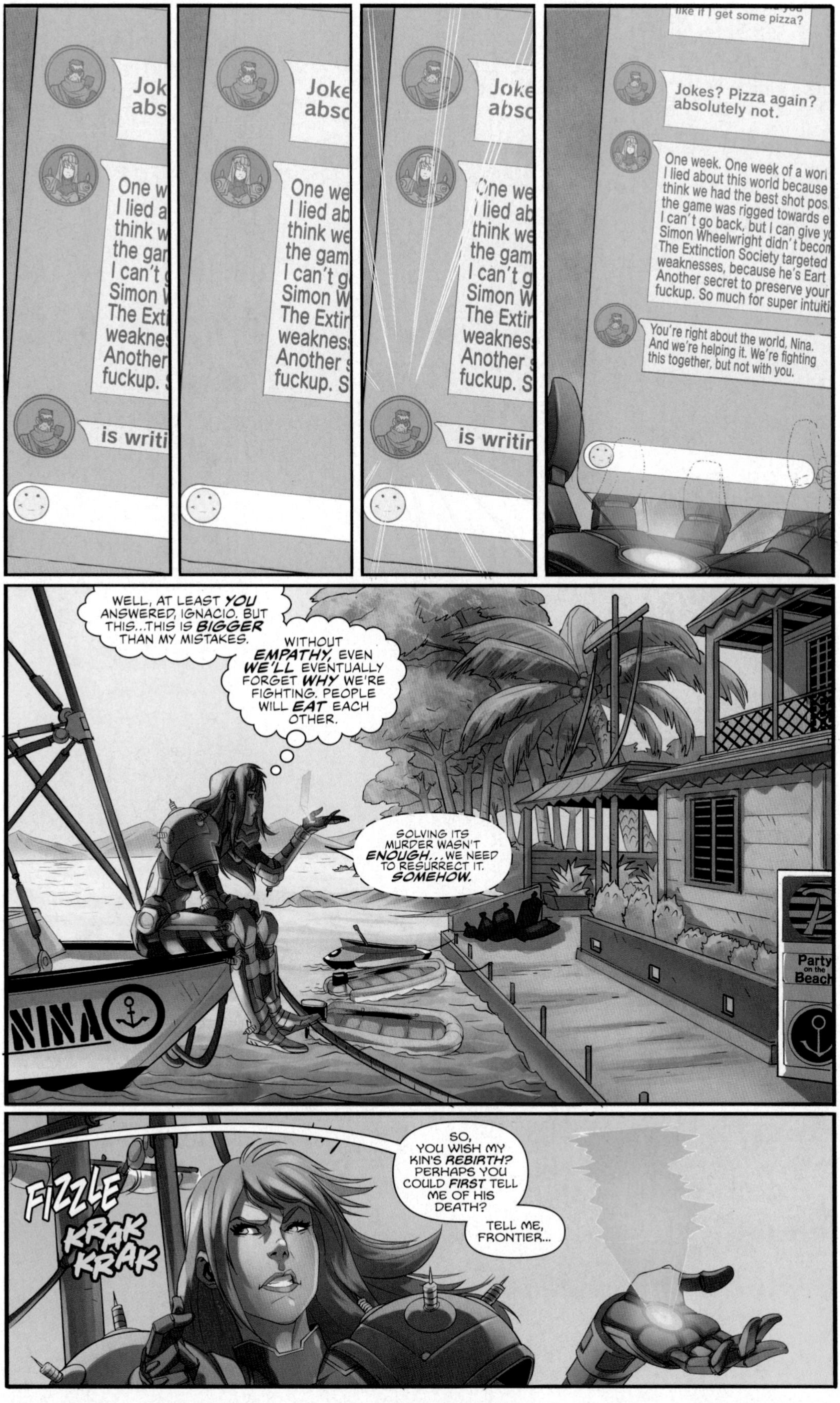
Jokes? Pizza again? absolutely not.
One week. One week of a worl I lied about this world because think we had the best shot pos the game was rigged towards e I can't go back, but I can give yo Simon Wheelwright didn't becom The Extinction Society targeted weaknesses, because he's Eart Another secret to preserve your fuckup. So much for super intuiti
You're right about the world, Nina. And we're helping it. We're fighting this together, but not with you.
WELL, AT LEAST YOU ANSWERED, IGNACIO. BUT THIS...THIS IS BIGGER THAN MY MISTAKES.
WITHOUT EMPATHY, EVEN WE'LL EVENTUALLY FORGET WHY WE'RE FIGHTING. PEOPLE WILL EAT EACH OTHER.
SOLVING ITS MURDER WASN'T ENOUGH...WE NEED TO RESURRECT IT. SOMEHOW.
NINA
Party on the Beach
FIZZLE
KRAK KRAK
SO, YOU WISH MY KIN'S REBIRTH? PERHAPS YOU COULD FIRST TELL ME OF HIS DEATH?
TELL ME, FRONTIER...

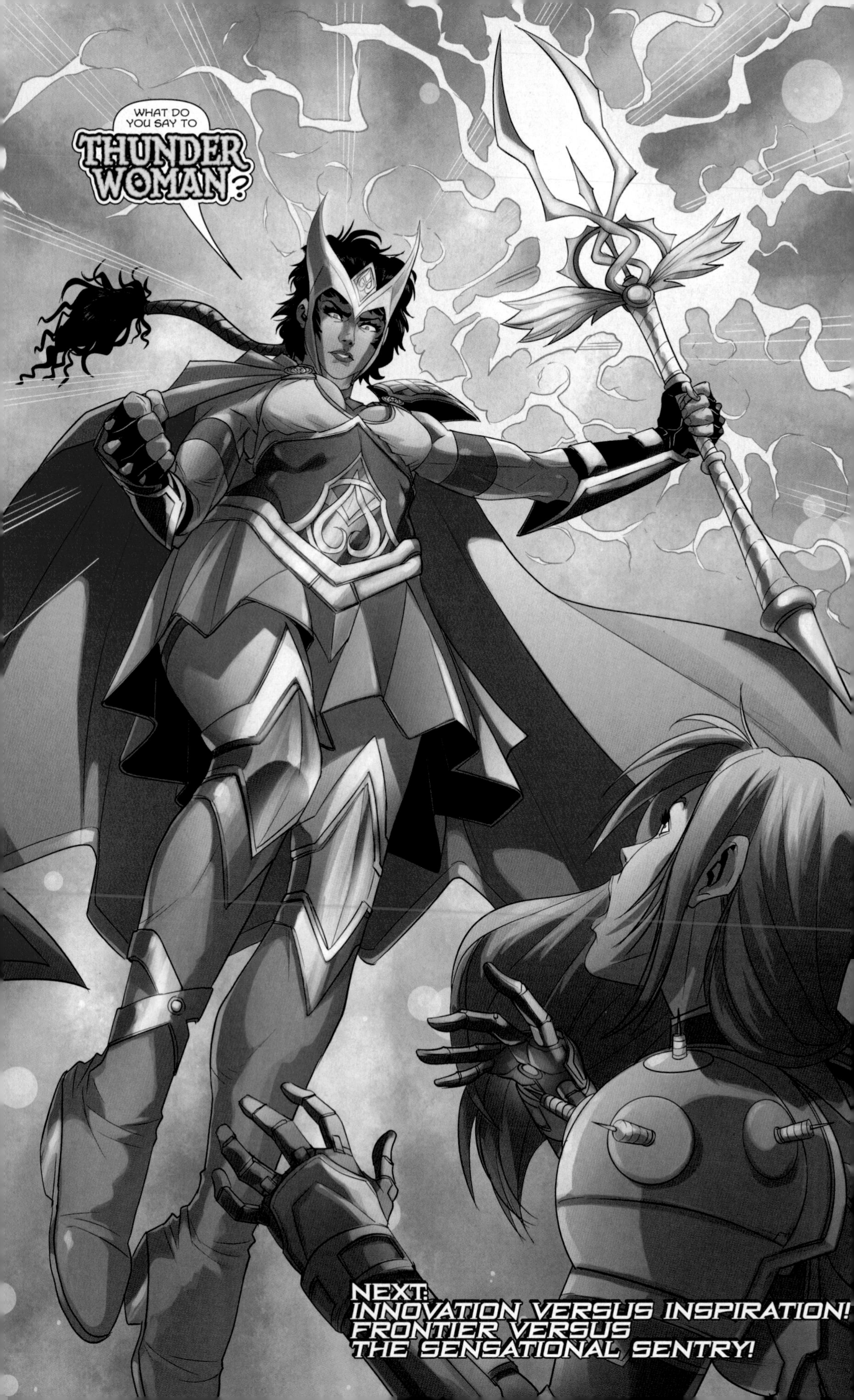

WHAT DO YOU SAY TO THUNDER WOMAN?
NEXT: INNOVATION VERSUS INSPIRATION! FRONTIER VERSUS THE SENSATIONAL SENTRY!

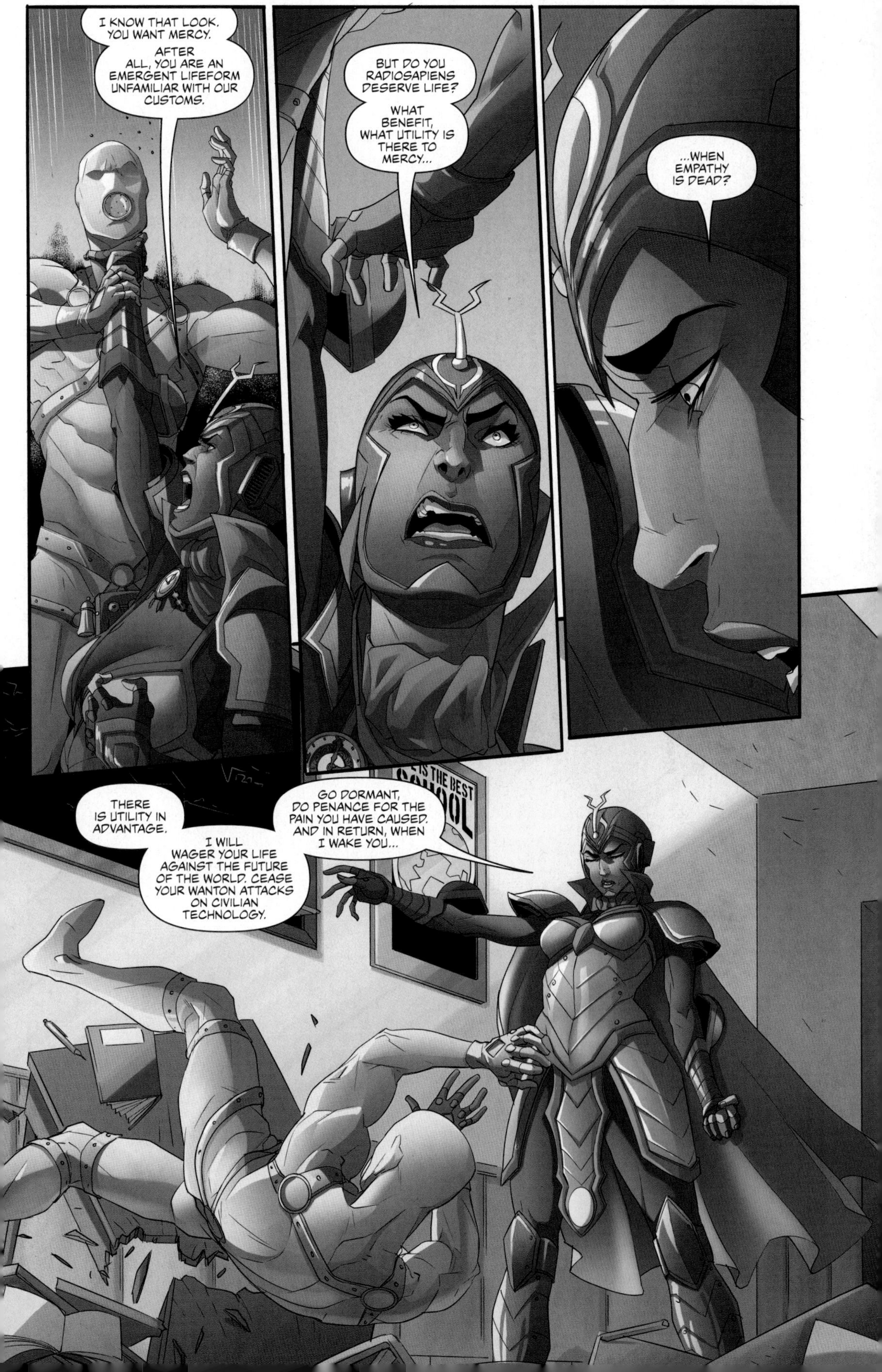
I KNOW THAT LOOK. YOU WANT MERCY.
AFTER ALL, YOU ARE AN EMERGENT LIFEFORM UNFAMILIAR WITH OUR CUSTOMS.
BUT DO YOU RADIOSAPIENS DESERVE LIFE?
WHAT BENEFIT, WHAT UTILITY IS THERE TO MERCY...
...WHEN EMPATHY IS DEAD?
THERE IS UTILITY IN ADVANTAGE.
I WILL WAGER YOUR LIFE AGAINST THE FUTURE OF THE WORLD. CEASE YOUR WANTON ATTACKS ON CIVILIAN TECHNOLOGY.
GO DORMANT, DO PENANCE FOR THE PAIN YOU HAVE CAUSED. AND IN RETURN, WHEN I WAKE YOU...

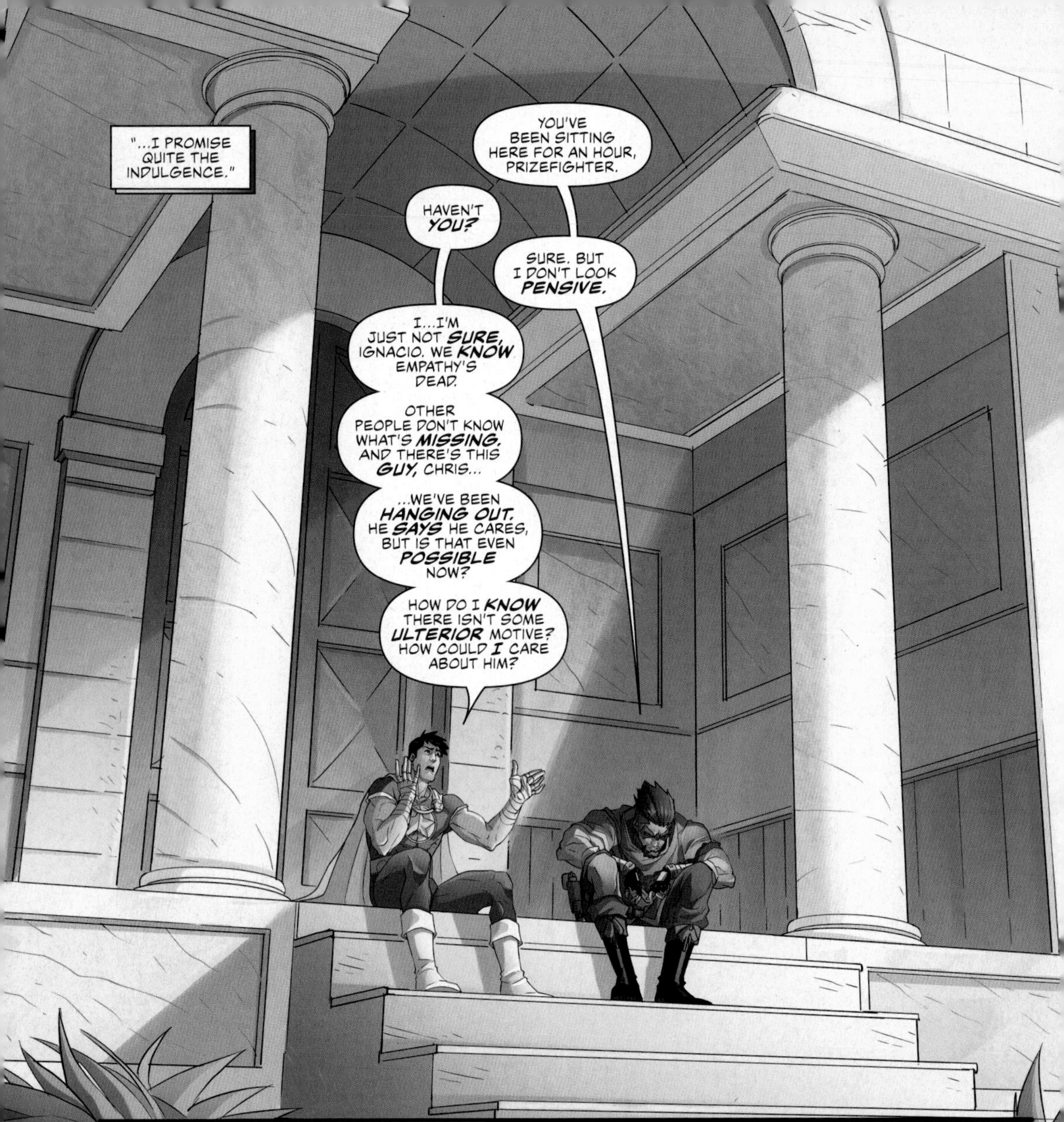
"...I PROMISE QUITE THE INDULGENCE."
YOU'VE BEEN SITTING HERE FOR AN HOUR, PRIZEFIGHTER.
HAVEN'T *YOU?*
SURE. BUT I DON'T LOOK *PENSIVE.*
I...I'M JUST NOT *SURE,* IGNACIO. WE *KNOW* EMPATHY'S DEAD.
OTHER PEOPLE DON'T KNOW WHAT'S *MISSING,* AND THERE'S THIS *GUY,* CHRIS...
...WE'VE BEEN *HANGING OUT.* HE *SAYS* HE CARES, BUT IS THAT EVEN *POSSIBLE* NOW?
HOW DO I *KNOW* THERE ISN'T SOME *ULTERIOR* MOTIVE? HOW COULD *I* CARE ABOUT HIM?

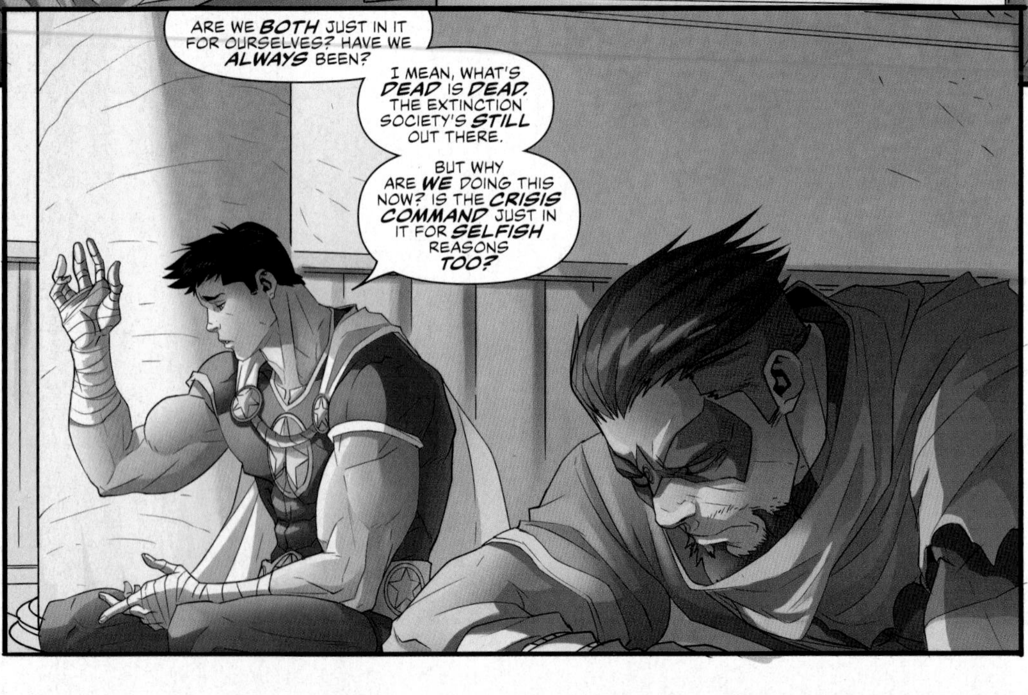
ARE WE *BOTH* JUST IN IT FOR OURSELVES? HAVE WE *ALWAYS* BEEN?
I MEAN, WHAT'S *DEAD* IS *DEAD.* THE EXTINCTION SOCIETY'S *STILL* OUT THERE.
BUT WHY ARE *WE* DOING THIS NOW? IS THE *CRISIS COMMAND* JUST IN IT FOR *SELFISH* REASONS *TOO?*

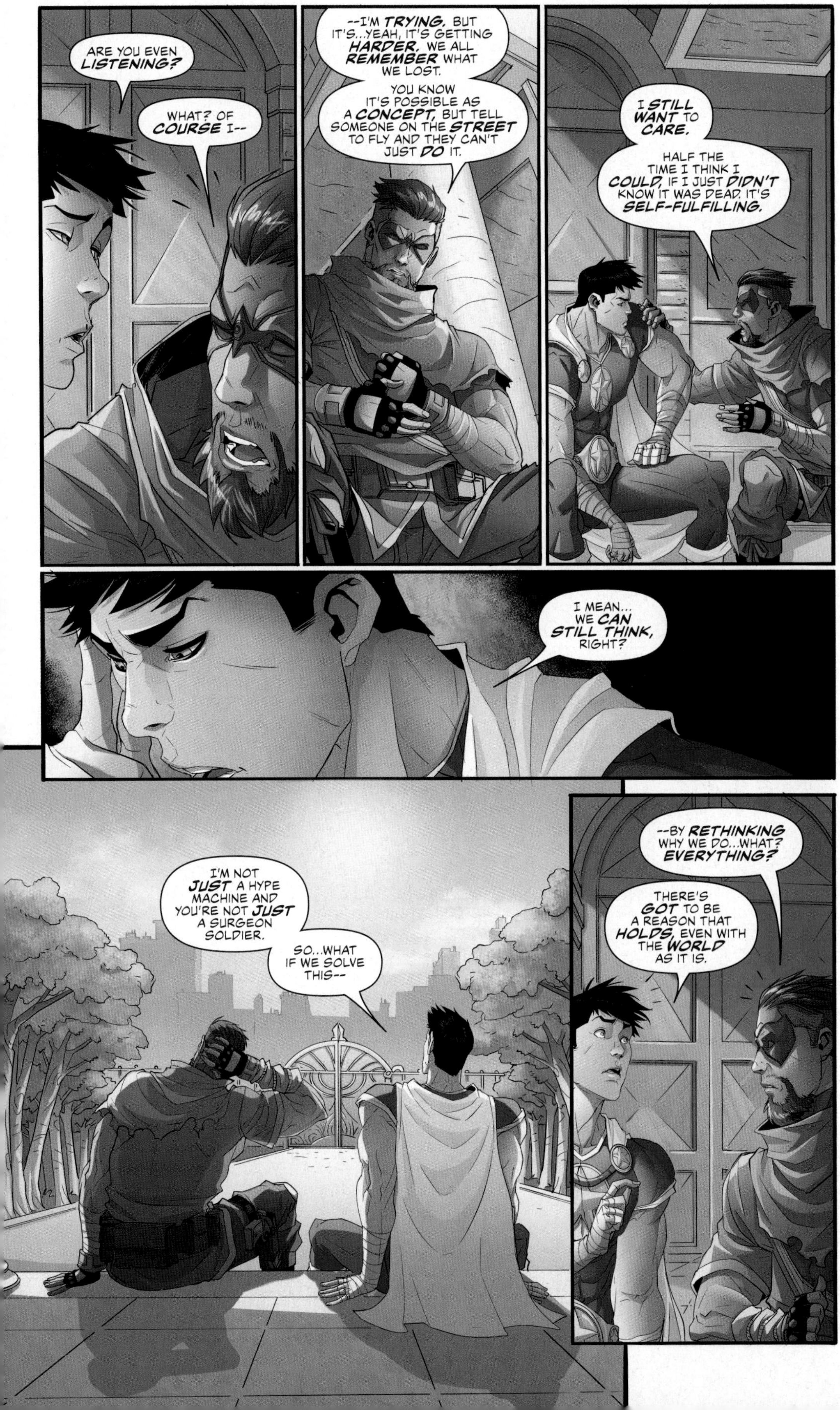
ARE YOU EVEN LISTENING?
WHAT? OF COURSE I--
--I'M TRYING, BUT IT'S...YEAH, IT'S GETTING HARDER. WE ALL REMEMBER WHAT WE LOST.
YOU KNOW IT'S POSSIBLE AS A CONCEPT, BUT TELL SOMEONE ON THE STREET TO FLY AND THEY CAN'T JUST DO IT.
I STILL WANT TO CARE.
HALF THE TIME I THINK I COULD, IF I JUST DIDN'T KNOW IT WAS DEAD. IT'S SELF-FULFILLING.
I MEAN... WE CAN STILL THINK, RIGHT?
I'M NOT JUST A HYPE MACHINE AND YOU'RE NOT JUST A SURGEON SOLDIER.
SO...WHAT IF WE SOLVE THIS--
--BY RETHINKING WHY WE DO...WHAT? EVERYTHING?
THERE'S GOT TO BE A REASON THAT HOLDS, EVEN WITH THE WORLD AS IT IS.

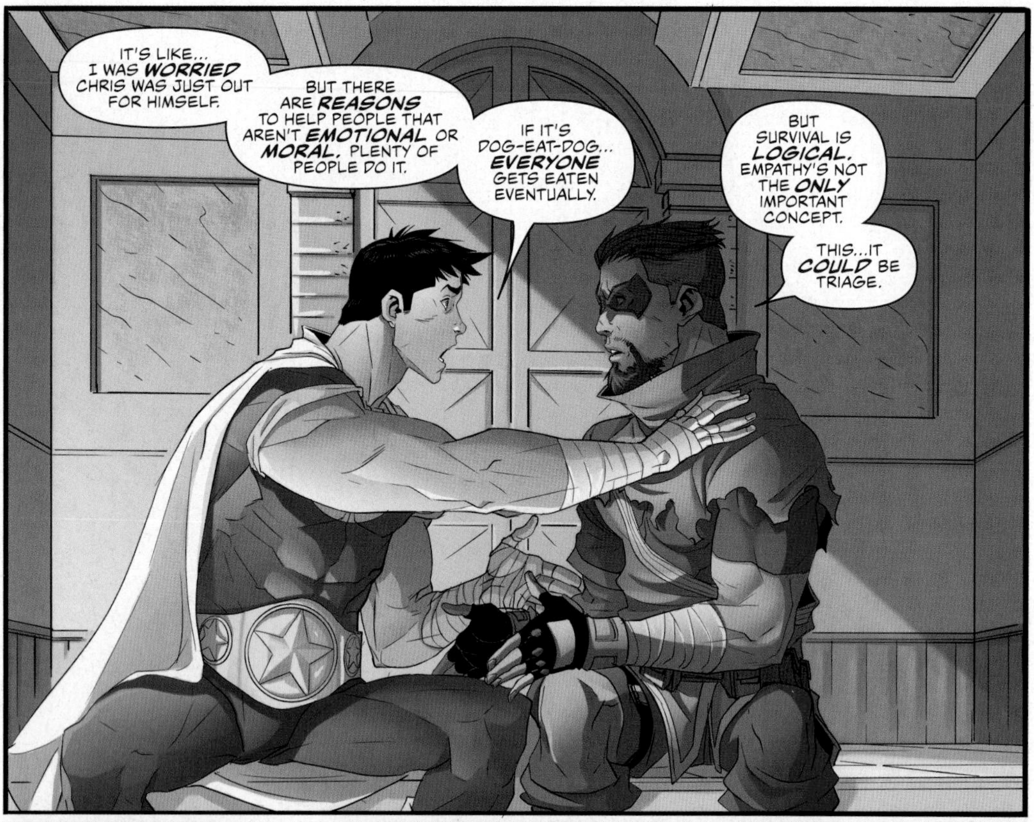
IT'S LIKE... I WAS WORRIED CHRIS WAS JUST OUT FOR HIMSELF.
BUT THERE ARE REASONS TO HELP PEOPLE THAT AREN'T EMOTIONAL OR MORAL. PLENTY OF PEOPLE DO IT.
IF IT'S DOG-EAT-DOG... EVERYONE GETS EATEN EVENTUALLY.
BUT SURVIVAL IS LOGICAL. EMPATHY'S NOT THE ONLY IMPORTANT CONCEPT.
THIS...IT COULD BE TRIAGE.
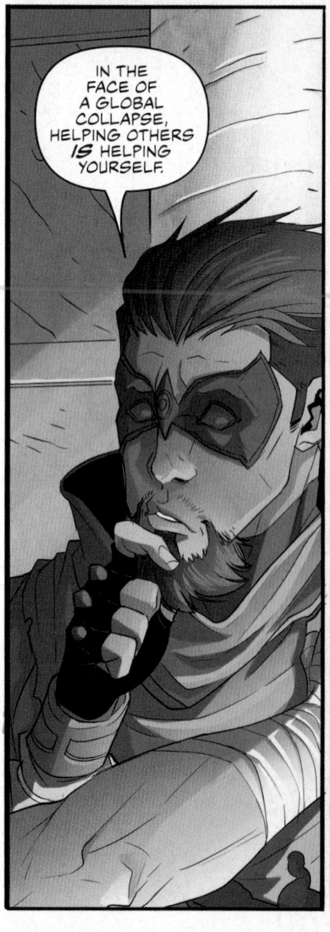
IN THE FACE OF A GLOBAL COLLAPSE, HELPING OTHERS IS HELPING YOURSELF.
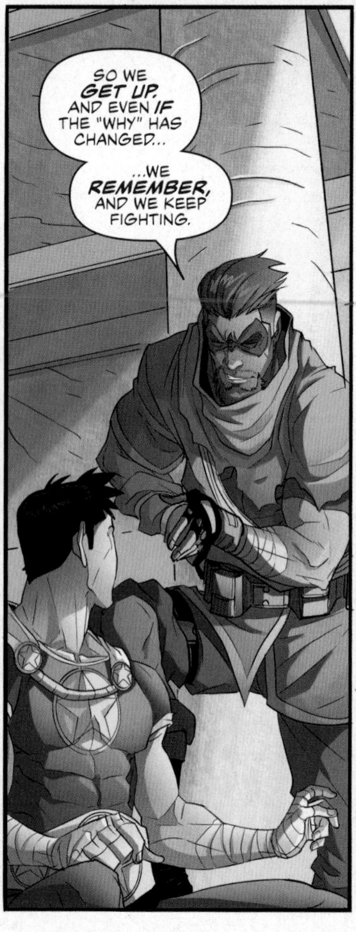
SO WE GET UP, AND EVEN IF THE "WHY" HAS CHANGED...
...WE REMEMBER, AND WE KEEP FIGHTING.
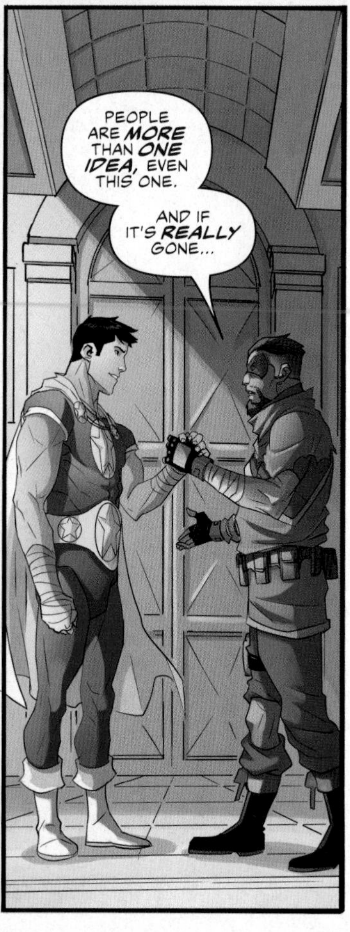
PEOPLE ARE MORE THAN ONE IDEA, EVEN THIS ONE.
AND IF IT'S REALLY GONE...

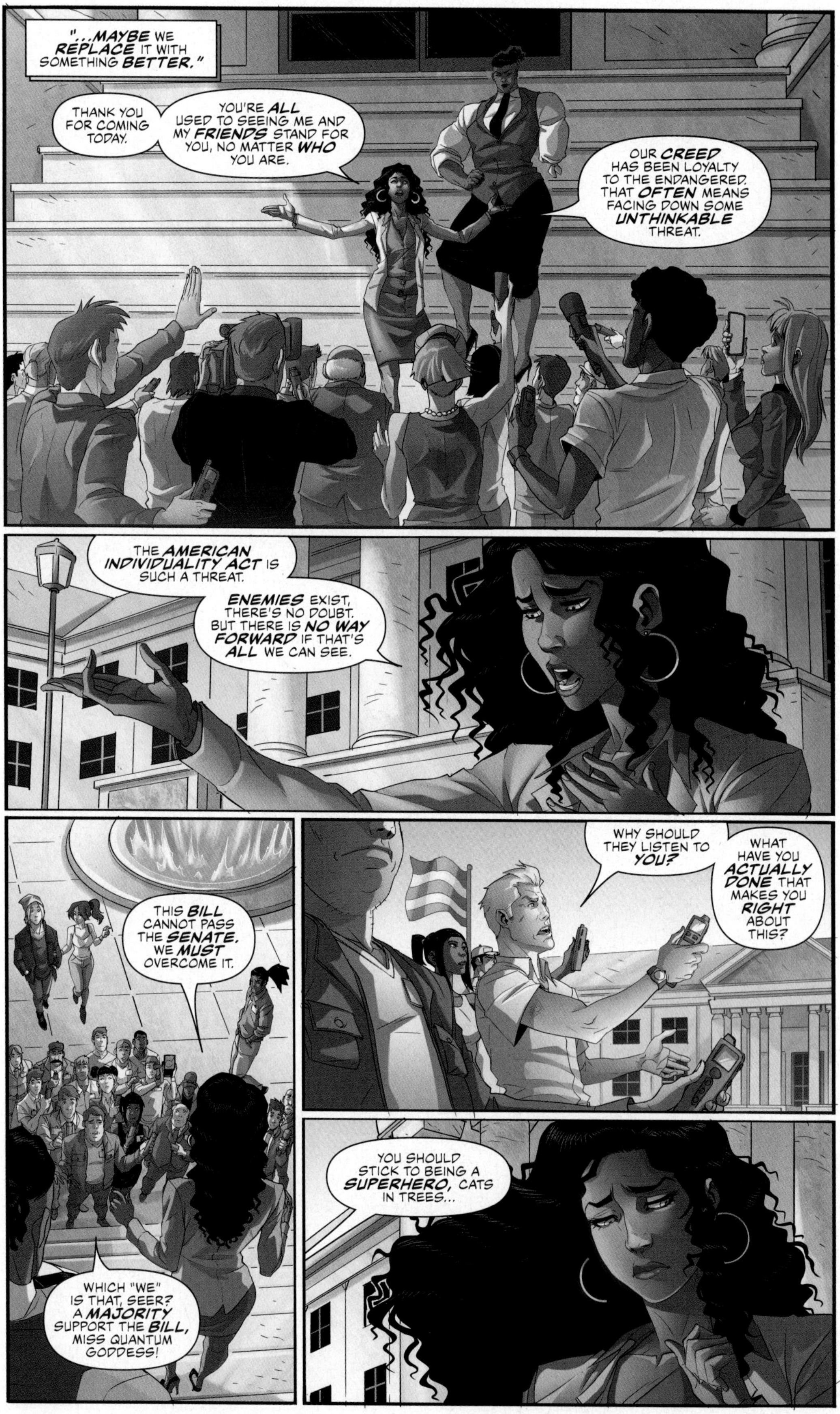
"...MAYBE WE REPLACE IT WITH SOMETHING BETTER."
THANK YOU FOR COMING TODAY.
YOU'RE ALL USED TO SEEING ME AND MY FRIENDS STAND FOR YOU, NO MATTER WHO YOU ARE.
OUR CREED HAS BEEN LOYALTY TO THE ENDANGERED. THAT OFTEN MEANS FACING DOWN SOME UNTHINKABLE THREAT.
THE AMERICAN INDIVIDUALITY ACT IS SUCH A THREAT.
ENEMIES EXIST, THERE'S NO DOUBT. BUT THERE IS NO WAY FORWARD IF THAT'S ALL WE CAN SEE.
THIS BILL CANNOT PASS THE SENATE. WE MUST OVERCOME IT.
WHICH "WE" IS THAT, SEER? A MAJORITY SUPPORT THE BILL, MISS QUANTUM GODDESS!
WHY SHOULD THEY LISTEN TO YOU?
WHAT HAVE YOU ACTUALLY DONE THAT MAKES YOU RIGHT ABOUT THIS?
YOU SHOULD STICK TO BEING A SUPERHERO, CATS IN TREES...

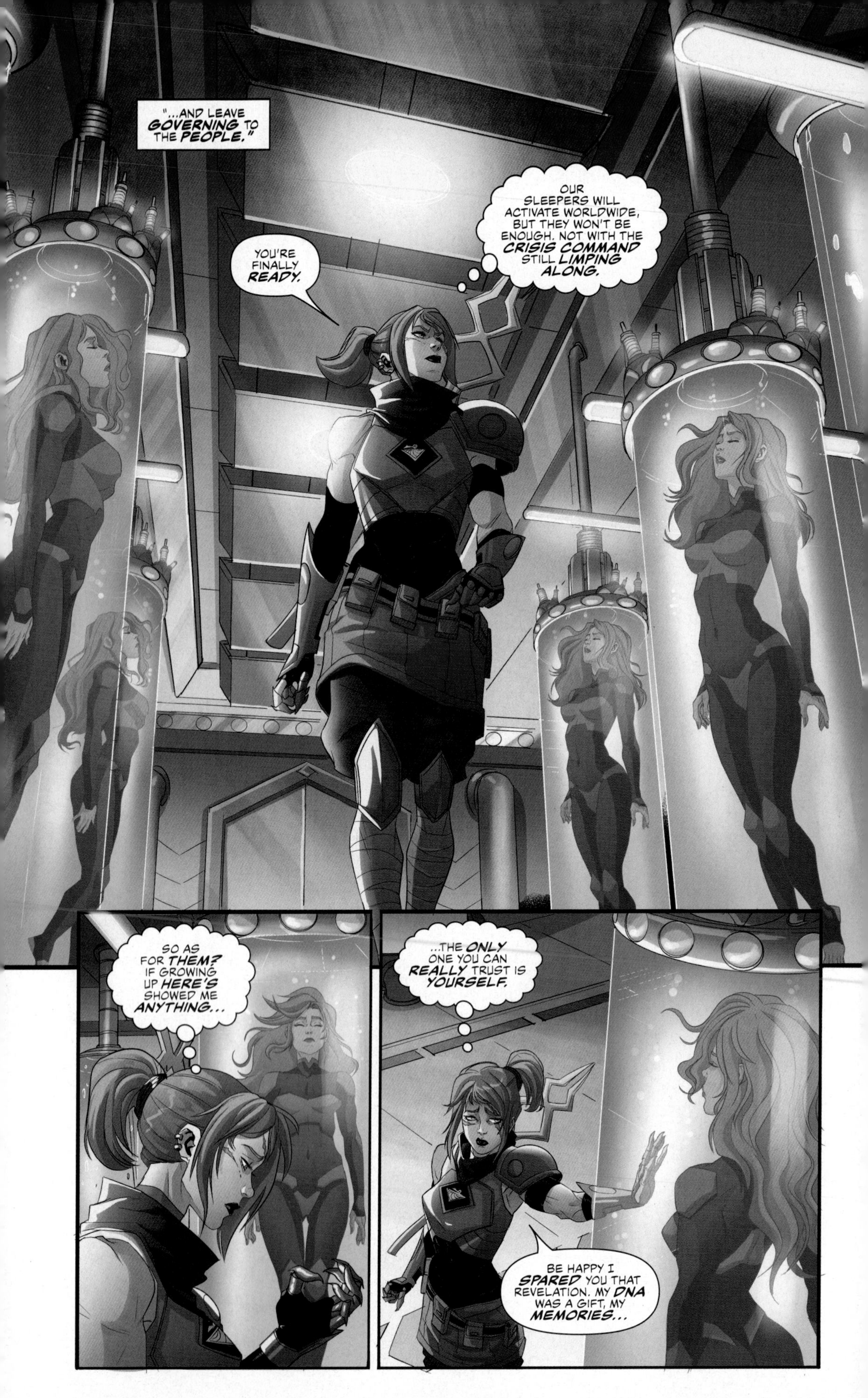

"...AND LEAVE GOVERNING TO THE PEOPLE."
YOU'RE FINALLY READY.
OUR SLEEPERS WILL ACTIVATE WORLDWIDE, BUT THEY WON'T BE ENOUGH. NOT WITH THE CRISIS COMMAND STILL LIMPING ALONG.
SO AS FOR THEM? IF GROWING UP HERE'S SHOWED ME ANYTHING...
...THE ONLY ONE YOU CAN REALLY TRUST IS YOURSELF.
BE HAPPY I SPARED YOU THAT REVELATION. MY DNA WAS A GIFT, MY MEMORIES...

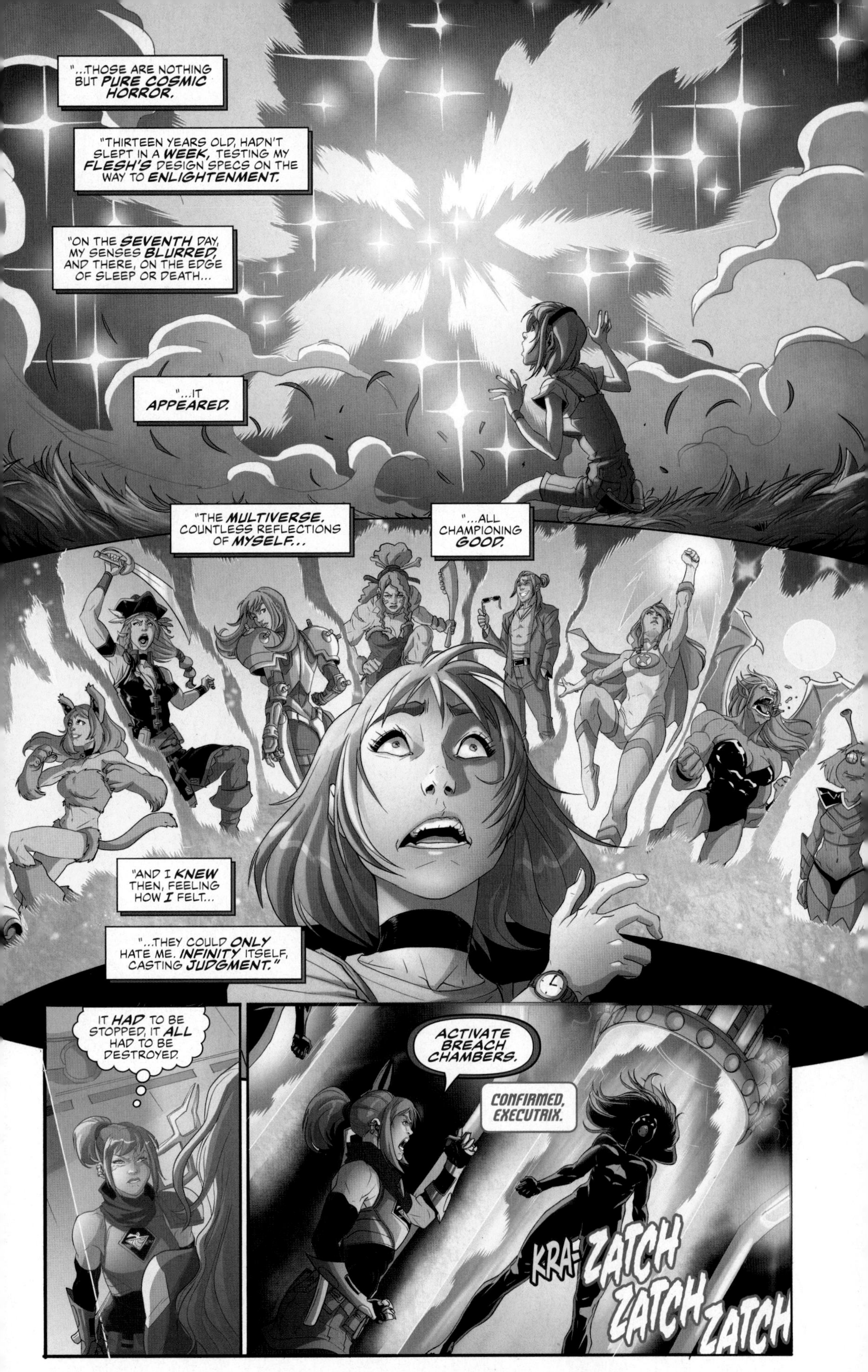
"...THOSE ARE NOTHING BUT PURE COSMIC HORROR.
"THIRTEEN YEARS OLD, HADN'T SLEPT IN A WEEK, TESTING MY FLESH'S DESIGN SPECS ON THE WAY TO ENLIGHTENMENT.
"ON THE SEVENTH DAY, MY SENSES BLURRED, AND THERE, ON THE EDGE OF SLEEP OR DEATH...
"...IT APPEARED.
"THE MULTIVERSE. COUNTLESS REFLECTIONS OF MYSELF...
"...ALL CHAMPIONING GOOD.
"AND I KNEW THEN, FEELING HOW I FELT...
"...THEY COULD ONLY HATE ME. INFINITY ITSELF, CASTING JUDGMENT."
IT HAD TO BE STOPPED, IT ALL HAD TO BE DESTROYED.
ACTIVATE BREACH CHAMBERS.
CONFIRMED, EXECUTRIX.
KRA-ZATCH
ZATCH
ZATCH

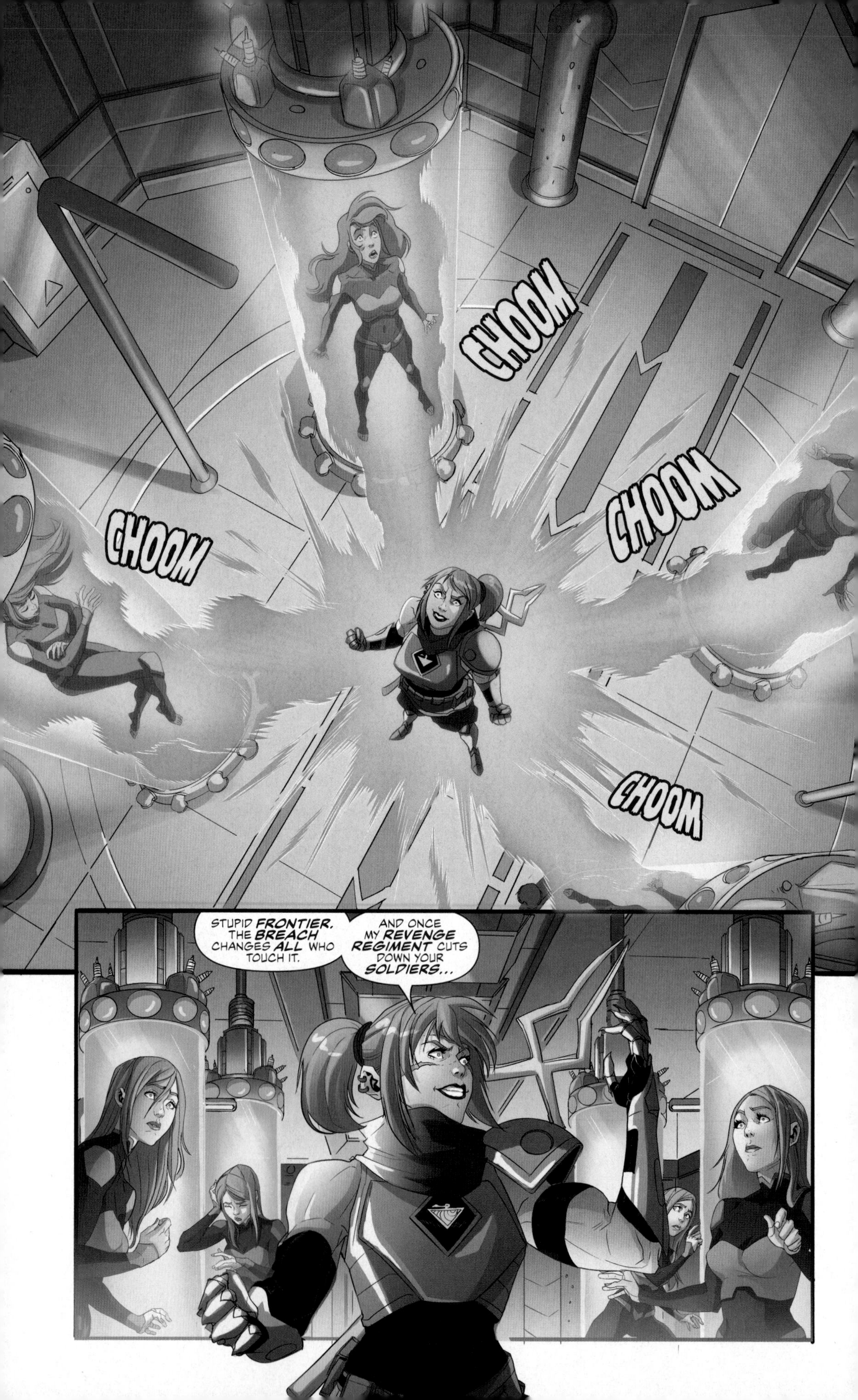
CHOOM
CHOOM
CHOOM
CHOOM
STUPID FRONTIER. THE BREACH CHANGES ALL WHO TOUCH IT.
AND ONCE MY REVENGE REGIMENT CUTS DOWN YOUR SOLDIERS...

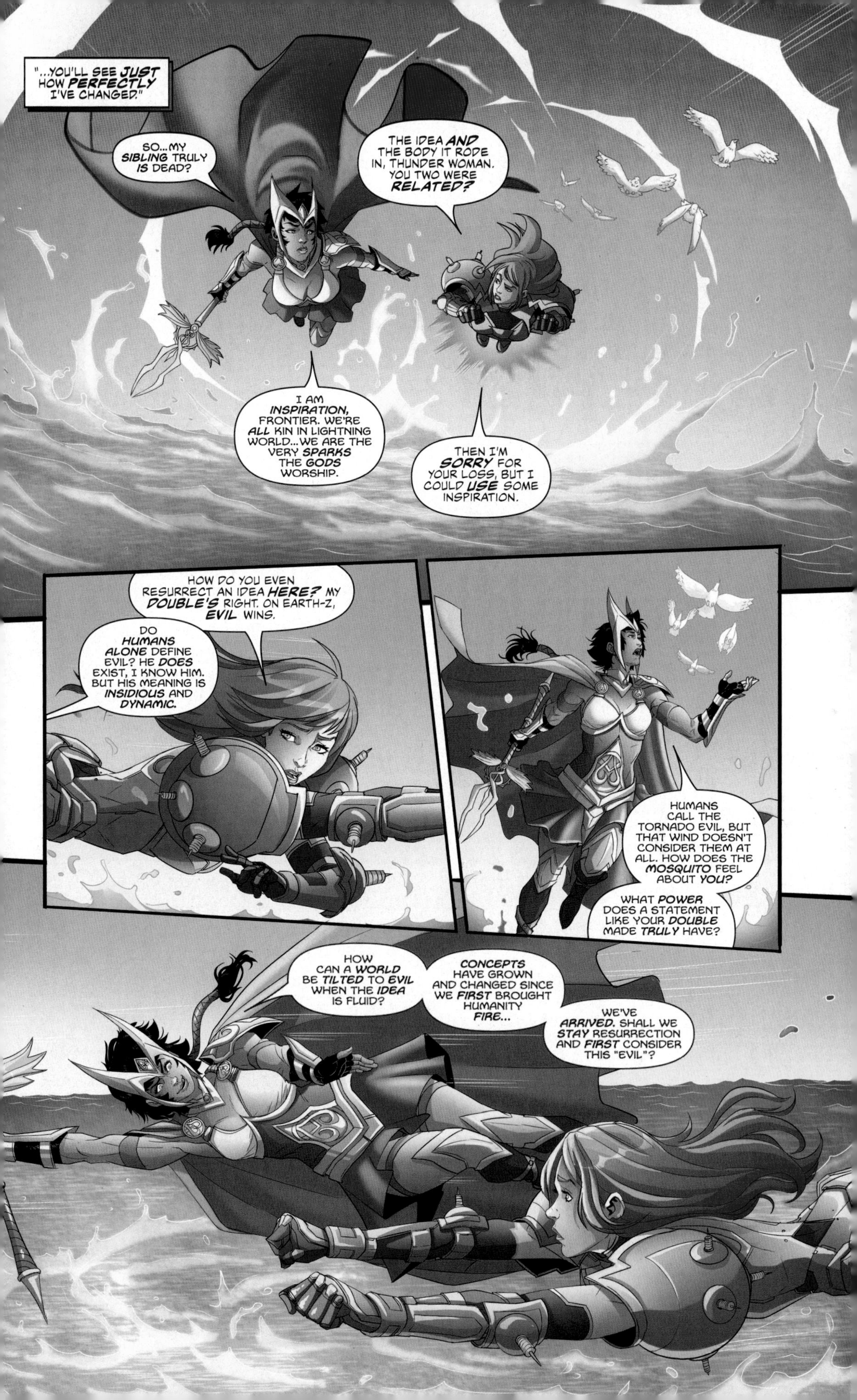
"...YOU'LL SEE JUST HOW PERFECTLY I'VE CHANGED."
SO...MY SIBLING TRULY IS DEAD?
THE IDEA AND THE BODY IT RODE IN, THUNDER WOMAN. YOU TWO WERE RELATED?
I AM INSPIRATION, FRONTIER. WE'RE ALL KIN IN LIGHTNING WORLD...WE ARE THE VERY SPARKS THE GODS WORSHIP.
THEN I'M SORRY FOR YOUR LOSS, BUT I COULD USE SOME INSPIRATION.
HOW DO YOU EVEN RESURRECT AN IDEA HERE? MY DOUBLE'S RIGHT. ON EARTH-Z, EVIL WINS.
DO HUMANS ALONE DEFINE EVIL? HE DOES EXIST, I KNOW HIM. BUT HIS MEANING IS INSIDIOUS AND DYNAMIC.
HUMANS CALL THE TORNADO EVIL, BUT THAT WIND DOESN'T CONSIDER THEM AT ALL. HOW DOES THE MOSQUITO FEEL ABOUT YOU?
WHAT POWER DOES A STATEMENT LIKE YOUR DOUBLE MADE TRULY HAVE?
HOW CAN A WORLD BE TILTED TO EVIL WHEN THE IDEA IS FLUID?
CONCEPTS HAVE GROWN AND CHANGED SINCE WE FIRST BROUGHT HUMANITY FIRE...
WE'VE ARRIVED. SHALL WE STAY RESURRECTION AND FIRST CONSIDER THIS "EVIL"?

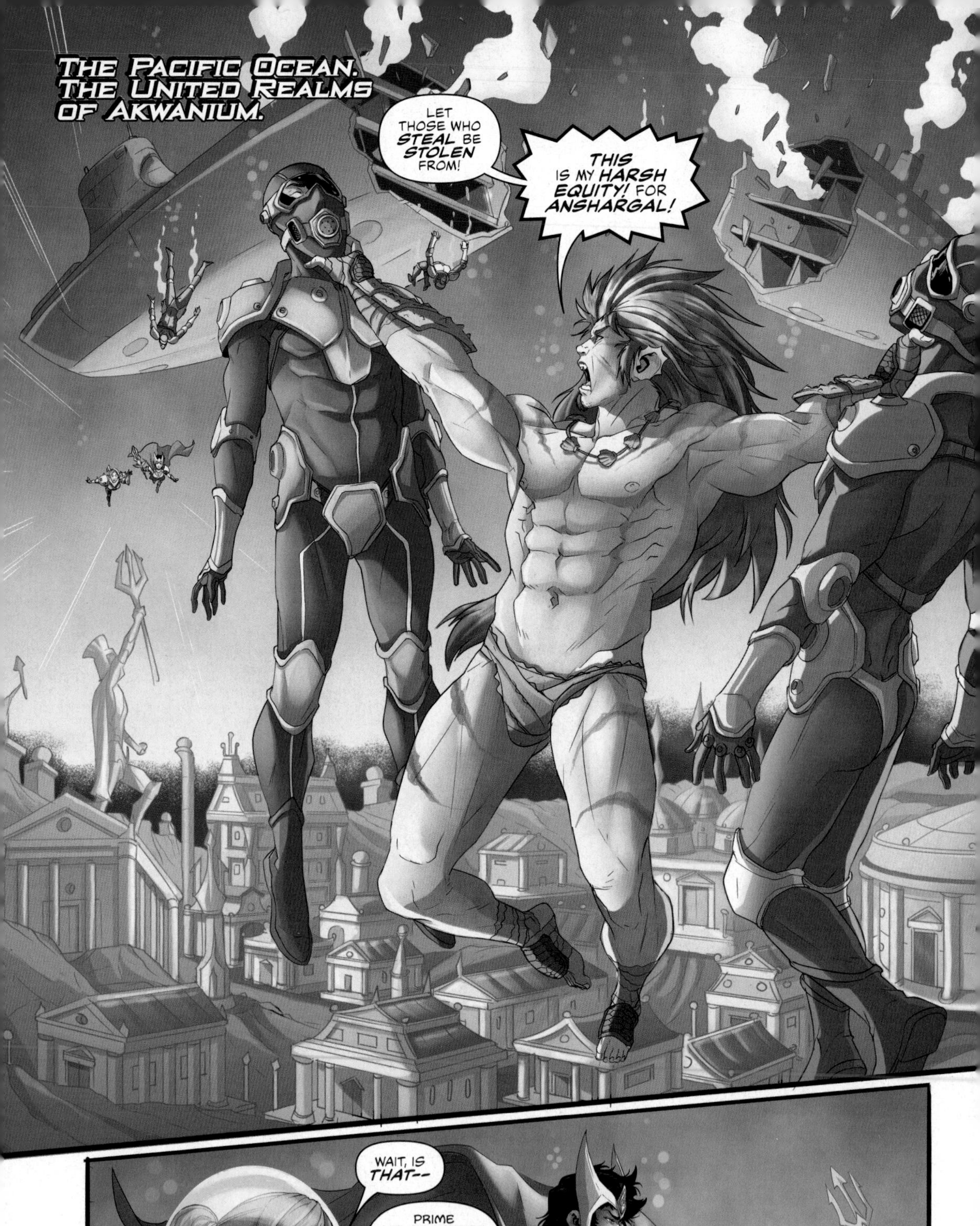
THE PACIFIC OCEAN. THE UNITED REALMS OF AKWANIUM.
LET THOSE WHO STEAL BE STOLEN FROM!
THIS IS MY HARSH EQUITY! FOR ANSHARGAL!

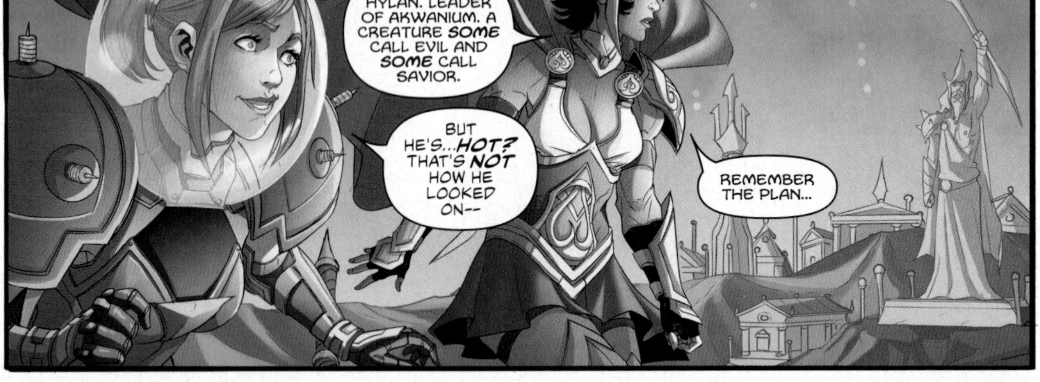
WAIT, IS THAT--
PRIME HYLAN. LEADER OF AKWANIUM. A CREATURE SOME CALL EVIL AND SOME CALL SAVIOR.
BUT HE'S...HOT? THAT'S NOT HOW HE LOOKED ON--
REMEMBER THE PLAN...

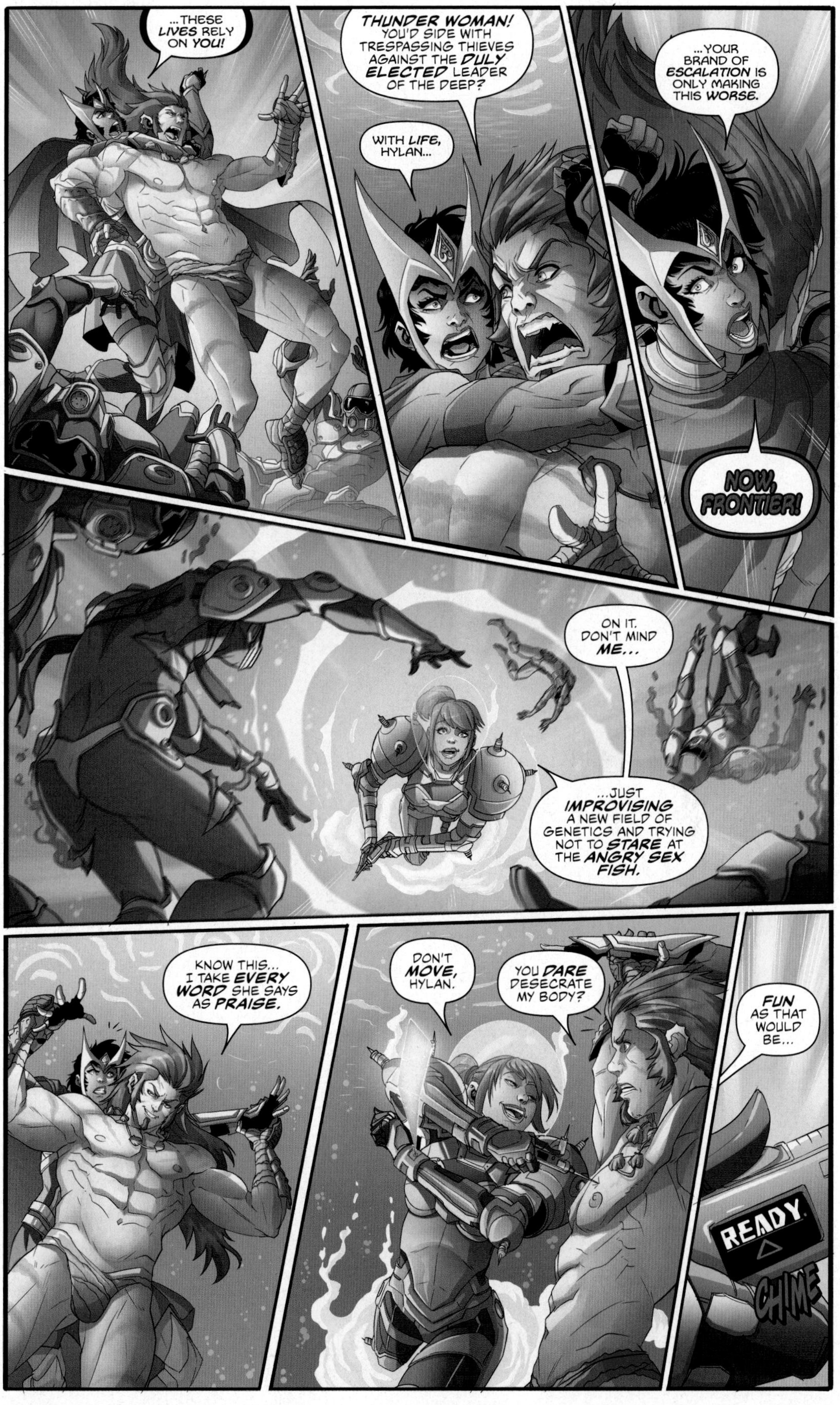
...THESE LIVES RELY ON YOU!
THUNDER WOMAN! YOU'D SIDE WITH TRESPASSING THIEVES AGAINST THE DULY ELECTED LEADER OF THE DEEP?
WITH LIFE, HYLAN...
...YOUR BRAND OF ESCALATION IS ONLY MAKING THIS WORSE.
NOW, FRONTIER!
ON IT. DON'T MIND ME...
...JUST IMPROVISING A NEW FIELD OF GENETICS AND TRYING NOT TO STARE AT THE ANGRY SEX FISH.
KNOW THIS... I TAKE EVERY WORD SHE SAYS AS PRAISE.
DON'T MOVE, HYLAN.
YOU DARE DESECRATE MY BODY?
FUN AS THAT WOULD BE...
READY.
CHIME

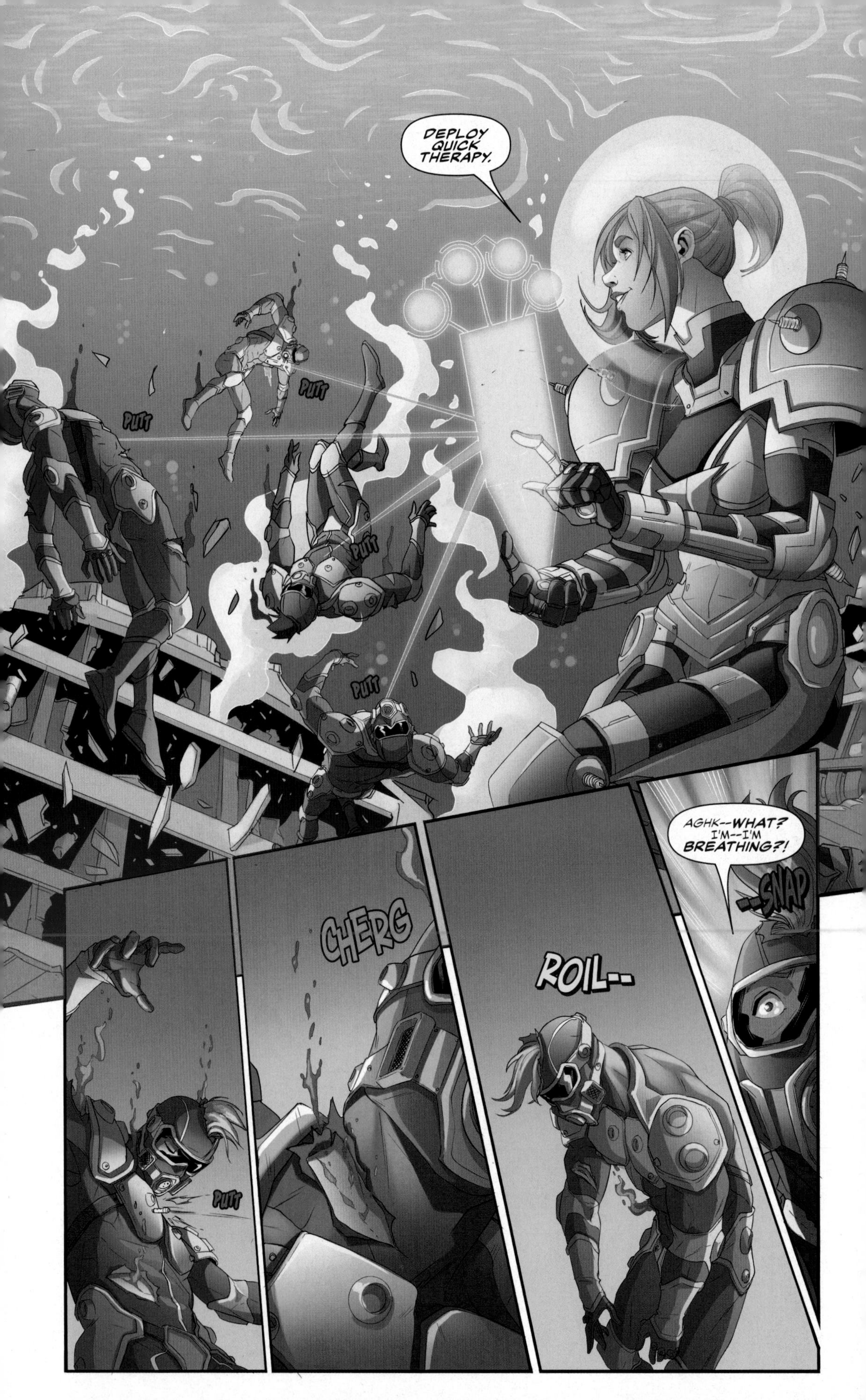
DEPLOY QUICK THERAPY.
PUTT
PUTT
PUTT
PUTT
AGHK--WHAT? I'M--I'M BREATHING?!
--SNAP
PUTT
CHERG
ROIL--

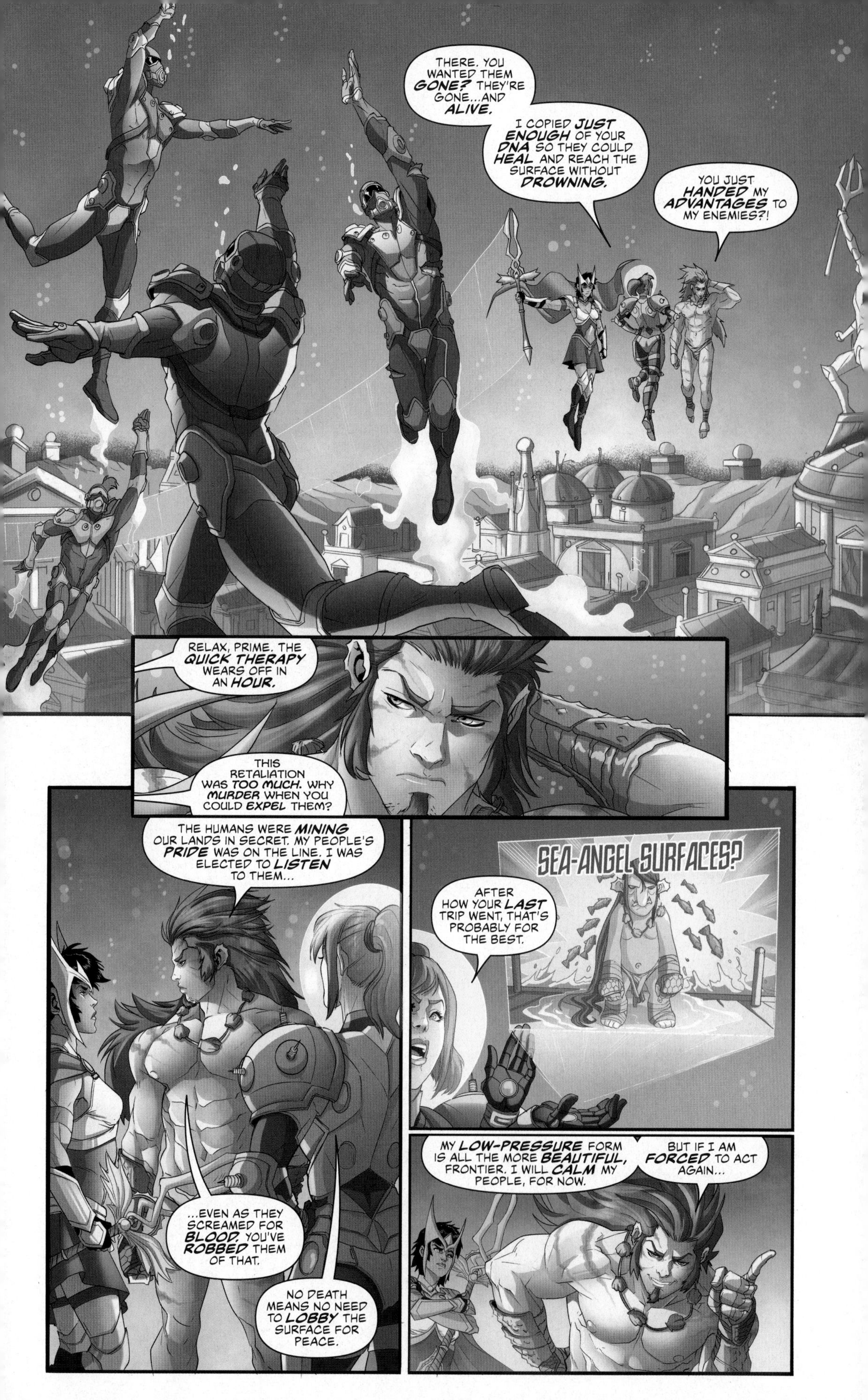
THERE. YOU WANTED THEM GONE? THEY'RE GONE...AND ALIVE.
I COPIED JUST ENOUGH OF YOUR DNA SO THEY COULD HEAL AND REACH THE SURFACE WITHOUT DROWNING.
YOU JUST HANDED MY ADVANTAGES TO MY ENEMIES?!
RELAX, PRIME. THE QUICK THERAPY WEARS OFF IN AN HOUR.
THIS RETALIATION WAS TOO MUCH. WHY MURDER WHEN YOU COULD EXPEL THEM?
THE HUMANS WERE MINING OUR LANDS IN SECRET. MY PEOPLE'S PRIDE WAS ON THE LINE. I WAS ELECTED TO LISTEN TO THEM...
...EVEN AS THEY SCREAMED FOR BLOOD. YOU'VE ROBBED THEM OF THAT.
NO DEATH MEANS NO NEED TO LOBBY THE SURFACE FOR PEACE.
SEA-ANGEL SURFACES?
AFTER HOW YOUR LAST TRIP WENT, THAT'S PROBABLY FOR THE BEST.
MY LOW-PRESSURE FORM IS ALL THE MORE BEAUTIFUL, FRONTIER. I WILL CALM MY PEOPLE, FOR NOW.
BUT IF I AM FORCED TO ACT AGAIN...

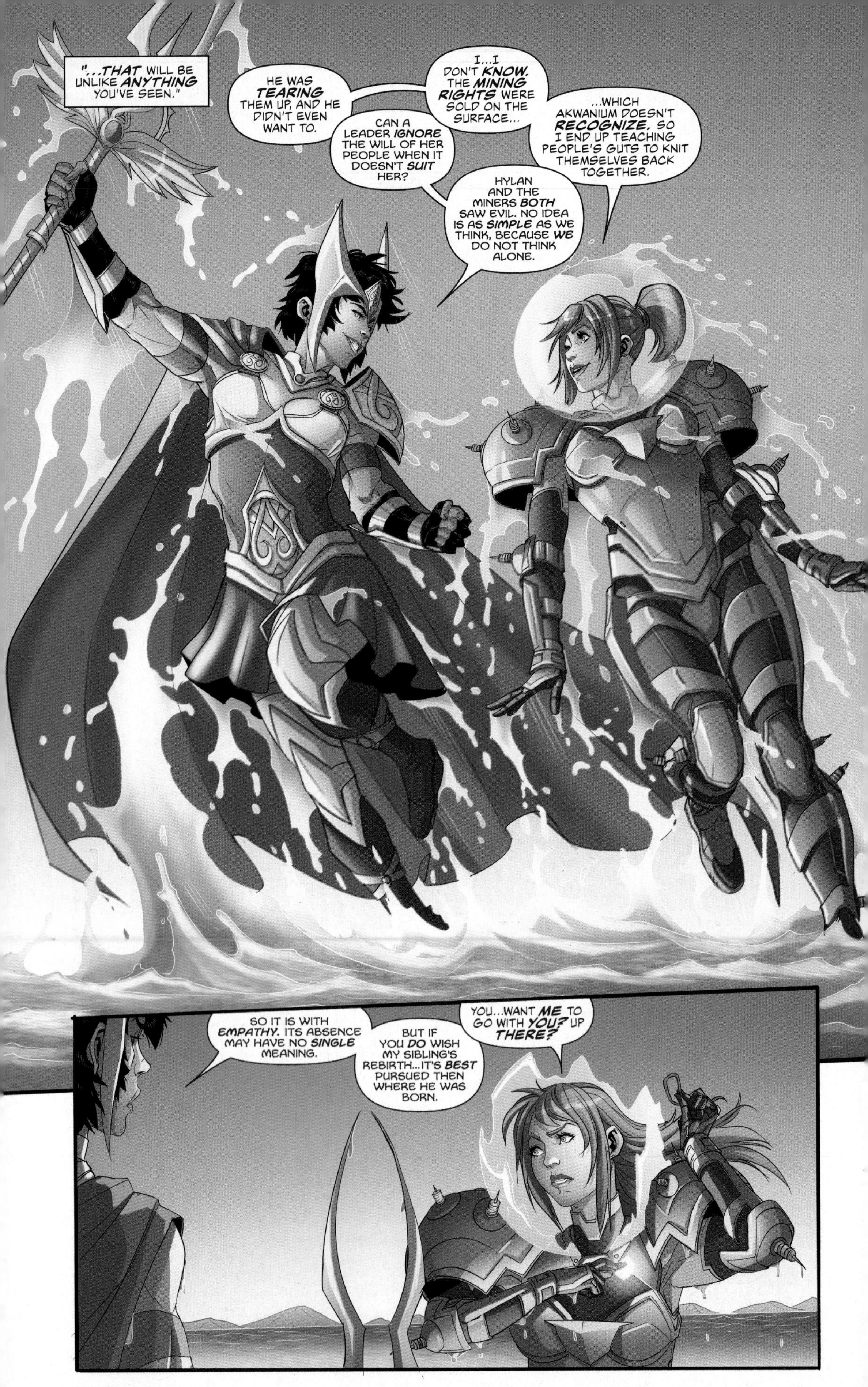
"...THAT WILL BE UNLIKE ANYTHING YOU'VE SEEN."
HE WAS TEARING THEM UP, AND HE DIDN'T EVEN WANT TO.
I...I DON'T KNOW. THE MINING RIGHTS WERE SOLD ON THE SURFACE...
CAN A LEADER IGNORE THE WILL OF HER PEOPLE WHEN IT DOESN'T SUIT HER?
...WHICH AKWANIUM DOESN'T RECOGNIZE. SO I END UP TEACHING PEOPLE'S GUTS TO KNIT THEMSELVES BACK TOGETHER.
HYLAN AND THE MINERS BOTH SAW EVIL. NO IDEA IS AS SIMPLE AS WE THINK, BECAUSE WE DO NOT THINK ALONE.
SO IT IS WITH EMPATHY. ITS ABSENCE MAY HAVE NO SINGLE MEANING.
BUT IF YOU DO WISH MY SIBLING'S REBIRTH...IT'S BEST PURSUED THEN WHERE HE WAS BORN.
YOU...WANT ME TO GO WITH YOU? UP THERE?

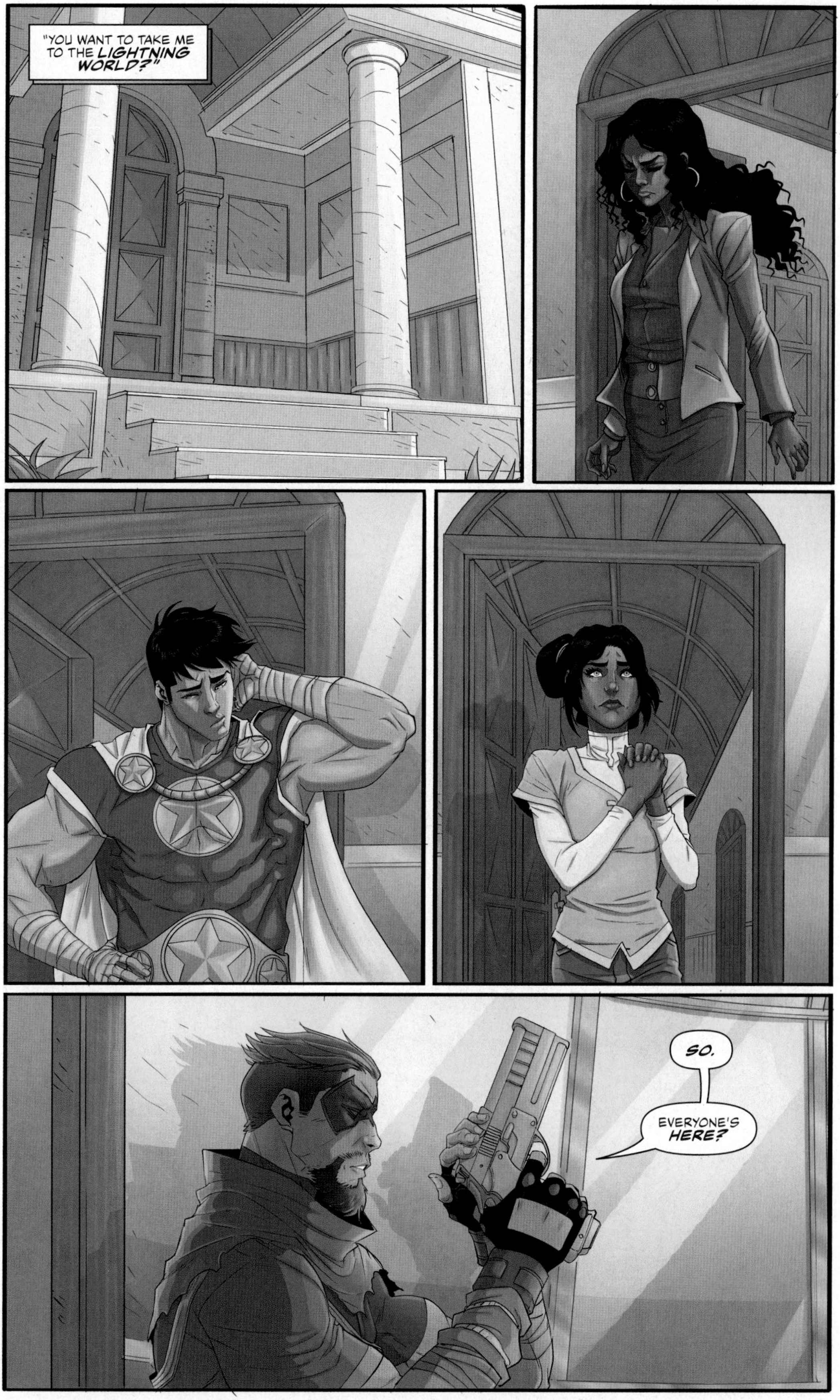
"YOU WANT TO TAKE ME TO THE LIGHTNING WORLD?"
SO.
EVERYONE'S HERE?

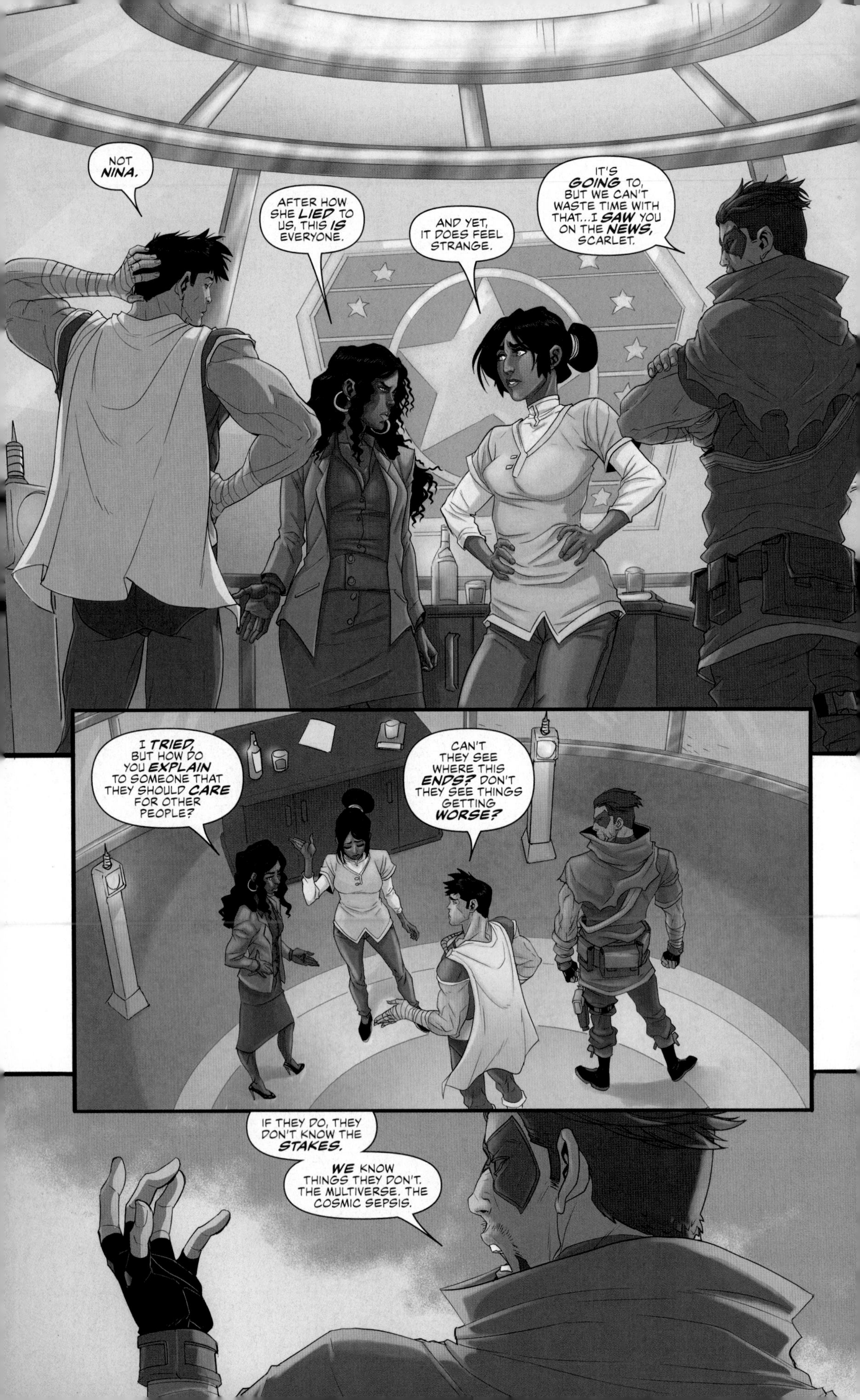
NOT NINA.
AFTER HOW SHE LIED TO US, THIS IS EVERYONE.
AND YET, IT DOES FEEL STRANGE.
IT'S GOING TO, BUT WE CAN'T WASTE TIME WITH THAT...I SAW YOU ON THE NEWS, SCARLET.
I TRIED, BUT HOW DO YOU EXPLAIN TO SOMEONE THAT THEY SHOULD CARE FOR OTHER PEOPLE?
CAN'T THEY SEE WHERE THIS ENDS? DON'T THEY SEE THINGS GETTING WORSE?
IF THEY DO, THEY DON'T KNOW THE STAKES.
WE KNOW THINGS THEY DON'T. THE MULTIVERSE. THE COSMIC SEPSIS.

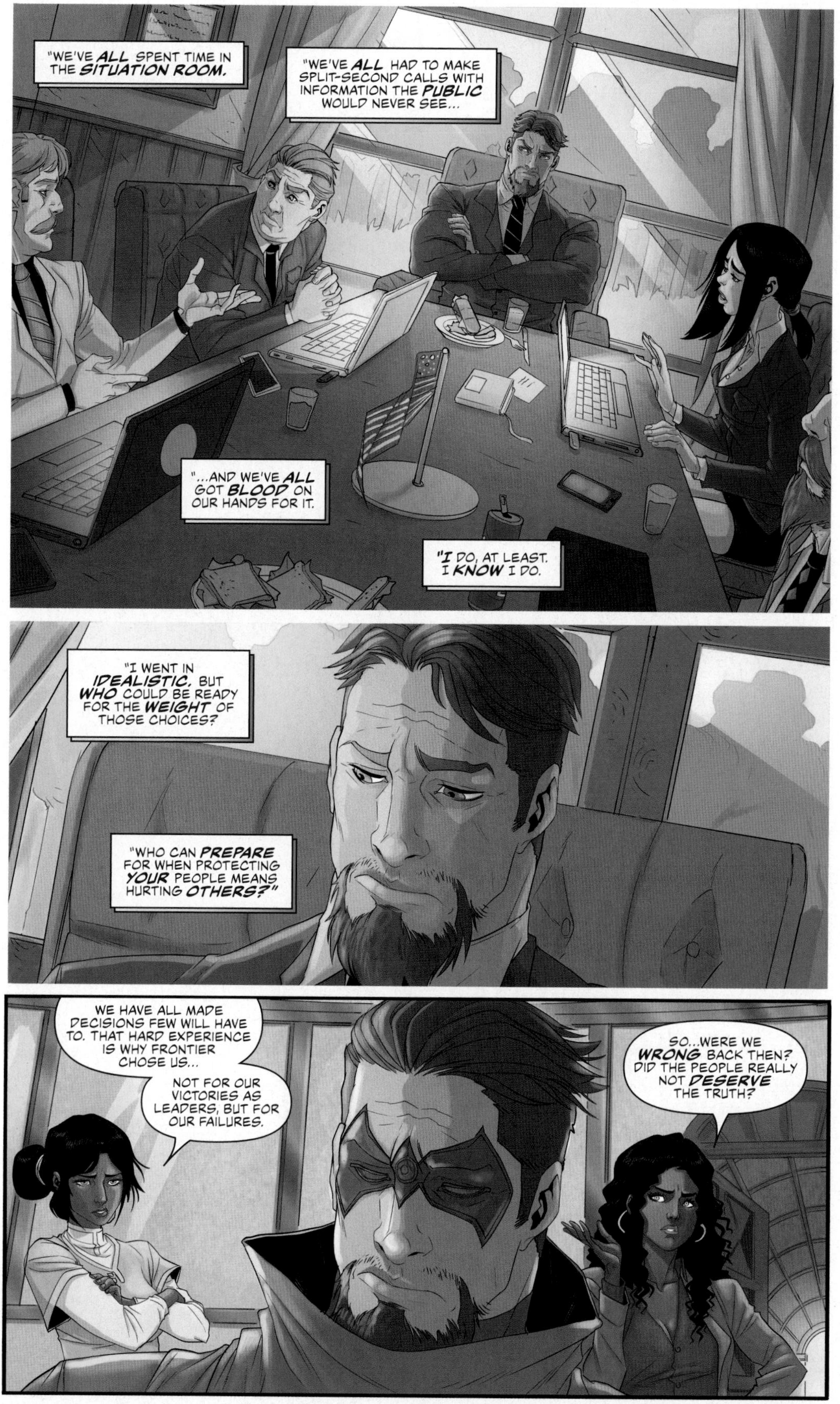
"WE'VE ALL SPENT TIME IN THE SITUATION ROOM.
"WE'VE ALL HAD TO MAKE SPLIT-SECOND CALLS WITH INFORMATION THE PUBLIC WOULD NEVER SEE...
"...AND WE'VE ALL GOT BLOOD ON OUR HANDS FOR IT.
"I DO, AT LEAST. I KNOW I DO.
"I WENT IN IDEALISTIC, BUT WHO COULD BE READY FOR THE WEIGHT OF THOSE CHOICES?
"WHO CAN PREPARE FOR WHEN PROTECTING YOUR PEOPLE MEANS HURTING OTHERS?"
WE HAVE ALL MADE DECISIONS FEW WILL HAVE TO. THAT HARD EXPERIENCE IS WHY FRONTIER CHOSE US...
NOT FOR OUR VICTORIES AS LEADERS, BUT FOR OUR FAILURES.
SO...WERE WE WRONG BACK THEN? DID THE PEOPLE REALLY NOT DESERVE THE TRUTH?

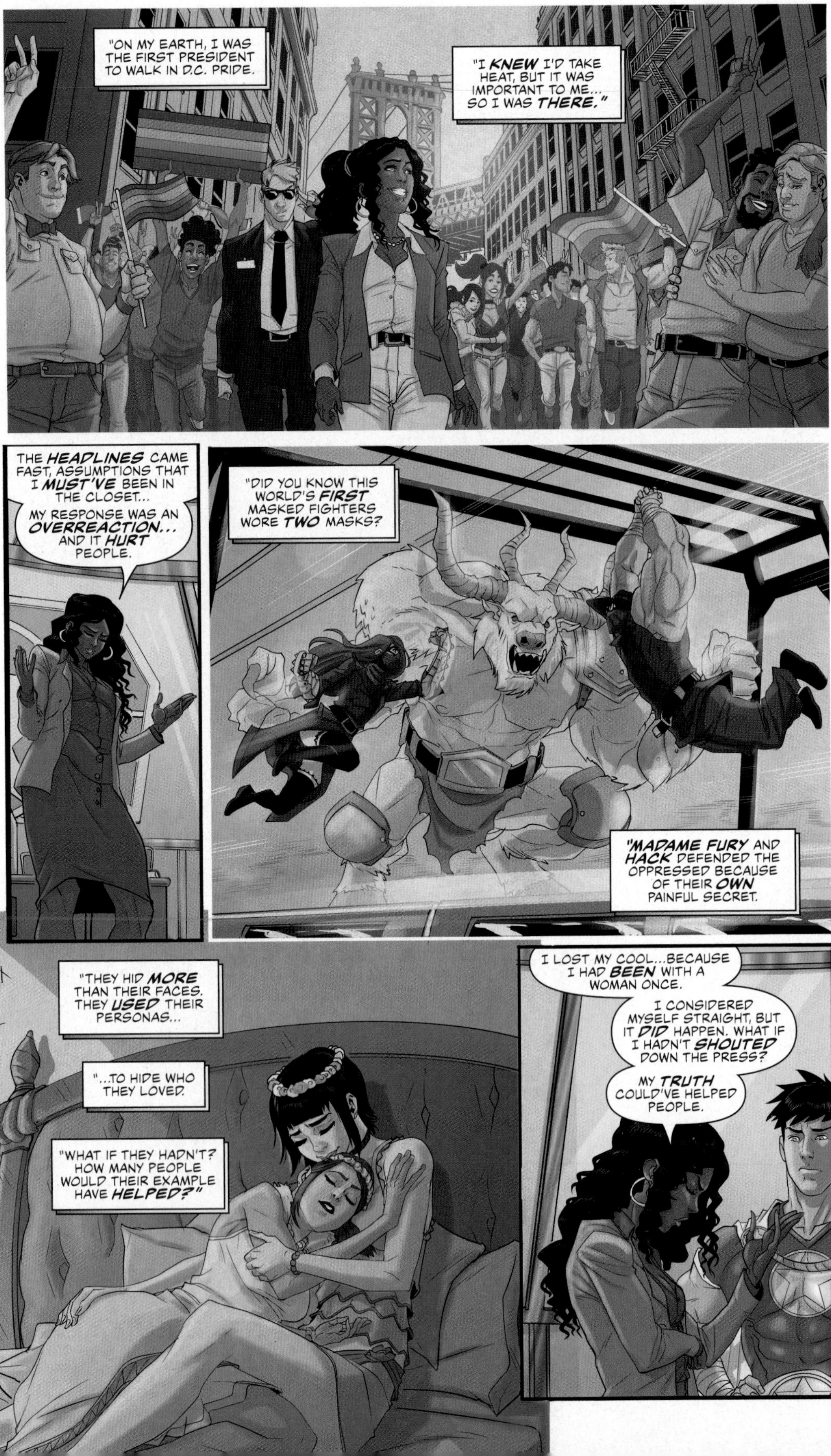
"ON MY EARTH, I WAS THE FIRST PRESIDENT TO WALK IN D.C. PRIDE.
"I KNEW I'D TAKE HEAT, BUT IT WAS IMPORTANT TO ME... SO I WAS THERE."
THE HEADLINES CAME FAST, ASSUMPTIONS THAT I MUST'VE BEEN IN THE CLOSET...
MY RESPONSE WAS AN OVERREACTION... AND IT HURT PEOPLE.
"DID YOU KNOW THIS WORLD'S FIRST MASKED FIGHTERS WORE TWO MASKS?
"MADAME FURY AND HACK DEFENDED THE OPPRESSED BECAUSE OF THEIR OWN PAINFUL SECRET.
"THEY HID MORE THAN THEIR FACES. THEY USED THEIR PERSONAS...
"...TO HIDE WHO THEY LOVED.
"WHAT IF THEY HADN'T? HOW MANY PEOPLE WOULD THEIR EXAMPLE HAVE HELPED?"
I LOST MY COOL...BECAUSE I HAD BEEN WITH A WOMAN ONCE.
I CONSIDERED MYSELF STRAIGHT, BUT IT DID HAPPEN. WHAT IF I HADN'T SHOUTED DOWN THE PRESS?
MY TRUTH COULD'VE HELPED PEOPLE.

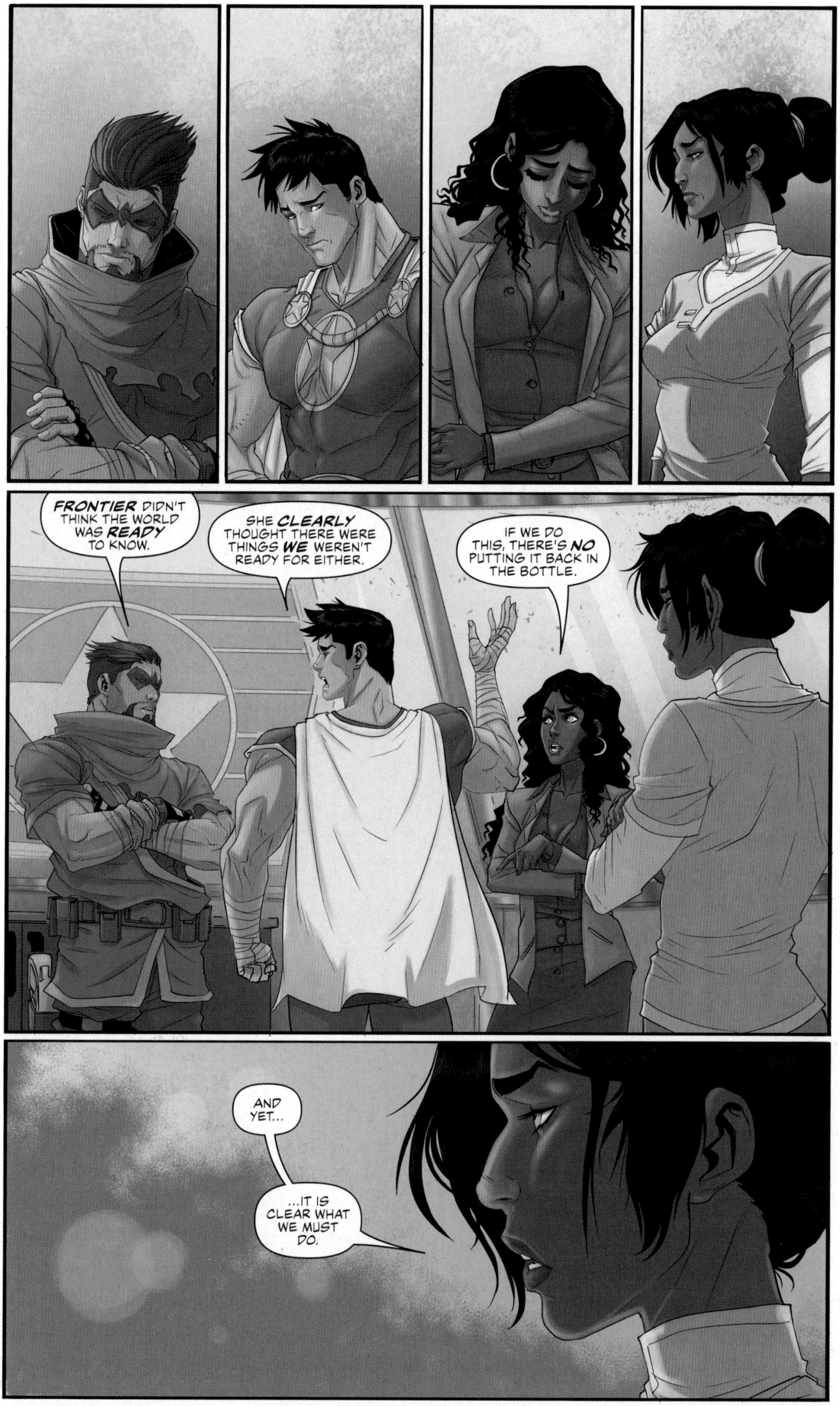
FRONTIER DIDN'T THINK THE WORLD WAS READY TO KNOW.
SHE CLEARLY THOUGHT THERE WERE THINGS WE WEREN'T READY FOR EITHER.
IF WE DO THIS, THERE'S NO PUTTING IT BACK IN THE BOTTLE.
AND YET...
...IT IS CLEAR WHAT WE MUST DO.

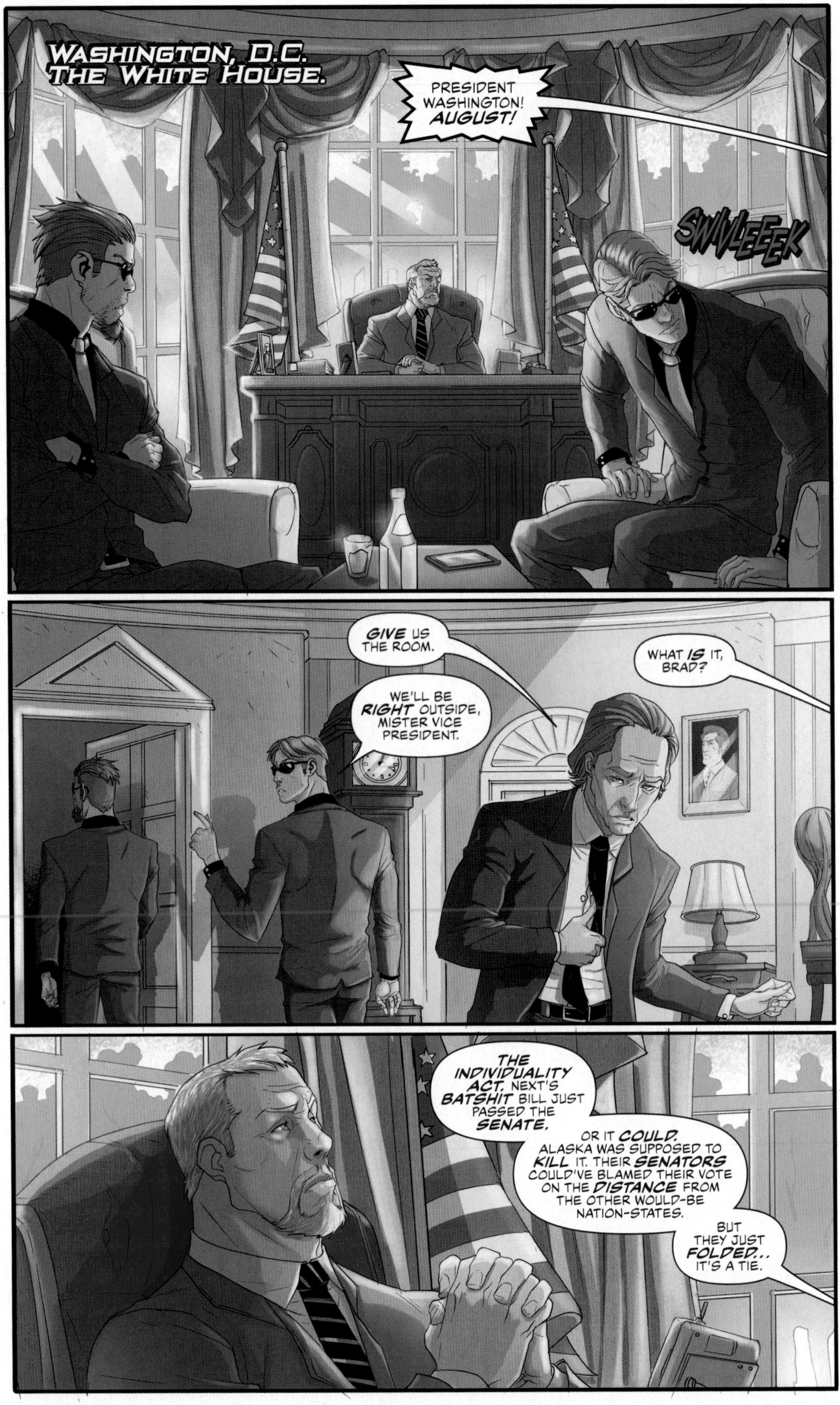
WASHINGTON, D.C.
THE WHITE HOUSE.
PRESIDENT WASHINGTON! AUGUST!
SWIVLEEEK
GIVE US THE ROOM.
WE'LL BE RIGHT OUTSIDE, MISTER VICE PRESIDENT.
WHAT IS IT, BRAD?
THE INDIVIDUALITY ACT. NEXT'S BATSHIT BILL JUST PASSED THE SENATE.
OR IT COULD. ALASKA WAS SUPPOSED TO KILL IT. THEIR SENATORS COULD'VE BLAMED THEIR VOTE ON THE DISTANCE FROM THE OTHER WOULD-BE NATION-STATES.
BUT THEY JUST FOLDED... IT'S A TIE.

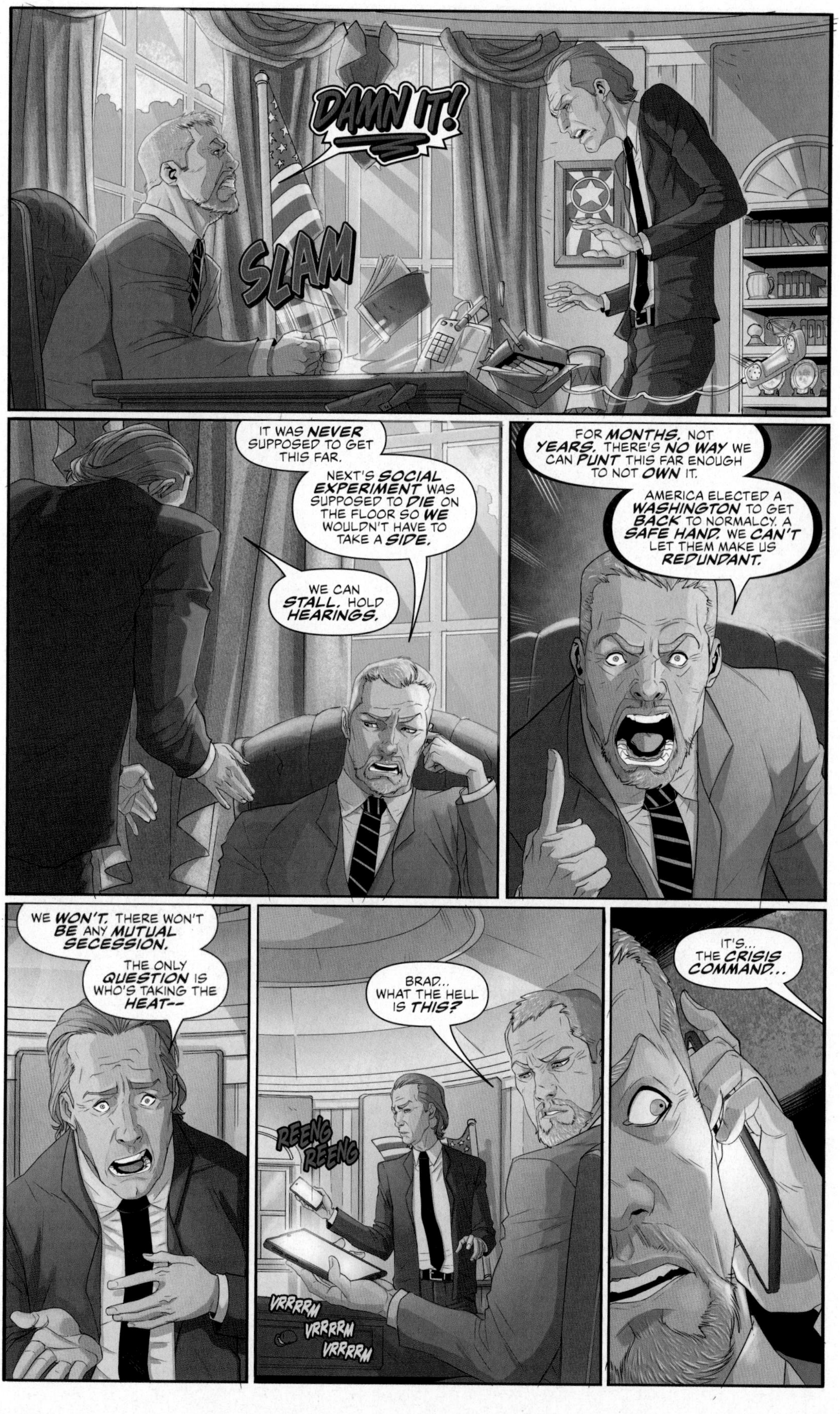

DAMN IT!
SLAM
IT WAS NEVER SUPPOSED TO GET THIS FAR.
NEXT'S SOCIAL EXPERIMENT WAS SUPPOSED TO DIE ON THE FLOOR SO WE WOULDN'T HAVE TO TAKE A SIDE.
WE CAN STALL. HOLD HEARINGS.
FOR MONTHS. NOT YEARS. THERE'S NO WAY WE CAN PUNT THIS FAR ENOUGH TO NOT OWN IT.
AMERICA ELECTED A WASHINGTON TO GET BACK TO NORMALCY. A SAFE HAND. WE CAN'T LET THEM MAKE US REDUNDANT.
WE WON'T. THERE WON'T BE ANY MUTUAL SECESSION.
THE ONLY QUESTION IS WHO'S TAKING THE HEAT--
BRAD... WHAT THE HELL IS THIS?
REENG REENG
VRRRRM
VRRRRM
VRRRRM
IT'S... THE CRISIS COMMAND...

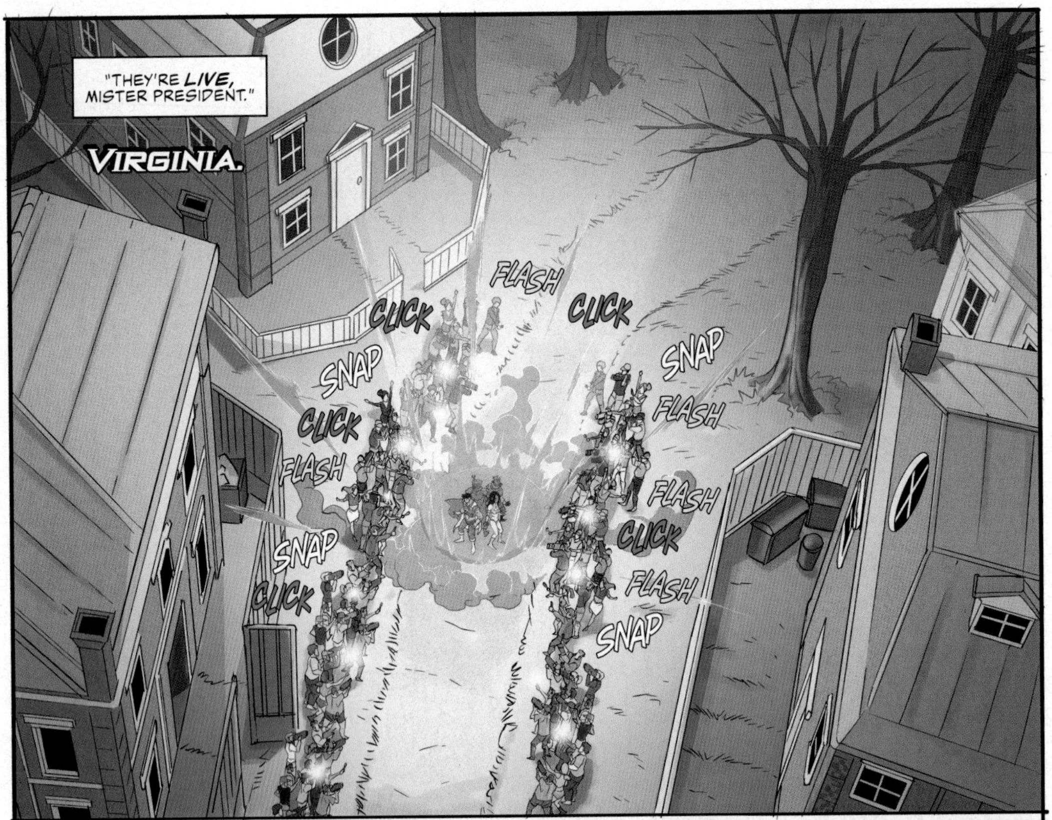
"THEY'RE LIVE, MISTER PRESIDENT."
VIRGINIA.
FLASH
CLICK
CLICK
SNAP
SNAP
CLICK
FLASH
FLASH
FLASH
CLICK
SNAP
CLICK
FLASH
SNAP

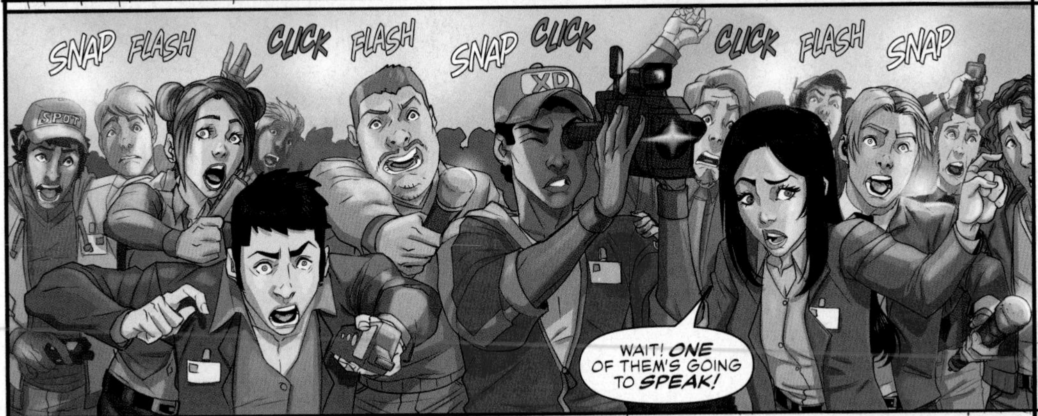
SNAP FLASH CLICK FLASH SNAP CLICK CLICK FLASH SNAP
WAIT! ONE OF THEM'S GOING TO SPEAK!

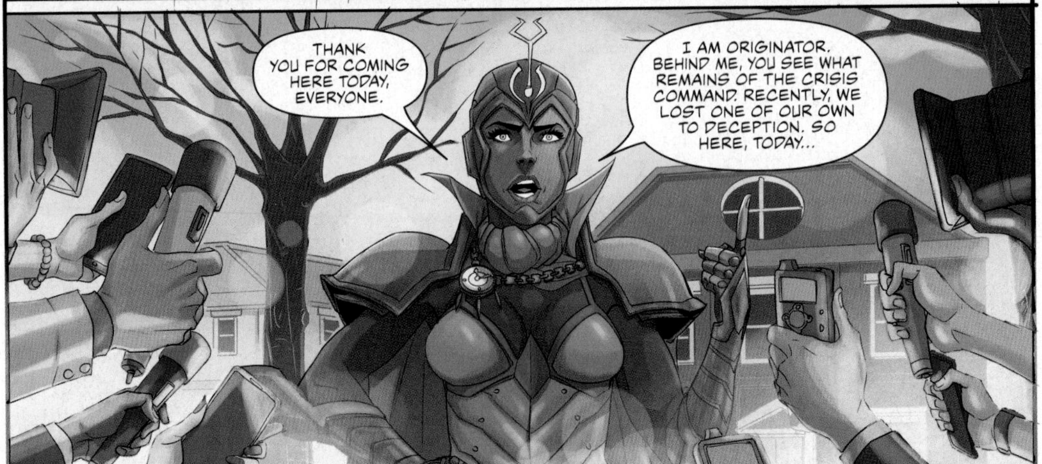
THANK YOU FOR COMING HERE TODAY, EVERYONE.
I AM ORIGINATOR. BEHIND ME, YOU SEE WHAT REMAINS OF THE CRISIS COMMAND. RECENTLY, WE LOST ONE OF OUR OWN TO DECEPTION. SO HERE, TODAY...

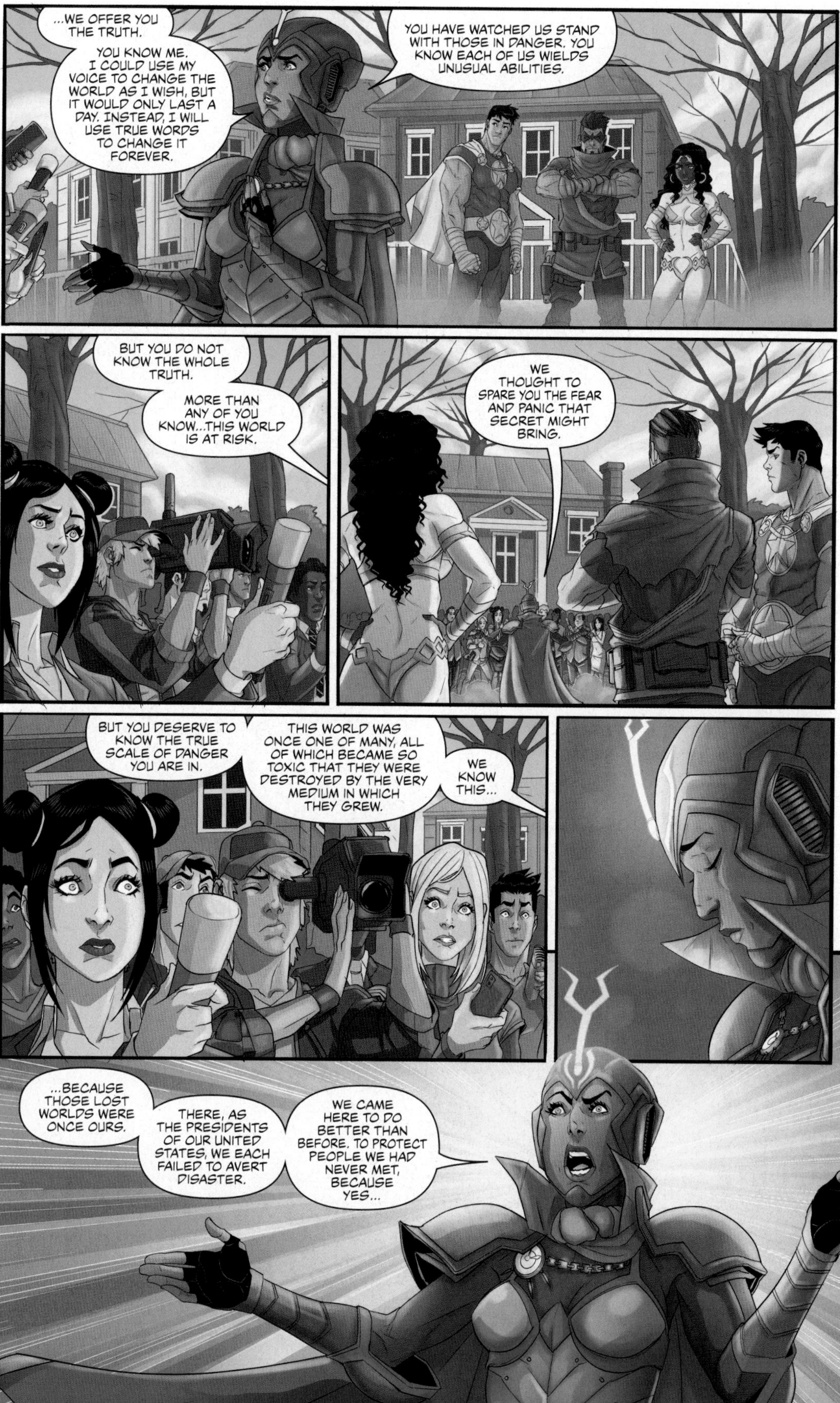
...WE OFFER YOU THE TRUTH.
YOU KNOW ME. I COULD USE MY VOICE TO CHANGE THE WORLD AS I WISH, BUT IT WOULD ONLY LAST A DAY. INSTEAD, I WILL USE TRUE WORDS TO CHANGE IT FOREVER.
YOU HAVE WATCHED US STAND WITH THOSE IN DANGER. YOU KNOW EACH OF US WIELDS UNUSUAL ABILITIES.
BUT YOU DO NOT KNOW THE WHOLE TRUTH.
MORE THAN ANY OF YOU KNOW...THIS WORLD IS AT RISK.
WE THOUGHT TO SPARE YOU THE FEAR AND PANIC THAT SECRET MIGHT BRING.
BUT YOU DESERVE TO KNOW THE TRUE SCALE OF DANGER YOU ARE IN.
THIS WORLD WAS ONCE ONE OF MANY, ALL OF WHICH BECAME SO TOXIC THAT THEY WERE DESTROYED BY THE VERY MEDIUM IN WHICH THEY GREW.
WE KNOW THIS...
...BECAUSE THOSE LOST WORLDS WERE ONCE OURS.
THERE, AS THE PRESIDENTS OF OUR UNITED STATES, WE EACH FAILED TO AVERT DISASTER.
WE CAME HERE TO DO BETTER THAN BEFORE. TO PROTECT PEOPLE WE HAD NEVER MET, BECAUSE YES...

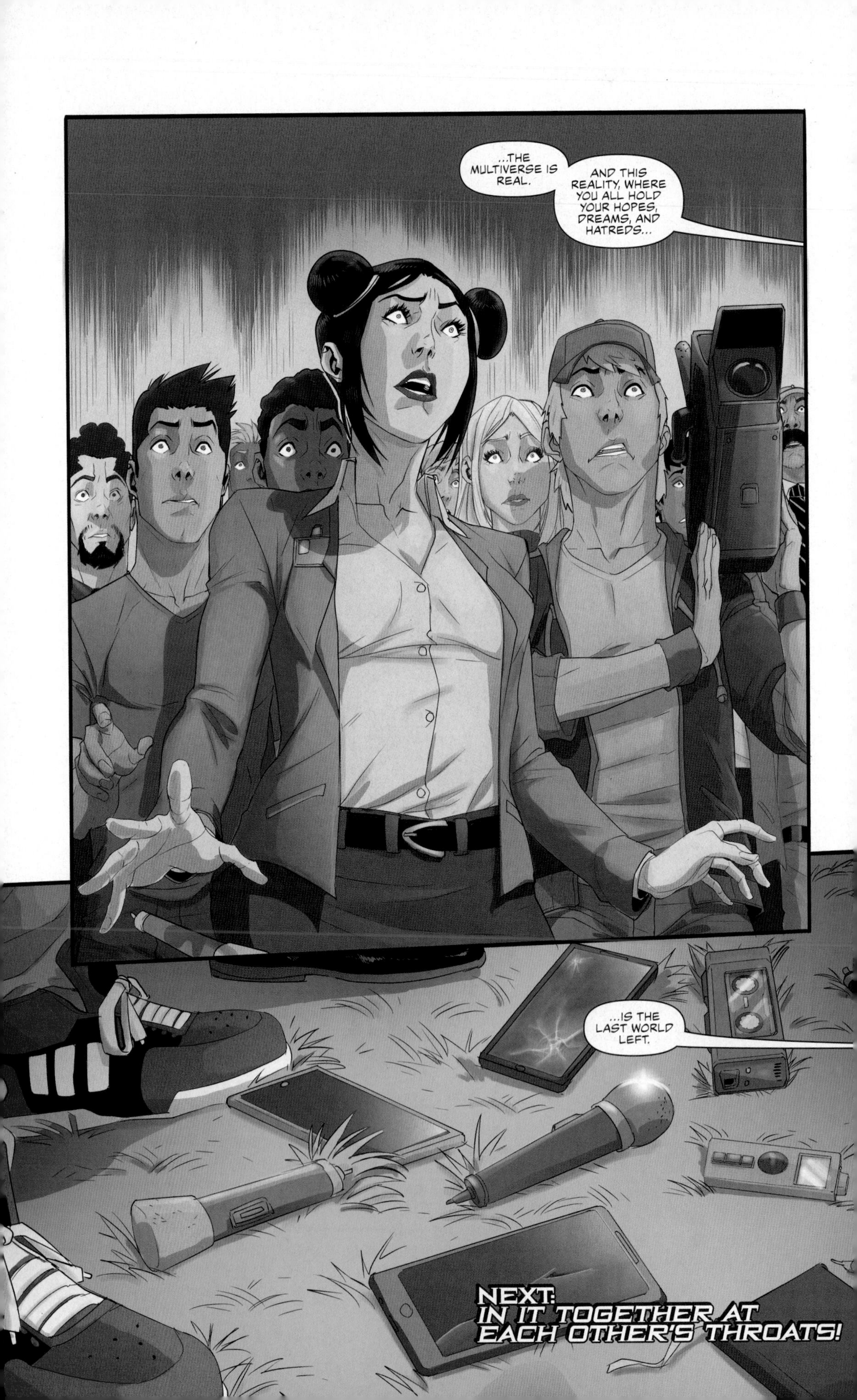
...THE MULTIVERSE IS REAL.
AND THIS REALITY, WHERE YOU ALL HOLD YOUR HOPES, DREAMS, AND HATREDS...
...IS THE LAST WORLD LEFT.
NEXT: IN IT TOGETHER AT EACH OTHER'S THROATS!

EXTRA CONTENTS

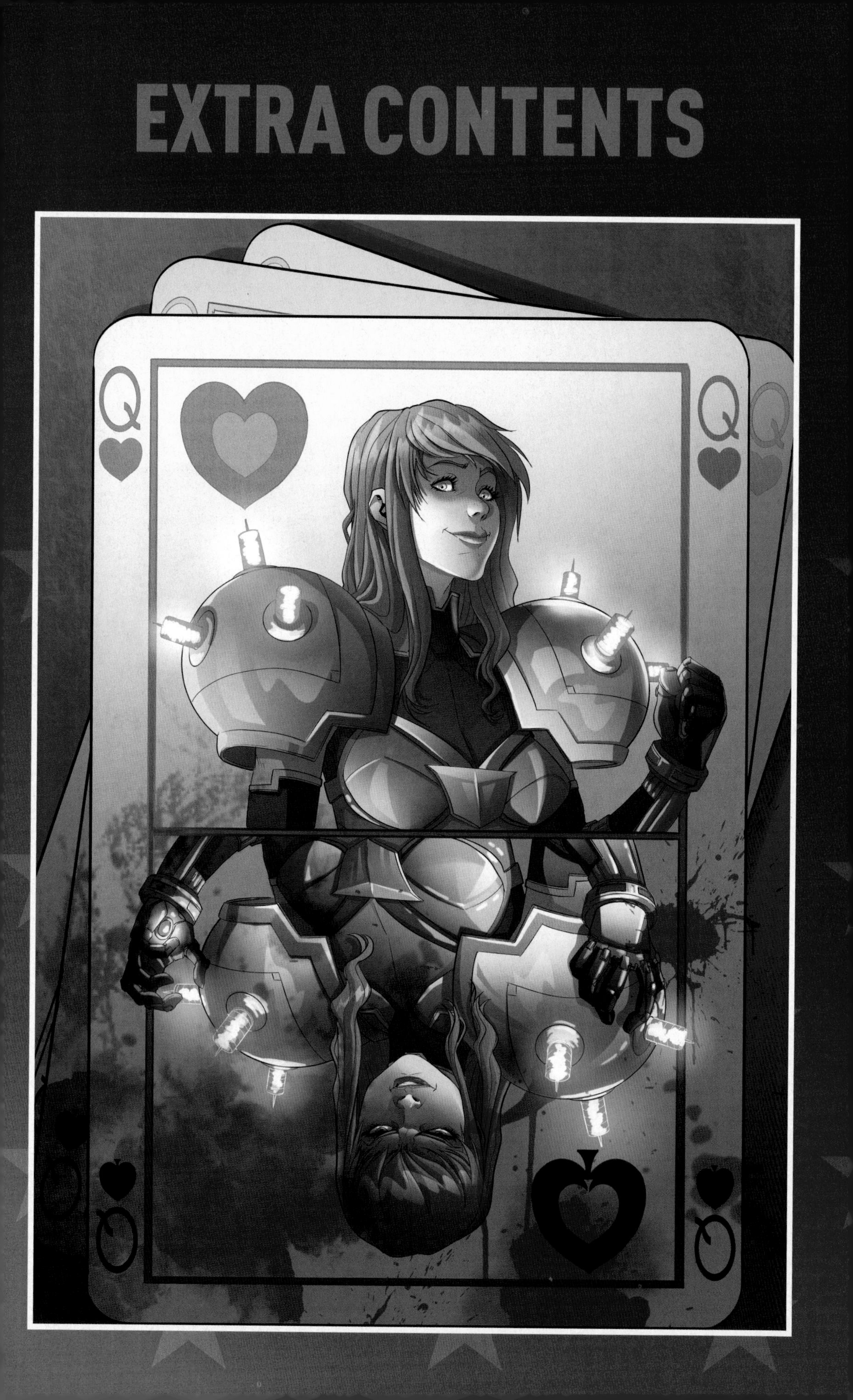

Q
Q
Q
Q

EXCLUSIVE INTERVIEW WITH
NOAH ROWE · PRIZEFIGHTER

The following was originally published in the October 14th issue of **The Washington Comet**. It is reproduced below, with the permission of all the parties involved.

The Crisis Command, the world's most mighty, the champions of tomorrow, the super-team of America. Every day we watch them save our world—a team of diverse individuals who fight off the absurdly abnormal with impossible ideas. They're a busy bunch, and they do difficult work.

But the Crisis Command has graciously agreed to take some time to sit down with us here at **The Washington Comet**, so that we may all better get to know the people who walk among us with such tremendous talents.
Over the next few months, we'll be covering each and every single member of the team closely. From what they're enjoying on TV to their stance on what they believe their super-team represents, we'll be digging into all the details. And who better to start with than the most popular of them all? The darling of the Crisis Command, The Golden Gladiator himself, Prizefighter!

It's a warm afternoon, as we sit down for lunch in a cozy restaurant in downtown DC. A whole legion of people swarm the space, forming a never-ending line that seemingly extends out the door and onto the bustling street. The staff does not look pleased, to say the least.
I look to the superhero sitting before me and nod, as though this were a completely normal situation. He simply grins before waving back to a child that yells out his name. He's a man that loves his crowds. Indeed, perhaps few love one as much as he does. Adorned with a gleaming golden belt emblazoned with majestic stars, akin to a wrestling champion, he's a man that isn't a stranger to public scrutiny. He watches them, smiling, waving, responding to their energy with his own, as we await our order.
His posture is relaxed despite the many eyes, while I remain stiff, still acclimating to the scenario. "Are you alright?" he asks, leaning forward, the concern clear through his eyes and voice. It's then I'm reminded why there is such a crowd at all. I smile.
The food comes in not long after, and the room grows silent. Prizefighter extends his arms and asks, "Well then, shall we begin?" And we do.

TWC: It's Noah, isn't it? May I call you Noah?

It is, I can't tell a lie. And it's your interview, for sure, and I'm pretty out of practice answering questions. These days, I try to go by Prizefighter inside the costume and out. Easier branding, you know? And with how busy we've been on the job, it's not like those identities are far from one in the same. So, Prizefighter to many. Makes it simpler! For you? Noah, if you want it.

TWC: Sweet. Noah, first off, thank you for doing this. I know you're a busy man.

We have been busy, for sure. Half the reason I dropped the secret identity, or didn't even really get one started. I've got friends that have been asking for interviews just like this for what seems like forever. Hell, they're going to kill me when they see I talked to you and not them. But what can I say? Right place, right time, and the more people know my name, the stronger I get, right? Easier to save the day with a readership like the *Comet*'s cheering me on. For some people that's a figure of speech. But for these muscles? It's literal.

TWC: Now, Noah, given it is my first time interviewing a superhero, I have to ask, what's the story behind the costume? Is there a story behind the costume? And where do superheroes get their costumes? Do you folks all have the same tailor, a super-tailor of sorts, or do your families and friends help put them together?

Ha! I'd have to have a family in the first place for them to put a costume together for me. No Midwestern mother sewed this thing up, that's a nice urban legend, right there with apple pie and cheddar as something I've never confirmed with my own eyes. For me? This costume is just like the name, it's all about hype. The Prizefighter persona is one in the same with my abilities. Lord knows if I trended globally I could probably crack the moon in half. So the belt, the wrist wraps, the cape, it's all to be instantly recognizable, make it easy for people to meme me, and to be perfectly clear: I'm a fighter, I fight for you, and the more you're in my corner, the harder I can fight. As for our tailor, well, I think that's a different interview with a different hero, I've never been the innovator. And as for my fashion, my late husband would've just choked on his drink at just hearing the question.

TWC: As a proud queer man, and a superhero, you mean a lot to a lot of people. You're a pillar of the community, and many people, especially young people today, find you an empowering figure, an inspiration. That's a heavy responsibility. To not only be a hero, but a hero as so many are watching, with so many expectations. How do you manage and deal with all that?

It's been a journey, most would say, a journey away from being an asshole. Can I say that? I'm saying it. I'm the one with the big gold belt, after all. Journey away from being an asshole. Because yeah, I know there's power in being who I am in public, and giving less than a fuck about it. But only since going public in the cape, as Prizefighter, did I realize I had been up my own ass about a lot of things. So I've had to learn to be more careful, and not make it seem like the way I'm queer is the way everyone has to be. My way isn't the right way just because it's maybe the most visible. There is no "right" way besides what works for each of us individually. I had a lot of internal work to do to get there. But when you're fighting for people, you're fighting for more than just the people like you. It's important people see me, but it's important too that they know they don't have to be just like me. They have to be their own selves, and know that if they're up against a wall because of it, I'll have their back.

TWC: As a young man, who were the people you looked up to, and found empowering, both real and fictional? Who were, and maybe still are, Prizefighter's heroes growing up?

Sports people, mostly? I was pretty mainstream as a kid, big into sports, hanging out with the guys, stereotypically masculine things. I didn't have many queer friends before I came out, and if I'm being honest until recently I still didn't. I did say I had to do a lot of work getting out of my own stubborn way. And I did, and I'm thankful for it. Damn so. But I did have queer icons, people like Emile Griffith, the bisexual boxer. Hell, even Jack Saul, the prostitute who blew up turn of the century English society. I read that book in the back of a bookstore, half embarrassed, half entranced, in baggy sweatpants. Then I'd go off to track and field and forget that I was that person for a few hours. If I'd really keyed in on what I liked about those people, the anger, the fact they didn't care about taking a match to expectations, I might've come out sooner. But I finally did, I made up for lost time, and now I'm trying to be the one to show people they can hold the match themselves.

TWC: What are your thoughts on the proposal in Washington right now? The American Individuality Act, as they're calling it. Where do you stand on that?
I wouldn't be Prizefighter if I didn't throw some haymakers, right? I think it's complete garbage. The American Individuality Act is the worst type of cynical take. They're taking the fact they want to give up on working together and helping our fellow citizens as some form of bullshit rugged individualism. If I acted like those suits out there making laws just because people are angry the world's changing, I'd have never lifted a finger to help anyone else. To me, the thing's a goddamn anchor pulling us into the deep, dark end of history, when what we could use is a life preserver.

TWC: Are you a man of faith, Noah? Are you religious at all? What's your relationship to God like, especially given all the powers you and your peers have?
When you've seen what I have, what everyone in the Crisis Command has, it's hard not to question things like that. I honestly don't know what the rest of the Command might say. You said it yourself, some of them are all but gods themselves. It's hard not to see how humans, in all our pettiness, use religion to keep people angry and scared. And I'm not about that. But faith, absent the human element turning it into a tool for manipulation? Who am I to tell someone what should and shouldn't get them through the day? I don't have all the answers, but I do know any time I think I've seen it all there's something new to prove me wrong. So I can't rule out a higher power, or higher powers. I know this reality is bigger than just us, but I'm no more up to date on just what those higher powers have in mind for people, if anything, than anyone else. You want answers? Talk to Thunder Woman. Aren't her people supposed to be the gods the gods worship?

TWC: Some conspiracy theorists, particularly right-wingers, believe you and the Crisis Command are an elaborate leftist ploy and act out together to destroy our nation and its values. Others believe you folks don't even have powers and that everything is staged, while some proclaim you guys are aliens disguised as comic-book superheroes to trick us, a recon party for an oncoming invasion. Meanwhile there's folks speculating about your team not even being from this universe. What do you have to say to all such claims and theories?
Honestly, I can't even hear half of that. Let's see if you still think that after you've met us in person, yeah? Theories are theories, people can think what they want, it's a free country while it's still a country, but I don't have an obligation to validate it. We'll be there for those people just the same.

TWC: Do you feel you guys are doing enough? How do you decide what problem to tackle and when, and what not to? There's so many problems in our world right now, and here you guys are, blessed with all these incredible powers. What is it that you'd like to have accomplished, at the end of everything? What is your goal and intended legacy, and what do you think the Crisis Command's ought to be?
We're doing everything we can. I don't think about the grand plan too much, I leave that to the smarter people on the team. Frontier's got the plans, Seer can see quarks having arguments. They can explain the Crisis Alert to you, I'm sure, if you can convince them that is. I step in when there's a fight to be had. We've got macro thinkers on the Command, but I'm about the micro. Is someone in danger, solve the danger, rinse and repeat. But along with that it means from my end, we're never doing enough. There's billions of people on this planet, fifty-two states of America alone, and we don't just protect one country. We're just trying to keep going, so the world can keep going with us. If you only knew what's at stake when people go bad...you know what? No. We'll be there, we'll keep being there for you.

TWC: If you had to describe each of your teammates in a single word, what would it be? And what's your relationship like to each of them? There's a number of fans for Sawbones, your peer, in particular.
One word? Okay, sure. I can probably answer it all in one word if I give it a shot. Frontier – coach. Seer – vision. Sawbones – soul. Originator – conscience. Yeah, I think those work, and if you think about it, they answer for my relationship too. So go think about it, I'd say.

TWC: Folks argue all the time about who your true arch-nemesis is, so, to set the record straight once

and for all—Who is your arch-nemesis?
Emotional attachment? That's what the reviews on my dating profile seem to say. My greatest series was probably against Brick Bat, back when I was starting out. But who knows? Word is he might've reformed.

TWC: The world is a strange, bizarre, absurd place right now, and we're in an especially trying moment. So what does Noah Rowe do to relax, beyond all the superheroics? What are your favorite films and books? And have you been reading or watching anything lately that you'd wanna mention or talk about?
I think you might've heard me mention a dating profile? I was maybe being generous with the term. These days I'm mostly fighting or blowing off steam, there's not a lot of time for stuff in between. But I've been watching a lot of those personal interest, self-renovation type shows lately, you know? The life coach type things. It's shocking to me how easy it is for people to write themselves off, and it's nice to see them be able to find their own strength. And it's a good reminder strong doesn't mean the same thing for everyone. I said it earlier, but I have been and I'm going to keep making an effort to learn that my way's not the only way, or even the best way, just another way. So I'm forcing myself, in my queer life, to look at parts of the culture that would've made me uncomfortable in the past and really ask myself why? More often than not I realize it's been my own bullshit that was the problem. So I'm throwing as much media in my face as I can to not be about that anymore, and be a better fighter. It's training, learning through experience, like anything else.

TWC: Your passion for wrestling is evident, clearly. Who are your favorite wrestlers, and do you have any obscure favorites or matches?
You think so? Maybe the costume's working, then, if you're making that assumption. But I do love competition, and I love being a champion for people. I like the personalities of wrestling maybe more than actually watching it? But I will always respect one of the originals, George Hackenschmidt. The Russian Lion! Hell yeah! The stuff he wrote about wellness and fitness is useful today just like it was over a century ago. And if I'm well, I can do my job better. Everyone's better off if they've got me fighting on their side, which means I need to keep myself at fighting weight.

TWC: Now, for one final question. Favorite alcoholic drink, go.
I've been getting hell for it for years, but I never moved past the college classic: Red Bull and vodka. Sometimes I do class it up and put it in a champagne glass, if I'm trying to impress a guy.
And that was Noah Rowe, Prizefighter! Join us next month, as we speak to the most enigmatic of the Command, Sawbones!

[Interview by: **Ritesh Babu**. Answers by: **Steve Orlando**. The other interviews with the squad members will be available in **COMMANDERS IN CRISIS BOOK 2: THE REACTION**.]

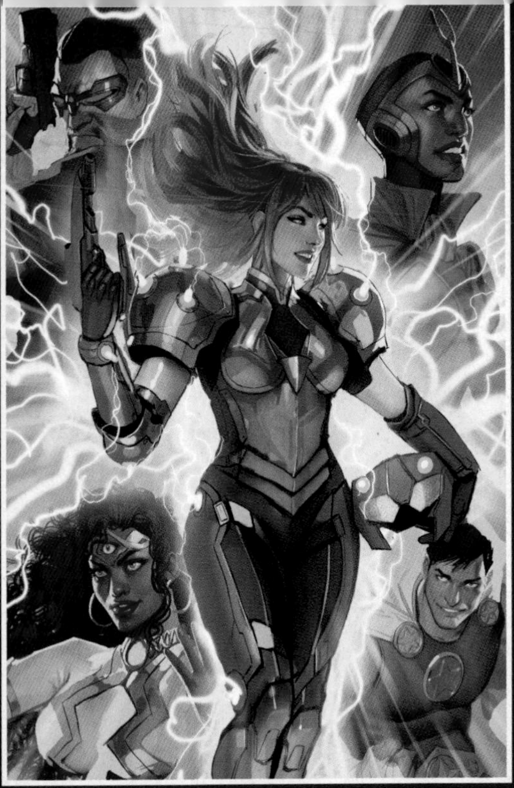

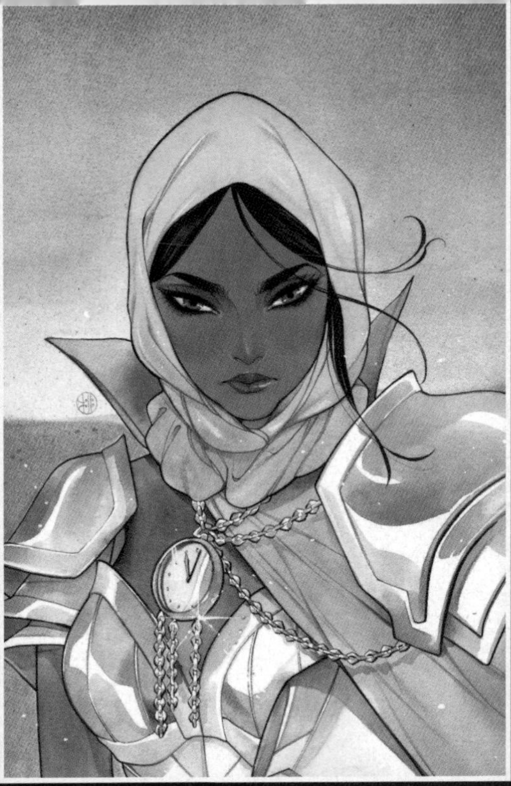

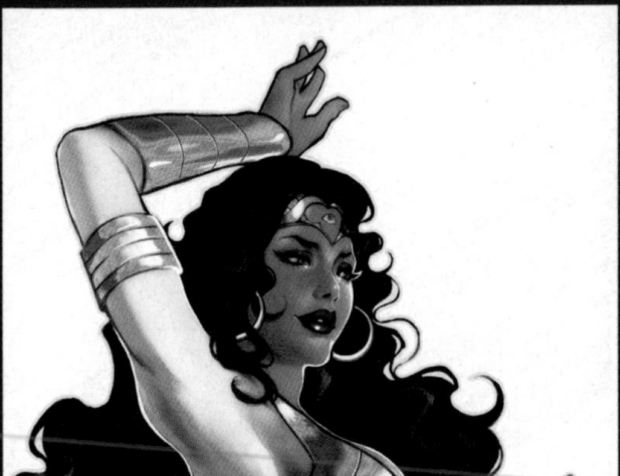

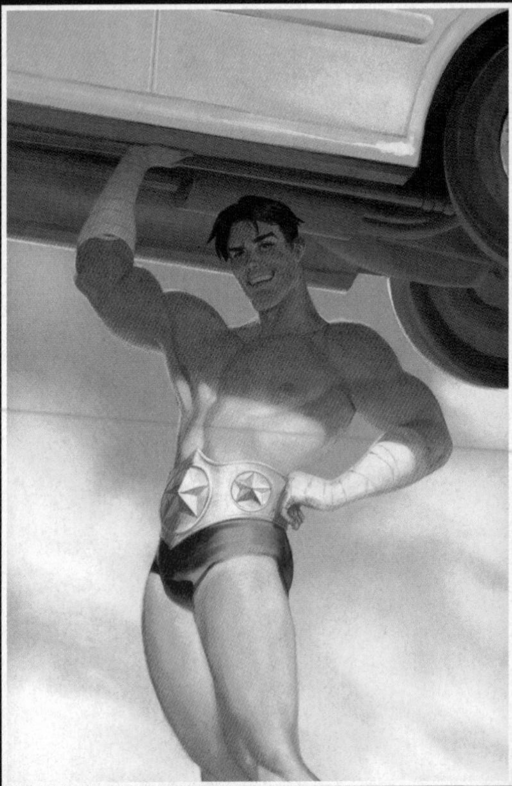

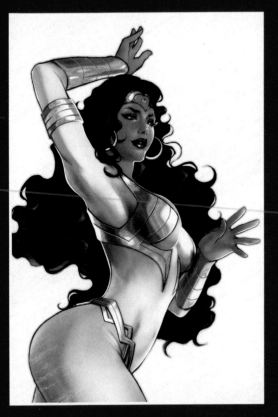

STJEPAN SEJIC [1], **PEACH MOMOKO** [2],
MAIKA SOZO [3], **DAVID TALASKI** [4].

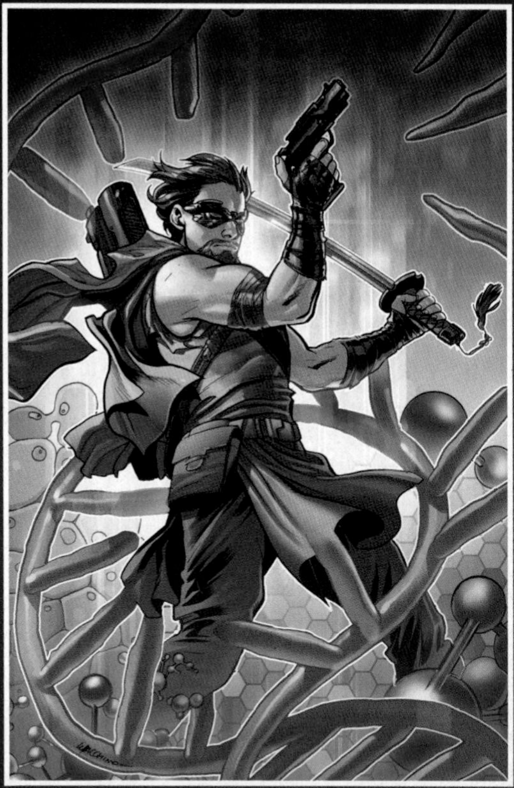

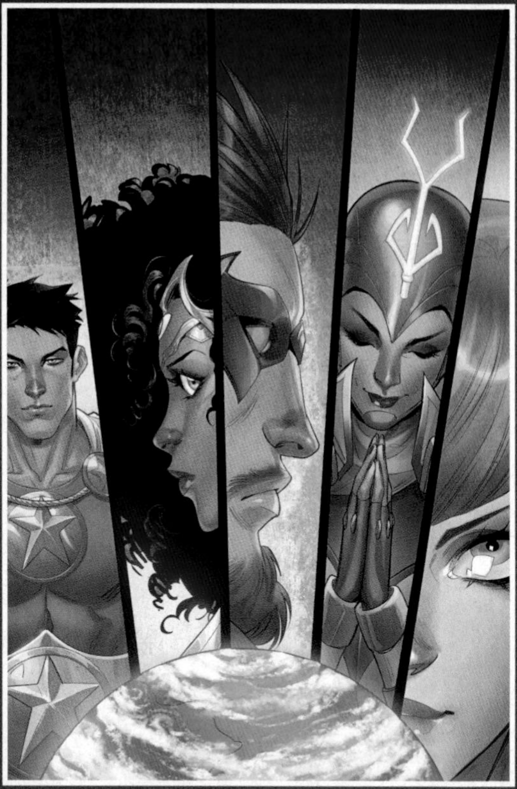

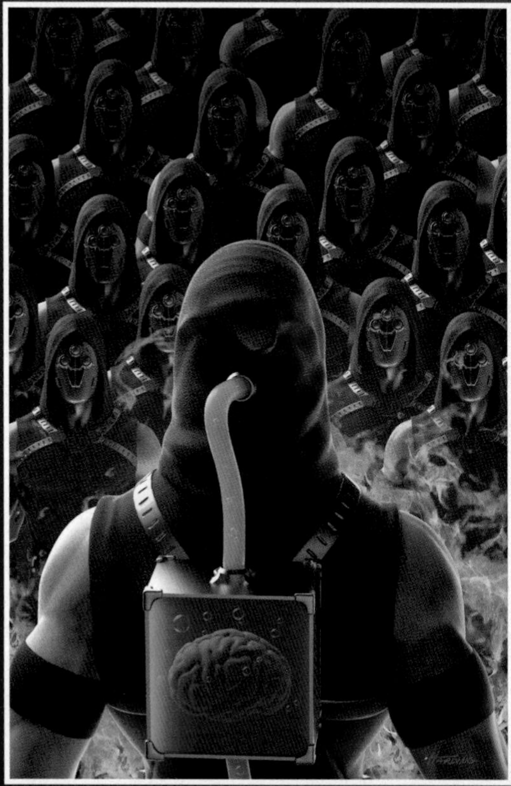

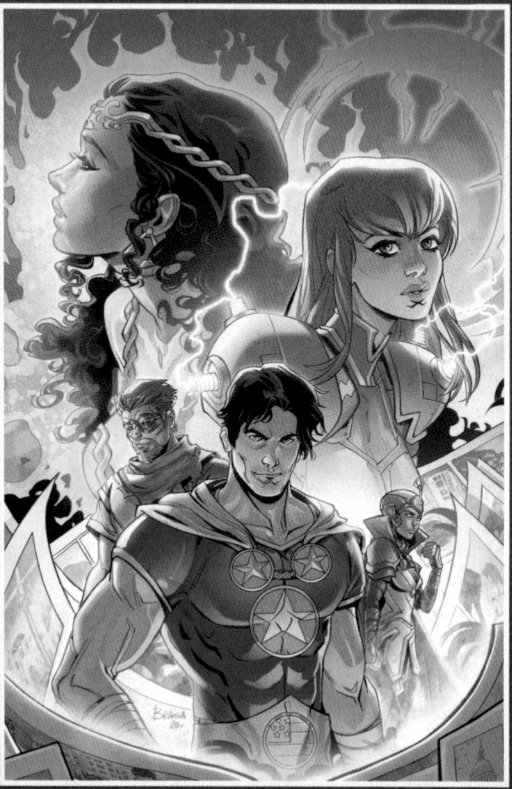

EMANUELA LUPACCHINO (art) & ANDREA MELONI (colors) [1]**,**
MIRKA ANDOLFO (art) & SABINE RICH (colors) [2]**, PAUL HARDING** [3]**,**
LAURA BRAGA (art) & ANDREA MELONI (colors) [4]**.**

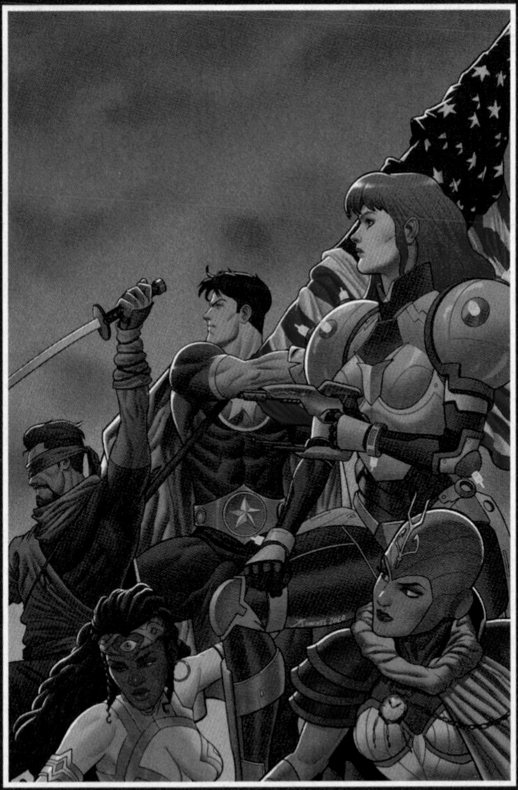

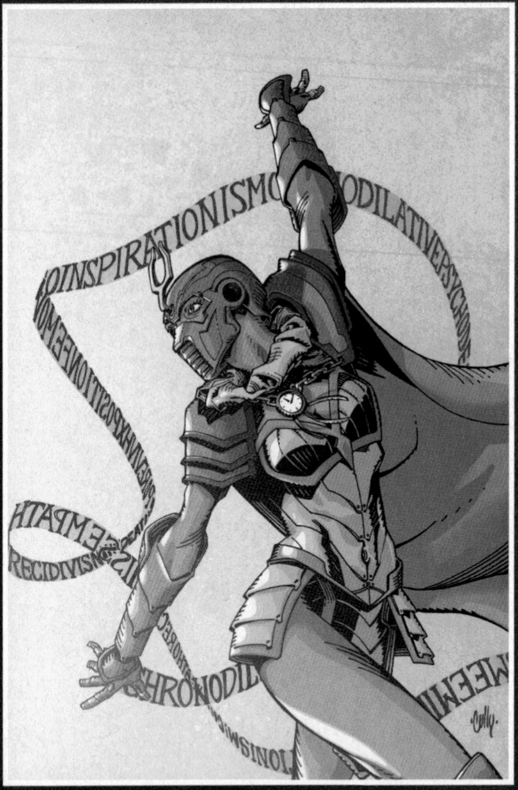
INSPIRATIONISMO
EMPATH
RECIDIVISM
CHRONODIL

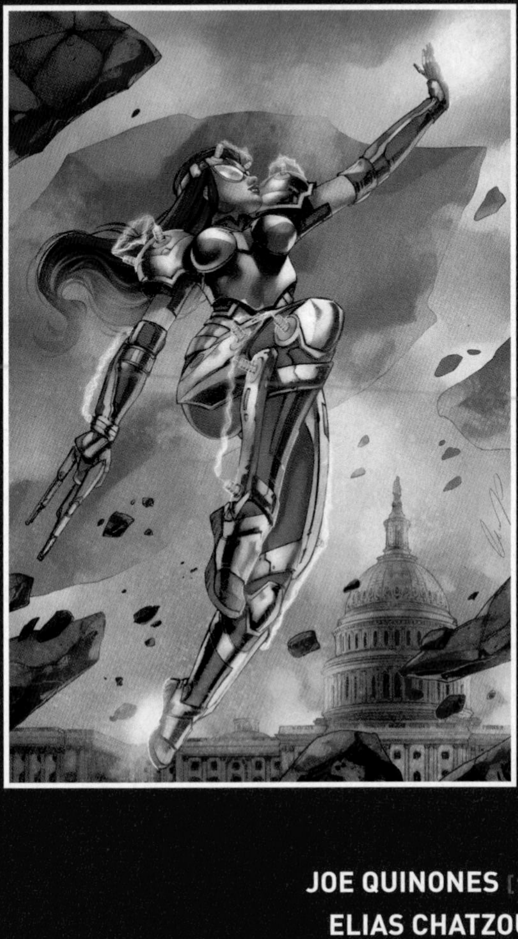

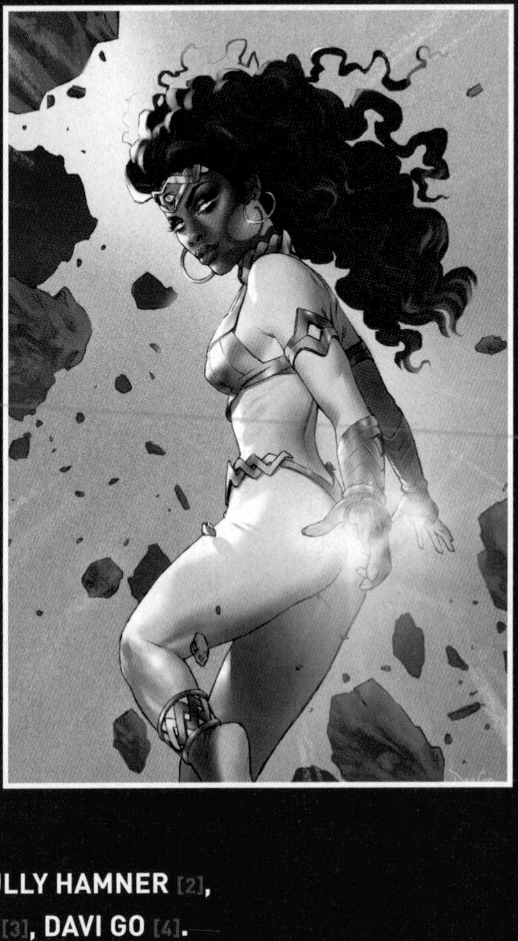

JOE QUINONES [1], **CULLY HAMNER** [2],
ELIAS CHATZOUDIS [3], **DAVI GO** [4].

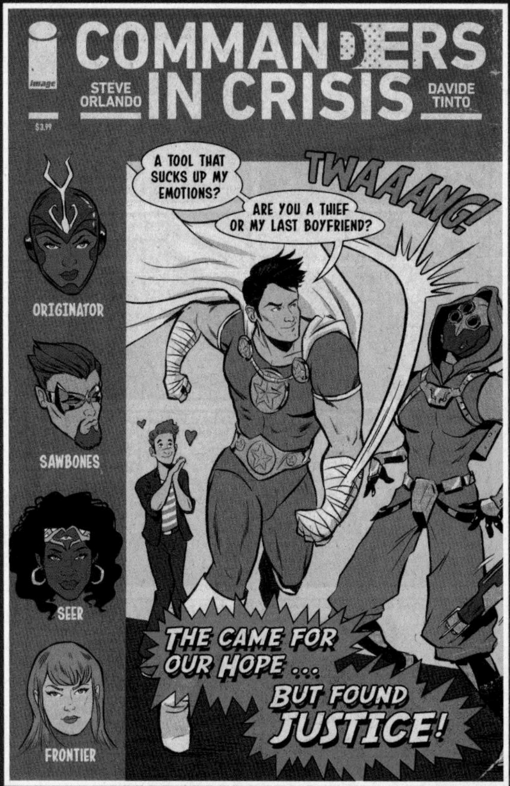
COMMANDERS IN CRISIS
STEVE ORLANDO
DAVIDE TINTO
A TOOL THAT SUCKS UP MY EMOTIONS?
TWAAANG!
ARE YOU A THIEF OR MY LAST BOYFRIEND?
ORIGINATOR
SAWBONES
SEER
FRONTIER
THE CAME FOR OUR HOPE ...
BUT FOUND JUSTICE!

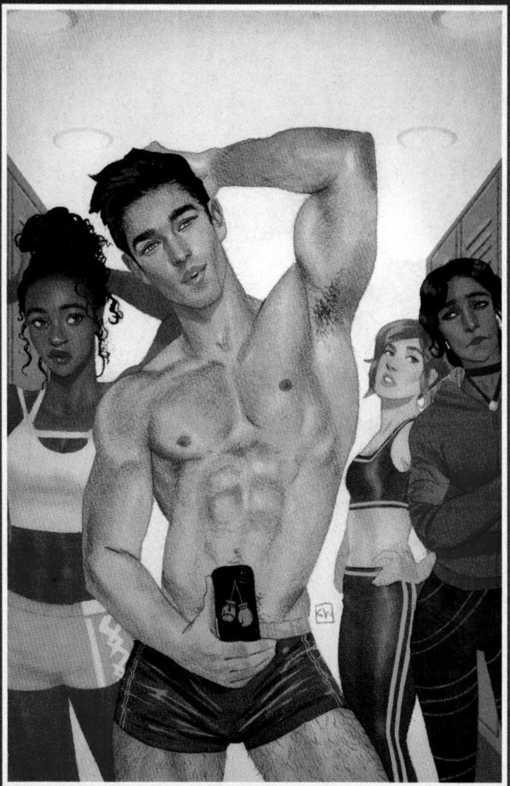

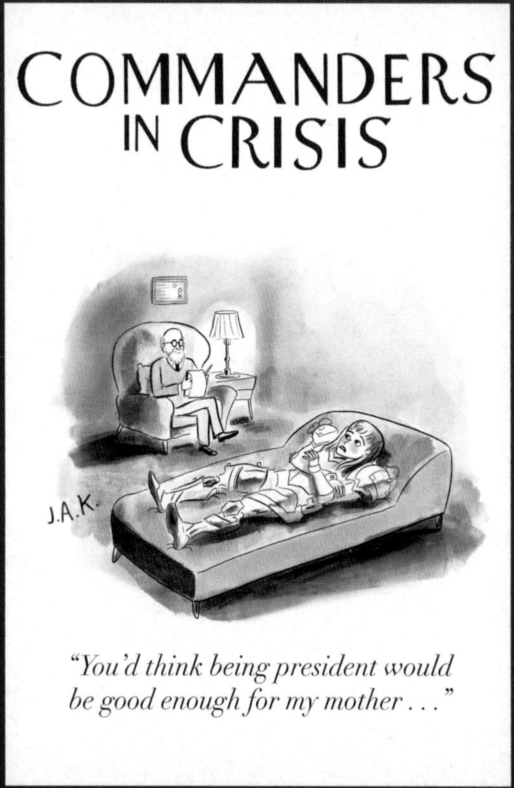
COMMANDERS IN CRISIS
J.A.K.
"You'd think being president would be good enough for my mother . . ."

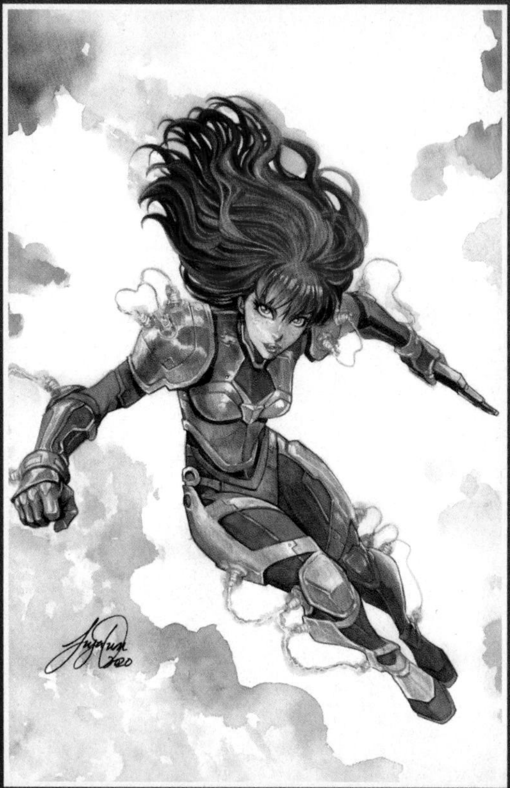

CHEYNE GALLARDE [1], **KEVIN WADA** [2],
JASON KATZENSTEIN [3], **SIYA OUM** [4].

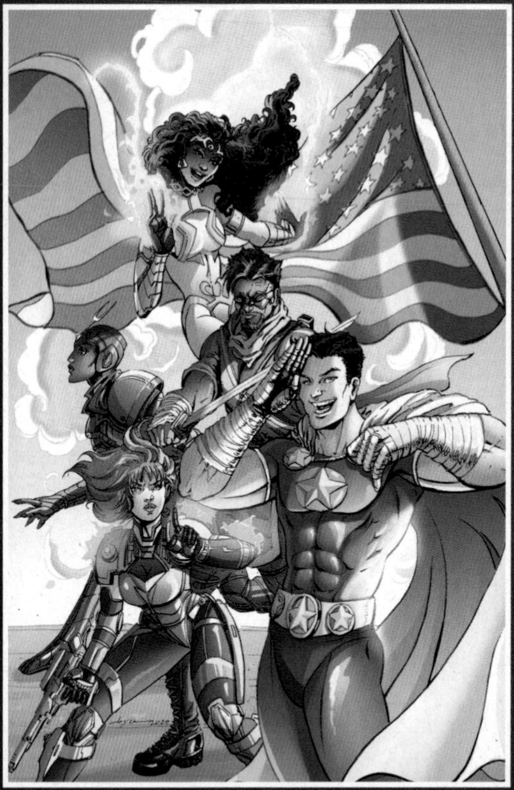

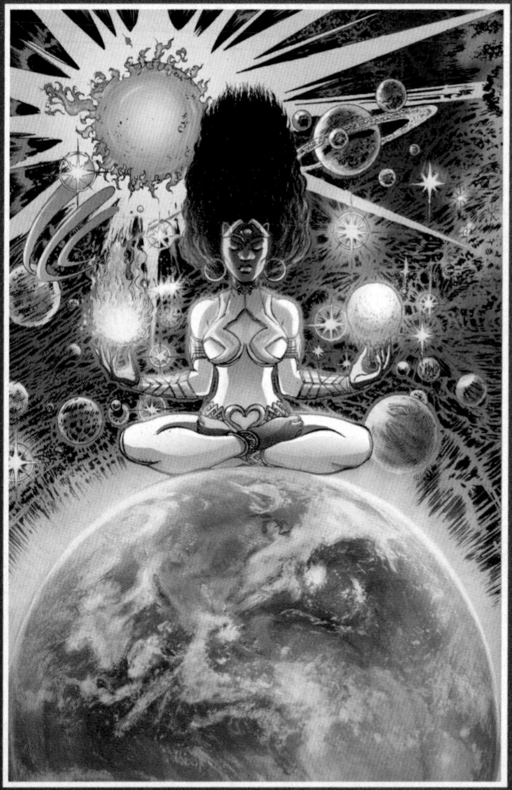

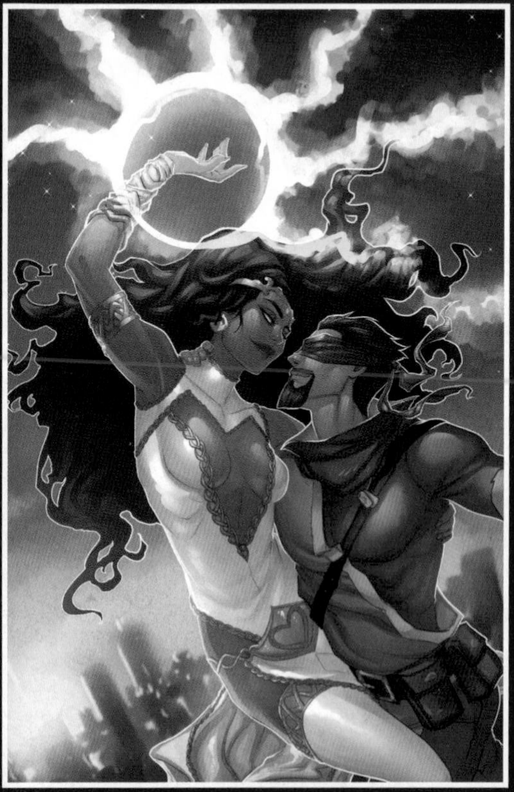

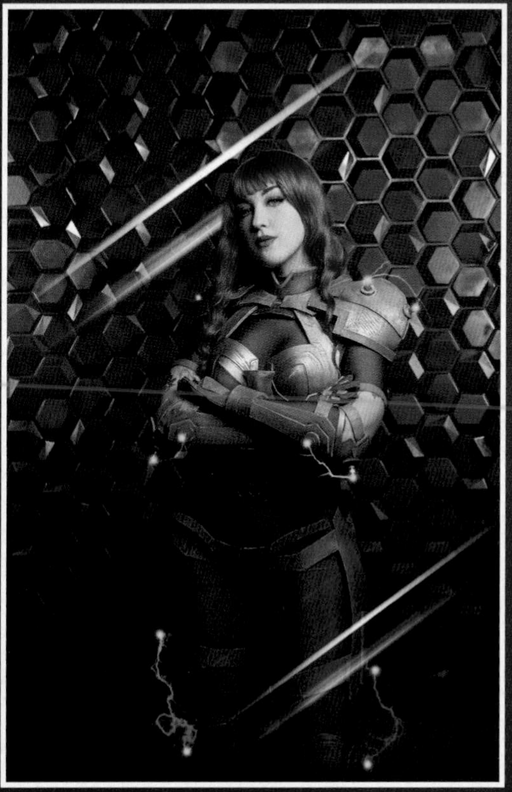

JOYCE CHIN (art) & FRANCESCA CAROTENUTO (colors) [1], TREVOR VON EEDEN (art) & FRANCESCA CAROTENUTO (colors) [2], MEGHAN HETRICK [3], KAT FOX (photo by MIKE SAFFELS) [4].